CHILDREN OF THE WEST

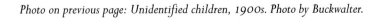

Photo on previous page: Unidentified children, 1900s. Photo by Buckwalter.

Also by CATHY LUCHETTI

Women of the West
(with Carol Olwell)

Home on the Range
A Culinary History of the American West

Under God's Spell
Frontier Evangelists, 1772–1915

"I Do!"
Courtship, Love and Marriage on the American Frontier

Medicine Women
The Story of Early-American Women Doctors

Children of the West

Family Life on the Frontier

Cathy Luchetti

W. W. Norton & Company
New York • London

Title page photo: Cowboy, Grand Junction, Colorado, ca. 1900s. Photo by Dean.

Printed in the United States of America

First Edition

The text of this book is composed in Perpetua
with the display set in Chevalier Stripes
Composition by Allentown Digital Services
Manufacturing by The Courier Companies, Inc.
Book design by Chris Welch
Production manager: Andrew Marasia

Library of Congress Cataloging-in-Publication Data

Luchetti, Cathy, 1945–
Children of the West : family life on the frontier / Cathy Luchetti.
p.cm.
Includes bibliographical references and index.
ISBN 0-393-04913-2
1. Pioneer children—West (U.S.)—Social life and customs. 2. Pioneer children—West (U.S.)—Social conditions. 3. Pioneer children—West (U.S.)—Pictorial works. 4. Family—West (U.S.)—History—19th century. 5. Family—West (U.S.)—History—19th century—Pictorial works. 6. Frontier and pioneer life—West (U.S.)— 7. Frontier and pioneer life—West (U.S.)—Pictorial works. 8. West (U.S.)—Social life and customs—19th century. 9. West (U.S.)—Social life and customs—19th century—Pictorial works. I. Title.

F596 .L84 2001 00-053287
978'.02—dc21

W. W. Norton & Company, Inc., 500 Fifth Avenue, New York, N.Y. 10110
www.wwnorton.com

W. W. Norton & Company Ltd., 10 Coptic Street, London WC1A 1PU

1 2 3 4 5 6 7 8 9 0

A large family of children [is] really a treasure to a man . . . a source of profit and wealth to him, as well as of domestic happiness.

—George Wood, Irish immigrant, 1840s,
quoted in *The Great Migration,* by Edwin C. Guillet

To my own true "riches"—

Zack, Micah, and J. J. Luchetti

Photo on previous page: Lebanese child in Utah, ca. 1900.

CONTENTS

Part 4 Growing Up

Part 5 Manners, Morals, Discipline, and the Great Beyond

Part 6 Ethnic Americans

Acknowledgments

In today's rich stock of historical writing, rapt attention has been given to the customs, cultures, music, food, geography, land use patterns, homesteading history, and settlers of the American West. Frontier children, on the other hand, have been less well served. Rather than examine how their roles had changed from the times of European culture, their means of education, adaptation to isolation, and need to work from an early age and religious influences, the journal keepers, diarists, and biographers of the nineteenth century were far too occupied with their own westward progress to reflect too deeply upon their children. Perhaps each was caught up in the role of the "child of Nature," in which adults acted out the stages usually reserved for children: "growing up" in new surroundings, learning new languages, trying to unlock meaning from the unexplainable, even the belief in "magical" abilities, usually associated with the forces of nature. Choices were few—either tame the wilderness or become a part of it. To them, the path of childhood was as inexplicable and inexorable as their own adulthood in a new land.

In the frontier thesis of Frederick Jackson Turner, men and women had come west to conquer and settle the land, and in doing so became changed themselves. Transformation or no, their children continued to sprout up, learn, stumble, soar, giggle, shove, and finally fly on their own. They were part of a domestic backdrop too often ignored, and deserving of further exploration.

To assist in this quest, the history of frontier children has fortunately been preserved in libraries, historical societies, research institutions, and archives around the country. Creating this book has been made possible through the supportive efforts of curators, archivists, and librarians, particularly the photo curators whose expertise helped to direct my efforts. Thanks to George Hobart, curator of documentary photographs at the Library of Congress; Todd Strand of the North Dakota Heritage Center; and the staff at the Colorado Historical Society and the Denver Public Library. Particular thanks to children's historian Jim Silverman for insights concerning advertising in early American children's books. To Jim Gasparini, for directing me to the story of Esther Whinery Wattles—a fascinating manuscript whose excerpts are sprinkled throughout—and to Ruth Arps, for graciously allowing me to quote from the manuscript. To Eli Leon, eminent authority on the art of quilt making among African Americans, for information about early midwives. Profound thanks to Alexis Kirschbaum, my research assistant, whose assiduous work at the Bancroft Library has formed the basis for this book; and to writer and professor Raffi del Bourgio, for thoughtfully introducing me to her. Alice Hamburg has lent inspiration as she writes her life story—many thanks. As always, I appreciate the informed recommendations of Bob Hawley. I thank Peter Hadreas for continual insights and loving support throughout the writing of this book. To Anne Edelstein, my agent, for her assiduous efforts on my behalf, and to Amy Cherry, my editor, for clear insight and imagination.

INTRODUCTION

All I can do for my country is to raise three children so that the world may be better for their having been in it.—*Mrs. G.H. of North Carolina*

His idea was that we must do better by our children than we had been done by.—*Mrs. Mortimer, a midwife*

In September our little daughter was born—it made no difference to me—I wanted this baby for two years.—*Martha Heywood*

CHILDREN OF THE frontier west were loved, coddled, sheltered as best as possible, clothed somewhat—all the essentials of a nurtured childhood. In the best cases, families were close, siblings numerous, and affection readily given. "O! When I look back at those bright loving days . . . with Father, Mother, brothers and sisters gathered in groups round about, how glad I am to have been one of them," wrote Esther Whinery Wattles of her childhood in New Garden, Ohio. "When I went to have a picture taken I always had a broad grin ready, never had any thing to make me look sad. My childhood hours were happy, oh! So happy," recalled Maggie Brown. Ideally, the frontier woman counted herself happy to have "energy, industry, and capability" as well as, like the grandmother of Bethenia Owens, "twelve children, all of whom grew to maturity, married, and went on giving vigorous sons and daughters to this young and growing republic."

The story of American family life resembles that of the country itself—a people maturing in a new land, striking out in search of freedom, and finding in their quest the ability to "grow up," as well as to move on. Free land was a beacon to thousands of immigrants who arrived daily by steamboat, wagon, train, and ships that sailed around Cape Horn, lured by the promise of work, bounteous food, and fertile acreage. "Urge my brothers to come out if they wish to free themselves from bondage," wrote one. "This is a land of independence to the industrious." Although the term *Frontier,* as applied to the West, was already an anachronism by the 1850s—since it denoted unsettled, and by then even Oregon had nearly five thousand inhabitants—the land continued to draw people with the Homestead Act, passed by Congress in 1862, which offered 160 acres for five years' continuous residence. Across the Continental Divide, into California, Washington, and Oregon, they trudged, determined to fill up the emptiness with optimism, children, productivity, and dreams.

From documents pieced together—scraps from old church records, family histories, letters, daybooks, and diaries—a picture of the cultural restlessness of the nineteenth century emerges. Not only did wanderlust and Old West nostalgia fill the air, but emancipation, too. Women were clamoring for more formal recognition of their position in society, raising the question, if the entire race of blacks in America could now vote, why not a gender, too? Even the question of children's liberation, although hardly formed at the time, would soon lead to new theories of nutrition, discipline, and education.

The cult of the young mother was an industry on the rise, presenting, in the latter half of nineteenth-century America, an idea nearly as sacred as freedom itself, and which was widely promoted in the Christian tract literature of the day. Who could influence more the ways of a child than a mother? Male scholars, pastors, and politicians addressed themselves to the issue of ideal womanhood, determined to keep order in their potentially restless ranks. A mother was "like a gardener!" exclaimed Daniel Chaplin to the Female Society of Groton, Connecticut, in 1814. "Angels of the hearth," echoed others. Sarah Hale, editor of the popular women's journal *Ladies' Magazine,* reminded readers that home was the woman's world, where she could transform the "crushed and ill-shapen" into those "made straight." Lives of the mothers of famous men churned from the presses in the 1840s and 1850s, pointing out that greatness began at home—just note Mary Washington! Integral to the child's destiny, a mother must exercise discipline and apply love, always on the lookout for "infant depravity," a Calvinist doctrine in which children were seen as potentially flawed. In urban Victorian society, mothers were preeminent, fathers withdrawn, and children, hopefully, quiet and well behaved. Fertility was tied not only to femininity but to professionalism and patriotism as well. With limited career options, childbearing was a vocation without limitation. While men flooded into the world of trade, business, and government, women could succeed in maternity, finding in it the "moral purpose" they sought.

The American style of child rearing had changed drastically from the Old World traditions. To the staid British, American children were seen as spirited and rebellious, although, as some admitted, their self-reliance was to be admired, and they were valued for their contributions to the growing Republic. "Of course they are having a hard time. What of it?" said one stalwart woman. "The very root of independence is hard times. That's the way America was founded; that is why it stands so firmly. Hard times is what makes sound characters. And them kids are getting a new hold on character that was very near run to seed in the parents. . . ."

Earlier Calvinist views of original sin—in which only the rod would adequately tame the innately evil nature and break the childish will—gave way in America. Inherent in the "new" approach was the idea that parents could influence a child's direction, rather than accept the child as simply being "that way." Thus the mother's role—as one who could best instruct in manners, morals, civility, and etiquette—took on new significance. The thoughtful and farsighted mother could dignify herself, as well as her country, by producing well-mannered children to equal those of European lineage—American children who were stylishly dressed, literate, spoke in low tones, used a fork properly, and said "sir!" with a flourish.

The frontier childhood, however, differed significantly from that of the Old World. Isabella Bird, a jaunty, outspoken British traveler

Girl in bonnet, 1885–88.

who loved the West almost as much as she loved to criticize it, believed that one of the most "painful things" she had witnessed in the western states and territories was the untrammeled freedom of American youth. "I have never seen any children," she wrote, "only debased imitations of men and women, cankered by greed and selfishness, and asserting and gaining complete independence of their parents at ten years old." Traditionally, interaction between adults and children had been as undemonstrative as language itself. In the proper Victorian world, "tedious" might actually mean terrible or life-threatening—it was hard to tell where emotions lay. In the West, with its daily dramas and near escapes, children and adults spoke directly. Shared trials encouraged a new kind of truth.

Yet Bird condemned the adult atmosphere in America, where "greed, godlessness, and frequency of profanity" seemed to reign. From this came a child-raising dichotomy: one particular view of child raising was to reject children in order to toughen them to the rigors of frontier life; the other was to overprotect them, so as to instill the dying-out concepts of European civilization.

Whichever was adopted, Americans continued to live out their dreaming spirits in the naming of their children. The devout prayed for virtue and fruits of the spirit, and filled their homes with youngsters named Prudence, Piety, Chastity, and Charity, and even that odd appellation, Barebones. Parents who dreamed of travel and adventure had "exotic" offspring—Persia and India, or the lesser destinations of Cincinnati and Philadelphia. Often, relatives' names cropped up—what better reminder of bygone friends and family? Wrote Harriet Shaw:

> Sometimes think my heart is so hardened that nothing has power to rouse me but when a letter reaches me & reference is made to the dear home of childhood & early friends are spoken of a fountain of feeling gushes forth & finds vent in tears, I never wanted to see Vermont so much in my life as I do now. The very names "Aunt Nancy" "Aunt Mary" "Uncle Hart" bring to mind instantly all the scenes of early life & I seem to be living in another state of existence.

Some names were so long they seemed to recall every friend and long-lost relative within memory, with none overlooked. Towheaded toddlers answered to a generation of family history—anything to make loved ones seem nearer. Wrote Elinore Pruitt Stewart:

> "What is the little girl's name," queried Mrs. O'Shaughnessy of Wyoming.
>
> "Caroline Agnes Lucia Lavina Ida Eunice" was the astonishing reply.
>
> Mrs. O'Shaughnessy gasped. "My *goodness,*" she exclaimed, "is that *all?*"
>
> "Oh, no," Aunt Hettie went on placidly; "you see, her mother couldn't call her all the names, so she just used the first letters. They spell Callie; so that is what she called her. But I don't like the name. I call her Baby Girl."

Others had the opposite problem—they simply couldn't come up with another name for another child. "We never did name him," a young girl confided to a Wyoming woman interested in adopting the girl's orphan brother. "You see we had kind of run out of boys' names. We just called him Buddy."

Parents and society had expectations, and prejudice could extend to children, too. Were they pretty? Smart? Girls? Boys? Unattractive children had "character," while those of great charm might be too attractive, or spoiled. Hard work and rough living taught lasting lessons, and children such as young Connie Willis came to terms early with their gifts. "All the Ford children are handsome, and smart, too. I am the only homely child Ma had." Family life, in fact, seemed a safe haven for clear evaluation. In the Rosenshine family of San Francisco, it was common knowledge that Annette's mother had been the favorite daughter, particularly since her sister "was much plainer looking . . . and had been relegated to an inferior role in their parental home."

In Annette's life, the same standards seemed to apply. Although a bright, lively child, she had a disfiguring cleft palate, which an operation had failed to mend.

> [This] interfered grievously with my speech during all the school years. My most painful experiences happened when I became aware that my speech defect bothered my father. It happened the day that he scolded me for some prank. I saucily answered back.

I remember how shocked I was when he imitated my nasal speech. Possibly this gave me my first vivid realization of my defect. Nevertheless in my active fantasy world I was most beautiful, a princess who was called "Alice," whose father took her to all the balls and parties, because her mother was dead. She was beautifully dressed and most popular, a success at every function and greatly admired with plenty of beaux, but never wanted any other escort but her father.

Girl pouring tea, ca. 1870s.

Yet other parents were tolerant and wise, and, as Ethan Allen Crawford wrote, could wish only that their children "had good reason and proper shapes."

More difficult to sort out than looks was gender, with the question perpetually asked: Which do you want, a boy or a girl? "Boys escape by the natural order of law and life," said Agnes Reid of Blackfoot River, Idaho Territory, on May 5, 1874; it was only beginning to dawn on her that, on the frontier, women could work as well as men, and sometimes better. Cultures and generations have always revealed prejudice through gender preference, and immigrant parents, particularly from eastern Europe, had definite ideas of gender and propriety. Girls were slated to tend the familial home first, their own futures second, and according to their responsibilities, their behavior was closely monitored. One daughter, either the eldest or the youngest, was selected to care for the younger siblings or the aging parents as time went by. "At fifteen, [my mother] was taken from school to care for the large brood of five sisters and three brothers. I always felt like they were her first family," recalled Annette Rosenshine. "We were more like her step children." Gender comparisons also colored the sibling relationship, already a seething mixture of overexposure and rivalry, gender issues aside. Yet in the West, there was a certain built-in respect for womanhood, and for its offshoot, girlhood, which showed itself in grudging courtesy given, boy to girl, brother to sister. Since men were often gone, why not have a daughter or two to fill in during emergencies?

Young Bethenia Owens felt equal to her younger brother in size, skill, weight, and instinct, at least until he gained enough weight and height to change her mind.

> My brother Flem and I were playing with the baby. He was two years my junior, but my constant companion. He grew rapidly, and soon overtook me in size, as I was small, and grew slowly, but I was tough and active, and usually led in all our pursuits. . . . Not until I was past twelve, did he ever succeed in throwing me. One day he . . . said: "Pap told me to go to the barn for two bundles of oats . . . now the first one that is thrown down must go for the oats." Instantly the dish-cloth was dropped, and we clinched.

I had noticed for some time that he was gaining on me, but I could not refuse to take a "dare" and he had not yet thrown me.

Round and round the room we went, bending and swaying, like two young saplings, till, seeing his chance, he put out his foot and tripped me. I fell on a chair . . . and I broke off a piece of one of my front teeth. Poor brother picked up the fragment of tooth, burst out crying, and ran off to the barn for the oats.

Family life was made beautiful or was broken by the relationship of husband and wife, which colored every aspect. When love was present, there was much to celebrate, and the writings of both men and women show overwhelmingly the sense of loss they felt when parted and the joy of reunion. "Mr. Shaw has come," cried his wife, Harriet. "I ran to see & I was caught in his arms before I had reached the front door, never was I more glad to see him. He had come on ahead of the rest to reach home sooner." The sexes inhabited very separate spheres, which ideally led to a kind of respect and delicacy when considering the other's privacy. Better not inquire too closely into unseen areas. Better leave some things unexplained. Francis Prevaux was discretion itself when it came to his wife's affairs. "Lil wanted me to get her a bottle of brandy a few days since. Whether she wanted to drink it or not, I did not inquire. It was provided and placed in the closet under the wash stand."

If rural life seemed slow at times, or hidebound by tradition, its rewards were found in the potential of freedom. Economically and emotionally, westerners gradually began to reap the benefits of their labor. As the age wore on, new horizons and general uplift caused taciturn Victorian traits to melt away. "What an experience Kansas was! I felt the very air was easier to breathe . . . it didn't matter a bit who your ancestors were or what you did for a living," wrote Nannie Alderson. "It seemed to me a wonderful thing."

Parents tried to maintain order, but were themselves struggling with the harshness of their new lives. Discipline gave way to a far deeper question—how to survive? To admonish, cajole, and threaten was not enough, and adults found themselves as bewildered as children as they pondered the enormity of fate, measured out in wagon tracks stretching into the horizon.

Perhaps no sentiment better expressed the western outlook than an account written by Solomon Butcher, the famed Nebraska photographer who found his subject—a young boy who was part of a family portrait—making a dash for the tall grass, tired of posing. Minutes later, another boy scampered off. With a sigh, the owner of the sod-hut homestead said to Butcher, "Take what you've got." Somehow, it would sort itself out.

Part 1

BIRTH

Photo on previous page: Confinement in a Colorado cabin.

1

Going West

They couldn't make us understand about mountains. "You just can't imagine a mountain," Papa said, " 'til you have seen one."
—*Blanche Beale Lowe*

I remember walking just ahead of that halted wagon, venturing out alone to gaze across that expanse of country. I recall so vividly the feeling of wonderment and perplexity at the bigness of the world and how I so eagerly struggled to stretch my childhood experience and imagination to comprehend some of its meaning and its promise.
—*Mary Ronan*

Traveling with a family across this American desert is the very hardest business I have ever followed. —*Richard Martin May*

I never felt so miserable in my life. I sat on the ground with my face buried in my hands, speechless. . . . What would become of us children?"
—*Mary Ackley*

THE EMIGRANT TRAINS lumbering west were like bulky, slow-moving villages—each bearing a small population to a new life in the West. Drawn by teams of ponderous oxen, each "schooner" crept along the 2,200-mile route, kicking up plumes of alkali at every step, eking out only ten miles a day, if that. Each boatlike wagon had a canvas roof that billowed overhead like a wind-blown sail. Inside, the cloth walls sagged from rows of sewn-in pockets that were filled to overflowing with household items. Children continually rummaged through them, looking for surprises.

Bushel bags, feather ticking, candles, medicine, and dried provisions were crammed in the wagon's interior, reaching a weight of two thousand pounds when fully loaded—a tremendous burden for underfed or thirsty oxen. Cooking utensils were lodged in the feed-box, and every cranny brimmed with home goods—patchwork quilts, kettles, dried peas, or a velvet smock, neatly folded around cedar chips to discourage moths. Possessions slid back and forth as if animated, a cane-back rocker colliding with a jar of honey as the wagon bumped and swayed.

Numbers of migrants varied. By the end of 1846, some eight or nine thousand travelers had reached Oregon, undaunted by news of Indians, starvation, or even skirmishes between Mexico and the United States. James Marshall's bonanza discovery of gold at Sutter's Mill in 1848 unleashed a flood of nearly thirty thousand fortune-seekers, of whom nearly fifteen hundred were children or

Unidentified family traveling west by covered wagon, ca. 1900.

young teens. Routes were varied; some parties inched along the piney, serpentine course of the Truckee River, while others found their way to the higher elevations of Nevada's Carson River. One route, the Oregon-bound Hasting's Cut-Off, was so deadly in terms of terrain and distance that its path was traced by the skeletal hulks of abandoned wagons, stark and foreboding. Parched travelers finally unhitched their emaciated oxen, shouldered their supplies, and set out on foot—either that or die. Hermann J. Scharmann, traveling from New York, saw "eighty-one shattered and abandoned wagons, and 1,663 oxen, either dead or dying." Thus Elizabeth Custer spoke for many when she reached her destination in New Mexico: "I then realized, for the first time, that we had reached a spot where the comforts of life could not be had for love or money."

Emigrants were usually middle-class greenhorns—small-town barbers, tailors, accountants, or teachers—who knew little about farming, or even travel. Over time, their pale faces toughened, turning grimy and sunburned as the three-month trek progressed. Hunger slowed their steps, and their children, often shoeless, stumbled with fatigue as they walked to lighten the wagonload, bent under knapsacks made of old shirts. Wrote Lucy Ann Henderson:

> When we started, my mother and sister and myself had each a new calico dress, made of the substantial cloth of fifty years ago.

These dresses were expected to last through the journey, which was to be about three weeks. The constant climbing in and out of a lumber wagon was ruinous to clothing, and, when the time of wearing was doubled, each dress looked more like a piece of wide fringe hanging from belt to hem, than the garment it was intended to be.

When the oxen failed, treasured possessions were cast aside to lighten the wagonload. Curious Indians would gather in their wake, quizzically inspecting the freakish assortment of sewing machines, dangling threads, embroidery hoops, rocking chairs, and carved "what not" shelves. Discarded delicacies fizzed and spilled in the heat, even an occasional bottle of champagne. Emma Shepard Hill, however, refused to part with a "little fancy covered basket, containing several strings of beads and a bead purse partly completed," as well as other trinkets such as her mother's gold thimble. She also clung to a little case holding a "set of false teeth, made on a gold plate," belonging to her father. "He was wearing one good set, but I suppose he thought he was going where there might be no dentists, and he would lay in a supply while he had the opportunity."

As heat waves tripped across the horizon, gathering strength as the day progressed, no keepsake was worth its weight in delay, and the pervasive cry, voiced by Kate Heath, in the deserts of Arizona, changed from "No, I cannot part with it" to "Oh, if I could have had a drink of water!"

The crossing came at the peak of most men's lives, but at an inconvenient time for young women, who often found themselves pregnant en route, and, worse, forced to slow down the wagon train to give birth. "I have heard of several children being born on the plains, though it is not a very pleasant place for the little fellows to first see the light of day," wrote Mrs. Francis H. Sawyer. The first "wagon" birth took place in 1843, and one Illinois couple gave birth successively in Kansas, Illinois, Iowa, and Idaho as they settled briefly in each state—emigrants embarked upon a private odyssey.

Between 1840 and 1860, according to historian Elliot West, more than a quarter-million people made their way to the Pacific Coast. Forty-six children registered at Fort Laramie in a single day in 1850. By the next day, the number had risen to ninety-nine. So closely tied was the crossing to family fecundity that a favorite memento of the day was a tiny tin cradle—a sly joke at the expense of the many young couples. Children, in fact, seemed to be everywhere, scrambling, jostling, and underfoot. One man "passed wagon after wagon with juvenile heads in front, juvenile heads behind, juvenile heads to the right, and juvenile heads to the left, literally rows of little faces, from two to a dozen years old, peeping out from under the covers all around . . . all dirty, healthy, and happy." One wagon had "eight holes cut in the canvas on one side, and a child's face peeping out of every one," as well as a multitude of "cats, dogs, beds, cooking stove, tin pans and kettles."

As the covered-wagon "village" rolled along, children would bounce up from the wagon bed or peer out the flaps. At rest time, while parents tended the animals or nursed infants, toddlers would find an apron to cling to—any apron, since every adult could pass for a parent when needed. "We were like one family," a woman recalled. "We just took care of each other and shared everything."

The presence of children on the trains influenced group behavior. Men grew more cautious, whether about Indians or oxen, and took extra precautions to make the campsites safe. Food was better cooked than it might otherwise have been, while child-laden trains were often slower, with daylong halts for every childbirth. Children were also late sleepers, and their weight in the wagon, if they were allowed to sleep in, added to the oxen's heavy load. "On stormy nights the men did the cooking while the women and children remained in the wagon, but we were usually so cramped from sitting all day we were glad to get out for exercise, if possible," said Sarah York.

The stunning obligation of daily travel, the endless vistas of windbent bluestem grass, seemed to daze the travelers, distorting all sense of direction or degree, leaving only a feeling of displacement from the ordinary world. "The West was so big and bare," said Elizabeth Hull, it made her feel "so alone and so sad she just had to cry." For Maggie Hall, the sense of space left her near dizzy. "We had to travel more than half way to California to get out of Texas," she marveled. But, she might have added, what a trip it was.

"The first part [of the route] is beautiful and the scenery surpassing anything of the kind I have ever seen—large rolling prairies stretching as far as your eye can carry you," wrote twelve-year-old Elizabeth Keegan in 1852. "The grass so green and flowers of every description from violets to geraniums of the richest hue. Then leaving this beautiful scenery behind, you descend into the woodland which is . . . interspersed with creeks." Mary Ackley was equally impressed with the swales of prairie grass, wild strawberries, and the "meadows . . . covered with beautiful wild flowers . . . [where] we find white popp[ies]," too thorn-laden to pick. Birds fluttered up from the dewy larkspur, the glossy black wings of the prairie blackbird like a flash of ebony. Birdsong swelled, from the low hoot of the owl to a bobwhite's confused stutter.

Such splendors were not lost on Ada Millington Jones, whose journal records her awe at what nature had wrought.

> Aunt Ollie and we children went up on the hill near by and had such a beautiful view of natural scenery. Near by us was a pretty natural bridge of rocks from one cliff to another. In the distance the Platte River wound gracefully around among the hills which in turn were tastefully ornamented with pines and cedar trees . . . [she then goes on to describe in detail houses that she sees] and all these unusual signs of civilization make our eyes stare and our mouths water.

Camping, for those who had never slept outdoors before, seemed a thrill, and children adapted quickly. One infant grew so familiar with the howl of coyotes that the ticking of a clock seemed terrifying. "He's become a child of Nature," the father concluded—and why not? After seven and a half months on the trail, it was all he had ever known.

There was also fun to be had, whether picking wild strawberries or sliding down a slick clay riverbank. Children scampered after prairie dogs that yipped in surprise and ducked into their pockmarked burrows. For sport, the boys would shoot and hunt, studying animal prints as if reading road signs, or play "Wild West," a favorite game that involved imaginary pony races.

Hiking appealed to these newly minted mountaineers, who garnished the rocks and redwoods with scrawled, carved graffiti. With all the unbroken land around, there was little sense of preservation or care. Ada Millington Jones described an outing with her cousin on Sunday, June 8, 1862.

> My cousin Fred Michael and I started to it [walking to the river] and after a walk of about two miles reached it. . . . We ascended to the top of it which is about 240 ft from the ground and from there had a beautiful view of the surrounding country. . . . We carved our names on the top of the rock and then returned to camp.

When Sallie Hester climbed Devils Gate, a place where the Sweetwater River thundered between huge, four-hundred-foot-high cliffs, she was in a party of young children, none older than fourteen: "We made our way to the very edge of the cliff and looked down," she wrote. "We could hear the water dashing, splashing and roaring as if angry." They were so late returning that the wagon train was stopped and men set out in search of them.

At sundown, heads were counted, and at any unexplained disappearance, the mood would suddenly shift. "We . . . had . . . 'excitements' when we camped," wrote overland child Maggie Hall. Suddenly, parents might recall an unfortunate prank, such as when the boys stole two bear cubs from their nest, which caused a near riot of angry protest from the camp. With every passing minute, wrote Hall, distraught mothers would "let up a wail how the Indians would kill them. So the Pa's would get out guns and off they would go to kick the boys [back] to camp, [but] next chance they had the boys would go off again." Maggie Hall's mother thought her lost when she awoke in a panic one night, searched everywhere for her daughter, and then called "everyone to go down to the river bed & find Maggie, that she had rolled out and hid under the edge of the tent." The girl was found fast asleep in another tent with several of her friends.

Children were often lost, as in the case of two girls who wandered down a rock-bordered trail that "looked like a romantic castle." When they saw Indian horsemen in the distance, they ran back to their wagons, only to find lone wagon tracks and settling dust. Frightened but sensible, the girls carefully followed the tracks back to their anxious parents, who assumed the girls had been kidnapped by Indians. Group politics had dictated their behavior: forced to move on by the rest of the train, they had left their children to an uncertain fate.

At night, the odor of pine or sage would waft skyward from the crackling cedar fires. Myriad stars wheeled overhead. A melody would break out, or a catchy tune on the harmonica, rising higher than the wind in the trees, or the constant coyote cries. At night, grime, fatigue, and cantankerousness melted away in the firelight glow, as, one by one, dancers would rise up and sway to the strains of "Money Musk" and "Zipp Coon." Life in a Conestoga wagon seemed a "continuous picnic" to seventeen-year-old Susan Thompson, California-bound via the Southwest Passage—always plentiful with surprise. When Eliza McAuley's train stopped one night near some sulfur springs, they spied a party camped a few rocks away. "A merrier set I never saw . . . just after dark we were treated to a variety of barnyard music . . . roosters crowed, hens cackled, ducks quacked, pigs squealed, owls hooted, donkeys brayed, dogs howled, cats squalled and all these perfect imitations were made by the human voice." Animal calls? Perhaps the joy of surviving one more day made even the somber pioneers giddy.

Each season brought its own weather, and in summer the heat fell heavy as a fist, smashing the travelers into weary surrender. To Emma Shepard Hill, the sere landscape along the open prairies of the Missouri River seemed Dantesque.

> The Plains that year were burned brown—not one trace of green was there anywhere except along the streams. The air was hot all day, even after the sun had set. Sometimes a little breeze would spring up; but instead of cooling the atmosphere, it felt like a breath from an open furnace door. At times the heat waves rising from the ground were as visible as the mist after a rain. Mile after mile of the road was level as a floor and deep with dust. The bushes and weeds were so dry that they crackled under foot. On each side of the road were hundreds of dead locusts, four inches or more in length. The bleached bones and skulls of buffaloes were everywhere, all over the Plains, hundreds of them shining white in the sun. The bodies of oxen and mules were frequently seen beside the road—worn-out creatures left by freighters to die. The stench from these bodies was at times almost unbearable. If we did not see or smell them, we should know they were there by the number of buzzards circling around.

Grandmother of Mrs. Leslie Curlew standing with horse and child in front of covered wagon just after arrival in northeast Washington.

Nature's violence was witnessed daily, from thunderstorms to torrential rains in which "tents would be blown down, and everybody and everything would be soaked with the driving rains," according to Lucy Ann Henderson, an eleven year old crossing the plains in 1846. Even more frightening were oxen whipped into a frenzied stampede by the startling display of summertime lightning.

Hardships mounted with every mile. "No one can form the most faint conception of the filth, lice, fleas, bugs, reptiles, etc., by which we are surrounded," wrote William Dangerfield. As conditions worsened and oxen weakened, walking was mandatory, even welcome, and children joined their parents in the dust of the road.

Daily tension turned to suspicion and querulousness. Quarrels broke out. Leadership faltered and anger flamed, causing parents to transform before their children's eyes. "I became so frightened [of her]," said one girl of her mother, who was a victim of severe melancholia. Adult anxiety was magnified in childish imaginations, thanks to campfire tales that reflected the inevitable dangers of the trail. In later years, asylums would dot the midwestern plains, offering solace and some treatment to those who suffered from depression. But without professional help, anyone could be affected by a "mental" condition. Why else the woman who talked to herself in low tones and abrupt screams? In another case, recalled by Elizabeth Dixon Greer in 1847:

> This morning one company moved on except one family. The woman got mad and would not budge, nor let the children go. I told my husband the circumstance, and he and Adam Polk and Mr. Kimball went and took each one a young one and rammed them in the wagon and her husband drove off and left her sitting. She got up, took the back track and traveled out of sight. Cut across, overtook her husband. Meantime he sent his boy back to camp after a horse that he had left and when she came up her husband says, "Did you meet John?" "Yes," was the reply, "and I picked up a stone and knocked out his brains." Her husband went back to ascertain the truth, and while he was gone she set one of his wagons on fire.

Wagon life proved dangerous to children in numerous ways. The towering box seat was at least five feet above the ground—a dangerous invitation to frisky youngsters to "pretend drive" the oxen. One jolt, and off they pitched onto the sod below. One young boy nearly bit his tongue off. Another lost an ear. If a wagon lurched into a large pothole or hit a rock, children shot off like sparks. One woman exclaimed to her granddaughter, "Hold fast or you will . . . be run over again." Mary Ackley's two brothers were playing on the wagon bed when a rut "jarred the wagon" and threw out her brother John. "A hind wheel ran over him, breaking one of his legs." Elizabeth Lord, a young overland traveler, had the fright of her life while jumping from a wagon.

> My skirt caught on the king pin; this threw me under the wheels. The first ran over my face, taking all the skin off that side. The next one across my abdomen. The . . . wheels both passed over me before they were stopped. . . . I was badly hurt, but the dust was so deep that it softened the weight and lightened the load.

With so much to occupy attention, who knew where the next danger might lie? Even the scrupulously careful might overlook the threat posed by domestic items—particularly medical supplies.

> I shall never forget [one] camp. Mother . . . hung the bag containing the medicine from a nail on the sideboard of the wagon. My playmate, the Currier girl, who was of my own age, and I discovered the bag, and so I decided to taste the medicine. I put a little on my tongue, but it didn't taste good, so I took no more. The Currier girl tasted it, made a wry face, and handed the bottle back. My little sister, Salita, wanted to taste it, but I told her she couldn't have it. She didn't say anything but as soon as we had gone she got the bottle and drank it all. Presently she came to the campfire where mother was cooking supper and said she felt awfully sleepy. Mother told her to run away and not bother her, so she went to where the beds were spread and lay down. When mother called her for supper she didn't come. Mother saw she was asleep, so didn't disturb her. When mother tried to awake her later she couldn't arouse her. Lettie had drunk the whole bottle of laudanum. It was too late to save her life. Before we had started father had made some boards of black walnut that fitted along the side of the wagon. They were grooved so they would fit together, and we used them for a table all the way across the plains. Father took these walnut boards and made a coffin for Salita and we buried her there by the roadside in the desert. . . .

Despite the tragedy, time was essential—the party simply had to keep moving. "Three days after my little sister Lettie drank the laudanum and died we stopped for a few hours, and my sister Olivia was born. We were so late that the men of the party decided we could not tarry a day; so we had to press on. . . ."

Children fell into fires, were scorched by gunpowder, and once, near Emigrant Gap, some prankish boys pushed a huge rock into the cattle, causing a stampede that nearly killed several men. Another young girl, running to catch a pet crow amid the oxen, was kicked in the forehead.

Encounters with Indians were frequent, but more prevalent was the fear of an encounter, which led to recurring nightmares and moments of anxiety. A young boy, obsessed by the idea of Indians, felt drawn to become what he most feared, dressing up in a blanket and startling the night guardsman patrolling by the river. The guard shouted out, the teenager ran, and the guard wounded the boy, who barely survived.

Worse than nature's storms or the Indian threat was the slow, pervasive hunger that seemed to settle in the bones, compelling every thought to food, driving children to search and forage for any berry they could find, any small animal to be chased. Young girls in tattered homespun were assigned to cook and bake, helping out mothers who were nursing infants or perhaps ill themselves. At first, such responsibility seemed like a game. Girls festooned the plank tables with wild roses, or chopped wild parsley and berries to make a bright condiment. Trench cooking was newly popular—no one had ever slow-roasted meat in the ground, over mesquite coals, before. Girls might shelter the yeast for bread at night in their own beds—in cold weather the delicate brew would otherwise die.

Young boys ran about, drawing water, fishing, finding blackberries. Tired of salt pork and pone, they fanned out from the train, keeping an eye on the wagons but distracted by rabbits, gophers, or

Unidentified pioneer family, ca. 1860.

birds. Fresh meat brought adult praise and culinary variety; they were hailed as little victors when they returned with food. "How we did relish the fish and venison and Buffalo steaks," recalled Rebecca Woodson, tired of the continual home-cured bacon and dry lumps of bread, often weevil-infested. Over time, lack of food weakened the travelers, who presented a pitiable sight when bent from scurvy and other diseases. As an antidote, they would gulp down vinegar, or eat vinegar-soaked potatoes, hoping to trick the body into a sense of well-being.

Food was too scarce to barter or buy, and besides, many were destitute—they had borrowed from friends and fellow travelers for the trip, and, by the time the Sierra was reached, had often paid out the last gold watch, or coin, to buy meat for their children. One family was so ravenous they put woodpeckers, leathery and tough, into a soup, adding a half pound of dried peaches to the broth. Two of the boys became "horribly sick" and disgorged it all.

At times, fodder was just as scarce, so women baked bread for the oxen to keep up their strength. Wrote Emma Shepard Hill: "We were now experiencing much trouble for lack of water, both for man or beast. Wherever we stayed long enough and there was water to spare, my mother cooked a large pot of navy beans, and occasionally made doughnuts; but they were gone so soon that we scarcely knew we had them." Said Elisha Brooks: "You need but one meal a day; you can eat dried apples for breakfast, drink water for dinner and swill for supper."

Burnt sagebrush and red mud for coffee sustained the family of Ada Millington Jones, traveling west in 1862, who shared boiled wheat and meager peas with her five siblings. Traveler Emma Shepard Hill noted that her "next-door neighbors, a man and a wife with two little boys, had at one time lived three weeks on dried apple sauce, and corn meal for flour."

They were as hungry as Elijah, but not as fortunate, pointed out Mary Ellen Applegate's father, describing to his girls the biblical story of the prophet who was fed by ravens. Mary, who could have eaten a peck of raw potatoes as well as the raven, wished for such a miracle, as she was "so hungry for green things" that she "chewed sticks and twigs." A single thought replayed through her mind, "Oh! for something green!" To stave off hunger, Eliza Donner's mother gave her own and other suffering children "wee lumps of sugar, moistened with a drop of peppermint, and later put a flattened bullet in each child's mouth to engage its attention."

But none suffered like twelve-year-old Virginia Reed, traveling with her family from Illinois to California with the ill-fated Donner Party. The party was slowed by lack of feed for the stock and split at Bridger's Fort, with eighty members taking the treacherous Hastings' Cut-Off. The lateness of the season brought winter's first snows, high in the California Sierra, at Donner Lake. After a long, harrowing entrapment and her final recovery, Virginia penned the following account to her cousin.

> My Dear Cousin,
>
> . . . I am going to write to you all about our trubels in getting to California. . . . We got to Donners and they were all asleep so we laid down on the ground. We spred our shawl down. We laid down on it and spred another over us and then put the dogs on top, Tyler, Barney, Trailer, Tracker and little Cash it was the coldest night you ever saw, for the season the wind blew very hard and if it had not been for the dogs we would have Frosen. . . . We staid there a week and hunted for our cattel and could not find them. The Indians had taken them . . . we got out of provisions and papa had to go on to California for provisions; we could not get along that way.
>
> In 2 or 3 days after pa left we had to cash our wagon and take Mr. Graves wagon and cash some more of our things . . . we had to walk all the time—we were traveling up the truckey river. We met a Mr. T. C. Stanton and 2 Indians that we had sent on for provisions to Capt. Sutter's Fort before papa started. They had met pa not far from Sutter's Fort, he looked very bad—he had not ate but 3 times in 7 days and the last three days without anything. His horse was not abel to carrie him—they gave him a horse and he went on so we cashed some more of our things all but what we could pack on one mule and we started. Martha and James road behind the two Indians. It was raining then in the vallies and snowing on the mountains—so we went on that way 3 or 4 days till we come to the big mountains of the California Mountains—the snow then was about 3 feet deep. There was

some wagons there—they said they had attempted to cross and could not. Well we thought we would try it so we started and they started again with their wagons—the snow was then way up to the mule's side, the farther we went up the deeper the snow got so the wagons could not go so they unhitched thare oxens and started with us, carrying a child apeice and driving the oxen in snow up to their waste . . . well the women were all so tired carrying their Children that they could not go on over that night so we made a fire and got something to eat . . . we seldom thot of bread for we had not had any since October. The cattel was so poor they could hardly get up when they laid down. We had to eat I can't hardly tell you and we had Mr. Stanton and the two Indians to feed. Well, they started over afoot and it come on a storm and they had to come back—it would snow 10 days before it would stop—they waited till it stoped and started again. I was going with them and I took sick and could not go. There was 15 started and there was 7 got through, 5 women and 2 men. It come on a storm and they lost the road and got out of provisions. Those that got through had to eat them that Died. Not long after . . . Ma and Eliza and Milt Eliot and I dried up what little meat we had and started to see if we could not get across the mountains and had to leve the children. . . . We went and was out 5 days in the mountains. Eliza give out and had to go back—we went on a day longer—we had to lay by a day and make snowshoes and we went on awhile and could not find the road so we had to turn back. I could go on very well while I thought we were getting along but as soon as we had to turn back I could hardly get along but we got to the cabins that night. I froze one of my feet very bad . . . we had nothing to eat then but hides. O Mary I would cry, and wish I had what you all wasted.

Eliza had got to Mr. Grave's cabin and we stayed at Mr. Breen's. [T]hay had meat all the time and we had to kill little Cash the dog and eat him.

O my Dear cousin you don't know what trubel is yet. Many a time we had on the last thing cooking and did not know where the next would come from but there was always some way provided. There was 15 in the cabin we was in and half of us had to lay a bed all the time. Thare was 10 starved to death while we were there—we was hardly able to walk. We lived on little Cash a week, and after Mr. Breen would cook his meat we would take the bones and boil them 2 or 3 days at a time. Mama went down to the other cabins and got half a hide, carried in snow up to her waist. It snowed and covered the cabins all over so we could not get out for 2 or 3 days at a time. I could hardly eat the hides. . . .

We had not eaten anything for 3 days and we had only half a hide. We was out on top of the cabins when we seen the party coming.

O my Dear Cousin, you don't know how glad I was. [W]e ran and met them. One of them we knew—we had travelled with him on the road—they stayed there 3 days to recruit us a little so we could go. Then 21 started, and went on a piece and Martha and Thomas give out and the men had to take them back. Ma and Eliza and James and I came on, and Mary that was the hardest thing yet, to come on and leave them there. . . . We did not know but what they would starve to death. Martha said Well Ma, if you never see me again, you do the best you can. The men said they could hardly stand it—it made them all cry, but they said it was better for all of us to go on for if we was to go back we would eat that much more from them. They gave them a little meat and flour and took them back and we come on. . . . We went over great hye mountains as straight as stair steps in snow up to our knees. Little James walked the whole way over all the mountains and snow up to his waist. He said every step he took he was getting nearer to papa and something to eat. . . . When we had travelled 5 days we met Pa with 13 men going to the cabins. O Mary you do not know how glad we were to see him. We had not seen him for 5 months—we thought we would never see him again. . . . He said he would see Martha and Thomas the next day. He went in 2 days what it took us 5 days. When he got to the cabins some of the company were eating those that had died, but Thomas and Martha had not had to eat any. . . . Thomas asked for something to eat once. Those that they brought from the cabins some of them was not able to come, and some would not come from the "starved camp" as it is called. Three died and the rest ate them, they were 10 days without anything but the dead. Pa brought

Tom and Patty in to where we were. None of the men Pa had with him were able to go back for the people still at the cabins. Their feet were frozen very badly, so another company went and brought them all in—

Mary I have not written to you half of the trubel we have had but I have written enough to let you know that you do not know what trubel is but thank God we have all got thro, and we did not eat human flesh.

Although far more extreme than the events recounted in the diaries of other children, the drama experienced by the young girl, and her party, was replayed daily, in varying degrees, by other emigrant children. When young Mary Ackley sat on the ground, her face buried in her hands, by her account, she had never felt so miserable in her life. She was terrified for her father's well-being, for her own, and for life in general. She asked herself the question that many must have wondered: "What would become of us children?"

2

BE FRUITFUL, BE FEARFUL

He said, mama How Does god Make Babeys out of Clay? If I knowed I would Be Making Babeys All the Time and sell Them. It is a grat Mistory To Him How children Comes. Shindel told Hime That When Adam Was made He Was Made out of clay And Sat up A gainst the Fense to dry. And Then When he was dry he Began to walk. . . . And That Was The way people Came (When) he Asked Me how Babeys came I told him that god Made them out of Clay two.—*Little Charley Malick*

FAMILY LIFE ON the frontier was a daily lesson in tenderness and devotion, want and privation, as well as some excess—particularly when it came to childbearing. Seemingly, nothing could halt the rising tide of towheaded, sun-bleached children who peered out from curtainless windows, and whose squallings echoed from shanties, sheds, soddies, log huts, and frame houses throughout the West. Childbirth, like Manifest Destiny, seemed limitless and autonomous, made possible, believed French traveler Ferdinand Bayard, by the prospect of plenty. In America, a father must only "cut down a few of these tall trees to provide for the needs of his large family. . . ."

Ideally, warm welcome was given to the children as they arrived, "little roley-poley things, whom it would have been in vain to have Marked this side up like . . . baggage," wrote Mrs. Caroline Kirkland. Parents, often little more than children themselves, were delighted to add offspring to their growing list of adventures, and felt, as did missionary wife Harriet Shaw, there was nothing better than a "healthy child & very little trouble" who "grows, eats & sleeps all night." Parents and children, it seemed, were all pioneers together, learning about frontier life from scratch. Even young children sensed the celebratory nature of bringing another family member into the world. "My little sister . . . was the cunningest baby that ever was," said Sarah Bixby Smith. "They rolled her up so close in blankets that My aunt Francina was afraid she would be smothered. What along time it does take for a baby to grow up enough to play with a person born three years ahead of her!"

Women spent most of their adult lives bearing and raising children, some beginning as young as fifteen, and continuing on into their mid-forties. Mothers and daughters might give birth within weeks of one another, adding to the tight-knit fabric of family life a litter of children, aunts, uncles, and grandchildren—all playmates. Utah settler Priscilla Evans nursed her own baby, along with her little granddaughter, Maud, "as twins." Even as the children grew, replacements would inevitably appear—the progeny of neighbors, children "passing through," or abandoned youngsters. "If our own little children need us no longer," said a Wyoming woman, Mrs. O'Shaugnessy, "[we] mother every child that [does]."

Birth brought a joy so intense as to make all other discomforts di-

North Dakota mother and child, ca. 1900. Photo by Cournoyer Fiske and Francine Fiske, Fort Yates, North Dakota.

minish, and often give rise to rhapsodic musings. The more educated the mother, the higher-flown the sentiments, and the outpourings of verse that accompanied woman's "highest achievement" filled the journals and daybooks of young mothers throughout the land. "My child is the consummation of all my earthly wishes," exclaimed Mormon mother Martha Heywood, stirred to heights of "reverence, love and esteem" by motherhood.

YET THERE WAS much to fear in pregnancy. "Prepare to die!" was Cotton Mather's admonition to expectant mothers, a sentiment echoed in their own minds and often reflected in the number of infant and maternal deaths throughout the country. In a society that had refused to recognize germs until the late 1800s, the idea of prenatal care was nearly nonexistent, bearing out the early American view of childbirth as "one step from the grave." According to historian Judith Walzer Leavitt, Elizabeth Holyoke bore two infants in 1710 and 1711 and died before her second wedding anniversary. Judith Pickman passed away only one month after her marriage from postpartum illness. "In those days," said frontier physician Urling Coe, "a large percentage of the mothers died." "It cannot be long now before the end, or the beginning," wrote expectant Elizabeth Cabot. "I hourly look at the hills . . . and think these may be my last glimpses. . . ." For her, maternity invited mortality—she was woefully familiar with the postconfinement deaths of friends and relatives. In one letter, she described the demise of her friend Isabella Appleton, who was six months pregnant. "I suppose her death was the result of that." Eight years later, Elizabeth's confidence had increased: "The weeks roll on, and my time shortens . . . sometimes I am full of dread; then the reward, and the thought that what I have borne I can bear again, gives me courage, and I think of other things."

As late as 1930, Dr. S. Josephine Baker of the New York City Bureau of Child Hygiene called the United States one of "the most unsafe countr[ies] in the world for pregnant women," with the "highest maternal mortality of the 25 industrialized nations." This, in spite of "scientific" equipment such as the forceps, used to pull infants through the birth canal. An 1879 medical instrument catalog offered fifty-three varieties of this tool, none of which managed to avoïd perforations. Without the ability to perform a cesarean section, doctors sacrificed many infants in order to save the mother. On the frontier, the link between filth and infection was vague, and even among physicians, antisepsis was a fledgling concept and germs rampant. Frontier fecundity loosed rounds of illness, death, and female melancholia, and the lack of proper medical care led to alarming rates of maternal mortality. So common was postpartum death that midwives, both on the East Coast and in the West, routinely explained a birth as "delivered" or "safe delivered," either one being a surprise. The rate at which American women died of childbed fever was reminiscent of that in the most fetid slums of London, causing them to call upon every charm, invocation, and good-luck measure that promised protection from death.

In fact, such grim statistics amounted to a kind of maternal mayhem, with women approaching confinement as if it were the guillotine. In a society that saw God's punishing hand in all natural disasters, childbirth, to many, thrust expectant mothers "almost beyond hope," and its fearsome inevitability was all too often borne out. "O . . . I wish there was no such thing as having babies!" fretted mother-to-be Mary Kincaid in 1896, in mortal terror of the host of woes that she believed would certainly befall her during delivery. Childbirth was, in fact, terrifying—particularly the first time. When Josephine Peabody swelled up with "an apocalyptic hugeness," she could only grasp biblical references for her ordeal. She was a "handmaiden of the Lord who expected a Time of Travail," her success in delivery dependent upon her piety. Yet, for all that, she would not "for anything give up the awfulness of it" for she so desired a child.

Such "awfulness" might take many forms, from the swelling of edema to diabetes and kidney problems, as well as the dreaded "milk leg"—a distension due to venial clotting that led to high fever and hemorrhage. Also common was "gathered breast," an abcess "cured" by lancing, while women only whispered about disfiguring, dropsical swelling, hemorrhoids, nausea, and the prolapsed uterus, in which the hard-worked members simply "fell" out of place and had to be gussied back into position. Most dreaded was childbed fever, often fatal, which would render a mother blind, sometimes unconscious, her breasts in slings, with inflammation of the bowels and blood poisoning. Poor nutrition often caused cases of maternal diabetes, which ironically resulted in extremely large children—babies over ten pounds were often mentioned in diaries and journals, although statistics about birth size were not documented in the 1800s.

Between 1790 and 1840, only 27 percent of the practicing physicians in the country had graduated from medical school, leaving maternal care to the questionable ministrations of herbalists, folk practitioners, empirics, bonesetters, hydropaths, animal magnetizers, and galvanists, whose typical advice might include, "For a headache, put a buckwheat cake on the head!" Midwives commonly provided adequate, sometimes excellent, care.

So lacking were most women in even the most basic information that, in 1909, the government launched the first in a series of White House Conferences on the health of children, sponsored by President Theodore Roosevelt. The result: a special department—the Government Children's Bureau—would attempt to deal with the flood of letters begging for information about parturition, nursing, birth control—even mental health.

> Dear Miss Lathrop,
>
> I live sixty five miles from a Dr. and my other babies (two) were very large at birth, one 12-lbs the other 10 1/2 lbs. . . . I am 37 years old and I am so worried and filled with perfect horror at the prospects ahead. So many of my neighbors die at giving birth to their children. I have a baby 11 months old in my keeping now whose mother died—when I reached their cabin last Nov. It was 22 below zero and I had to ride 7 miles horseback. She was nearly dead when I got there and died after giving birth to a 14 lb. boy. Will you please send me all the information for the care of my self before and after and at the time of delivery. I am far from a Dr. and we have no means, only what we get on this rented ranch. I also want all the information on baby care especially young new born ones. If there is anything what I can do to escape being torn again wont you let me know. I am just 4 months along now but haven't quickened yet.

The lot of the "older" mother was also to be feared. How could a late-wedded spinster, with mature bones already set, adapt to the physical changes of pregnancy? How would it affect a child's intelligence? Georgiana Kirby, an educated woman, was an older mother of thirty-four and remembered that her own mother had "not married until her thirtieth year." Kirby's sister, the younger child of this "elder" woman, was "thoroughly superficial and selfish." Would this happen to Georgiana's child? In a world where fate struck randomly, God seemed vengeful, and superstition prevailed, how could a woman protect her child? Kirby was convinced that her Georgie was born with a weak left eye because she herself had been doing so much sewing and her eyes were weak. With such "power" to alter a child, women were racked with superstitious fear and guilt. "Mother [was] nineteen when I was born," wrote a young Jewish girl, Annette Rosenshine, born with a cleft palate and harelip. "When I was about thirty a boy with a similar defect [cleft palate] was born to my first cousin. . . . It was then that mother confided in me her sense of relief in knowing that it could happen to some one else. Monthly migraine headaches and acute nausea were a high price enough to pay for her ignorance."

Motherhood, ca. 1880s.

MONSTROUS CHILDREN WERE dreaded, and the ways in which people thought they could be formed seemed endless. Wanton and irresponsible coupling during menstruation might lead to a punishing deformity, a sign that unrestrained lovemaking for purposes other than procreation could loose the furies. A chance "sighting" on the mother's part of a deformed animal might mark the child irrevocably and produce a hermaphrodite. Limbless beggars should be avoided, since even a quick glimpse might call down the beggar's same deformities upon the child. The mother alone bore responsibility for "scars, warts, moles and low intelligence" of the child, not to mention birthmarks, blemishes, or animal characteristics. An Indiana woman feared the presence of a "defarm[ed]" baby, its head "like a snake" that she had inadvertently gazed upon. Wouldn't it make her own baby "defarm[ed] as well?" Losing an infant in childbirth, perhaps strangled by an unusually long umbilical cord, was also the mother's fault, particularly if she had driven a wagon, or worse, an automobile, within a month of the baby's delivery. Mrs. G.B. from Missouri outlined her fears to Dr. Blanche Haines of the Children's Bureau. Her child had lived only eight days:

> [My baby] . . . was marked by Something. An open cavity in back of the head had Something Stuck up away into the bone; the place looked like the intestines of a chicken or something similar to it. I don't [know] how I happen to mark it, only one thing I remembered seeing. I had to go thru a pasture at my work and accidentally Saw a cow giving birth to a calf when I was almost 3 months a long, and I'm wondering if it was marked by that. [The

> baby's head] had [two] little skins hanging that I thought resembled the calf's [two] front feet the way they hung, and a bulge that resembled its nose. Tell me where it is possible that one can be marked this way or not? Some of the papers say they can't be marked. My baby was the Stoutest baby I ever had except that when the blood and water seeped out it was down smooth with the head and it died soon after.

Some taboos were simple—salt and egg meant good luck, and a baby should be carried upstairs before it is ever carried down. Others, mostly religious, were complex and threatening, as experienced by Jewish homesteader Rachel Calof. Settled with her husband in Devil's Lake, North Dakota, her first child, Minnie, seemed to bring out every dark fear and superstition that her mother-in-law could muster. "[She] was a religious fanatic and superstitious beyond imagination," Rachel recalled. "The force of her dark beliefs and suggestions found me terribly vulnerable." The older woman "placed a prayer book" in Rachel's bed to "prevent the devils" from harming her and taking the baby. Rachel's nervousness increased:

> I was afraid to examine [the baby] but when I finally got the nerve to unwrap her entirely, I became ill . . . when I saw her navel I screamed in terror. I thought that her intestines were falling out, but it proved to be the cord which was about twelve-inches long. . . . On the third day . . . my mother-in-law instructed me [that] to protect the baby and myself from the contrivings of the devil I must be certain to leave the prayer book in the bed with the child if I had to get out of bed. This was to prevent the devil from taking the child in my absence. For my personal protecting from the fiend, I was to carry a knife at all times in a belt around my waist. . . . The superstitious preachings . . . flooded my mind. My own fevered imagination added to the fantasies. I knew there were demons who looked like little people and whose specialty was the stealing of newborn babies.

When her mother-in-law began to snore one night, the sound "was frightening, particularly so when it began to sound less like snoring and more like devils whistling outside the cabin walls." Rachel continued to be anxious, seeing devils in the grass, feeling them lurking beneath the bed—after six weeks she finally confided in her husband. She showed him the large stones she had dragged into the house at the end of every day, and the household goods and furniture piled on top of the trap door—all to keep the devil out. He comforted her, "constantly reassured" her, and gradually, she "recovered a semblance of calmness."

No less foreboding were food taboos. If a child could be marked by events outside the mother's body, why not, then, by what she consumed? Wrote Mrs. W.M. to the Government Children's Bureau.

> I am pregnant a little over 6 months. I had a longing for strawberries for breakfast one day; I thought about them before I got up, and while in the bathroom combing my hair, I wiped out the corners of my eyes with my fingers. I thought, well, it doesn't matter even if I haven't eaten any strawberries yet. I asked a neighbor about it, and she told me I sure must of marked the baby. Is this possible? She told me if you have an appetite for anything and don't eat it and you put your hand on your face, or scratch your face, that will mark the baby sure. I'm just worried sick. Its on my mind all the time. I wake up nights and think of things to eat; it seems I just cant get that off my mind and what can you do when you long for watermelon or mush melon, or anything out of season? I can't get these things now. Can that mark or harm the baby in any way? Oh please tell me what to do. All these thoughts about marking the baby when you dont eat what you think of, or long for, just drive me frantic. I think of one thing, and then I think of something else, but I try to overcome these thoughts, and then I worry every time I wash or put my hand to my face that I'm marking the baby because I couldn't get or didn't eat what I longed for last. Does this come from worry? I never worried about these things the first few months, but here of late I'm just sick from worry. I couldn't tell this to anyone else but you, as I have no mother, and no one else cares. I have kept it to myself, but I just had to go to someone and I'm sure you will help me. I have your book on "Prenatal Care," but it doesn't say anything about longing for things to eat, so I just had to write and

ask your advice. Thanking you very much. Please keep this confidentially.

Some women believed they could alter the child's gender—perhaps by conceiving two days after menstruation to produce a boy, or indulging in sexual intercourse from the fifth to the eighth month, at the moon's waning, to bear a girl. Twins proved particularly upsetting, since, as one Illinois woman believed, the girl of a twinned pair would be infertile. Yet in the West, where every family counted its wealth in the addition of its family members, a child could only be an asset. As Mary Hallock Foote mused: "Son or daughter, it made no difference to me."

3

Lyin' In

You see how greedy I am for new experiences?
—*Elinore Pruitt Stewart*

She had reason to rest, lying down on prairie grass, and fancying the clouds were baby-carriages, for she knew she was pregnant again and worried that she would miscarry.
—*Russian immigrant woman*

Confinement, or "lying in," was first noted by feelings of "quickening," evident in the second to fourth month in swelling breasts, increased saliva, food cravings, vague stirrings of anxiety, general bloatedness, and even toothaches—not to mention morning sickness. Often called "feeling poorly," the subject was deemed so sensitive that, at least in the South, it was simply known as "that way," or "feeling delicate." Urban Victorian women were politely termed "invalids," or, more concisely, "in a family way," while more explicit terms in general use, such as the legal term *miscarriage of justice,* were thought indelicate.

Not only were references to pregnancy unseemly, but its very existence seemed to come as a surprise, at least to some. Girls married so young they were often confused about the symptoms, and even to older women, such as Martha Spense Heywood, the third wife of a Mormon hat merchandiser in the town of Nephi, on Salt Creek, Utah, the intricacies of pregnancy were so little understood, or discussed, that for many months she simply thought she had taken ill. Certainly she was feeling "poorly," but felt too embarrassed to discuss the matter with her newly acquired "plural sisters," the other wives of her polygamous Mormon husband. "I have had . . . poor health," she noted in her journal. "I have reason to think it is in consequence of a change going on in my system." Modesty and lack of terminology kept her silent. Her discoveries continued.

April 20th. Nature is rapidly growing greener every day. My health has been a little better last week but not so well as I could wish it.

June 8th—Sunday—For two weeks past I have felt rather miserable in health and some puzzled as to the true cause of it having some indications of pregnancy and some rather opposed to it. It tries me a little as to what is the matter with me.

July 13th—Sunday—Sister Susanna Richards called here on that day and having consulted her she told me what it was that caused my pains and prescribed for me. It has been a relief to my mind to have some little knowledge of what the matter was with me. Time seems to confirm my suppositions of being pregnant.

Even as early as 1860, physicians could diagnose pregnancy—scientific medical techniques included the ballottement, a cervical examination, ausculation (or the listening for fetal movements), and a Jacquemin's test to measure the color change of the vagina. But allopaths, with their penchant for fee charging, were not always on call, and many women lived in settings so remote they had no medical recourse.

Confinement, however, continued its inexorable pace, although differing with each woman. Some simply drank milk, loosened their apron strings, and proceeded with their lives, while those of a more delicate nature found the nine-month process a daunting experience, calling up a litany of fears. One woman was struck by such a "deep boredom" that her health failed and she fell into an odd decline "brought on by ennui," explained her puzzled husband. Another first-time mother, a "great big healthy girl," was so "lazy and afraid she would be in pain . . . she wouldn't work on the delivery," according to Dr. Lillian Heath, a no-nonsense physician from Rawlings, Wyoming. "She just laid there hour after hour. Finally I just rolled her over and swatted her backside good three or four times." The delivery started soon after, and she gave normal birth to a big, healthy boy "without any trouble!" Charlene Perkins Stetson found herself unable to move, and "lay about" as if under a spell. "Get up and do something and you will feel better," her mother remonstrated. Charlotte tried to oblige.

> I rose drearily, and essayed to brush up the floor a little, with a dustpan and small whiskbroom, but soon dropped those implements exhausted, and wept again in helpless shame.
>
> I, the ceaselessly industrious, could do no work of any kind. I was so weak that the knife and fork sank from my hands—too tired to eat. I could not read nor write nor paint nor sew nor talk nor listen to talking, nor anything. I lay on the lounge and wept all day. The tears ran down into my ears on either side. I went to bed crying, woke in the night crying, sat on the edge of the bed in the morning and cried—from sheer continuous pain. Not physical, the doctors examined me and found nothing the matter.

Labor provided such excitement that entire rural populations turned out, as if for a lecture, a tableau, or a hanging. In small communities, a "kind of tenseness" settled down from pregnancy through delivery. Exact symptoms and duration of morning sickness were broadcast daily, and the baby's sex "read" by the tilt or thrust of the womb. After delivery, the duration, gruesomeness, and general level of emotion were carefully detailed, as well as the baby's weight, family resemblance, and legitimacy.

As for the delivery itself—there seemed no end of crude and surprising settings for its occurrence. Shanty or shed, cabin or lean-to—no dwelling was too rude, too drafty, or too flea-ridden to serve both as surgical facility and nursery to the frontier mother. Margaret Archer Murray's baby sprang forth in a four-room house that sheltered two families who lived "practly in one room as [the] kitchen was to cold," where she shuddered throughout the delivery due to "icy winds [that] constantly blew in through a hole [in the wall] that one could throw a cat out through." Martha Spense Heywood delivered in a "wagon box that had been set off the running," the bumps and jostles recalling the "unnecessary pain and distress from taking a wrong position." Nor did she enjoy the "smallness of the wagon and its openness." Katherine Fougera, a young army wife in the Dakotas, witnessed a birth in an ambulance that was jolting over the Kansas plains as it carried passengers from one army garrison to another. The mother was the wife of an enlisted man.

> The day, as usual, was insufferably hot, the springless conveyance bumping and bounding in and out of holes . . . and, as they progressed thus violently, the officer noted from time to time that the woman would bite her lips, while beads of perspiration stood out upon her brow. . . . Suddenly . . . the woman spoke. Said she, white-lipped, "I'm sorry sir, but you'll have to stop the ambulance, for I'm going to have a child. . . ."
>
> Then the two men spread gunny sacks . . . on the grass, upon which they placed the suffering woman. Water, a few handkerchiefs, and a penknife had to serve as surgical instruments. Then,

following instructions from the patient, the young lieutenant did his best, and finally, beneath a blazing sun, a wee, very premature recruit blinked . . . and sent forth a wail upon the silent prairies.

Births regularly took place on the jolting, swaying, oxen-drawn, overland journey, without a doctor or even medication. When a "child was doubled up in the womb," said Mary Ackley, "it [was] a very serious and strenuous [affair]" in which someone had to reach in and handle the breech birth. Worse, the woman might have an impatient husband who would allow for only half a day's rest, afraid of losing time or being left behind by the rest of the wagon train. Another overland traveler, Mrs. Moss, delivered as she was riding along in the scorching sun. She suddenly gave a moan, slumped slightly, and "felt worse." Her husband simply "rolled up his sleeves, got into the waggon and received from his affectionate wife another little Moss." In one hour, "everything was put to rights and the wagon rolled ahead. Since he was their first child, they named him 'California.' "

Colorado homesteader Audrey Oldland survived the tortuous hours of her labor "moving beds" with a friend. "We just laughed and played and moved beds all night," she recalled, amazed that she had the strength to pick up the bed and shift it around "until the baby was born the next morning." Another lighthearted labor was enjoyed by Ann, a "generous and goodhearted" woman who ran a boarding house in Topeka, Kansas. Heavy with child and swollen in size, she was still eager to do-si-do at a dancing party "gotten up" by the Episcopalian ladies of the town and held at an old stone hall. The women believed that she "was not particular enough" about life's conventionalities, and knowing her instinct to dance, tried to keep the party secret. As soon as Ann discovered there was a dance, she insisted on attending, and "precarious state" notwithstanding, offered to bring a roast turkey as well. Cook turkey and dance? With a baby due any moment? The matrons shuddered:

> One of the first on the floor was Ann. She was dressed in a black silk dress, ruffled to the waist, and a black scarf knotted in front and looked very nice, but we watched her anxiously. She did not miss a set. . . . [After 12 o'clock] she went through that cotillion and started on another when [there was a] commotion in the set in which she was dancing and Ann [went] hunting her husband.

Unidentified woman holding her child, 1900. Photo by Tonnesen Sisters.

The baby was born almost as soon as the couple reached home, with no "doctor to introduce him to the world." The women tried to keep the news quiet, but, according to one observer,

Gertrude Burlingame, "it got out among the men and soon they were giggling all over the hall."

Even more idiosyncratic was the delivery of a determined young woman whose pregnancy hardly interfered with the more serious business of finding the child's father. It was hardly unusual for a man to "slip away" on the frontier, since a woman's only recourse to pursue was to advertise in newspapers. Yet, disguised as a male, she set out in 1806 for Moose Factory, then a part of the Hudson's Bay Company. Calling herself John Fubbister, she "worked at anything & well like the rest of the men," according to the account of Hugh Heney, her bemused brigade leader. On December 29 young Fubbister fell ill and asked to remain behind from a holiday celebration. Heney was "surprised at the fellow's demand," but that was only the beginning.

> I told him to sit down and warm himself. I returned to my own room, where I had not been long before he sent one of my people, requesting the favor of speaking with me. Accordingly I stepped down to him, and was much surprised to find him extended on the hearth, uttering dreadful lamentations; he stretched out his hands toward me, and in piteous tones begged me to be kind to a poor, helpless, abandoned wretch, who was not of the sex I had supposed, but an unfortunate Orkney girl, pregnant, and actually in childbirth. In saying this she opened her jacket, and displayed a pair of beautiful, round, white breasts. . . . In about an hour she was safely delivered of a fine boy, and that same day she was conveyed home in my cariole, where she soon recovered.
>
> Fubbister, her sex revealed, was renamed Mary and discharged from [the] Honours Service in September, 1809.

NOTHING COULD REVITALIZE spirits like a frontier birth. With only a few hundred trained physicians in the country in the mid-eighteenth century (growing by 1905 to approximately twenty-five thousand graduates of medical schools a year), the "vitalization" often depended upon family members or midwives. "Where there is no competent doctor, people try to help themselves as well as possible," wrote German traveler Goddfried Duden, with "one neighbor does it for another" being the usual standard of natal care. Help could wear an apron or carry a satchel, could be licensed or simply volunteer, but it was always welcome. "Such a long hard night with Mrs. O'Brien, her labor so protracted," wrote Emily French, who rolled up her sleeves and attended her neighbor, although her sole birthing experience had been her own.

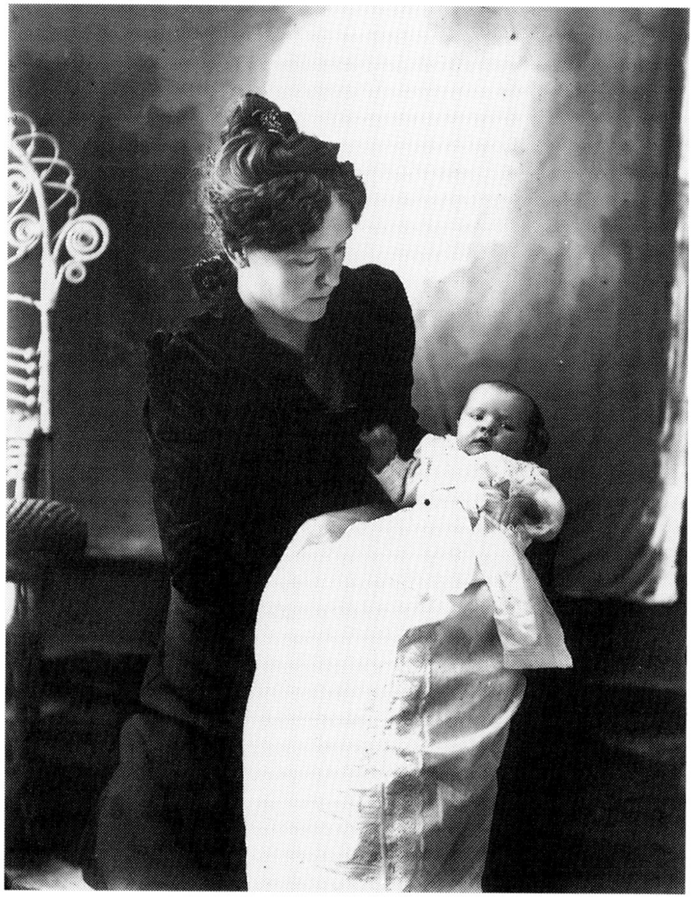

Unidentified woman, Fort Yates, North Dakota, ca. 1900. Photo by Frank B. Fiske, North Dakota.

Western midwives were usually neighborly women who came to midwifery somewhat by accident, and who often preferred not to profit from their calling. In fact, many were unaware they even had a calling, much less a practice, and were summoned in at the last minute by an overwrought husband at the onset of his wife's delivery. "When a neighbor . . . had a baby," mused Hilda Rawlinson, "I came in and took care of the baby, the mother, the children . . . did [the] cooking, the housework, the washing, the ironing, the canning, the baking: everything that the mother did." Rural birth invited a round of female-centered activity, much speculation and gossip, and offered women an opportunity to assist a friend or neighbor in need. Often, a "pye" was baked, the floor swept, the youngsters washed, combed, dressed, and fed. In New England, a festive "groaning board" of "boil'd Pork, Beef, Fowls, very Good Roast Beef, Turkey Pye, [and] Tarts" was set and served, thanking the helpers who had left their own homesteads and farms to tend the household of the delivering woman. According to observer Samuel Sewell, the groans came from the mother in travail, or from the weight of the heavily laden table, or both.

"I had always had a fondness for nursing," wrote Oregonian Bethenia Owens in 1860, "and had developed such a special capacity in that direction by assisting neighbors in illness, that I was more and more besieged by the entreaties of my friends . . . which were hard to refuse, to come to their aid in sickness." Tiring of midwiferey, she eventually graduated from medical school and continued her work, but as a physician. Colorado homesteader Sarah Farrell, cited by historian Julie Roy Jeffrey, "did a little midwifing and some practical nursing," deftly curing a snow-blind cowboy one winter in 1877 with "medication brewed from cedar leaves for tea and poultices." The two eventually wed, and she spent her remaining years affectionately known as "Aunt Sally," an unlicensed midwife who had conducted hundreds of babies into the world.

"Can you give me any information on how to deliver the baby myself?" pleaded a California woman to the U.S. Government Children's Bureau, afraid that her husband might be gone, her neighbors uncooperative, and the doctor, even if she could afford to pay one, difficult to find at the last moment. In the tiny settlement of Hot Creek, Nevada, "Mrs. F [the expectant mother] sent for her friend,

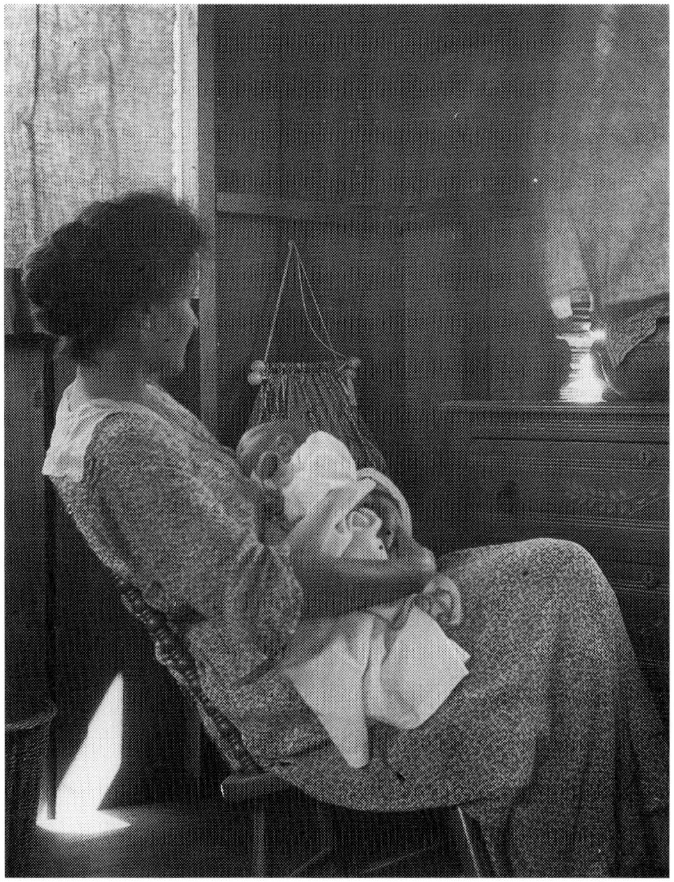

Mrs. Winifred Stanton Hill with baby Janet, Chino, California, September 1916.

Mrs. Smith, who declined coming. Mrs. Shafer then went for a Mrs. Potter who also refused to come, so we were all alone." Fortunately, the child arrived and the mother survived—a happy conclusion, no thanks to her neighbors. "Usually the children arrived before the doctor did," said homesteader Inez Whalin.

"A husband's hands alone are to have access to his sacred wife," wrote George Gregory, a zealot in the cause of female midwives over male attendants, in his polemic *Medical Morals Male.* Some men were not adverse to participation. One young spouse in southern Ohio clasped his arms to support his wife as she straddled his lap, straining to push out their child, becoming, as he did so, a human version of a centuries-long tradition used by women in travail—the birthing stool. A 1701 model had an adjustable seat, handrails to grasp, and a warming pot for the birthed baby—its U-shaped seat resembling a commode. Utilizing gravity's pull, the device allowed women to give birth seated, not prone. This "portable ladies' solace," used in Philadelphia as late as 1799, lent back support as well as privacy, but lacked the empathy and human touch of the Ohio woman's enterprising husband.

"My husband and I were alone, three miles from any woman or doctor," recalled Martha Ann Minto, a child-bride married at fifteen, who seemed oddly sanguine about bearing two children within a scant eighteen months. At "her most private moment," the husband actually delivered the baby, plunging her into a state of agitated embarrassment. Worse, he then had to "perform [the] women's work" of washing out the birth cloths.

When Agnes Just Reid of Blackfoot River, Idaho Territory, delivered a son on September 30, 1876, she was a veteran who "feared the birth with a dread that every mother must feel in repeating the experience of childbearing." This birth would be her last, she was sure, with no midwife or doctor to help out. Then, at "the eleventh hour," her husband stepped in to assist. "Nels acted as surgeon and I as a nurse," she wrote. Thanks to such cooperation, the baby's coming "was a marvel and still is."

Science had made few inroads into rural America, and expectant mothers, "out" of the United States, in one of the far-off territories, had little to rely on save myth, supposition, or dozens of nostrums prescribed by a host of quasi-medical practitioners of the day, such as Hostetter's Celebrated Stomach Bitters or Kickapoo Indian Sagwa. "We can't get anything here for syrups," wrote Harriet Shaw about the New Mexico army outpost. "This country was not made for sick folks or grunty folks." Without prescribed medications, women relied upon elixirs steeped or brewed from home recipes, or from those of their friends.

Nature yielded up a wealth of postpartum remedies to be rubbed in, sipped, or inhaled, as administered by the attending midwife. Herbs to ease the "anguish . . . and great distress attending . . . delivery" were feverfew, slippery elm, cramp bark, squaw vine, orange peel, bitteroot, and blueberry root. Spikenard Tea, priced at 25 cents, "surely helped" a California woman whose first two deliveries were marked by "horrible suffering." After a sip of tea brewed from Spikenard leaves, she didn't "suffer nearly so much." The leaves contained an ingredient found in digitalis, which strengthened the heart during contractions and slowed the pulse. Cramp bark effectively "relaxed cramps or spasms," while a small infusion of slippery elm bark or marshmallow root relieved the itching caused by urine.

Folk remedies were largely empirical, and stories of their use were whispered from woman to woman, invoking tradition as well as founding new ones—yet another aspect to western family autonomy and heritage.

4

Tin Bottles and Baby Care

The rest of us went to bed, all except Mrs. O'Shaughnessy, who was so cranky and snappy that we left her by the fire. . . . She was still sitting [there] . . . absently marking in the ashes with a stick. I happened to be the first one up next morning and as I stirred up the fire I saw "Baby" written in the ashes.—*Eleanor Pruitt Stewart*

I want to play with my babies, I want to have time to love them and laugh with them. I have wanted babies for years now. . . . I love them until it hurts and know that, when they are out of their babyhood, I can never forgive myself for not making more of these precious years.
—*Mrs. N.W. of Seattle, Washington, March 4, 1920, writing to M. Lathrop of the Government Children's Bureau.*

Will you be kind enough to send me bulletins suitable for home care of babies that I may . . . pass on to the few mothers who can read?
—*Mrs. E.M, July 15, 1917, writing to the Government Children's Bureau*

He Is Avery Butiful child And grows Fineley.—*Abigail Malick, speaking of her grandson*

Infancy brought its gifts to parents and children alike, turning sober adults childlike with happiness as they admired the new addition. Like a child herself, Josephine Peabody, writing in 1908, could hardly wait to share her "high spirits and light feet" with her new little companion. "I've been such a child . . . all my years, that the natural sequence of times and things is a marvel to me, always." For Peabody, infant care was simply part of a vast, swooning tide of adoration and parental pride, in which her "delight grew with the reality of the thing." She was unfailingly inspired:

> If our First Born isn't an Armful of Chuckles, there's nothing in heredity. He must have Begun when I was so filled with the October sunlight setting my own happiness a-sparkle that I could do nothing at all but run about this house with wings on my heels, making a merry noise unto the Lord.

Yet an infant's first months could also be tense with unspoken dread, with the verbal precaution "if he lives" repeated almost as an incantation to ward off the probability of the child's death. Only after the infant "proved up" could a family relax into tender approbation. To help with the "proving," a mother must keep the baby safe, fed, warm, and protected—duties that every woman took seriously. A west Texas mother sewed flour sacks into a tiny mattress that she had stuffed with grass cut from a riverbank in order to

Unidentified baby in christening dress, ca. 1890.

"make the sweetest smelling bed." A Colorado infant rested snugly in a cotton-lined wooden box set over a rubber hot water bottle, a makeshift incubator to keep him cozy. For extra comfort, the baby was laid in front of an oven, "set down real low, & the oven door opened for warmth, and fed milk through an eyedropper." Sickly, weak "blue babies" were bundled in swaddling clothes, their tiny limbs massaged with oil to restore circulation. Russian immigrants practiced brauching, which combined prayer with massage, as the child's arms and legs were smoothed with a concoction of vinegar and fat, then moved back and forth in rhythmic motions. The mother, sunk into holy meditation, would utter a prayer at every stroke, and if the baby continued to cry, she would comfort it with a sock filled with heated oats, laid across its chest as an impromptu hot water bottle.

Instinctively, women knew that their own tranquility would contribute to the child's well-being. Lydia Child and Lydia Sigourney, popular domestic authors of the mid-1800s, implored mothers to adhere to a "season of quietness" during lactation, so as better to perform their "sacred office." Nursing mothers found in the tug and flow a comforting reassurance of their own vitality, as well as relief from the symptoms of milk abscesses, headaches, and general engorgement. Poor milk led to malnourished, sickly infants, a reason for fretful concern. Wrote one mother to the Children's Bureau in 1910:

> 5 years ago . . . I gave birth to a baby boy. After having been obliged to go without food myself so my other 2 little girls could have enough to eat and not go hungry, then my baby was born. And ther I was, no food for me, only what was given to me by kind neighbors.
>
> I nursed my baby mornings and night, at night time after working all day then nursing my child. Every drop it swallowed it would throw up. At the same [time] I [was] suffering the awfull torture with my milk, pumping it and throwing it into the sink, while my baby starved and my husband refused to provide for us. At the end of one month my milk had dried up. There [I] was without the fountain nature had provided me with to feed my child. . . . He will be 5 years old next Nov. This is only one reason why mothers cant nurse their babies.

Another reason was vanity. For more cosmopolitan women, some of whom had begun to settle in the West but were still tuned to the vicissitudes of fashion, the lure of small waists and discreet breasts remained important—any hint of a sagging shape would cast them out of vogue. Gathered breasts, not to mention tired or sagging ones, were bothersome and outmoded, and among many urbanites, nursing was viewed as a short step toward total decline, thrusting women into the early realm of the old and the haggard. "Nurse a child, lose a husband" was whispered from one to another, although nature's way usually prevailed. Yet, when one young wife was informed by her mother-in-law that "giving her baby breast" was a sure way for a young woman to look old, the girl simply shrugged. Nursing, to her, was one of the "grandest sights to see and one she would not relinquish."

Willis Hayden Gray in a high chair, ca. 1890.

Wise instincts, indeed. Between 1832 and 1842 half the children born in the West died before their fifth birthday—more suckling might well have prevented an even greater toll. Lactation protected the child from cow-borne intestinal disease—health hazards due to lack of sanitation, pasteurization, or refrigeration of milk. Cow's milk might also be steeped with deadly tremetol, the result of grazing on milkweed. Harmless and even enticing to a cow, this deadly plant was fatal to humans when processed into milk and accounted for the sudden deaths of many. Breastfeeding also circumvented the use of tin or pewter "sucking" bottles, which were favored by women during colonial times but had a lead content so high that many children were slowly poisoned through prolonged use.

If suckling seemed natural to most, weaning was a more complicated process, burdened with the chill of emotional separation and dependent upon the coaching of neighbors, friends, and even instructions from faraway relatives. "I wrote you a long time ago about the signs of weaning, but you never told me," Harriet Shaw complained to her mother in Vermont by letter. "Perhaps I have weaned her at the wrong time & that makes her sick. . . . Is it a whim or do the signs make a difference? Do tell me . . . or send me a leaf of the old Abels Almanack with the signs." Harriet finally decided to rub both breasts with coal, which so startled the child she recoiled, calling it "dirty," and then "wanted the other & behold it was dirty too." Although effective, weaning left the child "looking sad" and Harriet with excess milk, which she relieved by letting her "other children draw my breasts once a day." A San Francisco matron, the mother of Annette Rosenshine, was also engorged, and without the yet-to-be invented breast pumps, she finally found release when "a puppy was provided to relieve [her] of her milk." Mothers felt possessive about their milk to varying degrees. While some shared their bounty—even became wet nurses—others shunned the prospect. Caroline Kinkaid, documenting her life as a sophisticated woman in the wilds of Michigan, noted the penchant for borrowing in village life—until it came to children. When "little Ianthe Howard, dirty as ever, sat down and stared a while" and then informed the women that her mother wanted Miss Doubleday to let her have her baby for a little while, "cause Benny's mouth [was] so sore that . . . ," she had no time to finish her sentence. Miss Doubleday's outraged scream, "Lend my baby!" cut her off. Ianthe was immediately ousted from the room.

Mary Hallock Foote, in the spring of 1887, noted that her newborn was wan and listless and failing to gain weight. "She was not holding her own." Foote was suspicious of the doctor's injunction "not to wean her until the heat of her second summer was over." Physicians and medical advisers were unanimous in the decision that mothers should suckle for as long as possible; it was the assumed "mother's religion." But not all children received enough nutrition from breastfeeding. Foote finally nerved herself up to disobey orders and fed the baby cow's milk instead, rejoicing in the instant improvement she found.

Once weaned, an infant had to be fed, usually with scraps and bits from the family table mashed in milk, or a combination of cow's milk mixed with brown sugar and bread, called "pap" in the South and used as a common replacement for mother's milk. According to Pauline Diede, Russian babies were raised on "kindes brei" (baby mush), a slather of flour and water or milk mixed together, then simmered on the stove to a saucelike consistency.

> Ma took a spoonful of it and swished it around in her mouth then fed it to the baby. Every midwife recommended mixing the brei with the mother's saliva before being fed to the baby. It was considered the proper way, and no worse than the baby sucking from a mother's breast. Even as a child of four years, it made me gag.

Mothers were warned against giving solid food to their toothless offspring, yet they somehow knew better, and would slip an infant eggs or cake or potato scraps at the first signs of hunger. As children grew, their diets expanded to include milk-soaked chunks of dense baker's bread, canned milk, fork-mashed meats, soup, and stews. Infants generally shunned green vegetables—not unlike their parents—and savored thick puddings and soft fruit. An Iowa woman worried about the digestibility of foods queried the U.S. Children's Bureau. She had already consulted her battered copies of *Mrs. Max's Child Care* and *Milk's the Indispensable Food for Children* by Dr. D.R. without success.

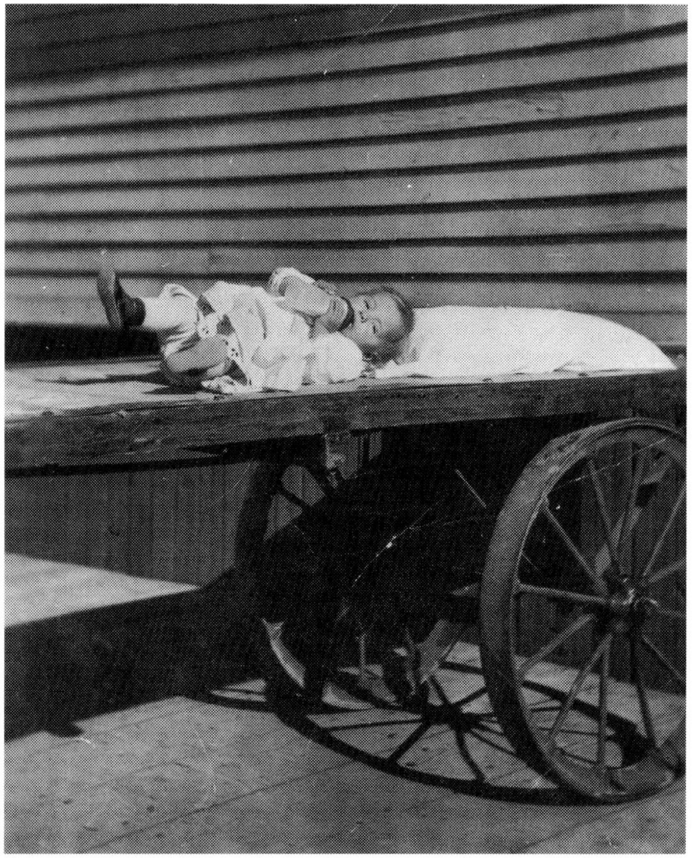

Unidentified child with bottle, ca. 1914.

> I have a little boy one year and nine months old, and some people insist on giving him cake, pie, cookies, doughnuts, etc. in spite of my objections. They have even said he could have pickles. Why should pickles be any more digestible because they are "well Spiced?" Are not spices constipating? I was shocked beyond measure when after my baby swallowed a prune seed, [and] a lady

said, "It wont hurt him, is good for him, the rough surface will hold particles etc." Am I not right when I say that the stomach starts to work on anything it receives, and if it is some indigestible thing that . . . is harmful to the child? I am trying to raise my baby to a strong healthy boy, but it is hard to always know the right thing to do when older people say some such things as I have mentioned.

Recently my husband asked, "how old must he be when he can have pickles," and I could not answer that, only I know he can't have them now.

On the frontier, poverty was the norm and want was so predictable as to be respectable, as much a part of the landscape as scrub creosote or windswept mountains. Daily reckonings with the safekeeping cookie jar, or the match tin, or wherever stray pennies might be hoarded was an ongoing disappointment, raising the perpetual question, How to feed a family on nothing? After food for the children and fodder for the flock, plus seed, medicine, and savings were factored in, family life often turned into a breathless fiscal marathon, broken by occasional celebration, but more often than not, borne along on a mounting tide of despair. Even those fortunate enough to earn wages, such as post office workers or county assessors in government employ, brought home less than one hundred dollars a month, scarcely enough to feed a family.

Usually, the question of food had more to do with its existence, not quality. "Was it nourishing?" gave way to "Is there any?" as hope for variety, balance, and freshness grew dim. One rural mother could find no edible fruit or vegetables locally, leaving "nothing to feed [her child] but macaroni and [canned] tomatoes." Fresh milk was scarce, and infants in mining communities or remote homesteads might be raised on Horlicks Malted Milk or Allenbury's, an imported powdered milk substance from England.

Nutritional disorders were common in families who lived year-round on available staples such as dried apples, spices, sugar, molasses, herring, sardines, flour, corn meal, and salt pork. Vegetables often arrived in tins, and if free of corroded solder that "may have dissolved out" with the juices, they were also free of nutritional value. Children from the sunless Pacific Northwest, who lacked citrus fruits and vegetables, were often splayed by rickets, with bowlegs, misshapen heads, and sunken chests. Such symptoms attested to severe vitamin D deficiency, reversible only by doses of Phillips' palatable cod liver oil emulsion, administered daily. The lack of fresh vegetables and fruits and the use of powdered milk substitutes also caused scurvy. "Our meals often consist of ham & bread & a dish of milk, but a person here, on account of scurvy, has to be cautious in eating salt," wrote Harriet Shaw. Advanced scurvy in an infant was both terrible and irreversible, seen in the telltale swollen eyelids, emaciation, dehydration, thin bones, rapid respiration, spongy gums, and faint heartbeat of a fevered child.

Dietary success was quickly registered by the baby's bowels, a bellwether of health brooded over attentively and read like tea leaves. Constipation? Looseness? The symptoms were myriad. "Our baby had not had an unaided movement of the bowels for more than a year when he died this June, at the age of two and a half years, [too] worn out to cut his last two baby teeth," one mother grieved, perhaps unfamiliar with the popular "soap stick" suppository taken with lime water to free up the system through invasive action—a process not always successful. For another bereaved mother, science was the culprit:

> I gave birth to a beautiful fat boy and it lived but 3 days. The Drs. claimed the baby had a leaking heart; he died in convulsions. I would like to know if the injection the woman gave him of soap & water threw him in these convulsions as he just moaned like a pigeon & his whole body shook after that & at night he was dead.

In fact, many so-called heroic measures, named after the invasive and often fatal techniques of Civil War doctors, were too extreme for a child's system. Harriet Shaw, for one, refused to call in the doctor for as "long as she dared," fearing his recommendation of calomel, a purgative so filled with mercury that mouths were ulcerated and teeth and jawbones rotted by its fiery effects. "I could not stuff him with mercury," she confessed, throwing away the doctor's prescription for her Georgie's diarrhea.

Instead, folk remedies passed from midwife to mother to daughter to child, and the brewing, stewing, steeping, and administering of them was an act of love and lore, both reinforcing family ties as well as the prevailing traditions. Home remedies were often recorded in journals or daybooks, as was this backwoods favorite:

> How to cure a sore throat in children.
>
> Take a small piece of pork and fasten it to a string. Thrust the morsel down her son's throat, and then with the string draw it up and allow it to be swallowed and drawn up again, repeating many times.

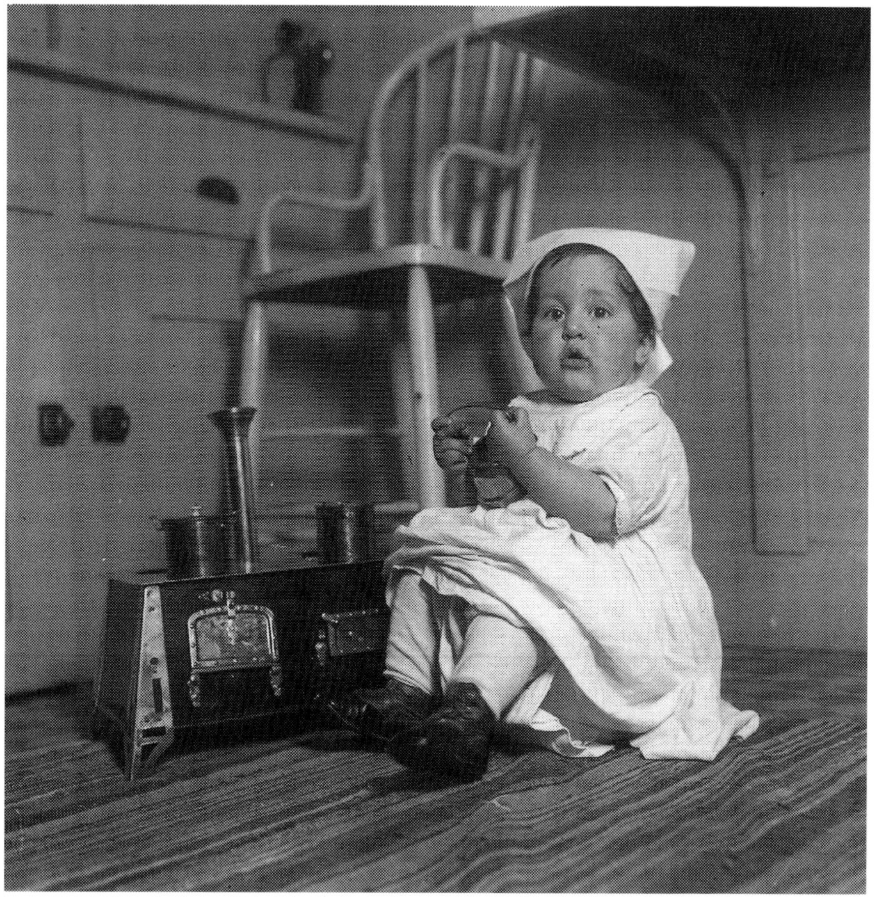

Harriet Rhoads playing with toy stove, ca. 1900s. Photo by Harry Rhoads.

When it came to dosing children, "Sandhill pioneer people had not medicine cabinet nor were there any filled prescriptions," wrote one young girl. In fact, medicine was "almost nil." Instead, frontier women turned to pantry and root cellar, or gathered wild herbs and bark in the springtime for use yearlong. Baking soda soothed the child's sour stomach, sulphur laced with molasses or honey or syrup buoyed up the constitution, while skunk oil, goose grease, sorghum, rhubarb, and teas of butternut, boneset, burdock, sassafras, and smartwood were natural digestive aids. Failing those, minute doses of quinine, morphine, and particularly whiskey were an "eye-opener" and a "victual settler," serving as an exhilarator to stimulate and as a medication for both children and adults. Coe's Cough Balsam deterred "tickling of the throat," while Ayers' sarsaparilla purified the blood, cured tumors, ulcers, sores, and skin diseases. Anyone sick with alkali poisoning "was doctored with the usual antidotes—vinegar fat meat etc." Children were slathered on feet, wrists, and neck with mustard poultices, dosed with ginger tea, had their limbs rubbed with whisky, and a rough bag of asafetida or gum resin hung around the neck to ward off colds. Infants were "greased up" as thoroughly as wagon springs, in the belief that no baby could be properly raised without goose grease to prevent their taking cold. Inspiration struck a Colorado woman, Emily French, who simply "put a raisin in the navel" of a newborn to sooth the inflammation.

When Sarah Gillespie's "ears [were] very sore," her mother did not wait around for professional help. She simply "opened one [ear] . . . & squoze an awful lot out." What was "squoze" was never named, nor the degree of pain experienced, yet by Sarah's account, the problem was apparently solved.

Wrote Sylvia Dye:

> I could still feel the warmth and grease of poultice made from turpentine and lard heated, soaked, and wrung out of a piece of flannel which she put on as hot as I could stand it on my chest and back. Sometimes goose fat was used and many times skunk grease which, though just a wee bit off in smell, seemed most effective. Once I even had on my chest hot fried onions for a phlegm breaker. Some used mustard plasters. Once when a teenager, I had a boiled flax-seed poultice around my arm to cure a stubborn

boil. It was soft as breakfast cream of wheat, and each time I raised or lowered my arm, the cloth bandage couldn't hold, so it seeped out, running up and down my arm. I wore it one day and that was enough for me.

In Idaho, the favorite folk cure for colic in children was to blow tobacco smoke into a saucer of milk, then feed the milk to the baby. In Mississippi, catnip tea was given to babies until they were five or six weeks old. Why? Because, said one woman, "Mother gave it to her children & I am giving it to mine."

To the new mother, every aspect of a child's behavior was inexplicable, including the ubiquitous penchant for "self-play." In repressive Victorian times, even the notion of adult sexuality was off-limits—for an infant, it was unthinkable. Adults were deeply disturbed by the implications. "My Baby has masturbated since five months old," wrote Mrs. W.D. of North Dakota. "I told Dr. K . . . and he could not believe it. . . . Dr. K. said he never heard of a child under the age of four masturbate. I am certainly much grieved over her condition as I think this is the reason for her being so delicate."

Mrs. R.C., in a letter to the Children's Bureau, was horrified. "The baby . . . has, what you call in one of your books . . . masturbation. [W]hen [diapered] she sits up and works herself backwards and forwards. I tried folding it square and keeping her washed clean. But it does no good." The mother could not "hold up much longer under the strain and worry of it" and "would rather die now" than have her daughter persist in "grow[ing] up that way." As a young girl, she had seen some of her friends, no doubt depraved, "riding their seats," and she couldn't bear to think of her own daughter so possessed. Mrs. D.F. was equally horrified by her eleven month old's "habit of crossing her legs and rocking to and fro and sort of bearing down at the same time." How to stop such behavior? One doctor offered to brace a stick between her legs, or tie her legs to the crib, despite which, the girl continued to "rock and breathe heavy." "A most disgusting thing," said her mother. "It is making a nervous wreck of me."

Also puzzling to parents was the baby's foreskin, which, left intact, might subject the child to the prevailing theory that the uncircumcised were "mentally dumb" and would always be impaired. But

Unidentified Colorado child in high chair, ca. 1880.

its removal, for religious or hygienic reasons, was dangerous, since the procedure was frequently botched by unskilled medics, leaving the child in a state of delayed healing, swelling, and bleeding, often with the skin cut too far back. Common wisdom dictated that the foreskin was perfectly satisfactory as long as a mother simply pushed it back, kept it clean, and applied occasional unguents—what else was needed? One mother worried that the baby "pulls at himself so

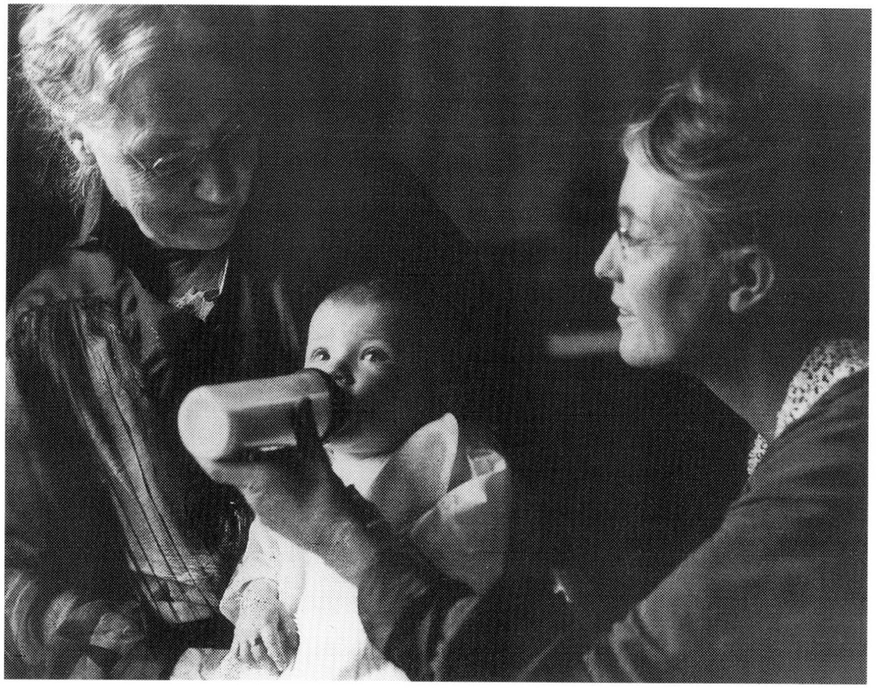

Robert Hopkins with his two grandmothers—Mrs. R. D. Hopkins, Bismarck, North Dakota, and Mrs. Collinson, Devils Lake, North Dakota—December 1915.

much . . . at times it gets as red as blood." Should the baby keep the foreskin, or not? For Jewish children, there was no question that the circumcision ritual be performed on the eighth day, or shortly afterward, according to Jewish law. The officiant, however, must be ritually trained and acceptable—in many rural settings, there were few proficient enough to turn back the foreskin without resulting infection. Arizona settler Isaac Goldberg delayed his son's circumcision for five months after the child's birth, until he could find, in San Francisco, "the Great City of the West," a ritually fit practitioner to read the prayers and perform the ceremony.

⁂

HYGIENE PRESENTED OTHER pressing concerns. On the frontier, ignorance prevailed, poverty was the norm, and in the midst of such attendant grimness, fresh food, clean hands, and boiled water seemed remote. The notion of linking germs to infection seemed dubious, a "new bit of nonsense," and even as late as the early 1900s strict rules of hygiene were the exception. "Dirt and dust, how many mothers as well as myself can't afford soap to help clean with?" admitted one mother. "I regretted taking my tiny infant among people where might lurk the germs of every dread disease," wrote Agnes Reid in 1879. "We never go anywhere to expose the children." Another mother came up with her own remedy: birthing clothes sterilized with carbolic acid, baked in the ranch oven.

Even the advent of teeth could cause a crisis, as when Harriet Shaw's youngest, Lilly, "looked more like a corps than a living child" due to teething. "I have used warm bath, castor oil, rhubarb & magnesia," Harriet noted, yet still, the child was "so pale & weak she could hardly walk without staggering." Babies could also have colic, a common debility dispelled by oil, calomel, brandy, or the innovative use of a suet-and-turpentine chest plaster. Mumps, measles, and whooping cough were rampant, with little remedy other than patience. Since most ailments went undiagnosed, the best remedy was "water, breast milk, flannel clothing, cool baths and wool stockings" and waiting for an illness to run its course. Isabella Bird nursed a woman suffering from cholera and, after searching for a baby bottle to feed the patient's starving infant, finally saved the child with a milk-filled sponge. Cholera infantum was a widespread childhood affliction, often attributed to miasmic conditions in hot, swampy climates, or in some cases, simply to teething. Mysterious as the malady was, the true causes were undoubtedly spoiled food and cow's milk given to recently weaned infants, resulting in severe diarrhea and death. Rhubarb and magnesia were prescribed for children, as well as purging with calomel, leeching behind the ears and blistering the stomach. Castor oil would cleanse the digestive tract, followed by a mild cathartic, such as Dover's Pills, or soothing, opium-laced drinks.

Evidence suggests that serious illness took an equally taxing toll upon the mother, who, like one woman, "almost got to be as bad as the Child." For Mary Hallock Foote, "going to bed was a waste of time," while watching over restless children at night. "We sat under a lamp at the dining room table, surrounded by measles in the rooms adjoining and there we read half through the night."

When not scrounging for food or embroiled in a medical emergency, women faced the unending duty of hand-washing soiled diapers, a daily round of boiling water and lye soap, celebrated by a line of ragged cloth diapers lofting high in the wind. Cumbersome and unlovely, diapers were made from fabric nearly a yard wide and folded repeatedly into four dense layers of material, then snapped closed with a large safety pin. "In the summer time . . . even the little babies had their three-cornered pants pinned on with common pins," said Iowa settler Margaret Archer. Children wetted themselves so frequently that fabric would be oiled, in the hopes of keeping the dampness from spreading.

Occasionally, children were swaddled, an old-world, Russian custom of tightly binding the child's abdomen, then wrapping the baby around in extra cloths to shield him from the dangers of night vapors, although not from the possibility of poor circulation or broken bones. By the mid-1800s, gowns were loosened and petticoats encouraged, giving the infant untold new liberty in its roomy cotton or linen shifts, its need for perpetual motion satisfied. Loosely gowned babies, it was believed, learned to walk earlier.

While cuddling an infant, a mother might sing and sew, croon and crochet, interweaving her loving responses to the child with the everyday concerns of fashioning a wardrobe in which style and cut were secondary to sheer availability. In a flour-sack economy, "store-bought" clothes were unheard of. Well-worn pants, shirts, and jumpers were fished out of the church charity barrel to be torn apart, hemmed up, then redistributed to friends and neighbors. The ruffle from an old slip might turn into a sack gown; an old pair of denim pants, softened by hand-washing over the years and ripped into shabby strips, was stitched into diapers.

More immediate by far than financial needs was a mother's need for help with the children, though she rarely got it. Tending an infant led to extreme exhaustion—everyone knew it. On the overland journey, "There were nine babies under a year old in the company; everybody was willing to tend a baby."

"I know mothers ought to get used to such things," wrote Mrs. Caroline Kirkland, "I have heard that eels get accustomed to being skinned, but I doubt the fact." Said Georgiana Kirby: "Directly I exert myself I get ill."

Mrs. James McLaughlin and grandchildren, ca. 1880s. Photo by Frank B. Fiske, Fort Yates, North Dakota.

> During the three years . . . it was a constant strain on my powers, bodily and mental. . . . I trembled all over from weakness constantly, and it was so discouraging to go to bed at night feeling that notwithstanding such exertions the work was all behindhand. Ora was a most troublesome child till she was 3 1/2 or 4 years old. No one could imagine the mischief such a really

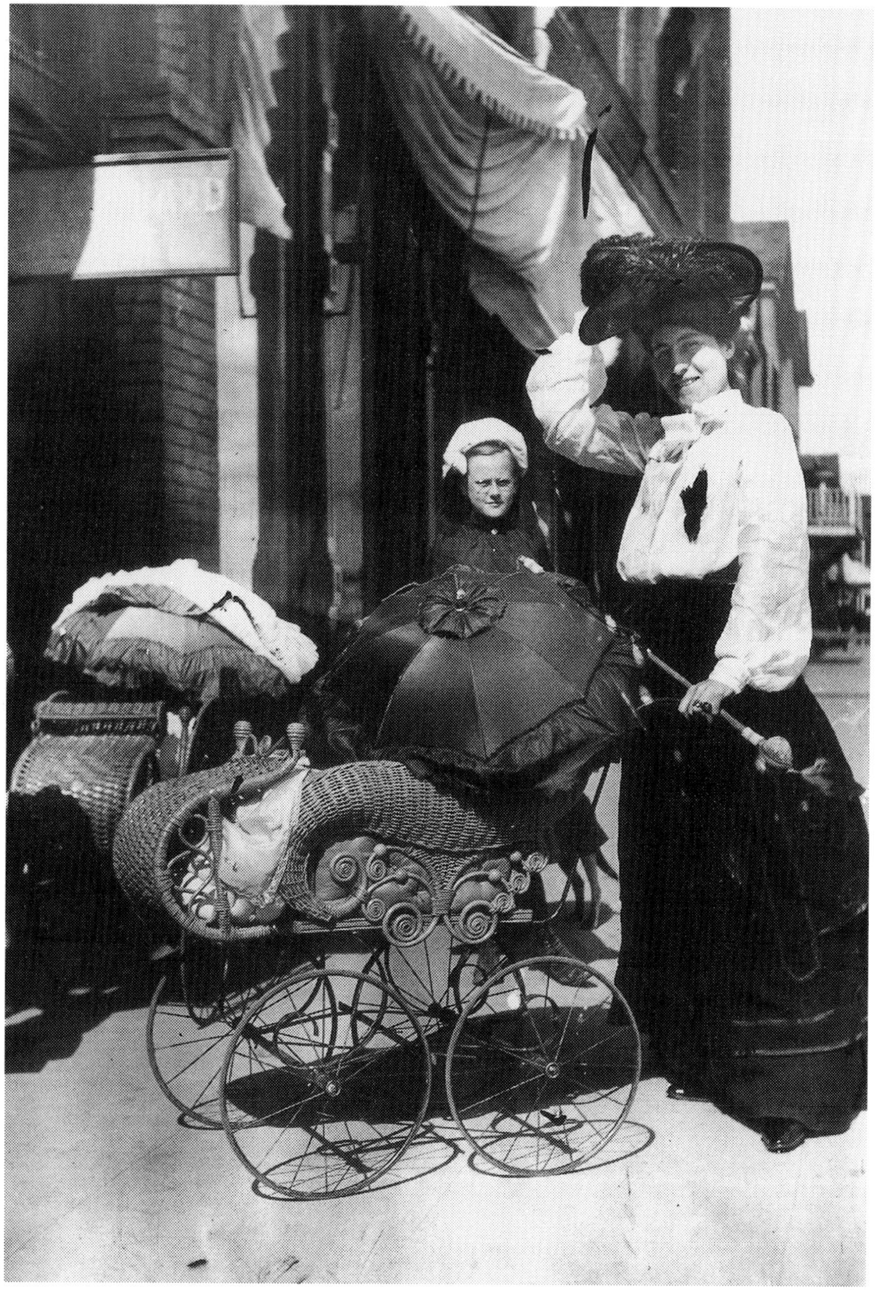

Lucille Van Solen in Bismarck, North Dakota, ca. 1890s. Photo by Frank B. Fiske, Fort Yates, North Dakota.

good child could accomplish. Then to cook, wash, iron, house-clean, bake, mend, nurse, write letters, receive and pay visits, read, etc. all of which was necessary if you would really live like a civilized being, was too much for one person. I feel that at forty my constitution is gone and even if I had a boy he would not be what we should expect.

Another mother expressed her worry in a letter to the U.S. Government Children's Bureau:

I need advise. I am a farmers wife, do my household duties and a regular field hand too. The mother of 9 children and in family way again. I am quarrelsome when tired and fatigued.

When I come in out of the field to prepare dinner my Husband and all the children gets in the kitchen in my way. I quarrel at them for being in my way. I tell them I will build them a fire if they are cold. I also threaten to move the Stove out on the porch. What shall I do? My husband wont sympathize with me one bit but talks rough to me. If I get tired and sick of my daily food and crave some simple article, should I have it? I have [helped] make the living for 20 years. Should I be denied of a few simple articles or money either?

When a farmwife, Tillie Mae W., also complained to the U.S. Children's Bureau, it was because of pains, headaches, weak legs, and exhaustion, thanks to six children and the terror of another pregnancy, and worse, the weekly specter of "nail day," a dreaded, mid-week event in which she cut all the finger- and toenails of six children, plus those of her husband and herself, a scattering of 160 dirty nails! Had she known of such a thing before marriage, Tillie sobbed, she would still be single.

OFTEN, SIBLINGS OR grandchildren helped with baby care—no reason the young couldn't help the younger, since the responsibility of the assignment added to their sense of self-worth. One young boy found that "he was to take care at night of each two-year-old whenever its place in the cradle was taken by a new baby." Thanks to his participation, his older sister, Francina, managed to escape the usual fate of an oldest daughter, that of secondary mother. Bethenia Owens, a twelve year old growing up in Oregon, was the appointed family nurse.

> "It was seldom that I had not a child in my arms, and more clinging to me. Where there is a baby every two years, there is always no end of nursing to be done; especially when the mother's time is occupied, as it was then, every moment, from early morning till late at night, with as much outdoor as well as indoor work. . . .
>
> When the weather was fine we fairly lived out of doors, baby and all, I hauling the baby in its rude little sled, or cart, which bumped along, and from which baby was often thrown out, but seldom seriously hurt, and never killed. [I always had] a two-year-old on one hip, and a four-year-old hanging to my skirts . . . so we went, playing here, and working there during all the pleasant weather. When it rained, we had access to the barn . . . and many a time I have carried the children to the top, from where, with the baby in my arms, and the two younger clinging to me, I would slide to the bottom, to their great delight.

Neighbors and friends could be counted on to help, particularly if they were gathered at a worship service. A meeting should be a place of welcome for all, fretful children or not. Ohio homesteader Keturah Penton observed a mother with her colicky baby.

> She was fixing to go out dores with it and the preacher said dont go out Dear sister the child will soon get quiet, and he asked the congregation to give him their Prayerful attention while the sisters took care of the dear little child, and by that time Mother had some water boiling in a tin cup on the coals and her root of Calamas and had some warm tea, so she took the baby from its young excited mother and gave it a few spoonsfull of the tea then made it comfortable and turned it on its Stumach with its feet to the fire and in a few minutes it was asleep and this was all done right in meeting, and nobody thought it any thing out of the way.

The husband of Anna Waltz was a cheerful contributor to her

The Beaulieu family, ca. 1880s. Photo by Frank Fiske, Fort Yates, North Dakota.

well-being, with ideas that seemed to her inspired. Both knew that the dry-bone South Dakota prairie was "no place for a baby buggy, for it would be impossible to push it more than a few feet from the soddie because of the rough ground." So her husband built a little wagon, "sun or rain proof," that she could park outdoors when not in use. "Oh yes," she said admiringly, "my husband has thought of almost everything." Milton Shaw seemed equally supportive, making a "very good" nurse and rendering his wife "much assistance." "Sometimes the babe sleeps with him on the floor & some times with me for we are so poor we have but one bedstead & that so narrow it will not accommodate us all," wrote Harriet. But even the most thoughtful spouse faltered when it came to diapering and dinners, and would retreat to the fields to get on with the "man's work" of seeding,

Young girl with mother in garden, Humboldt County, California, ca. 1910–15.

mowing, or furrowing—anything to avoid the anxiety of wailing babies and sodden diapers. Mothers thus left to themselves had to devise child-care methods that allowed them to keep on with their own work, usually by stowing their infants in baskets or boxes stationed along the work route. Matilda Peitzke Paul dragged her infant into the fields in a large wooden box, so she could continue harvesting while the baby slept. When she hauled water from the well, the nursling was rolled into her apron and securely tied around her waist to prevent his falling to the ground and being "trampled on by thirsty cattle." When in the house, she "done all my rubbing and rocking the baby's cradle with the other foot." Toddlers were often tied by the wrist to cornstalks, which kept them in one place, as well as harnessing their furious energy to shake the stalks and scatter the crows.

What could make the task easier? Every mother needed help, including one who had "not undressed to lie down for 6 weeks" because of her child. "Most of the children were well and good-natured" on the overland crossing, according to pioneer Keturah Penton—and no wonder. She was startled to see a "woman out by the roadside with a little bag and her baby asleep in the wagon under a strong opiate." The baby was, in the popular phrase of the day, simply "stupid from opium," which, along with laudanum, was a popular form of tranquilizer.

Comfort also came from companionship, and despite distance

and isolation, women would inevitably find support in loose-knit maternal associations, where troubles, recipes, and medications were shared. Women were supported by their friends, unleashing a heady and contagious spirit of independence. So alluring was the idea of female friendship, that one woman, over her husband's objections, pushed her infant in a collapsing baby buggy over five miles of furrowed fields to attend a mother's meeting, returning home the same day. He never knew she had gone.

Family love renewed itself, season after season. As the morning sun slanted across the fields of wild rye grass and the giggle of toddlers stirred up the chickens, a parent might survey such a scene of tranquility and give thanks—hardships or not.

5

No More Babies for Me!

Will you please send me one of your birth control? I am married woman of 23 and have two children, and I hope I wont have any more for a present time, because I am having lots of trouble from my husband. He won't hardly work.—*Mrs. H.H., Michigan, writing to the Government Children's Bureau*

What I want to know is Why can't We poor people be give Birth Control as well as Dr's. & the Rich people. . . . We need help to prevent any more babies.—*Mrs. E.S., Kansas*

The forces of nature that ruled over frontier life knew no constancy, save one: confinement and delivery were as predictable as the yearly harvest cycles, and following the rhythms of the moon, would complete the long, cold nights of winter with a bumper crop of children each fall. Such seasonal periodicity was predictable as sun-up, and exceptions to the rule meant either infertility or the "unnatural practices" of contraception, abortion, or infanticide. Otherwise, rural women had no choice but to produce vast numbers of children. A midwife, asked at the end of her life how many babies she had delivered into the world, had "lost count" but figured "up to more than a thousand." Similarly, in a ten-year period, Dr. Mary Glassen delivered "nearly 1,000 babies, mostly in homes." A young physician from the Medical College of South Carolina wondered if all women shouldn't be considered pregnant unless proven otherwise—a statement borne out by the growing numbers of children on the frontier.

Pregnancy was hardly unusual in a population with wives so young they had at least ten extra childbearing years, compared to their European counterparts. Women, it seemed, were duty-bound to procreate. Rural settlers counted children as beloved assets, and the average number born from the eighteenth to nineteenth centuries could be as many as twelve or as "few" as seven, each of whom would give rise to a surfeit of grandchildren and great grandchildren beyond recording. Judity Turner bore eight children in eighteen years. Sarah Everett Hale had eleven pregnancies in twenty years. "As I write," said Mary Ann Humble Case, "I have nine children, thirty-six grandchildren, thirty-seven great-grandchildren, and one great-great grandson." Katharina Hohn Reimann bore fourteen children in twenty-three years—and once had two born in the same year. Of Mary Vian Holyoke's twelve children, only three lived to adulthood, while Charles Kiney, age seventy-two, a farmer—not Mormon—living on the Blue Ridge Mountains in 1852, saw nothing amiss in having four wives who "together raz 42 children." Mary Gibson, matron of a remote sheep ranch, recalled the summer of 1891, when the "old Universalist minister, Dr. Tuttle" came to visit. To best utilize his time, he performed a "bargain" baptism, christening Paris, Louise, Valeria, Donald, Dorothy, Margaret, Greely Ladd, Aline Chowed, and Bobby Sweat all at once, proving that the scriptural injunction to multiply was happily in effect on the American frontier. Harriet Shaw, wife of a Baptist missionary in New Mexico, summed up the scene for her mother in Vermont. "Oh I wish you could step in here and see us. Babies & bottles all over the house . . . every chair is full & every corner."

Every culture has its tradition of fecundity. For the Irish, virility resulted if men ate "more potatoes and oatmeal and drank more milk," while in rural America, a man's right to sexual congress was supported by "the volcano theory," an odd Victorian hypothesis, acknowledged although not widely held, in which men would "explode" into poor health if their sexual activity was interrupted. Although many women were desperate to prevent or delay new pregnancies, husbands seemed oddly impervious to cause and effect, either disbelieving, unable to refrain, or unconcerned.

"Where there is a large family or a thoughtless husband the woman pays with her life," wrote one mother, recognizing how a family could be disabled by the overproduction of children. What good was an extra child or two—in terms of farm economy—if the mother lay incapacitated from childbearing, ill, feeble, and unable to work? And worse, what if her children were left motherless?

Margaret Sanger, in an attempt to give women and their children the option of a better life, exhorted:

> *Mothers! Can you afford to have a large family?*
> *Do you want to have any more children?*
> *If not, why do you have them?*
> *Do not kill, do not take a life, but prevent.*

Yet her missives were slow to reach the frontier. Another overworked woman, Malinda Jenkins, protested:

> I didn't want no more children. I had my home, my work and everything that a woman raised like me could wish for. Two children was enough. There wasn't no quarrel with Willie, no words. I was his good wife in every respect—but I wasn't going to have no more babies. And when I said that it meant something because I was posted (term for contraceptive). The many times I lived with my sister Betty, the doctor, I was poking my nose in medical books. I knowd more about how such things was than the girls around me. When I found out I was having another baby I wasn't only unhappy, I had an awful bad feeling towards Willie, too. I had one thought all the time, I wanted to run for it, get clear away from everybody, to live among strangers.

"My soul rebelled against having more children," lamented another. "But my husband was dead to my prayers and my tears, though he himself was opposed to my having any more children, and insisted it was my fault if I did, though he persisted in his right to his sensual indulgences." Aware of the "unfaithfulness on the part of the husband where families are limited," she finally submitted. "We must let the men know we are human beings with ideals, and aspire to something higher than to be mere objects on which they can satisfy themselves," wrote another. "Owing to . . . worry [and] also having to be up again too soon after confinement, and for want of rest," another felt her "health giving way." In her weakened condition, she "became an easy prey to sexual intercourse, and thus once more . . . became a mother in fourteen months."

In some cases, concern shifted, and it was the man who sought to limit family size. Martha Farnsworth, a young Kansas housewife, had to "make a fight to be allowed to become a mother. . . . Johnny says, if it is a fact that I am pregnant as everything indicates, I must do something to prevent it; that he is not ready to commence to raise a family and that I should not bear the child." A church deacon confided to his pastor, "I will tell you . . . I love my children, I am proud of them, I wouldn't take a million dollars for a single one of them; but I wouldn't give fifteen cents for another."

Given the heedless manner in which families grew, little wonder that, as frontier physician Urling Coe noted, "many of the babies . . . were not wanted but were merely the result of accidents." "Surely," he continued, "birth control would be of benefit to the human race . . . and an incalculable blessing through the number of abortions it would prevent." Couldn't women declare a truce on having so many babies for a little while? Motherless children and early graves were all too frequent reminders of the dangers of repeated deliveries by worn-out women who failed in childbirth.

In kitchens and gardens, while quilting or canning, rural and urban women alike would discuss in hushed tones the manner and means of controlling their destinies—although few in the early nineteenth century would have couched birth control in such liberal terms. Instead, they refrained from comment when one or another nursed a child year after year, since each understood that prolonged suckling was the simplest way to avoid conception. Depending upon the length of nursing, women could manage to space their pregnancies at least two years apart, or more.

Folk contraceptives abounded, from the inexplicable "blowing on the wrist" (to discourage passion) to the rhythm method, which timed ovulation and encouraged lovemaking during periods of "natural infertility." Failing this, there was always withdrawal, hot water douching, ice water baths, and alcohol or rusty nail water, taken externally. Also touted as abortifacients were fresh tansy, ingested gunpowder, hot baths, balsam, cold baths, a milk diet, cooling cathartics, a silver probe, and sulfate of zinc, applied externally, or in one case, the unexplained use of cocoa butter. Dr. A. M. Mauriceau's favorite was "half an ounce of a strong decoction of red oak bark . . . thrown into the vagina by means of a female syringe, two or three times a day." Deadly indeed were "last resort" abortifacients, such as the black fungus, ergot, that sprouted in brittle rye grass and, when ingested, threw the uterus into violent contractions and caused premature ejection. Too little was ineffective, too much was toxic, with the prescribed dosage one to two teaspoons, taken six times a day. When Emily French's employer, Mrs. Dake, "started her menses" again—code for a forced miscarriage—Emily "fixed to soak her feet, [gave] her four doses Ergot [and] her menses started again good."

CONTRACEPTIVE CANDOR WAS rare in diaries and journals, yet nineteenth century books, such as *Psychological Views of Marriage* (1885) by E. DeLaCroix, as well as periodicals and newspapers held mysterious references to "medical prescriptions" and offered women "confidential advice concerning their many interesting complaints," as well as potions or concoctions, discreetly labeled "do not drink in the event of pregnancy," code for "take in order to miscarry." Abortifacents such as Morrell's Magnetic Fluid, Yellow Dock Sarsaparilla, and Henry's Invigorating Cordial were discreetly called "female drugs." By the late 1860s, more than twenty-five different chemicals clamored for attention, each promising to solve the sexual dilemma and reassure women that motherhood was choice, not destiny.

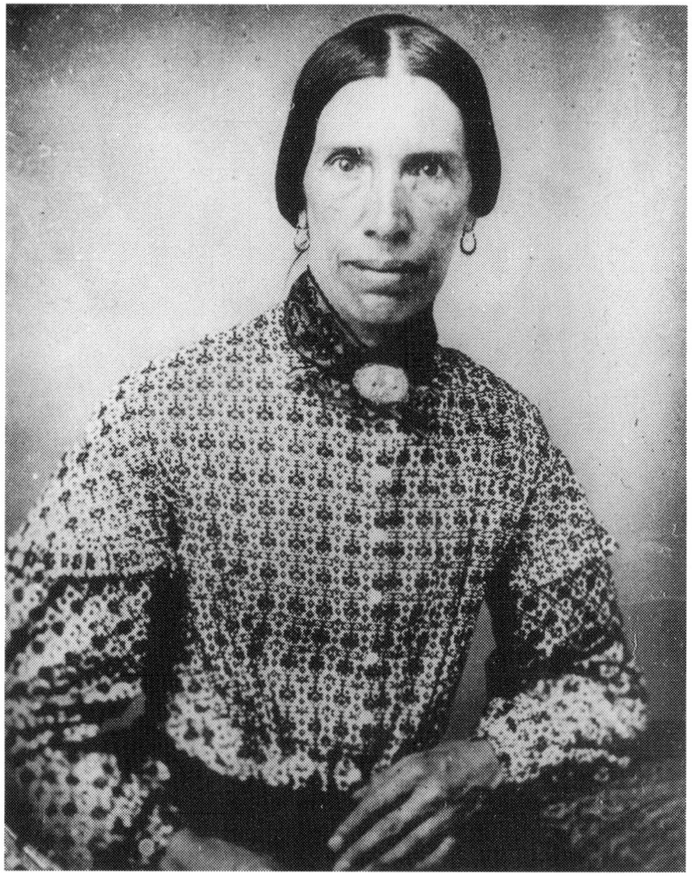

Martha Spense Heywood, Utah, ca. 1880s.

In the larger western cities, more contraception was available. Men were advised in newspapers about oiled silk sheaths and rubber goods, while women could turn to the mysterious "French Preventatives," sponges, a diaphragm called "The Wife's Protector," rubber uterine caps, female syringes filled with alum, sulfate of zinc or iron, as well as the ubiquitous "Malthusian appliance," probably a diaphragm sold in Europe as early as the 1890s but unavailable in the United States until the 1920s. Also popular were pessaries, the lightweight, interior devices of wood, cotton, or sponge, designed by Dr. Marie Stopes in 1920, which popped open like a tiny umbrella when inserted, preventing the womb's feeble habit of "falling in" upon itself. Dubbed the "female preventative" for those too reticent to whisper "pisser," the pessarie's inner "discipline" was so rigid as to be attributed moral values—inner structure, outer character! Rose Williams urged her young friend Lettie Mosher to get fitted. "Just ask for a female preventative. They cost one dollar [and] the directions are with it." Failing that, Williams remonstrated, "Well, plague take it, you sleep in one bed and your man in another."

Gwendoline Kinkaid, writing to her friend Mamie Goodwater, of Grand Forks, Michigan, in March 1901, was candid about contraceptive options. "Mamie I am going to send you an ad I answered.

Polygamous Utah family, ca. 1870.

The lady has sent me several times her circulars, and I will send you one. I think the pills would be fine, for just what they say in case any one should get caught."

From cocoa butter to rusty nail water, women's contraceptive efforts proved socially threatening. Taking command of the female destiny resulted in stiff legislation to prevent abortion, as in the Sheppard-Towner Act, and to forbid the advertisement of birth control devices, as in the Comstock Act of 1873. Despite such interdictions, by 1870 books on family limitation had been widely circulated, with one, Dr. Frederick Hollick's *The Marriage Guide,* reprinted thirty times in twenty-five years. In 1825 the average number of children per family in the United States was six, and by 1850 it was five, according to historian Daniel Scoto Smith. By the turn of the century, these efforts had taken even greater effect, reducing family size to an average of 3.5 children.

Despite its illegality, abortion had always flourished. Patients were "put on the kitchen table, & given a glass filled with chloroform-drenched cotton" to self-administer as an anesthetic. The mangled results of "kitchen table" surgery were common, with hemorrhaging and infection the all-too-often results. Abortions were performed by female practitioners ironically called "female physicians" in eastern newspapers, or "healing women," whose skills could switch from midwifery to abortions with ease, using dilatory and curettes and an unsterilized catheter of gut elastic around wire for stiffening.

There is no way of knowing if abortion was more common in the West or less. With limited access to pharmacies, medications, or the newspapers that advertised contraceptives, as well as living far-distant from other women, frontier women undoubtedly had more unwanted pregnancies. How many western women used herbal remedies or bought prescriptions to prevent or abort pregnancies or used other methods of birth control will remain their private secret.

Part 2

Family Bonds

Photo on previous page: Unidentified frontier family, ca. 1870s.

6

For the Love of a Family

Those wer the days that tried mens souls and bodys too, and womans constitutions they worked the mussle on and it was their to stay.
—*Keturah Penton*

I stay alone but fear nothing.—*Harriet Shaw, Fort Defiance, New Mexico*

Mother took the babies and fled to her retreat in the woods, where she often goes to gain her equilibrium.—*Mollie Dorsey Sanford*

How to understand the frontier? Many had been warned by their families "don't go!" but drawn by love or bravado, they blithely set out upon the two thousand or more miles that would separate them from their families and rob them of the bloom of youth, even while pointing toward a life of great promise. Although everyone hoped to return, few were ever able to—after years most bowed to the realities of time, distance, and economy.

"Only three months," Elizabeth Burt had exclaimed. She had joined her husband on Lookout Mountain, Arizona, in 1865, for a brief visit, but when departure day dawned, Elizabeth was struck by pangs of loneliness. How unkind to let her husband face such hardships alone, and in such freezing December weather! "Wherever orders took him, baby and I would go," she bravely announced, and then readied herself for the flood of urgent protests from her family. How could she take a two-year-old baby into such a savage place in the middle of winter? Countless letters from home "painted Wild Indians [and] tent life . . . in vivid colors," and her cousin, searching for an image so awful that Elizabeth would lose heart, finally predicted the trial of having "no servant," and being forced to "make [her husband's] trousers and coats" alone. Undaunted, Elizabeth stayed on.

Over time, homesick memories faded, replaced by the sweep and grandeur of the dramatic new land. "I had never seen a pine until I came to Colorado, so the idea of a home among [them] fascinated me," wrote Elinore Pruitt Stewart. Marian Russell recalled her pretty, dark-haired, adventuresome mother, Eliza, who loved the route between Kansas City and Santa Fe so much she was like a trail boss, always riding back and forth along the route. Said Marian: "She was planning my wedding with the left ventricle of her heart, while she used the big right one to plan going out west." Finally, her daughter could not stand the idea of missing such fun, and broke her engagement, preferring "hoopskirts in an old covered wagon" to the diamond engagement ring. In Eliza's later years, Marian described her as a "lovely woman . . . courageous, educated and cultured. . . .

At times I seem to see her standing by a flickering campfire in a flounced gingham dress and a great sunbonnet. Behind her looms the great bulk of a covered wagon. I think I can hear her singing. Flow gently sweet Afton, among the green braes."

Women living in the wilderness, caught up in the vast indifference of sky, prairie, or forest, faced great stretches of empty time alone, kept company at night only by their young children and the lonely yowl of coyotes. They fondled and rocked their children, finding in their warm presence comfort and reassurance. They wrote letters home and dreamed of finding a sympathetic, female neighbor in whom they could confide. Once settled, they found ways to explore the new terrain, children in tow, making every outing a history, biology, or geography lesson as well. Recalled a twelve-year-old Texas girl, Tommie Clack:

> My mother . . . brought special meaning to frontier life. Sunday afternoons were her time with her children. We never had naps at our house, never had them in our lives, and on Sunday afternoon she would take us for a walk. . . . She loved the outdoors and would tell us about trees, the flowers, the rocks, the birds and the animals that lived up and down the creek. . . . At night she would take her astronomy book out into the moonlight and teach us to recognize Ursa Minor and Ursa Major, how to locate the North Star, and explain the phases of the moon. Mother made adventures of small things.

Children—particularly daughters—took to heart every aspect of a mother's skills, moods, and interests. She was inspiration, education, and heritage, too, the source of all art and whimsy, of music, debate, prayer, and life's mainstay, food. "The first home I remember was a three-room sod house on the North Dakota prairie," wrote Jeanette Wrottenbert, a North Dakota settler, quoted by author Linda Mack Schloff. "Our resourceful young mother . . . papered the walls five layers deep with flamboyant posters left behind by a traveling circus," while Margaret Archer's mother, perhaps less the artist, "made all our clothes, she hand knit all our stockings and mittens by lamp light." Even Sophia Gelhorn Boylan's crippled mother was continually "knitting and sewing and baking and browning," and in summer, turning the rich earth of her garden. Despite her handicap, "she made all our clothes," recalled Boylan, "did all the baking and cooking, and nearly always had a baby at her breast."

If a mother allowed independence in children, they would be adaptable, strong, and fearless. "We were taught to take care of ourselves. We grew up without some of the fears which plague today's children," wrote Tommie Clack. Her mother might as well rely on the children themselves—it was only realistic. No matter what precautions she took, a mother's children would inevitably fall outside her circle of safety. Tommie, living on Lytle Creek, Texas, provided a glimpse into the "secret" life of children.

> One night when I was about 12 I went down to the creek to fish at Blue Hole. Mother did not know where I was, but she knew I was safe. If she were to call, I would hear her. The moon was gorgeous, lighting the water and the trees along the bank. All at once, about ten o'clock, I saw the glitter of a man's watch fob. The man was approaching along the path by the edge of the creek. He walked right up to me and I recognized my schoolteacher, Thomas Bledsoe. "What are you doing out here this time of night?" he asked. I replied, "I'm fishing." I hurried on home, however, as fast as I could and for months after that arranged my fishing excursions at an earlier hour in the daylight.

Despite numerous children, women longed for husbands who had gone to the mines, or hired out as farm hands, or had simply left from boredom or despair, leaving their wives in charge of domestic duties, including the heavy farm work and all financial accounts. "Five American women here & no husbands," noted Harriet Shaw of her rural desert home near Socorro, New Mexico, 1861. "When [my husband] disappeared from view," said South Dakota homesteader Anna Waltz, "I had a sickish feeling at the pit of my stomach. I was truly scared . . . but would not let myself be beaten into defeat. Here I was at last, a lonely homesteader." When urbanite Caroline Kirkland found herself alone with her young children in a mud-and-log hut in the wilds of Michigan, she was sure that its terrors would "never fade from . . . memory. Excessive fatigue made it impossible to avoid falling asleep, yet the fear of being devoured by wild beasts, or poisoned by rattlesnakes, caused me to start up after every nap with sensations of horror and alarm, which could hardly have been increased by the actual occurrence of all I dreaded." "[I] was afraid of Indians behind every tree or rock . . . [I] imagined every soap weed was an enemy running," wrote Sarah York. One woman so despaired that she took to the fields to sleep among her sheep, seeking warmth from their wool and comfort from their peaceful, synchronous breathing.

Hardships abounded, but women could look about them and understand the worth of their choices, their children able to grow in a new land and freedom. Spunk and enterprise defined the efforts of a Nebraska woman, Mrs. Kopac, who was left alone by her husband when he went in search of work. "It was in the late fall of the year, her provisions were gone, nothing was available but the melon-patch. The poor woman lived on it during the whole melon season. She had a small baby to take care of, and grew so weak she could scarcely walk," observed a neighbor, Frank Cejda. Why not call on her neighbors and beg for food, he wondered? A woman of strict traditions and generous spirit, she knew that her fellow Czech settlers were also starving, and hated to worry them with her condition. Rachel Bella Kahn, a Ukrainian immigrant who settled near Devils Lake, North Dakota, had to struggle to gain her composure at "what awaited" in her pioneer home. According to author Linda Mack Schloff, this meant a bed, a rough table, and two benches. The "kitchen held a stove and beside it a heap of dried cow dung. When I inquired about this, I was told this was the only fuel this household had. . . . I silently vowed that my home would be heated by firewood and that no animal waste would litter my floor. How little I knew. How innocent I was."

But even the bravest suffered moments of doubt, and might dive deep beneath the comforters at the scream of a panther, or turn stupid with fear as a branch scraped the window, or a shadow whispered past. Sheltered women had no sense of the wilderness, and found foreboding in every rustle or hoot or scrape of a broken twig. Occasionally, the worst imaginings of the fearful mind came to pass. The Scotch-Irish immigrant mother of missionary Stephen Riggs, raising her family in an unfinished cabin in the Pennsylvania woods, never lost her fear of *Ursus horribilis,* particularly after one unforgettable night "when a big bear, pushing aside the quilt that served for a door, sat down on his haunches and calmly stared at the frightened family and the fire roaring in the big chimney." Even though it eventually lost interest and lumbered away, nothing could erase its image for her, or the children.

Mrs. John Murrey washing clothes, ca. 1890s. Photo by Lasera Rose, South Dakota.

Families lived in whatever refuge they could scrape together, stack up, nail down, or drape about, and whether tent or garrison, every effort was made to keep children in and wildlife out—with limited success. Nature could not be deterred, as Martha Summerhayes, a young socialite recently married to an Army officer living at a remote outpost in the Arizona desert, discovered. The house had walls, floors, doors—even a cook provided by the commander. One night while sleeping, "like lightning, [a] huge creature gave a flying leap in our window, across the bed and through the living room." Her husband jumped up with a shout, "Jehosophat!" and began "poking vigorously under the divan" with his sword. The mountain lion exited as it had entered, with a farewell pounce across the bed. Katherine Davis of New Mexico, her husband, and children were "pretty close to stark nature . . . with two glassless windows, [and] the ground squirrels came in at both the windows and the door. . . . One night while we were deep in sleep, the night air was pierced with a scream from a mountain lion. [Our dog] must have halted the beast. There was nothing to prevent it from entering."

Women with emotional stamina persevered no matter what, determined to make a better life for their children under any circumstances. Often religious, of Puritan stock, they viewed self-abnegation as repentance, hard work as character building, and were not afraid to buck tradition. Such women would, according to Texas settler Tommie Clack, "lay a sleeping baby in a fence corner, sometimes guarded by a faithful dog, sometimes with only the Good Lord watching from above, while she picked cotton, planted a garden or perhaps hoed the weeds from a crop that might furnish bread for them in the bitter winter ahead. [She] was gallant enough never to complain about how hard life was and to run back to mama and tell her a sad tale of woe." Sarah Bixby Smith's mother took her two children on a long trip from California back to Maine—she was one of the few women able to return to her home for a visit. Sarah recalled:

> It was a harder trip with two children and so my mother planned to simplify it in every possible way. She invented for us traveling dresses of a medium brown serge, with bloomers to match, a whole generation before such dresses came into general favor for little girls. With these, fewer bags and satchels were necessary, and we looked as well dressed at the end as at the beginning, and moreover, I was able to stand on my head modestly, whenever I felt like it. I am glad that I did not have to be mother of restless me on such a long, confined trip. I am also glad that I had a mother who could cut out such fascinating paper boxes and tell stories and think of thousands of things to do.

Widows had to decide whether to raise a child alone or remarry, and their decisions were very often based on their child's needs. Agnes Reid was so convinced her baby must "have a home built by a stepfather," she abandoned her much-loved stage career to find a suitable candidate. Utterly pragmatic, her marriage seemed the ultimate in self-sacrifice, resulting in periods of self-loathing and deep introspection.

> We had a queer wedding journey. . . . I was sitting in the covered wagon with my little boy, while the prospective bridegroom trudged along in the dust and sand trying to get two yoke of oxen over the ground fast enough to reach a justice of the peace before we were overtaken by winter. . . .
>
> The journey was not unpleasant. . . . At night the air would be crisp and cool, but my good comrade tied the cover down tightly over the wagon, so my boy and I were safe and snug while he stood guard over us. The country is full of wolves and Indians, but neither seem at all hostile toward us. As you know, the greatest fear the traveler entertains is that his oxen may stray away.
>
> Don't worry about me, father, there will be no drunkeness in this marriage, and therefore no divorce. Sometimes I feel uneasy because of my lack of real, all-forgiving love that guided my other marriage, but again I wonder what that great love gave me but misery. There is no deception, for my husband knows that I do not care as I should, but he, foolish boy, thinks that he cares enough for both of us. I call him a boy, though he is two years older, but he looks so very youthful. [I, however,] . . . feel very ancient.

Several months later, her feelings had shifted.

> You remember, I told you it was not through sentiment that I married Nels but because I considered it the sensible thing to do.

Think of it, Father! Think of trying to found a home without that prime essential, love. Of course I tried to be reasonable and think that romance for me was a thing of the past. I tried to believe that my love for Freddie's father was the only love that was ever to come into my life, but I failed to take into consideration that I was only twenty-one years old, so I cast my lot in that wilderness with a man for whom I could never feel anything more sacred than respect. . . .

When the spring came . . . I concluded it was a hopeless task and I would put an end to it. Yes, I was going to run away. . . . My plans were all laid, even to giving up my little boy. I could not take Jimmy from his father so I steeled myself to leave him as a sacrifice to the man I had wronged. I was to go with the older boy to the nearest county seat and secure a divorce, which is a very easy matter, then go farther east where I have friends. I was to leave all this barren life and go where there was civilization and cheer. I was to go where there was something besides hard work and where sometime the love of my womanhood might come to me! The love that is called the grand passion! The love that makes life worth while!

After years of agonizing, she finally decided that life with a man who treated her well, loved her dearly, and provided adequately for their expanding family far outweighed the glimmer of stage lights, now only dim, in memory. Although victim to periodic bouts of depression, her courage consisted in finally deciding to settle down and stay.

FRONTIER LIFE WAS not for everyone. Some women, trapped by walls of log or plank or sod and by the incessant, screaming howl of the "Northers" that swept across the plains, turned morose and bitter. Fears rose up; they shuddered and grew faint, and found only slight consolation in family life. "I thought I'd come help you a spell," offered one neighbor to Caroline Kirkland, a "city woman" alone for the first time with her children in the wilds. "I reckon you'd of done better to have waited till the old man got back."

"What old man?" Kirkland asked.

Unidentified mother and child washing clothes, wringing them dry, ca. 1880.

"Why, your old man to be sure," said he laughing." Said Kirkland: "I had yet to learn that in Michigan, as soon as a man marries he becomes "th' old man," though he may be yet in his minority."

Nothing, however, struck terror so deeply into a woman's heart as the fear of Indian depredations. Death by massacre had been witnessed or reported far too often—it was not idle speculation. What to do—fight or flee, or simply fall to the ground in a faint? Some used humor to boost their spirits, as when missionary Harriet Shaw joked that "Indians don't want my scalp and if they do they can have it," while others were matter-of-fact, showing the aplomb of Mrs. Anna Kalal, a Nebraska widow who was "home alone [when] about twenty Indians" came in asking for bread. "I cut slices and spread them with syrup and they went away satisfied." She was never afraid of them, finding them, in fact, "reliable and friendly." But the mother of Frank Cejda, recently emigrated from Bohemia and unable to fathom the many aspects of her frontier setting, was so terrified when a group of Indians came, begging food, that she changed color, becoming "so white" the Indians were startled, thinking her a ghost. Idaho settler Agnes Reid, also terrified, was on the point of "killing my children and myself that we might be spared an Indian uprising." She confided this to her father by letter, echoing the popular view that death was better than capture. Reasonably, she wondered if it was a "mark of insanity" to wish to take her own life, although she had never actually been attacked, or even threatened. Soldiers at Ford Verde, Arizona, even gave their wives guns for self-destruction, should Indians overtake the fort.

Some stories were so terrible as to be mythic, graven into the popular mind, embellished with each repetition, and bearing dire predictions for future Indian encounters. One was the tale of Angie Mitchell Brown, an Arizona pioneer from 1854 to 1909, whose day was transformed from the ordinary into the terrible, when surprised by a wandering band of Apaches in 1881:

> This morning we rose about our usual time. Alice, Clara, Abbie, Mrs. H. and I. Clara went to Vineyards for milk and the other four of us and oh yes, I forgot Janie & the baby—well, the other 5 of us (baby don't count) were eating breakfast when a great hullabaloo arose at the creek crossing just below our house . . . [and] up to the house with a horrible whoop rose a band of Indians. The chief rode his horse into the house but when he found he could not sit erect on the animal after he got inside . . . he dismounted. . . . Then [entered the rest of] the Indians till they quite filled the small room. . . .
>
> We sat as if petrified thinking our time had come when Mrs Harer (who is as brave a frontier woman as ever lived) arose put on a brave face and stepping to the Chief held out her hand. . . . The Chief only gave a savage grunt and put his hand behind him. Janies baby on our bed in the corner cried. . . .
>
> Janie was trying to hush her baby & the chief glanced her way as if anxious to see the child. . . . [N]ow usually the greatest mark of friendship one can show these savaages is to exhibit their tiny white & pink babies to them & usually the Indians consider it an honor, so Janie plucking up courage moved a little nearer & unrolled the shawl & showed the chief what a tiny morsel he was but he only frowned the fiercer & made a motion as if to seize the child & fling him down but Janie clasped him closer & carried him to the farthest corner & deposited him & then resumed her seat at the table near me, close by her baby & between the Indians & it. The Chief and his band surveyed us in ominous silence, three lone defenseless women, one old, small & gray, one a slender girl, & the third, weak from recent confinement & now pale as death; then after a few gutteral sentences to each other, they seemed to decide on a plan. Grasping Mrs. H firmly the chief held her hands behind her while one of the others tied them tightly with a buckskin thong. Then she was led to the opposite corner from us placed in a chair & tied to the chair while a handkerchief lying handy was bound over her mouth. She struggled desperately but uselessly. During this performance Jane & I sat motionless—I could not have moved an eyelash . . . and I believe Janie was in a similar condition. . . .
>
> One of the ugliest & most hideously painted Indians came & stood as nearly in front of me as my position permitted . . . [and put] his hand under my chin and jerked my head back with a force that nearly broke my neck. I looked at him then straight, & unflinchingly in his cruel gleaming eyes. . . . With a wild whoop . . . he grabbed that great knife of his & grabbing me by my hair threw my head back & drew his knife, I thought, over my throat but he did not touch it. . . . I think he must have touched my flesh with the back of the knife for I am sure I felt the cold of the steel. . . . Then he tore my sleeves open & pinched my arms & shoulders till I am blue-green & black most all over them, he slapped my cheeks

pulled my ears & pinched them—& then grabbed me by my bangs & pretended to scalp me & not a sound did I utter all that time—I really believe if he had tied me to a stake & set fire to me I could not have even groaned, & I'm sure I could not have resisted. At last as if tired he paused a minute & I glanced at Jane. Poor girl—she had been submitted to the same torments only she wore earrings & the brut had torn one entirely down thro' her ear & the other nearly & the blood was running freely from them. She like myself had not made a sound & for a similar reason. . . .

Suddenly Jane's possessor grasped me by the arm, jerked me out of the chair & led me to the third & unoccupied corner of our brush house . . . while my Indian—who had had the rifle at my head came in & up to me and said, "Heap brave squaw, mucho brave—mucho. Una pocita (that's not spelled right but it sounds like it) muchacha esta mucha brave!" Then they turned to Jane and called her "mucho brave," "una bravisto mujer" & lots of such phrases, all meaning that they thought we were "brave." At first I thought they were making game of us but soon realized they were serious & really thought that it was courage that had prevented us from screaming or fainting or crying when they tormented us and that while we had been so paralyzed with fear & terror as to be utterly powerless to scream or even speak or to move hardly of our own volition, they had ascribed it to pride & bravery. Well! That's good! . . .

The Apaches are great admirers of courage in anyone particularly white women.

The Indians finally tired of their sport and, as mysteriously as they arrived, left. The women were uninjured, although badly frightened.

Nor were Indians the only ones to be feared. Outlaws, border ruffians, and rebels were only part of a shiftless population that roamed the countryside, jumping claims or stealing horses. Armed, lawless men, they were only marginally conversant with such truths as the "sacred duty" of motherhood, so touted by ministers and polemicists of the eastern establishment. In fact, they raided, plundered, and robbed at will, often seeing women and children as ideal ransom opportunities, striking terror into the lives of the vulnerable and undefended. The frontier was a land in flux—where cultures mingled, traditions died, expectations became fulfilled, or were dashed. Even a "timid sort of a person naturally" such as Mrs. Marsh, might find herself a heroine. Living in Lawrence, Kansas, with her two small boys in the aftermath of the Civil War, she recalled "those terrible days" in which "we felt as if we carried our lives in our hands all the time." Nightly she lay awake, listening to every sound, expecting the terror of a Rebel raid. The state was filled with Union sympathizers, and, after the war, disaffected, former Southern soldiers roamed the land. Stories of the depredations were rampant.

One morning, it was warm weather and the doors and windows were all open and I was about my work, my husband came running to the door, all out of breath, with his face as white as a sheet, and said to me, for God's sake save yourselves if you can the raiders are coming!" Well from that day to this it had always been a mystery to me, a timid, nervous creature as I was, and worn a good deal too, with nursing the sick child, that I didn't die with fright on the spot! I shut the door and windows, and then I took the baby out of the cradle and Johnny by the hand, and went up stairs and put on a new calico dress. . . . You will think it a queer thing to do at such a time, and so it was, but we all do strange things sometimes you know. All this time I heard the most terrible noise in the street that you can imagine. Men, women, and children screaming, groaning and crying, and then came the raiders galloping like mad, shouting, cursing and firing right and left as they rode. They held the reins in their teeth, and a pistol in each hand, shooting down everybody that came in their way. . . . We were in the center of the town and when they were opposite our house some of them dismounted and began setting fire to buildings. I was looking out of the window, when one of them came to the door, knocked and shouted to me to open the door. I went down stairs taking the children with me and opened the door. He looked at me and asked if there was a man in the house. I told him no. "Damn You," said he, "that's a lie." I looked straight at him and making as if I felt myself insulted I told him he could come in and see for himself if he didn't believe me. So he pushed me aside and came in and went up stairs and looked all through the rooms. Sure enough he didn't find anybody. When he came down he lighted a match and set fire to the curtain. I dropped the baby in the cradle and quick as a flash I pulled the curtain down, rolled it up and put it in the stove. He never said a word but set fire to the other one, and I ran into the kitchen and got a pail of water and put it out. There were some clothes hanging on hooks against the wall and he next set fire to them. I tried to throw more water but he pushed me away and swore he would kill me if I didn't stop. When I found the house was going to be burned sure enough, I took the children and went up stairs again and Johnny and I took a trunk that I had some things in that I valued, little keepsakes and some articles of clothing, and we brought it down and set it out in the yard in front of the house. Then I went back and threw some bedding and a few other things out of the window. By this time the smoke was getting thick and I took the children and tried to go down stairs but the stairway was blazing. I ran into the kitchen chamber, threw up the window and stepped out on the roof of the kitchen. The villains saw me and one of them galloped up and asked me how I was going to get down. I told him I could jump on the back of his horse. He got off and held the horse by the head while I jumped on his back. Johnny began to cry but I called out to him to jump, and heaven knows how I did it, but I caught and held him with one of my hands. You know I had the baby in my arms. I took the children and sat down on the pile of bedding leaning my back against the truck and there I sat three hours, hearing sounds and seeing sights that nearly froze my blood in my veins. Men, women and children were running up and down the street screaming and crying like crazy people, and every few minutes some one being shot down dead before my eyes. An old colored man who used to help about the stable came long with the crowd, and when he was near me, one of the raiders shot him in the head, at the same time shouting, "take that, you d——d nigger!" I saw my husband's partner fall, being shot in the breast. There was a hotel just below our house and another farther up on the same street. Word came that one of them was on fire and the women and children had been sent to the other with a promise of safety. It was terrible you may be sure, to hear the shrieks of the women and crying of the children as they ran by me up the street. Some of them fell down overcome with fright and were actually killed under the feet of the horses. Several called out to me to come, but I sat still where I was, not daring to move for fear that it might be worse for me. Three or four other women, seeing me sitting there unharmed, came with their children and staid near me. None of us knew where our husbands were but supposed them to be killed. About one o'clock the terrible news came that a party of Indians were coming to kill the women and the children. At this, Johnny who had been as brave as a little man all the time, began to cry and cling to me, but I soon quieted him. This rumor proved to be false, and by two o'clock the raiders were all out of sight. You can imagine what my feelings were as I looked around me upon that scene of desolation, but I doubt if you can realize my joy when I saw my husband alive and unharmed, coming towards me. He with many others had escaped by hiding in the ravine near by. The raiders had taken our best horses and burned our house and stable, but our lives were spared and we forgot all else for the time.

Part of a mother's protective instinct was to guard the family interests—difficult enough in the best of times, but particularly so during the post–Civil war upheaval, when the maxim "the more civilized, the more civil" was often disproved. Dandies, carpetbaggers, tax assessors, and "county" men flooded the South, making inroads into Kansas, Ohio, and further into the western territories, evicting widows and families in a trice, all chivalry ignored. In the opportunistic scramble for homestead lands, anyone's holdings were fair game, and mothers, in order to protect their children, had better learn the means of their own defense. Esther Wattles, whose husband had recently died of brain fever, was left with three children below the age of ten. Her goods had to be appraised. "No help from their father and the law not favorable to women . . . the home was not yet preempted and because I owned 160 acres I had to get out letters of administration and then take a long trip to the land office with witnesses to get the home. There was a long series of annoyances in settling up our affairs." Esther was more fortunate than most frontier widows—her husband had insisted that the land stay in her name, knowing the difficulties she would face.

And occasionally, family rewards were reaped by chivalry, which might be found particularly in the Catholic regions, where adoration of the Virgin Mary translated into respect for motherhood. Men responded to the sight of a woman protecting her children, as Flora Spiegelburg quickly discovered. Called the "tenderfoot bride" of Santa Fe, she had spent her honeymoon jolting over the plains in a stagecoach with her young husband, Willi, en route to the family dry goods store in Santa Fe. One night in 1877, her husband was called out to join a group of vigilantes lynching an outlaw. "Oh my God, boys," Willi objected, seeking their sympathy. "How could I leave my wife and young baby alone?" The men were unmoved. Flora then held her baby tightly to her breast, and showing a "deep look of anguish," claimed she would "die of fright" if her husband had to leave that night. Then she leaned on Willi's shoulder, sobbing weakly:

> There was a dead silence for a few minutes, then some whispering and the leader of the lynching party, a dear friend of ours . . . said . . . "Your request will be granted, as we all have families . . . and on that account [we] will let Willi off this time."

Then these old pioneers turned their horses and silently rode away in the moonlight. The two murderers were hung. To her knowledge, it was the first lynching party in old Santa Fe.

❖ ❖ ❖ ❖

DESPITE TOUGH TIMES and an unforgiving landscape, women found themselves increasingly under the spell of their wild new homelands, and conveyed the joy they found to their children. The scenery delighted them—they were tickled by the strange birdsong, awed by the bursts of spring flowers and looming mountain peaks that caught and played with light and shadow, as well as the vast, changing skies." Elinore Pruitt Stewart, describing an all-woman camping enclave in Wyoming, recalled the joy of cooking "big elk steaks on sticks before an open fire, and roast[ing] potatoes in the ashes. When our fear wore away, we had a fine time. After a while we lay down on fragrant beds of pine." A frequent traveler with her daughter, Jerrine, the two would ride alone through the Wyoming backcountry, sleeping at night under the stars, catching fish and roasting them for dinner, waking sometimes to find themselves blanketed with snow. Chill winds, blue haze, ripening grain, quaking aspens, clumps of rabbitbrush, even fossils, were part of their wanderings—and they nearly always laughed together as they rode. "I am a firm believer in laughter," said Stewart. "I am real superstitious about it."

Children viewed their mothers as heroines, albeit quiet ones. Who else would nurse them to health, plaster their chests, stitch

Esther Wells and Kathleen Reedy, Fort Yates, North Dakota. Photo by Frank B. Fiske, Fort Yates, North Dakota.

Daisey DeGraff, ca. 1890. Photo by Frank B. Fiske, Fort Yates, North Dakota.

their clothes, fill them with steaming oats or roasted corn? Mothers knew that the youngster would one day preside over another brood, passing on the same skills as the previous generation—such was life.

Hard work hardly brought recognition, yet women knew that their efforts mattered. "At this late time of my life," wrote pioneer Rachel Emma Woolley Simmons, then forty-five years old in 1883, "I feel impressed . . . to keep a journal . . . for my own satisfaction, knowing it will be a pleasure to my children to have it to look at and read, no matter how little merit it may contain or how poorly done, they will cherish it, not for great and noble deed, or sacrifices made for others, but they will like it to read Just because it was Mother."

In the West, bravery created a greater sense of equality for women—their efforts were integral to the family, and the farm, economy. And the impact of their personal courage would, over time, come to be known. Ultimately, strength could be inherited, as was that of Bethenia Owens, who "possessed a strong and vigorous constitution, and a most wonderful endurance and recuperative power. These qualities were inherited, not only from my parents, but my grandparents as well." In the words of Elinore Pruitt Stewart, speaking of homesteading, but, implicitly, of childraising as part of the process, "any woman who could stand her own company, can see the beauty of the sunset, loves growing things, and is willing to put in as much time at careful labor as she does over the washtub, will certainly succeed."

7

A Father's View

I like babys very much but not until they arrive at a certain age.
—*James Henry Gleason*

Little Henrique is the finest little boy out of jail, he is very forward of his age and his parents (of course) believe he will make a smart man.—*James Henry Gleason*

When I first knew there was to be another baby, I went to Nels and told him that I thought I had better drown myself and was very much astonished that he should disagree with me.—*Agnes Reid*

I never thought of disobeying him, I'll tell you! I feared, respected and loved him.—*Mary Ronan*

Papa, is this California?—*Lorenzo Waugh*

FATHERS, IN THE taciturn, Victorian sense, were often gruff, no-nonsense men so old-fashioned they would never dream of calling a youth by his first name. Such would be "obscene and exhibitionistic," wrote Jack O'Connor, whose father simply called him "boy." "In the years I knew him I can recall only a couple of tentative hugs and a few pats on the head. He seldom talked to me and never talked idly."

Such was the prescribed lot of the typical father and son. Men aspired to be solid and decent, honest and forthright, respectful and fair—all the traits that contributed to American caliber. But they also needed ambition, luck, and steely discipline to forge a path that their sons and daughters would one day follow. Yet more and more, they found that formalities counted for very little in the West. Westward expansion had broadened the notion of fathering, and when traditional, birch-rod authority confronted the frontier, age and youth alike reared up in surprise. How to discipline in the face of daily danger? It was all newly sprung and unforeseen, from gold to grain to grasshoppers, and parents and children alike wondered what would happen next.

Men faced difficult choices. Not only had they brought a defenseless family into the vast unknown, but they lacked the possessions and professions that once defined their lives, and which were not easily reclaimed. The great myth of Manifest Destiny assured them that enterprise alone could "tame" the land, yet the vast emi-

Unidentified man holding daughter, ca. 1890.

grant army of bookkeepers, factory workers, and shopkeepers who now puzzled over seed, soil, rakes, and harrows, found much of their labor so daunting as to be impossible. They had thought America a patriarchy, an "anyman's land," in which every aspect of commerce, the professions, and government catered to male enterprise and its attendant success. Yet also failure could loom.

What happened when men, thrust out of their element, failed in "manliness"? Young overlander Maggie Hall had reason to wonder one night, when her wagon train was attacked. The "night alarms" were sounded, the cry "Indians!" rang out, warning of "an Indian hiding behind the bush—or heard an arrow etc." Volunteers were summoned, but, Maggie noted, "it did not take long for a number of men to sit down as cowards." Shocked, she watched "grown men" crawl fearfully into their wagons, behavior that "made the women nervous, [and] sick." The West was a new land, in which men's bravery and resolve were sure to be tested.

When men became fathers, the results could be as diverse and wide-ranging as humanity itself. Some were overjoyed and welcomed the process. Others fled the scene, as did "the man in Ohio when his wife had 3 at a time, [just] putting off through the cornfields," according to New Mexico Baptist missionary Milton Shaw. Some took to the whiskey jug while others moved in and out of the birthing room, either trying to supervise, or else boasting about the grace and ease of the delivery that the spouse had achieved.

James Henry Gleason, an immature young man with a slightly arch view of his impending parenthood, joked to his sister that "my wife tells me that I shall be a father in about 6 or 8 weeks . . . of course she ought to know." A frisky and youthful puer, he wondered if he could really appreciate anyone more boyish than he. When his charming, bright-eyed Spanish wife delivered a boy in San Francisco in 1850, Gleason recovered from the stressful event by taking a brief trip, "partly to get clear of a squalling baby."

By December, his indifference had flown. He was proud of his month-old boy, who had "large blue eyes that flash and sparkle like a metior and [a] pretty little mouth that will at times curl itself into a smile." Very soon, he had settled into fatherhood, even overseeing the child's menu:

> March, 1851.
>
> we feed him on beef-steak [five months old!] poor little fellow got a piece down his throat the other day & it came very near making a finish of him
>
> January 15, 1852.
>
> Henrique is by my side kicking up considerable excitement because the nurse delays bringing in his dinner   I think he will be

> some pumpkins when he has a few more years on his head he can fight now when there is cause. his main ambition at the present days is to throw the lasso over the dogs and lambs and throw them down as the rancheros do the cattle.

Gleason was ready to admit, after several cases of smallpox and the onset of four small children, that his offspring were "smart as steel traps" and full of "fun and mischief." Fatherhood continued to strike, leaving him with mounting concerns.

> My wife is now about being confined again Heavens! what shall I do with so many babies in less than a fortnight they will call me father of five children Mr. Hartnell an old resident of this place & now in his grave was one day asked how many children he had. his reply was, twenty one in all but thank God half of them died young otherwise they would all have been beggers. . . . I think when a man has five children to feed clothe and educate it is full time for him to abandon the thought of adding more unless he has the resources of a Rothschild to back him.

A good citizen was a man who had "built a house, planted a tree and got a child," according to a popular adage. But what of he who produced many children—two, three, or even more? On December 3, 1861, Howard Havens, a young cashier at the Sacramento Valley Railroad, bragged to a friend that despite his wife's "very tedious" and "often severely trying" labor, she had "given birth to a female infant, with Comparative Ease." Then, shockingly, her labors continued. Another child was born—twins! He wrote to a friend:

> Now I suppose you will congratulate me, but I really cannot appreciate it. I suppose we must accept of whatever the Lord sends, but certainly, I should thank his Lordship, if by dispensation, could have been made in homeopathic doses. I have slept but six hours In the last sixteen; feel entirely unstrung, not to say used up, but hope to get right in a day or two and straighten out matters in abeyance at present.

The expanding population of young Americans grew to adolescence in the parental shadow. Boys were coached to be "little men,"

Edward and Cherry Johnson family photograph, ca. 1900. Photo by Frank B. Fiske, Fort Yates, North Dakota.

well-practiced in virtue and sober behavior. Girls of middle-class homes were "little ladies," which demanded a certain amount of protectiveness, even coddling, on the part of the parents. Frontier fathers made every effort to maintain the comforts of home, while keeping children safe, as well. "I just love you, Daddy," said little Dave Mortimer to his father, catching him by the leg as he went through the gate. Big Dave bent down and kissed him, saying, "You're a man, son." What better way could a father show his love?

One father, concerned for the safety of his children while they traveled on horseback, built a "travel box" to carry them, lashing the wooden crates filled with squirming offspring to the swaying pack saddles. "At first . . . the children set up a terrible clamor, since many of the horses were not saddle broken and . . . they would run and buck. [But] when they found they were not spilled out, they greatly enjoyed the excitement." Girls snuggled in one box and boys in the other as they skidded and bumped down the steep Pacific Slope toward Oregon's Klamath River, testing the ingenious design. The human "travel boxes" soon caught on, delighting children with the new mode of transportation.

Another California-bound father, concerned by the sniffling and crying of his fretful children, tried to pacify them with the most soothing sound he could recall—the monotonous creaking of a rocking chair, just like back home. He tied a split-bottom rocker to the back of his horse, hoping that its thumps and bumps would somehow bring them peaceful memories. When Sarah Bixby Smith traveled with her father as a toddler, she began the day "very erect and alert at papa's side" but before long "would droop and retire to the bottom of the buggy, where, wrapped in a robe, and with his foot for a pillow," she would sleep contentedly for hours. Annie Pierce was so lovingly attended by her father as they traveled by wagon train from Missouri to Southern California, she hardly felt the pangs of leave-taking. As the family wagon lumbered along, her gaze traveled over the flowering plain, a "vast sea of blue and pink as far as [she] could see," while her father, a minister, recounted lessons of natural history, each example a "treasure" to her. "He spied a prairie hen and held me up to see it [make] its escape among the flowers. . . . At night, when we would camp, father would always make mother comfortable in the coach, and then after a prayer

Unidentified Wyoming man and woman with infant, ca. 1880.

with us, for our safety, would take me in his arms where I slept as sweetly as at home."

The father of Mary Ellen Applegate knew his youngsters were distressed by the dangers of the overland crossing, and thought to cheer them with frequent bursts of song. If Mary Ellen awoke, startled by a nightmare, he offered a thoughtful rendition of "O Happy Day," his usual hymn sung to the sick or dying encountered along the trail. Although an odd practice, she knew his unusual chorus flowed from a loving nature, and she found him a hero in her eyes.

SUCH MEN WERE heroic—they could thresh and build, shoot and hew, feed a family, and pass on wisdom to sons and daughters—particularly to sons seeking a model of adult behavior. Floy Emhoff remembered his father as a hero so stalwart as to face down any danger, including a piercing Iowa blizzard that nearly froze out the entire family. As quoted by Glenda Riley: "When father went to do the chores he would often tie a rope to the house to guide him back in safety."

Clues to approaching manhood were detected in a father's behavior, even the "manly pleasures of smoking." John Barrows first used a "frontier mixture of plug smoking tobacco and the dried leaves of the barberry, l'herbe, [in a] hot and fragrant blend" with his father during his teenage years in Montana in the late 1800s. For Jack O'Connor, the mark of maturity was "possession of a cigar box full of bands," allowing him to puff and fume his Western Bee cigars along with the men, becoming "cigar-band and cigarette-coupon misers, gloating over our hordes with deep satisfaction." Milton Shaw's son, Georgie, "mimics every thing he sees, gets him a paper & makes him a cigar & smokes & spits with the Indians which amuses them very much. There is nothing that he does not try to imitate." Any male pastime could be shared with a son, including that favorite Texas diversion, cockfighting. "It was a sport as old as the nation," wrote housewife Tommie Clack. "While the women were 'trading' Papa and the older boys headed east to the stockpens. . . . Anyone could participate, if he owned a chicken big enough. The fee for admission was the ability to climb the stockpen fence. The sport was thrilling and colorful; it gave a man the opportunity to indulge in the exercise of gambling a dollar or two."

And, there were always guns.

No father left his son ignorant of marksmanship; guns could bring blackbirds, sparrows, or doves to the table, or in a more dreaded case, be used to defend a homestead. Young boys at the end of the

Unidentified Washington frontier couple with child, ca. 1880. Photo by Barnes.

nineteenth century could be found with Daisy air rifles or even shotguns, a model 76 Winchester or little, single-barrel, 20-gauge ones from down at the hardware store. Sons would hunt with their fathers—in Arizona, they might stalk the white-winged dove, one of the most popular game birds, that flew in from Mexico to nest. Wild pigs, turkeys, and mule deer abounded, scattered in the high mountains and plateau country.

NOT ALL SONS took to the typical male sports. "The boy went out with a new gun that had been given him, but came back telling me that he could not shoot turtle doves who sat in so friendly a fashion together on the fence rail and made mournful sounds, neither could he shoot rabbits, for they looked at him," wrote Sarah Bixby Smith. He was a sensitive boy—a lesser-sung entity on the frontier.

A man's relationship with his daughter was more complex. For one, society encouraged sexual discrimination against women, while blessing girlish freedoms—up to a point. The natural affinity between fathers and daughters flourished in childhood, but budding maturity brought a host of urgent restrictions. "Thou shalt not" replaced "Oh, why not," as young girls moved toward the protected realm of being young and marriageable. The urban middle class upheld maidens of the "seen-and-not-heard" variety, who practiced scrupulous obedience, nunlike modesty, and the tiny, neat crochet stitches they would need as wives.

Girls were often caught up in the timeless clutch of father-love, longed over as parent and soul mate, kin and idealized lover. "I like papa, I love him," enthused Nell, a young Kansas Quaker girl, about her kindly Dad. Edith Stratton Kitt shared a "small, chunky, fleabitten gray called Little Bill" with her three siblings, but had learned to ride "in an old sling made of a tablecloth knotted around [her father's] neck and shoulder, forming a hammock." Before long, she had graduated to a pillow. Californian Sarah Bixby Smith remembered tenderly the "gimlets, chisels, pliers, brads, rivets, and screws" of her father's work shop, where he prepared her to be a "general handy man" and able to fend for herself. "It was in this shop that papa made me a fire-cracker holder, a willow stick with a hole bored in one end in which to place the lovely red symbol of patriotism, so that I could celebrate without endangering my fingers." She also made a habit of placing her feet next to his while he was shining his boots, to come away with a gleaming shoeshine. For Sylvia Dye, her father was the repository of all good things, including a year-round cud of "Yankey Girl" chewing tobacco at which he was always "working away," ready for any emergency.

> Once while playing near barbed wire fence, I tore a deep gash in the side of my knee. Papa left the cows he was milking, put his cud of tobacco on the cut, and tied his big handkerchief around my knee. I'm not sure about it having any other medication.

The simple chores of hacienda life drew Sarah Bixby Smith close to her father. Although privileged, her girlhood on a sheep ranch in San Juan Bautista, California, during the Spanish heyday was one of work. "At one time papa and I were very occupied clearing a field. We cut down several large oak trees, cleared out underbrush, and piling it up against the great stumps, built fires that roared for a time and then smoldered for days." Her father had a tender side, particularly one day when she had torn her skirt "from hem to band." "As he sewed up the rent for me with nice big stitches . . . he told me it was a shoemakers stitch, and [brought] the edges together just as they had been originally. The children of Rev. Francis Prevaux were introduced gently to the workaday world when he decided to find out first what "delighted" them. "I made the work rather a pastime," he recalled. "On the trip I took up Frank, Anna and Johny. Anna walked home. I took a rope & tied Frank on the load and tied Johny in his lap. When we got home, I called Lil out to see my load of wood. She was very much amused to see the children so securely lashed on top of the pile."

FATHERHOOD HAD LITTLE to do with a child's own degree of maturity—many were as thankless as Lucy Ann Henderson, who hated giving up the plush comfort of her East Coast finishing school to traipse into the wilds of Oregon in 1846. Her new home was outside the United States proper, inhabited by Indians, trappers, and wildlife, and was wet and foreboding. The transition from giggling with her friends in marble halls to standing foot-deep in chilly seawater, wearing ragged clothes, and facing a bleak, mist-shrouded Oregon coastline nearly, she felt, ruined her. Life had become unthinkable. Live in a lean-to? Eat beans? She cried. She sobbed. She was so heartbroken that her father finally reconsidered, and instead of settling with his family in Oregon, decided to go alone to California to find gold to let her return to school! So delighted was Lucy at the prospect that she blithely dismissed the dangers he would face:

> Father shipped aboard a small sailing boat bound for California. Mother said that was the saddest day of her life, as she never expected to see father again and she would be left a widow with a brood of fatherless children. I was not sorry to see father go, for we were poor and I wanted to go to school and he told me that

if he had good luck he would see that I went to school. In those days, there were no free schools.

As a typical, post-Victorian daughter, she had little autonomy and depended upon her father in all matters. He, in turn, knew she must be sheltered until marriage. He would remain her caregiver as long as she remained under his roof—such as it was. A generous parent, a demanding child—how did it turn out? Although her journal entries stopped before telling the outcome of his trip, the drama no doubt unfolded for them both as life in the West moved on.

Other men tried to school their daughters as they would a boy—with the practical wisdom of balancing accounts, figuring sums, and developing writing skills. Nellie McGraw's father, a successful attorney, observed that finances were her weak suit—she needed an education.

I was quite a big girl when I first saw a copper penny. A nickel was our lowest coin and when the pennies made their appearance, they were treated with contempt; we did not trouble to pick them up from the counter when they were offered in change. Their advent raised prices somewhat. Where materials were 12 1/2 cents a yard or two yards for two bits, they were priced 15 cents a yard straight. The same applied to fruits and vegetables and groceries. Father started a banking system with the youngest sisters. He supplied himself with a roll from the bank and each night gave them each a penny. When they had saved five he would put it to their account in a small notebook and when they had five nickels to their account they could draw two bits or let it remain. This was their first lesson in saving money and they became quite adept at it. Only a few years before his death, he wrote to sister Doll that in looking over that old account book he found that she still had $3.50 credit and sent it to her with interest that had accrued through the years!

McGraw was a charming parent. Although gruff and prone to discipline, he thrilled his children in unexpected ways, often pushing aside sheaves of paperwork from his busy practice in admiralty law and Spanish land grants to hustle the children off on an outing—a delight for them, and a respite for his wife. Looking at the faces of his eight children, scrubbed, expectant and ready for a holiday, he could only sigh. Discipline was futile. The best he could hope for was that no one lost a limb, drowned, or ended up missing. As observed by fourteen-year-old Nellie:

Dr. Edward Bass reading his newspaper with Everetta, in Montello, Wisconsin, 1890.

Wherever we went we considered wading a part of the day, and someone was invariably falling in the water and having to be fished out and dried out as well. Then Father himself was sometimes to blame for the misadventure, and that did not add to his serenity. He was always in a hurry and on one occasion when we were headed for some desirable spot along a Saucelito railroad and the train stopped for some signal Dad said "Here we are! Get off quick." We were all scattered along the car, each one having rushed for a seat at a window. Jane and the heavy lunch basket were at the forward end of the car and, in her usually leisurely way, started to walk up the aisle. Father had dragged the rest of us off when the train started off. He yelled but it did no good. Jane calmly rode to the end of the line—about ten miles—and we found ourselves in a field of brush with no house in sight and nothing for company but a railroad switch signals; and no lunch. . . . Father grabbed the conductor and told of his lost daughter. He said he would send her back on the down train—if he could find her—and jumped on the train before Father realized that he might have boarded us and gone on. Well Jane came back two hours later! And we all boarded the train with her and went home. We tackled the lunch basket as soon as the train was in motion. Jane had sat at the station and eaten her lunch and was quite serene.

The father of young Arizona settler Edith Stratton Kitt decided that she should not be denied the use of a gun—however, his inability to keep her in ammunition might have been deliberate.

I learned to shoot at an early age. When I was ten years old my grandfather presented me with a sixteen-gauge, single-barrel shotgun. I learned to shoot fairly well, but nothing fancy. I preferred to shoot on a rest and never learned to shoot on the wing. The reason? I never had the ammunition. Dad did not go into Tucson often for supplies, and shells were expensive. I had only two brass shells, and when I went hunting I would carry a tin pail with powder, shot, wads caps and the tools with which to reload my shells. Whenever I used one shell, I would sit down and reload it. I have sat at a water hole for hours waiting for two or more doves to get in line so that I could kill more than one with a single shot.

Growing families and little income drove many men to despair. "My father once had a beautiful voice, but he's had seven children, and it is just ruined," said Carrie Williams. Kansas homesteader Edward Fitch would gaze out over the cloud-dappled plains and daydream about freedom. Although "tied to" his wife and baby and unable to "go anywhere or do anything," he could still imagine that "by and by the baby will be a little girl who can run alone and take care of herself somewhat."

And then what?

Such reflections were apart from reality, and the more a man imagined his freedom, the more confused became parental urges. "O, why did I leave Molly and the Baby!" queried a sign painted on the rough planks of a California-bound wagon—a question asked by absentee fathers whose dreams had driven them to the gold fields, where they vanished for years among the shadowy reaches of the California Sierra. Although still married, their wives became grass widows, women abandoned but not free to marry again. Their children were virtual orphans.

Others, more conscientious, tried to parent by Pony Express,

Unidentified Colorado girl with older man, either her father or grandfather, ca. 1880.

having their wives describe home events and the children's progress in minute detail by letter. The men, in turn, instructed their wives in the intricacies of land sale, crop harvesting, educating children, and forestalling claims, bills, and tax collectors. "When little Sis begins to talk, learn her to call me, won't you?" pleaded forty-niner David de Wolf in a letter to his wife.

"The baby looks at every man he sees to find some one that he Can call Pa," chided Sarah Dresser to her husband, William, in a letter of January 21, 1848. Perhaps she was trying to temper his voluminous outpourings. Or was irritated by his incessantly jolly and high-spirited missives, in which he demanded that they "recolect" him. He, in turn, would pray for them every day. "What can please a Father more than to learn that his children are trying to be good children and will try to learn all they can . . . and are good boyes and love each other and love their Mother?"

As the years went by, children lost all memory of their vanished fathers, although not all hope of their return. Twelve-year-old Thomas Booth had heard only stories of the mythic man who had supported the family for so many years. Daily, the boy would sit on a woodpile in front of the family's ramshackle frame house, gazing down the street, just in case. One day he was surprised.

> Away down the street perhaps a quarter of a mile distant, I saw a traveler approaching. As he came nearer I observed that he was carrying a carpet sack in one hand. Surely it wasn't anybody I was acquainted with in this locality.

Just then, he saw his mother "fly out of the back door and throw her arms around the stranger's neck and kiss him," an eerie performance that "terribly scandalized" Thomas's sister. When the big man came straight toward Thomas, "put out his hand and exclaimed, 'Home at last!' I knew it was father!" the boy exulted. "I verily believe I was the happiest boy in America at that moment."

Edmund Booth had finally yielded to his wife's entreaties to return to Iowa after years in the gold country. He had raised his children through letters and maintained his relationship with his wife, who was deaf, through correspondence. Finally in 1854, he had returned to tend his family.

✧ ✧ ✧ ✧

WIDOWERS ROAMED THE West, since women were far more likely to die than men. In Dakota, Nebraska, Utah, and Washington between 1859 and 1860, the death rate for women was 22 percent higher than the mortality rate for men. In Ohio and Illinois women between twenty and fifty years old had a mortality rate 50 percent higher than that for men.

Widowers might advertise in the matrimonial papers for a "helpmate of the feminine gender" to replace their lost wives, hopefully "motherly females" versed in sewing buttons and giving, according to David de Wolf, "poor motherless children an occasional spanking."

Some were shameless in their searching—like the bachelor who rode from door to door with a long pole, not taking the time to dismount, only leaning down and rapping the window with his pole, calling out, "Is there anyone to marry in there?" In another instance, Mary McNair Mathews of Virginia City opened the door one morning in 1896 to find a man perched on her steps. "I wish to the Lord you would marry me," he blurted out. "I have got four or five children, and I have not time to take care of them. I want a good, smart woman to bring them up—some one who will be kind to them." Mathews smartly informed him that she disliked all children but her own and would certainly be a cross stepmother. She was not "on the marry" and disliked men who were.

Just as motherhood had its special aura of saintliness, fatherhood set the standard of excellence in mining camps throughout the West. Miners, as well as the footloose men who rode the range or worked the mines or who were simply bachelor uncles, were drawn, mothlike, to the brightly lit kitchens and hearths of any available family. They appointed themselves surrogate fathers, or at the very least, mentors to the young children growing up in their midst. Such men might board with a family or just take in meals, standing in as "uncle" to children of absent fathers, or those so hard worked there was no time for play. Every community had its share of unmarried men—bachelors were the mainstay of western life. Living alone, they naturally heaped affection, instruction, gifts, and sympathy on their young friends. When a miner spied a child passing by and jokingly asked him, "Whose little boy are you?" the answer, "Mother's," caused the man to break down and weep. Henry S. Bloom, a husky "man of the frontier" thought children "pleasant." On February 22, 1851, he held a "Gathering of the little folks at our house tonight; some seven or eight little girls present; they had a jolly time." Anne Ellis, who grew up in rowdy, unsupervised fashion in the Colorado mining camps, always had a procession of kindly bachelors to help her out. One told her hunting stories, "Picnic Jim" took her camping, and Eli the freighter instructed her in cooking techniques. Young Jesse Applegate, an Oregon pioneer, always bunked with a lone bachelor, "Uncle Mack." Said Jesse, "I had always slept with him before my earliest recollections, when he was with us, as he almost always was."

Parents viewed such men with caution, but found them generally dependable. They gave the children freely what so many parents found difficult to provide—time and attention. Magnanimous miners were always "passing the hat" to raise subscriptions for orphaned or sick youngsters. They were repaid in family love, even if not by their own family.

8

FAMILY DISCORD

I love my children and am willing [to] have as many as possible but never before have I dreaded the ordeal of childbirth, as I am afraid to look upon its little face. How can it be human and a perfect child after all that I have been through this last time? Each place I have asked for advice what to do, or for to compel my husband to work and provide for me and the children, the best I receive is, "why do you live with him and have children for such a man? You deserve no pity."—*Mrs. H.B.*

THE HARMONY OF family life was often shattered by strife, bringing discord into the already bumpy progress of domestic life. Life in the West provided no buffers against emergencies—there were seldom family members to help out and inexperienced young parents were particularly vulnerable. When illness struck, the burden of care and anxiety caused partners to despair, or in some cases, to secretly make plans of escape.

Francis Prevaux, a minister living in California in 1858, found himself growing evermore suspicious of his wife as his unexpected illness progressed. Would she stay with him? Was he a burden? He tried to help her around the house, or tend to the children, but his secret musings, stemming from poor health, colored the scene. Did both plan their dissolution as they sat in the parlor, she busy hemming her hoops, he scratching pen to paper?

> I don't know, but Lil & I will have to dissolve partnership. By the advice of several physicians . . . Shes fearing that I am not well enough to go beyond good medical attention, and wishes for a few months of a year to live in San Francisco. Unless she comes round pretty soon, we shall have to separate, or split the difference by remaining where we are.

A new arrival invariably caused tension to mount in the small frame homes and dugouts of the frontier, sparking up friction, making parents "harassed & vexed, & perplexed constantly," as was Milton Shaw, a missionary in New Mexico, who worried constantly. Others felt the same. What if another child was still in the cradle? Would the wailing cries of one infant touch off those of another? How to sleep with all the din? How to live? Mounting debts added to the fray. "I write this confidentially. Our place is mortgaged & you will see that I feel much anxiety," wrote Harriet Shaw about her husband, a minister little suited to the snags of commerce, who had "entered into trade with a friend and was not doing well."

Urban families also encountered poverty, as did Mrs. H.B., trying to raise children in Illinois without her husband's help:

> God help the poor mothers of today. The cry is Save the babies, but what about the mothers who produce these babies? Now, Dear Sirs, No hard feeling for what I have written. But would it

> not be better to enact a law that, when a man marries a woman and she bears his children for him, that he be compelled to provide for the babies he caused to be brought into the world, and permit mothers to properly care for their babies, and give [a man] a life sentence for bringing home disease and inflicting his wife with it. And if possible start an association to protect mothers who are to give birth and after that help them to help themselves, and enable them to do for their babies. The Soldier receive[s] his pension. What do mothers' receive? Abuse, torture, slurs, that is the best they receive. Men in long service receive their pension. Mothers deserving receive nothing.

Sons could prove a blessing or a threat, depending upon how they were viewed by their parents. Charitable and loving men came to terms with their heirs, while others, so stunted as to view children as chattel, took unfortunate paths. Some men were unwilling to transfer manhood to a rival within the family, as was Mr. Wilson, who disliked his son, Henry, so much that he "sold" him to a traveling couple with the understanding that the boy would receive six months' schooling in return for his hard labor, and the father would receive twenty-five dollars for the bargain. According to diarist Helen Carpenter, the "sale" was more than agreeable to the seventeen year old, who had been sorely mistreated at home and at least would now have a change of scene.

Another boy, noted by Mrs. Hugh Fraser, an English traveler in the Pacific Northwest, was a victim of miserliness and religion. His father, a "stiff-necked Methodist" known for "grasping stinginess and downright cruelty," was a prosperous rancher in the Cascades with a "good many thousand dollars" in the bank and a valuable house in Spokane. Yet he kept his children so starved that all their ambition to learn failed to help them—their "underfed brains" were too malnourished to learn.

> In the bitterest weather the boys, who sometimes came to do chores for us, were shivering in ragged cotton shirts and bare feet, while the children of men who could not raise a dollar for months to come were running in warm sweaters, double stockings and thick shoes. There were three nice, handsome boys, ranging in age from ten to sixteen. In a country where meat was cheap they lived on potatoes, and all three had voices like old men, and articulated so indistinctly that it was hard to understand what they said.
>
> The two youngest still had some spring left in them, but the eldest, at sixteen, was a hollow-chested, broken creature, from whom it was impossible to extract either a cheery word or a smile. The father had always told them that he was a very poor man, that it was impossible for him to buy them warm clothes, and that all the hard work they did for him was due in payment of their food and lodging.
>
> And he worked them unmercifully. They rose at five and slaved away till a quarter to nine, when they started off to school on a breakfast of "mush." Returning at four they had to go to work again till night fell, when, after a supper of bread and potatoes, they went up to their bedroom to prepare their lessons. I could see the window from my house; the light used to burn there till eleven o'clock night after night, and I knew that those poor starved brains were straining at tasks which well-fed children, with a quarter of these boys' good-will, had got through in the hour before supper, without an effort.
>
> More than once during our stay a child was born, and when it was a boy the father was radiant. "Yes, more help!" he would exclaim when he was congratulated on the happy event. The girls were less enthusiastically received. Only a small amount of work could be got of them!

In the family of Bethenia Owens and her husband, Legrande, a baby led to the breaking point. He had already proved himself "shiftless" after having been given several fresh starts by her father, and failing every time. Finally, he proved himself cruel, too.

> Our trouble usually started with the baby, who was unusually cross. He was such a sickly, tiny mite, with an abnormal, voracious appetite, but his father thought him old enough to be trained and disciplined, and would spank him unmercifully because he cried. This I could not endure, and war would be precipitated at once. A few days before our separation, his father fed

him six hard-boiled eggs at supper, in spite of all I could do or say. I slept little that night, expecting that the child would be in convulsions before morning.

Early one morning in March, after a tempestuous scene of this sort, Mr. Hill threw the baby on the bed and rushed into town. As soon as he was out of sight, I put on my hat and shawl, and, gathering a few necessaries together for the baby, I flew over to father's.

ABUSE WITHIN THE family had untold consequences—children failed to learn, turned speechless, cowered, or became angry, and left home early, always remembering their improvident fathers, who fell into passivity or turned brutal, taking out their anxiety on wives and children. A North Carolina woman, writing to the Government Children's Bureau in 1917, lamented that "Only the other day he said right before the children that He and they ought to kill me. He just keeps me ill all the time. . . . [T]he children are afraid of him and dare not let him know they are ill." During the late 1880s, there was little in the way of government help to protect women from domestic violence or homicide.

Abigail Bailey lived in fear of her husband, Asa, and sorrowed over a marriage that was a litany of abuse. Yet her concerns were for her middle daughter, the victim of repeated acts of incest. As the mother lay ailing, the father turned to his daughter for companionship, and in later years, sought out other young women for his pleasure.

One night soon after he had retired to bed, he began to talk very familiarly and seemed pleasant. He said, now I will tell you what I have been studying upon all this while. I have been planning to sell our farm and to take our family and interest and move westward, over toward the Ohio country five or six hundred miles. I think that is a much better country than this, and I have planned the whole matter. . . .

But alas; words fail to see the things which followed.

Mr. B. said . . . he would take only his daughter. . . . [She] must go and cook for him.

He now commenced a new series of conduct in relation to this daughter who he selected to go with him. A great part of the time he now spent in the room where she was spinning [away from] the rest of the family. He seemed to have forgotten his age, his honor, and all decency, as well as all virtue. He would spend his time with this daughter in telling idle stories and foolish riddles and singing songs to her, and sometimes before the small children, when they were in the room. He thus pursued a course of conduct which had the most direct tendency to corrupt young and tender minds and lead them the greatest distance from every serious subject. He would try to make his daughter tell stories with him, wishing to make her free and sociable and to erase from her mind all that fear and reserve which he had ever taught his children to feel toward him. . . .

For a considerable time I was wholly at a loss what to think of his conduct. . . . I was loth to indulge the least suspicion of base design. . . . Every thing must lie neglected while this one daughter engrossed all his attention.

Through all the conduct of Mr. B. from day to day seemed to demonstrate . . . that he was determined . . . to ruin this poor young daughter. . . . No words can express the agitation of my soul.

I soon perceived that his strange conduct toward this daughter was to her very disagreeable. And she shewed much unwillingness to be in the room with him. . . . I often saw her cheeks bedewed with tears on account of his new and astonishing behavior. But as his will has ever been that of the family, she saw no way to deliver herself from her cruel father. . . .

If I even dropped words to her he would find out what I had said . . . and then be very angry with me so that on time I feared for my life. I queried with myself which way I could turn. How could I caution a young daughter in such a case? My thoughts fled to God for relief, that the Father of mercies could protect a poor helpless creature marked out for a prey and turn the shears of a cruel father from every wicked purpose.

After a while Mr. B.'s conduct toward this daughter was strangely altered. Instead of idle songs, fawning and flattery, he grew very angry with her and would see her dead and buried and he would correct her very severely. It seems that when he found his first line of conduct ineffectual, he changed his behavior . . . and was determined to see what he could effect by tyranny and cruelty. He most cautiously guarded her against having any free conversation with me . . . [fearing that] she should expose him. He would forbid any of the children going with her to milking. If at any time any went with her, it must be a number so that nothing could be said concerning him. . . . Never before had Mr. B. thus confined her, or any of his children. None but an eye witness can conceive of the strangeness of his conduct from day to day and of his pain to conceal his wickedness. . . .

One morning Mr. B. rose from bed, while it was yet dark. He immediately called this daughter, and told her to get up. She obeyed. And as she knew her daily business, she made up first her room, and sat down to her work. He sat by the fire in the kitchen. As my door was open, I carefully observed his motions. He sat looking into the fire for some time, as though absorbed in his thoughts. It soon grew light. The small children arose and came round the fire. He looked round like one . . . vexed. He sprang from his chair, and called his daughter. . . . She left her work in her room and came immediately to him. In a great rage, and with a voice of terror, he asked why she did not come to him, when he first called her? . . . He then fell to whipping her without mercy. She cried and begged. . . . He continued to whip her as though he were dealing with an ungovernable brute, striking over her head, hands, and back, nor did he spare her face and eyes, while the poor girl appeared as though she must die. No proper account could have ever prevailed to [excuse] this conduct.

It might appear surprising that such wickedness was not checked by legal restraints. But great difficulties attended to such a case. While I was fully convinced of the wickedness, yet I knew not that I could make legal proof. I could not prevail upon this daughter to make known to me her troubles or to testify against the author of them. . . . My soul was moved with pity for her wretched case and yet I cannot say I did not feel a degree of resentment, that she would not, as she ought, expose the wickedness of her father. . . . But no doubt his intrigues, insinuations, commands, threats, and parental influence, led her to feel that it was in vain for her to seek redress. . . .

The next morning I took an opportunity with Mr. B. alone to have solemn conversation. My health being now restored, I thought it high time . . . to adopt a new mode of treatment. . . . I calmly introduced the subject, and told him, plainly and solemnly, all my views of his wicked conduct, in which he had only lived with his daughter. He flew into a passion . . . and seemed to imagine he could frighten me out of my object. But I was carried equally above fear, and above temper. Of this I soon convinced him. . . . I reminded Mr. B. of my long and unusually distressing illness, how unable I had been to check him in his awful wickedness, which I knew he had pursued. . . .

I therefore had not known what to do better than to wait on God as I had done, to afford my strength . . . to introduce the means of his effectual control. This time, I told him, had arrived. . . . I would not suffer him to go on any longer as he has done. . . .

Mr. B. seeing me thus bold and determined, soon changed his conduct. He appeared panic-struck and he soon became mild, sociable and pleasant. He now made an attempt, with all his usual subtlety and flatteries, to induce me to relinquish my design. He pretended to deny the charge of incest. . . .

We spent the whole day in the most solemn conversation. . . . He begged me to inform him what he could or should do, so that I could once more trust him, and see if he would not prove as good . . . as his promises. He did not feel free to confess the worst crime, laid to his charge, yet he said he would feel quite content that I should think I had forgiven him. . . .

Mr. B. then begged of me to banish from my mind all that was past. . . .

For several weeks nothing more was said upon the subject. And Mr. B.'s conduct toward me and the family was pleasant and agreeable. I really began to hope that I should never again have occasion of any such distressing perplexities.

But God, in his infinite wisdom, did not see fit that my peculiar trial should [end.]

I again clearly perceived that the same wicked passions, as before, were in operating in Mr. B.'s heart. . . . Upon a certain sabbath I went to meeting. Mr. B. did not go. Before I reached home at night, I met with evidence, which convinced me, that the same horrible conduct had of this holy day been repeated in my family! I rode up to the door. Mr. B. stood waiting for me. He seemed very kind, and was coming to take me tenderly from my horse. I leaped from my saddle, before he had opportunity to reach me. My heart was disgusted at the offer of his deceitful help. I said nothing upon the dreadful subject this day. Some broken stories of the children corroborated the information I had received. But Mr. B. probably pleased himself with the idea that all was concealed, and he was safe.

The next day, I took him alone, and told him of what he had again been guilty, even after all his vows. . . . He started, and seemed very angry.

Mr. B. now attempted again to flatter me. He renewed the most solemn promise. . . .

Our unhappy daughter now became eighteen years of age, and thus legally free from her father. She immediately left us, and returned no more. As she was going, I had solemn conversation with her relative to her father's conduct. She gave me to understand that it had been abominable. But I could not induct her to consent to become an evidence against him. I plead with her the honor and safety of our family, the safety of her young sisters, and her own duty, but she appeared overwhelmed with shame and grief, and nothing effectual could yet be done.

Sexual abuse was considered so shameful, even by the victim, that, as in Abigail Bailey's daughter's case, it was rarely reported. But discipline could also go too far and enter the realm of physical abuse. But who was to decide where the line was crossed? With Calvinist notions of "purging, firing, and tempering" setting the disciplinary standard, cruel and unusual treatment was often confused with a family's style, and despite proof to the contrary, critics would withdraw until evidence swayed them one way or another. Abusive parents seemed secure in knowing they would not be challenged within the limits of their own homes. In one case, a girl, "ill-treated by both her father and stepmother, was often beaten with stove wood or whatever was handiest for any little thing," recalled J. H. Williams. Her suffering was complicated by the additional burden of threats to her life if she told. Despite her father's obfuscation, relatives found out the truth and decided to spirit the girl away under the cover of a stepmother's visit. When the father discovered her escape, he was "very angry and swore if he found her he would whip her until there was not a sound piece of skin in her body." Sadly enough, cruelty toward children took place with agonizing frequency, and pallid remonstrances from nearby neighbors were not enough to check the practice.

Democracy, privacy, and patriarchy contributed to the notion of family hegemony. A child was chattel under the nineteenth-century legal system of guardianship, and in a man's—or woman's—"castle home," there was a deep aversion to interference. Thus when fur trader Andrew Pambrun found that a half-breed had "put his child on a hot stove and burnt it to death, because it was crying and disturbed his sleep," he could only shake his head in dismay. The man was "inhuman, [a] Devil incarnate," but Pamburn stuck to the western code of "hands off," suitable perhaps for adults, but certainly not for children.

Part 3

PIONEER TIMES

Photo on previous page: Raising a cabin in Idaho, ca. 1880s.

9

Rural Lives

I knew having the baby would now complicate homesteading and often debated about . . . it.—*Anna Langhorne Waltz*

Punch cows! I've been punching cows all my life . . . from the time I was born, I think.—*Oma Jensen Graham*

Those moving west saw in the vast, boundless plains a "new Eden" of rolling hillsides carpeted with sage, sweet peas, honeysuckle, star daisies, goldenrod, and giant, breeze-ruffled sunflowers as far as the eye could see. In Nebraska, the hills were dotted with small pink roses that exploded through the tough sod, scattering color across the foothills. Where cactus leaned in the heat, their shade gave relief to panting lizards and an occasional tortoise. Such wilderness was imagination's playground, filled with exotic shrubs and blooms, Promethean vistas, oddly carved buttes and canyons, and rivers alive with fish.

Wild sand cherries clustered in the fields, ripe for plucking, their dark, shining globes stirring up the memory of pie, or dark, spicy preserves. After picking, children plunged the pitted fruit deep into the cool water of an artesian well to keep them from spoiling, then later, ate the cooled fruit as dessert, slathered with cream and sugar.

"O! to be a child again," wrote popular author Fanny Fern in *Ginger-Snaps*. "To love nothing but maple sugar. . . . To wake up with a shout. . . . To be able to *believe*."

Droning bees announced summer, as well as frequent cloudbursts. When rain drummed into the parched ground, everything turned delightfully cool and suddenly, there were choirs of unseen frogs, freed from the monotony of dusty hibernation.

Settlers found themselves living in a vast and surprising natural zoo, lavish with new breeds of animals and reptiles, from whippy garter snakes to fist-sized, burrowing mud clams. Sunfish were snapped up from the river, along with bullheads and carp, as children in torn clothes and tanned feet dangled willow poles over deep water. To Wyoming homesteader Elinore Pruitt Stewart "it was all so beautiful—the red rock, the green fields, the brown sand of the road and [the] bare places, the mighty mountains, the rugged cedars and sage-brush spicing the warm air. . . ." "I remember the smell of dust and sage and a kind of animal smell too," recalled Colorado homesteader Ethelyn Whalin Crawford. "It was magnificent. I just stood there . . . worshiping, I guess, what I was seeing."

The land was bereft of human imprint, patterned with the tracks of muskrats, civet cats, skunks, coons, and weasels, and wrapped in a silence so heavy the settlers felt bound to dispel it. Human hubbub was raised at every opportunity, from ball game to a taffy pull. "I have always thanked the Lord for a contented mind, a home and something to eat," said Utah settler Priscilla Merriman Evans. "The Lord has been mindful of us," added Rachel Emma Woolley Simmons, writing in 1870.

When a barn rose up, so did children's expectations. "The boys and girls knew . . . that something would be doing and spruced up for the occasion. As soon as the accordion player struck the first note, the festivities were on and kept on until day-break," wrote Czech settler Frank Cejda. Some happy-go-lucky couples skidded right across the floor, spewing shavings and sawdust behind them in a piney wake. Amid all the adult hoopla, children were overlooked, usually falling asleep under heaps of coats and blankets. One exhausted group of parents, bleary-eyed from dancing, dragged their drowsy offspring home at four o'clock in the morning only to find that those retrieved were not theirs at all. The next day was spent quietly redistributing youngsters.

The frontier home was the sum total of rural civilization—a haven of long evenings where yarns were spun, songs sung in faltering harmony, and musical instruments plunked and strummed. "Everyone likes to come here," said Emma Shepard Hill. "I think it is because we have the piano and my mother can sing." Fiddles whined out the strains of "Money Musk" and "Turkey in the Straw" to claps and shouts. "Home was something of a picnic for the . . . pioneers, still young enough to be boys and girls together. They had a good time, and were glad that their isolation allowed as much noise as they pleased," Sarah Bixby Smith recalled. She treasured the memory of one night by the fireplace, as her father was having a good time reading and smoking with his feet "high up against the mantel." She thought she would do the same. "I climbed up and . . . seated myself beside him, put my feet as high as I could on my side of the fireplace, adjusted my newspaper, lighted my squill cigar, and in [smoking] it, managed to set my front hair on fire. That attracted papa's attention."

In Keturah Penton's Ohio home, for entertainment, there was "always . . . a fund of aneckdotes to tell." Likewise, in the home of Susan Newcomb:

> Supper is over, and we are now quietly seated around our fireside. Pa is sitting in one corner, and Bettie is in the other playing her acordeon. Sallie is sitting by the table reading poetry, and ma is at my elbow chatting with pa. The men have gone down the lane to their "hall" and Gus [her five-year-old son] has gone with them to hear Mr. Fosdick pick on his banjo.

Any event could turn festive. "Nobody missed the arrival of the afternoon train in early Abilene unless the snow was too deep or a tornado hovered in the sky," recalled Tommie Clack. Everyone gathered at the depot, and afterward, the men would drop into a saloon on the way home. On that same day, women might go trading, swapping eggs, butter, or preserves for dry goods such as thread or salt. Women passed from door to door, meeting friends, chatting. "On Saturday afternoons there were no strangers," noted Clack.

Scarcity always bred such homespun offerings as "Gosh," a heap of moistened bread crumbs garnished with minced sage and a scatter of chopped wild onion, and greeted by an outraged question, *Gosh!* Do we have to eat *this* again?

Families lived however parents could manage, from frame shacks with tar-paper walls to the confines of a corncrib for one Iowa family. In the Michigan log hut of Mrs. Caroline Kirkland, "A quilt . . . was stuck up before the window and the unhinged cover of one of the chests was used as a lid for the stair-way, for fear the children might fall down." Said Kirkland: "I do not remember experiencing, at any time in my life, a sense of more complete uncomfortableness than was my lot upon awakening the next morning." Blanche Beale Lowe and her siblings slept in a barn, where "after we were all tucked in, Grandmammy came up those steep steps to hear our prayers. She kissed each one of us with quick little . . . kisses, and asked God to bless her babies. I don't think Grandpa let [her] go out to the barn to kiss the boys goodnight—they slept in the haymow."

For many settlers earth-hewn dugouts, or "soddies," were home, tucked snugly into the earth like a prairie dog burrow. Hand-hewn bricks, cut from buffalo grass sod, were slathered with clay and stacked tightly together for insulation. In the spring, wiry tufts of rye grass roots pushed down through the clay, dropping seeds and tassels on the swept earth floor. Storms dumped rain through gopher holes, as if they were rainspouts, shooting torrents into the homestead below. Umbrellas popped open at bedtime—how else to sleep?

Wrote Edith Kitt, daughter of an Arizona homesteader:

The small house in which I was born had dirt walls, a dirt floor and a dirt roof . . . The walls were . . . adobe. It was cool and nice, except when it rained. The ridge-pole and rafters were made out of rough-hewn timbers. Small branches, brush, and bear grass were laid on these, then finer grass or hay, and finally the dirt—no, last of all were the weeds which grew in the dirt and looked quite gay in the spring. If this roof sprang a leak, it was just too bad. First there would be a drop or two of water. Then the hole would widen—a fine example of erosion—and Mother would grab buckets, tubs, dishpans, anything to catch the muddy stream.

The Clack family of Lytle Creek, Texas, used their covered wagon as a dwelling, with "a sheet spread under the vehicle to serve as a sitting room and the wagon itself was the bedroom." Later, they moved to a picket house, a "fairly large dwelling [with] walls made of saplings set upright in small trenches and sealed together with mud."

"I felt confident I could build a house," said young emigrant C.V. Svoboda, who was sixteen when his family emigrated from Bohemia to Nebraska. New to manual labor, he had watched carpenters in the old country—surely, with the help of his father, he could build a sod hut in several months. "After completing the framework, we made several thousand dry bricks, which my father bricked the spaces between the studding and finished plastering the walls."

"I remember reading off the 'wallpaper' in our new ranch house," recalled Texan Tommie Clack. "It was great fun, picking out letters from the *Taylor County News* stuck to the wall. Later we had regular wallpaper, which cost 10 cents a roll, 15 cents for a double roll."

Heating was always a problem—a house could be so icy the mopped floors turned slick as a skating rink and frost rimmed the tables when washed. Snowflakes often drifted through chinks in the ceiling, melting into puddles from the early-morning firing of the stove. Insulation, as with Keturah Penton's backwoods cabin in Ohio, came from "Jams of damp dirt pounded in [so] solid between timbers . . . it would last for years." Emma Shepard Hill's first cabin was "warm and comfortable, being made of logs; but the front door is not very heavy and does not fit close at the top."

As for bedding? Every settler aspired to a good feather bed with goose down pillows, thick wool blankets, and an extra quilt, but

Unidentified women in front of frame cabin, ca. 1880.

Unidentified North Dakota family, ca. 1880s. Photo by Frank B. Fiske, Fort Yates, North Dakota.

could make do with less—which, in most cases, was a "wall bed" or rough shelf that protruded from the wall, balanced on two legs, like a table. Indoor plumbing was nonexistent, leaving an outhouse, or, for indoor use, an "earth closet," with its supply of stove ashes or charcoal for hygiene. Early settlers had no wood-burning stoves, hanging their pots from an iron crane over the open fire. A long, smooth griddle set directly on the hot coals gave rise to heavy, yellow hoecakes, which were turned with a knife until brown. Although the Hills' house was consistently "unfixed," her father took a philosophical tone: "Our lives are passing all the time," he mused, "and we should make the best of ourselves and our opportunities wherever we are."

Along with wilderness and isolation came the deep need to visit, and even though the Hills were eighteen miles over steep mountains from the nearest neighbors, "a good deal of company evenings" took place. Thick white ceramic plates were set out, bent steel forks collected, and pans were burnt sooty preparing food for a crowd. Bunking space was always needed—there were never enough beds. In Miriam Colt's Kansas dugout, "We fill the one bed lengthwise and crosswise; the family of the house take to the trundle-bed, while the floor is covered . . . with men, women and children, rolled in Indian blankets like silk worms in cocoons." When "twelve people spent the night" with Kansas homesteader Anna Biggs Heaney, "Mother took her own little son and the woman with the smallest baby into [bed] with her. The other two men and two of the children bunked crosswise in the treadle bed. . . . Father rolled in his old army overcoat and a buffalo hide beside the stove while small Stella slept snugly on the table with her head on the flour barrel. And," she added, "none of the guests of the hotel had to ring for ice water, because every once in a while a ruder-than-usual blast sent icy particles through unchinked crevices to sprinkle the weary sleepers." Typically, Kansas settler Lavina Gates Chapman "cooked breakfast one morning for fifty-two" guests, who were scattered about on quilts and bedding throughout the house.

As families grew, so did the number of beds per room needed to accommodate them. Idaho homesteader Nels Reid "built on a nice big room for five" a foul weather haven where animals and people could huddle for warmth. Not so, however, in Grandma Wilson's house: "Ol Brindle the cow was brought in to milk," wrote Wilson's granddaughter, Sylvia Dye. The children wanted to keep her out of the storm. Grandma, always fastidious, refused to let the beast stay. Once turned out into the blinding storm, "Ol Brindle" wandered about, sank into the snow, and unfortunately died.

Amenities were few, food was simple, and bathing rare, especially in winter, when any venture into water called for fortitude, as well as a tub and soap. Children dreaded the enforced soaking of the Saturday bath, even if the water *was* heated to boiling. They knew what awaited them was a long dash across a cold room to throw on icy, stiff clothes. Worse, they hated the lather of homemade soap, which stung their eyes and rimmed their ears and besides, tasted like fat and ashes. "Spit" baths were the common solution, with scummy washpan reused, over and over.

Keeping clean was chore enough, as was firing up the stove to heat water. Cold ashes were shaken down from the stove, the fire grates were cleaned, the trash box emptied, and the stove pipe draft regulated to suck air through. Unlit, the stove had to be scoured with sand and water to flake away carbon deposits.

Recalled Sylvia Dye:

> First we put some paper or fine sticks in the bottom, then a few cobs if we had some, and then the cow chips up to the stove lids which we left off so as to get the boiler closer to the fire. We carried water and filled the boiler, then lighted the paper under the fuel, and the stove did the rest.
>
> Leonard said he knew how to make the fire start sooner, so after we had cleaned out the ashes, set the drafts, filled the stove, he said he would pour in some coal oil and get a quick fire. With the filled boiler all in place and everything ready, he lit the fire with a match and, sure enough, it went like wild; and we, not having to wait to see if it would start, went to the pond about half a block away and were trying to find the snapping turtles that were killing Mama's ducklings.
>
> We had played only a few minutes when Leonard said there sure is a lot of smoke coming out of the wash house. Sure enough, it was billowing out of the pipe and also beside the pipe on the roof. Effie ran to call mama. Leonard and I ran for milk pails and to the horse tank for water. The stove pipe was red hot and some little red flames were coming out.
>
> Luckily a neighbor was passing by, saw the smoke, came galloping up, climbed to the roof, and with mama handing him the pails of water and we children making a water brigade, he soon had the fire out; but there was a big hole in the roof clear around the stove pipe and we children were really excited—as Leonard said, "the wash water surely got hot fast!

The stove grate yawned like a huge mouth, always hungry, demanding endless armfuls of kindling, brush, stalks, or sticks, as well as logs from a dwindling supply. "For fuel we had to depend on sunflowers, cornstalks, weeds and straw," wrote a Nebraska settler, who, along with nearly everyone, hated the stove and its fierce appetite. "Stoke the stove, get out flour, stoke the stove, wash hands, mix biscuit dough, stoke the stove, wash hands, cut biscuit dough, stoke the stove, wash hands, put biscuits in oven, keep on stoking until the bread is baked and ready for table."

KITCHEN TASKS SEEMED endless. In summer, children had to pour milk into thick crocks set in shallow troughs, then keep enough water in the trough to chill the milk. Wet clothes were reapplied over and over, utilizing evaporation to keep the crocks damp. Even

Mrs. Adeline Hall at work in her kitchen at Orchard Ranch, Wyoming, 1907.

getting honey was a chore, according to Edith Kitt. Children would wait for a bee to fly in, attracted by a bowl of sugar water, then "sprinkle him with flour" to better follow its "bee line" home. Recalled Edith: "A cell containing honey would be right next to one containing bee bread. . . . Mother would be days getting the honey extracted and put into jars."

In the Texas home of young Tommie Clack:

> We bought flour and molasses by the barrel. The sugar in the molasses barrel would settle to the bottom, so we had plenty of brown sugar. . . . In winter we kept a "starter" of yeast for bread when we had no milk or buttermilk. The starter was kept in a pitcher on the back of the stove. The last thing to do at night was to mix up yeast for the next morning and put it close to the fire so it would rise and bubble. It made the most delicious sourdough biscuits you can imagine.

Irritations abounded. In summer, horseflies and houseflies were so thick they often dropped into the food by mistake—hence, "shoofly" pie. To clear them away, boys would tack up mosquito net traps while girls drew the curtains, turning the room dim and the flies drowsy. Stealthily, the children would sneak up on the dozing insects, throw open the windows, and scatter them like cinder, then, gleeful, screaming, running, they would swat the flies in all directions, having a fine time. Any fly that escaped soon ended up stuck on flypaper, called Tanglefoot, which curled down from the doorways like ribbon, swaying with angrily buzzing flies. Groceries, pharmacies, and butcher shops were also a-buzz. "I can remember strips of flypaper six and eight feet long and black with struggling flies hanging from lighting fixtures," Jack O'Connor recalled.

Lacking luxuries and scant on necessities, the pioneer homestead invited innovation of every kind. No rolling pin? Fetch a wooden stick, freshly peeled, or a green ear of corn to flatten out the biscuit dough. No milk? Use egg whites. Raisins gone? Try wild grapes, dried in the sun, or perhaps cherries. "Ice cream" was fashioned from moss, cooked slowly with sugar until it swelled up, gelatinous and slightly green. For shampoo, mothers washed children's hair in a froth of hand soap and raw egg, making conditioner with a final rinse of vinegar and water, leaving the hair clean, fluffy, and shining. Without the slick new curling iron from the Sears catalog, girls resorted to setting their hair with the smoking-hot glass chimney of the kerosene lamp. To soften skin, buttermilk was slathered on. To ease the cracks and calluses of work-worn hands, girls gingerly pulled on gloves filled with chicken fat, wearing them all night while sleeping to soften the work-roughened skin. Toothpaste was sprigs of wild mint, chewed to freshen the breath.

Work was the mainstay of early American life—no one escaped, everyone toiled—even the disabled had a full regimen of duties. Sophia Gelhorn Boylan's crippled mother was continually "knitting and sewing and baking and browning, and in summer working in her garden. She made all [the family's] clothes, did all the baking and cooking, and nearly always had a baby at her breast."

Predictable as childbearing, expected as the seasons, work was age-blind, continuous, and indiscriminate. No one dodged it, no one expected to—children, as "little adults," must perform like other family members, pitching in to support the farm, gaining experience that would give them an ever-stronger voice in family decisions. Laborious, ubiquitous—work was the mainstay of frontier life. "Every child had something to do," wrote Keturah Penton of her early Ohio homestead. "We would gather nuts to Send to town and the money was layed up we never thought of buying candy . . . so we all had to learn to work. Then when it came time to go to market . . . we had to gather the vegatables in the after noon load them up in the evening and then get up a bout three oclock and drive six miles into town and back up to the side walk . . . and take out the . . . a little of evry thing too tedious to mention." So why not use imagination? "I do hate to sit down alone to pick wool," she added, deciding to invite "about a dozen old ladies in and in a day they will do it all up." "Mother . . . [taught] my sister and me to sew. Before I was five years old I had pieced one side of a quilt, sitting at her knee half an hour a day, and you may be sure she insisted on tiny stitches," recalled Edith White. A young Nebraska boy, Sid Ingles, found that he could watch his herd of cattle by sitting daily on top of the highest hill in the Cedar Valley, sitting there for so long that the rise became "Sid's Hill," while a hollow in the hill, or a "blowout," was called "Sid's Blowout." The deep, natural cistern on the northeast side was known as "Sid's Hole on the Cedar Creek."

Reinhardt Porath family, Elk Creek Precinct, Nebraska. Three of the boys are wearing material from a bolt of Montgomery Ward calico.

IN WINTER, CATTLE sheds vanished under huge snowdrifts, and it was the children's work to tunnel down with shovels to rescue the livestock. "As fast as we dug the snow away, the wind would blow the drifts back. So we decided to dig a hole through the top of the covering of the shed. As this was of straw, we soon accomplished it and I was let down. Then father got a basket filled with hay and lowered it down by a rope, and I fed the animals," recalled Nebraskan Frank Cejda. Toddlers, already low to the ground and naturally intrigued by sharp sticks, were assigned the task of planting, first digging shallow depressions in the flinty soil, then hammering the sod into fine dust to strew over the seed eyes. The best ones were sown on Good Friday, with the rows furrowed deep and the seeds planted exactly twelve inches apart. Typically, one boy followed along, dragging his hoe to cover the seed. Once the plants sprouted, it was the job of older children to stroll down the rows of potatoes, knock off the reddish-brown, striped potato bugs into a bucket of coal oil, then kill the eggs coating the undersides of the leaves with a dip in the same bucket.

In the henhouse, everyone's favorite chore was slipping china eggs beneath the laying hens, oh so carefully, to trick them into greater productivity.

Frontier life settled into an endless routine of scrubbing, scrap-

"Home Sweet Home" for unidentified Montana homesteaders, ca. 1890s.

ing, sowing, and tinkering, with little demarcation between toiling in the house or in the field. When Herbert Stubbs complained once about the mountain of housework expected, his mother simply looked at him and said, "Well, you're the oldest!" Haying, furrowing, digging vegetables, pruning trees, cooking for a work crew, hauling water by sled—it all blurred into a ceaseless workaday regimen. "We children had to go over the whole field and gather up the roots in piles and when they got dry we used them for fuel," recalled Iowa youth Matilda Peitzke Paul. "After harvest and haying was done we had to dig the potatoes and husk the corn ready for winter."

"There were chores the boys did and chores that the girls did too, but it always seemed to me like I wasn't considered a boy and I wasn't considered a girl!" said a Colorado woman, trying to understand the versatile nature of her assignments. Fifteen-year-old Keturah Penton voted for boy's chores, and was relieved whenever her mother felt "strong and well so she could do the work in the house," which freed Keturah to work with her father and the boys. She stacked debris into "big brush heeps to burn nights." Keturah could "trim up a tree soon as my Father could . . . and made a prety good hand."

Boys, conversely, could just as well fill the heavy iron kettles and help during the springtime soap making, hefting wooden paddles to mix the lye in the greased kettle, or stoking the fire until the liquid boiled and foamed "just right." Thick and ash-colored, its viscous stream poured out into wooden frames to cool, hardening into flats of creamy-looking soap, like maple candy. Then, it was cut into bars.

Agent's home at Fort Yates, North Dakota. Photo by Frank B. Fiske.

Barn duties were greeted eagerly, as children delighted in struggling up a swaying ladder into the haymow, barely avoiding suffocating between the huge bales of straw, to scramble about, tipping over the sprawling bales on the startled horses below, pumping water to fill the troughs. Later, the horses were curried, stables cleaned, cows pastured and milked by boys with strong hands and large wrists, whose job it was to strain the milk through a cheesecloth, then pour it into crocks to lay away in the musty dark of the root cellar. "I used to dread to have mother call me and tell me to help with the churning," recalled Matilda Peitzke Paul. "It seemed as if the butter never would come sometimes it did take for hours to churn."

As fledgling carpenters and handymen, boys might rehinge fallen doors, fling out the chamber pot contents, and clean out the air-cooled storage spaces for vegetables and butter storage. "Little Henry left the butry door open & my clean dishes, milk & all got covered with flies, so I have to take them all out again," complained Emily Hawley Gillespie. What good were brothers, anyway?

For girls, spring cleaning worked its brief, annual miracle, as they pried free the heavy, nailed-down carpets, shook them out, then walloped them with curved wire paddles, or flails, to loosen the dirt. "Beat-sweep-beat," echoed in muffled fashion, as the carpets exploded outward with every swat. In finishing, the girls pushed a thick layer of straw or newspaper matting under the freshened rug. Also, girls would tuck strips of rag around the trembling window panes to keep in warmth. They scrubbed walls and porches as well as every pot and pan in the kitchen, then painted the kitchen stove with blacking. "Tick time" was dreaded—the bed ticks were emptied of tired straw and afterward, the children would hand-wash the ticks, dry them on the line, restuff them with fresh straw, and then sew up the opening. Feather pillows were washed, wrung, dried, and fluffed in the sun and bedsprings buffed to a shine with coal oil to discourage bedbugs. Woolen blankets were home to countless moth eggs, and had to be rinsed frequently and sprinkled with doses of black pepper to prevent more moths. At night, girls drained the coal oil from the smoky lamps, washed the glass chimneys, and polished them to a sparkle with an old flour sack. After dinner, soapy dishwater was dashed on the cabbages to kill worms. Families too poor for lamps used old-fashioned tape soaked in a plate of grease "for illuminating purposes."

NO EXCUSES WERE were accepted—all had to do their fair share. In the face of such ubiquitous demands, only a shirker of unmentionable delinquency would avoid his or her part, perhaps slipping off to the privy right after dinner to hide out, gazing at pictures in the catalog. "Every child as they grew up was given a responsibility and they were held to that responsibility," said Audrey Oldland, who homesteaded with her parents in Colorado.

Clothing, or lack of it, played a significant role in the saga of rural life, with even the Indians—as recalled by overlander Martha Ann Minto, remembering the Oregon Indians—disdainful of the bedraggled hordes of emigrants. Once middle class, at times the settlers could scarcely recognize themselves, huddled around their smoking fires, bereft of every essential, rigged up in remade flour sacks. Many young children simply went without items that could not be replaced.

Not that half-clad children escaped all notice. Sadie Martin, a newcomer to the exigencies of Arizona desert life in the late 1880s, was amazed that a nearby family of five "wore very little clothing [over] tummies podded out full of melon." Nearby was the house of a "Mexican family, with little naked children playing around the door." As a boy, Mr. Parrish wore a blanket "doubled over" his shoulder with a string that served him both "as a coat & as a bed." Completing his backwoods couture were pants of unsmoked antelope skin, soaked and stretched by the perennial rains of Oregon. When sodden, they ballooned out to twice his size, and when dried in front of the fire, they shrank so that he "literally [had to] cut the dried skin off" to change into a pair of corduroy trousers. For men eschewing buckskin, the frontier uniform was usually a chambray shirt and pair of blue, bib overalls.

Clothes-happy young girls had little recourse than their own sewing skills, since the dream of ready-made clothes remained . . . just that. "[I] cut out a new pair of Drawers & skirt & made me a new part of a chemise," planned fourteen-year-old Sarah Gillespie, but when she tried to "stitch & sew on my white Dress," she lacked the skill. "Help ma! help ma! help ma!!!" she confided in her journal in near despair, unable to voice her needs to a mother so overworked that Sarah refused to ask for help.

Although the images that danced from the pages of *Godey's Lady's Book* were of taffeta, black silk, and high-heeled, sharp-toed boots

The Cooper homestead, Cheyenne, Wyoming, 1886.

Children at the Silver Queen mine, Colorado.

that laced to the calf over lisle stockings, a girl's reality was more often fetched up from the bottom of an old trunk and resewn to fit in the ubiquitous frontier fabrics of calicoes, ginghams, and handspun wools.

Mother Hubbards, pinafores worn over a gown, were in style, sewn from cool and loosely woven cheesecloth, and giving women and teenage girls the air of benevolent nuns as they "floated" about in their handmade gowns. For the more daring, full skirts with tight waists could be sewn from striped bedticking. While formfitting, they were so durable and stiff no thorns could tear their determined folds.

The hot sun called for long-billed poke bonnets, while freezing winters demanded thick stockings, heavy wool mittens, mufflers, and bulky wool wristlets, all smelling like damp sheep when wet. Warmth came from layers. "Mama dressed us in long-legged heavy underwear, long black stockings, overshoes, several slips, bloomers, and warm dresses, coats, bonnets, scarves, and leather mittens. We had long, shining, blonde braids tied with ribbons, and she kept us very clean," wrote pioneer Sylvia Dye.

FOR FRONTIER BOYS, the ineluctable chasm between manhood and childhood was bridged by long pants, which banished forever the embarrassing reminders of adolescence—short knickerbockers commonly worn until thirteen, or worse, as late as fifteen or sixteen. For every boy who "crossed over," there were others whose mothers were obsessed by the economy of short pants, which used less material. When, they cried, could they get long pants like everyone else? Trousers were homemade, high-waisted, and usually without pockets since they would only be weighed down with "rocks, strings, dead beetles, dried fish worms, chewing wax, nails, tops, toy pistols, crullers, doughnuts, fishing tackle, bullets, buttons, jewsharps, etc." According to Jesse Applegate, the "strain on the suspenders would become too great."

Scant wardrobes were supplemented by barrels of charity clothing, shipped from eastern cities to the needy folks out west, including items not always practical for sturdy wear. Boys with dangling, exposed wrists rummaged through the barrels seeking size, rather than style. One discovered a swallow-tailed evening coat that almost fit. He wore it, tails and all, to school.

> During a rough game of pull-a-way at recess time, my mother, then a big girl, tried to catch him, but missing, caught one of the flapping coat tails, and off it came. She says he wore the coat until school was out in the spring and that the one side with the tail still intact made it through all the rough school games and on windy days looked like a flag flapping behind him.

Split, worn shoes were replaced by hand, using homemade wooden "lasts" to wedge into the leather shell, no matter the foot size. "There were no rights or lefts to homemade brogans," recalled one pioneer. "At night the shoe that was to go on the right foot was put where the right foot would step into it in the morning, and the left one was put handy to the left foot, and gradually they wore to shape." Keturah Penton's father "bought a side of upper leather and one of sole leather and had a shoe maker come to the house with his [bench] and tools and shoe the family." The children took special care of their footwear, "washing and greesing the shoes every Saturday night so as to have them nice for Sunday."

Children who owned matched shoes were fortunate indeed. A young Wyoming girl, Connie Willis, "thought it a streak of luck" to find two spare shoes, although of different sizes and heel heights. One had low heels for a larger foot, while the other was a high heel. But Willis was not deterred. "I chopped the long heel off with the cleaver, and these shoes have saved me enough to buy Lennie [her little sister] a pair of patent leather slippers to wear on the Fourth of July." Shoes were saved for the week's biggest event—Sunday churchgoing—and even then, were scarcely worn. Ada and Ida Boyd, twins born into plantation life in Murfeesboro, Tennessee, in 1888, although privileged, practiced careful economy. On Sunday, the girls walked to church unshod, slipping on the prized brogues just before entering. On the way home, the action was reversed. Shoes were taken off and carried as they walked behind the buggy.

The practicalities of frontier life created dependency as well as enterprise, drawing families together to reap the benefits of their ingenuity. In the words of Mary Jane Anderson, "We had a home of our very own, we were young and hopeful, and with our little family and life before us, and always work to do and the strength to accomplish it, what more could we ask?"

10

Prairie Hardships

Men and women were not easily frightened in those days.
—*Bethenia Owens*

The river is high and looks terrific.—*Keturah Penton*

Each morning found us surprised that another night had passed and we were still alive.—*Emma Shepard Hill*

We have been tried by flood, by whirlwind, and by fire. I would like to try something else.—*Esther Whinery Wattles*

DANGER IN THE West was drunk like mother's milk, inhaled from the atmosphere, and spun out in wild yarns that startled children and adults alike. "There is hardly a fireside in Colorado where fearful stories . . . are not told," worried English traveler Isabella Bird, noting the widespread use of terror to caution unruly children. Fear caused them to grow up too quickly, she believed, and would surely prove the "extinction of the child," at least in the protected, Victorian sense. Unlike fairy tales, such cautionary yarns were often true, and bandits, grizzlies, and Indians were the underpinnings of a child's deepest imaginings. Why else would Mary Gettys Lockard, as quoted in *Pioneer Women,* have the "fixed idea that Indians rose up from the ground at times and killed everybody in sight?" "We children talked about Indians so much it got on my mother's nerves not a little," she recalled. Young Annette Rosenshine spent "night after night alone in bed," terrified by haunting fears and dreams." For young overland traveler Emma Shepard Hill, "each morning found us surprised that another night had passed and we were still alive."

Fear took fantastical, as well as realistic, shapes. Sleepless children could blame the presence of imaginary Indians, or animals, since every night was filled with dreadful rustlings and stealthy sounds. Recalled Edith Kitt of Arizona:

> It was not the most comforting thing in the world to wake up in the night and listen to the coyotes calling from one hill to the other. Many a night the blood absolutely congealed in my veins at the near and unexpected howl of a coyote which would be answered first from one hill and then from another until it seemed as if the souls of the dead were moaning and wailing and closing in on me. I would lie and sob to myself, but I did not dare to cry out because I feared Dad's scoldings worse than the coyotes.

Like the young girl stricken by mountain fever who was terrified, not of death, but that wolves would find her grave, children learned to think in terms of their own demise. The girl begged her sister to "dig her grave six feet deep" and to "pile rocks on." How else to keep herself "safe"? Sometimes, it all seemed too much. "I tell you a person learns a good many things by coming out to this country," an eight year old from Virginia City, Montana, sagely told his visiting grandparents.

DANGER ALSO LURKED in nature, and could strike with the quick fangs of a rattler, in a scorpion's thrust, or in the toxins of innocuous roots, leaves, blossoms, and bark. Frequently, Basque or Italian immigrants, trying to recreate the dishes of their homeland, died from the "succulent, poisonous wild parsley" that flourished in Nevada and parts of California. Mothers worried greatly. How could Jane Bell, of Oroville, California, have known that the "simple piece of wood" upon which she hung her wash one day in 1859 was actually poison oak? It affected her son very badly. "He is covered with it from head to foot."

Nature's unpredictability could be fierce, and no settler from Appalachia to the Rockies went unscathed. Nature had its own harsh reality, whether it be extreme temperatures, flood, tornado, or drought. In the Midwest, temperatures would soar to 120 degrees. On some days, a dusting of light clouds might tantalize, but without gathering into a storm, they would float silently away, vanishing into

Survivors of Sioux massacre of eight hundred settlers in the Upper Minnesoty River Valley, Minnesota, ca. 1870s. Photo by J. E. Whitney, part of his series "Gems of Minnesoty Scenery."

Blinding sandstorm, Midland, Texas, ca. 1860s.

the blue of the sky. "It was like opening an oven door and walking in. Everything I touched was hot—not warm, but hot—as if it would burst into flames. The very air seemed to scorch one's body clear through to the bones," wrote Dakota homesteader Anna Waltz. So intense was the heat of her sod hut—like a kiln—that she would "spread a large rubber sheet on the floor, put baby on it, get a basin of water, and keep sprinkling her with it, telling her it was little raindrops from heaven." Finally, they were overcome. Without trees, ice, or refrigeration, wilted by the sun that beat down with relentless fury, she and her infant daughter would retreat to a low-ceilinged cave for shelter, lying listlessly upon a cot. "We actually lived in the cave," she recalled. Small animals always took refuge underground—why not she?

When summer drought scorched and parched huge sections of the country, well water grew scarce and settlers were forced to buy it from vendors, or travel for miles to haul the sloshing barrels home. Even a well as deep as ninety feet could be "dry as dust." If water was to be had, it lurked in waterholes and coulees, causing settlers to travel miles to find it. To conserve, families gave up bathing, scrubbing hands and faces in the early-morning dew of the grass. "[Thirst] was the greatest hardship of all," sighed Montana homesteader Pearl Price Robertson.

Winter, inevitable as any other season, dashed the settlers with its freezing, blustering, soaking effects, that were either inconvenient or fatal. Blizzards dropped temperatures so low the bread froze in the oven even while it was baking, tables and chairs grew slick with indoor ice, while snowflakes drifted through the chinks and cracks in the cabin walls, turning furniture as white as the plains outdoors. Temperatures dipped to thirty-five to forty degrees below zero, and children were warned never to touch their tongues to metal, lest they freeze it solid, blistering their mouths. Woolen underwear, wool trousers, and wool socks were standard, and at night, only a heap of wool blankets and feather quilts helped them survive the icy chill. "In winter, men and boys wore boots with rags wrapped around their feet, in place of socks. The women and girls managed to knit stockings for themselves and [only] later made them for the male folk, who usually wrapped gunny sacks over their boots to keep from freezing," according to Frank Cejda. Arthur James Cowan of Harleman, Montana, remembered the subzero winter of 1906–7 as being so cold that "it was forty below zero for a long time, and . . . during the cold stormy weather [we] broke all the fork handles . . . on the ranch." Children often had the chore of spotting steam coming from the snow banks, indicating where cattle were trapped and huddled in the snow.

Winter brought storms, chills, and hypothermia. Dry blankets and extra clothes were scant, and those unfortunate enough to be caught outside shuddered as they waded through the freezing streams, or were fanned by bitterly cold winds. Young John Breen of the Donner Party recalled: "We crept closer together, and when we complained of the cold, papa placed all five of our dogs around us." "A picture lingers in my memory," recalled another young traveler, "of us children all lying in a row on the ground in our tent, somewhere in Iowa, stricken with the measles, while six inches of snow covered all the ground and the trees were brilliant with icicles."

Winter turned the small towns dangerous. Plank boardwalks only ran the length of an individual building, with each segment ending abruptly where the buildings separated, or if an alley intervened.

When snow blanketed both the boardwalk and the intervening gap with the same smooth layer of white, anyone striding thoughtlessly along would pitch off the edge of the boardwalk into a deep drift, surprised afresh by the hazardous footing.

Fire was a constant threat, devouring in minutes what had taken years to build. The hewn log and plank homes of the settlers were tinder dry, and their sagging cloth roofs could quickly combust into flames. It's a "wonder that more of the cities and villages do not burn up," said emigrant DeWitt Seaver in 1853. They were hastily assembled from flammable pitch pine and were "generally lined with cotton cloth [that gets] so dry in summer . . . it seems they would take fire from spontaneous combustion." Winds that rollicked through the shanty towns during the fall and winter were nearly gale force, and would sweep the flames ahead "with racehorse speed," recalled young May Crowder.

Nor could human error be discounted. Lanterns were toppled easily during chores, or matches carelessly flung.

To Sarah Bixby Smith, "fire, candles, matches, revolvers, all held a fascination." On one occasion, she was moved to "carry a shovelful of live coals out through the door to the porch, and there coax up a fire by the addition of kindling wood. That same spirit, or another, suggested a compensating action," she recalled. "I summoned my mother to see my 'nice fire' to the salvation of the house."

With near-biblical predictability, floods might follow fires, collapsing mountains like anthills, surging through frame houses situated too near the high-water mark in a standing wall of dirty water that roared down river beds, smashing bridges, homes, and villages. Worst of all was being struck at night. Recalled Mary Ackley, a recent arrival in California who was still trying to recuperate from the stress of the overland crossing.

> I remember being awakened in the night by the sound of logs being dashed violently against the house, and hurrying out of bed to look from the window at the great flood of dark waters surrounding the building, stretching away as far as I could see, and rushing in a swift, powerful tide past the front piazza, carrying along with it great beams of wood, broken branches of trees, and splintered boards, all on their journey toward the Sacramento River.

Kids playing in flood waters, Denver, Colorado, ca. 1880s. Photo by Harry Rhoads.

Although her house was nearly underwater, she was spry and courageous. Spying a turnip that had washed up to the windowsill, she splashed over, reached out, and grabbed it. Suddenly, she began to eat the root, recalling, "I have never eaten such a turnip." The simple act of eating what the flood had washed up helped the girl regain her calm.

After bouts of fire, famine, and weather exigencies, children were also warned against nature's other offerings, such as spiders, snakes, and carnivores. Rattlesnakes, in particular, were a threat to children whose body weight was insufficient to combat a full-grown viper's toxin. "I remember Mother's bed because she used to tie me to the bedpost for safety," recalled Arizona pioneer Edith Kitt in 1881. "Dad killed fifty rattlesnakes in our first year at the ranch." The soddie houses of the Midwest, set underground in snake-infested regions, were havens for reptiles, and many residents recalled with horror the sudden appearance of their great bodies,

Tornado levels the church at Herman, Nebraska. Photo by Rowe, Little Sioux, Iowa.

looping down through the earth ceiling. "One of them got into a neighbor's bed [and the] boy cried incessantly. When his parents . . . threw the covers back, they found the reptile, which had bitten the child," recalled Frank Cejda.

Agile as monkeys, children had their own means of courting disaster, including surprise plummets through barn beams, off wagon boxes, down haylofts, or into streams. "Dick fell off of this here clift and died" was emblazoned on a rock wall in Wyoming, in great black letters, noted by homesteader Elinore Pruitt Stewart. Disaster lurked in childish pranks, as Jesse Applegate discovered while accompanying his parents overland to Oregon with a team of ox-driven wagons. He was simply playing grown-up one warm spring day and swung a whip overhead, emulating his father as he "popped" it over the oxen's backs. Its heavy pull jerked him out of the wagon gate, into the road, and under the welter of sharp hooves. Although rescued in time, the hind wheel rolled over his leg, leaving him battered, as well as in terror of his mother. "I think I suffered more mental than physical pain," the boy recalled, "for I had disobeyed mother and got hurt by it." Even the ice wagon loomed dangerous, tempting a nimble youngster to dart suddenly into the street, directly into its path.

No less dangerous was the frontier kitchen. When an iron skillet dropped on Blanche Beal Lowe's little finger, her mother was ready with a home remedy. "She tore a strip from a clean dish towel, wrapped it round and round [the] finger, and poured turpentine on it, to help it heal."

Farm machinery was inevitably attractive, as children plotted how to emulate their parents, using such grown-up equipment as the sharp-toothed harrow, plows, and horses. Success sped them toward adulthood, but occasional failures caused parents to grieve and wonder "why?" for years to come. "Little Dave begged to be allowed to plough. Every other boy in the neighborhood did," recalled a midwife, Mrs. Mortimer, telling the sad story of her son's death. "I could hear little Dave begging his father to let him. . . . His father said he could if I said so. I will never forget his eager little face as he began on me. He had a heap of freckles. I remember noticing them that morning." The mule kicked little Dave in the stomach—he was dead within hours.

Sylvia Dye had her own misadventure with a hay stacker.

> I was playing under the hay stacker. The stacker team . . . lunged forward . . . pulling the large rope so fast through my hand that the end of my little finger above the first joint was nearly destroyed. . . . My screams brought Papa and again his cud of tobacco tied on with his handkerchief was repair for the moment. We went over the hills where Mama was mowing hay. She at once took me home, cleaned the wound, and applied thick separated cream.

Proximity to risk matured children quickly, teaching them to think in advance, value the moment, and slowly, over time, to develop an awareness of consequences. Viewed sternly as little adults, they were expected to show maturity, to act with grown-up courage when called upon, to defend a homesite as well as to build it. Such maturity often exposed them to adult experiences that were far from acceptable. Violence, prisons, murders, and lynchings were a frontier constant, with the local jail exerting as perverse an attraction as the sight of outlaws, who were often dragged to justice by citizens' groups, or vigilantes. Although religion preached forgiveness, it had a special tolerance for retribution, and in the lawless West, where strong example was the best deterrent, the hanging was seen by many as a quick way to stop the devil's work. It was not unusual for young children to watch a gallows' trap spring open and a man plummet through, meeting his death. Young overland traveler John Breen, no stranger to horrific sights on the long journey west, thought hanging was the worst. "I will never forget the day, the ground was covered with snow, the skies with clouds all nature seemed to mourn over the cruel act being done."

During the Civil War years, and immediately after, the North and South played out allegiances in other locales, such as Kansas or Ohio, where "armed bands of desperate looking men" hung around the train stations, and, in the mind of young Emily Shepherd Hill, were either bloodthirsty Southern rebels or Northern sympathizers who would end up, as had many others, dangling from trees along the track. As the trains passed slowly through the countryside, ominous clearings were glimpsed, where ugly "tar-and-feather" events

The burning of the Congregational Church on Central Avenue, Pacific Grove, California, March 14, 1910.

had occurred. Men were snatched from their homes, tarred, and then driven away because of their Union sympathies.

"Though we grew up without fear, we did learn to be careful about personal safety," recalled Tommie Clack, whose own, rural setting in west Texas seemed far removed from the troubles of war. Nevertheless, they never locked a house. Once, when her father forgot and locked a door, the family returned to discover that "some hungry cowboys had come by. They managed to get inside through a window, find some food, then had scrawled a note on a shingle saying, 'Thanks, Mr. Clack, for your hospitality.' "

ALTHOUGH RICH WITH geographical diversions, the rural West offered little to alleviate mental distress, and often, weighed heavily on everyone—men, women, and children alike. Many, like Melora Espry, discovered there was no greater hardship than to "leave permanently one's home and friends, parents, brothers and sisters; to journey a thousand miles . . . to a strange land inhabited by savages." It "required a poise of soul few possess . . . to forsake culture, plenty, prosperity and peace, for crude living, poverty, adversity and war." Without such "poise," many succumbed to their own worst imaginings, turning melancholic or mad. Abigail Malick's daughter, Jane, finally broke down in the fall of 1859.

> She destrois All that Xome Before Her When She Has Her Crasy Spells on her And Wantes to kill All Derest Frendes And her Little Babe And . . . I Have Had to Tak her Babe and Not let Her See it for two And thre dayes At A Time And tie her down on the Bed and it took Three of us to do it At that. So you May think I Have Had a hard time of it with her.

The pressures of parenthood were also eruptive, creating a fear-ridden domestic life, even threatening children's safety. In 1914, Fitch Hyatt Marean's father, Jason, grew strangely troubled.

> [He] had an injury that caused him to be insane and he had to be kept chained to the floor three years in order to protect the children from his violence. His wife kept the family together as best she could, but they had hard times. I heard one of the children tell of seeing the tears run down through her mothers fingers as she asked the blessing over the potato and salt she had for them. The same girl told of trying to eat grass because of hunger; the youngest boy, Jason, when about ten, worked for a man at Newark Valley and told of lying down in the cow path and holding his breath in an effort to kill himself because he was so tired; it seemed he could not go another step after the cows. He remained there for three years and then ran away because of the man. He did not grow any more until he was seventeen.

Suicide was whispered about—although children's own comments about it are not in evidence, the knowledge that it occurred must have been frightening for them. "O, what awful news, Lucy Ann Sims has killed herself & her four children," wrote Iowan Sarah Gillespie. When "sister" Campbell leapt out of the family buckboard, was it a leap of despair, or an accident? No one knew—perhaps she had only stumbled. But, according to Mormon Martha Heywood, she was treated carefully thereafter.

Such constant exposure to danger took its toll, finally breeding a kind of calm detachment, in which children could discuss fearful possibilities as if passing scenes of a play. Unfortunately, and all too often, the "scenes" would turn into frightening realities.

11

Motherless Children

Sweat Little Fellow . . . He Alwais Calles me [Mother], poor Motherless Child. But He Hardley knows the Difreance Now Wether I Aint His Mother. . . . And I Alwais Treet Him As My own Child.—*Abigail Bailey*

I have sent my other three little innocents to their dear relations, will you my dear Sir, assist in the distribution of them?—*E. Pettigrew*

I know, when I speak of Jimmie, that I am glad I stayed to be his mother. —*Agnes Reid*

Children are taken into the Boarding schools too young. A child under no circumstances should be taken from its home and its mother's constant care at so early an age.—*Mary Collins*

The deepest-held fear of a frontier childhood was that of being orphaned—perhaps left behind by mistake, or having parents fall ill and die. Little wonder there were fears. Illness and death were commonplace, nature's cataclysms routine, and the threat of Indians, wild animals, disease, or starvation habitual. Time and again, young children witnessed the breaking up of families. "The baby . . . wanted his mother and I could do no other than hold him all night and try to comfort him," wrote an Ohio flood survivor. "Not only was his mother killed but two half-brothers and a half-sister. Fortunately he had a grandmother living in the neighborhood, who came and took him away." Children were plunged early into the darkness of adult concerns. Young Mary Ackley, an overland traveler whose mother had recently died, was convinced that her father would also die if ever out of her sight. When he decided to leave the train for a brief mission on horseback, she panicked. "I never felt so miserable in my life. . . . What would become of us children?" Her despair continued until he returned safely home to her. Such journal entries were common: "Yesterday passed grave of a woman, today saw husband buried, with children left to go on with strangers," wrote John H. Clark, on June 11, 1852. Later he added: "M. Burns drowned while swimming in the river leaving two little boys fatherless. Frank and Buck."

The emigrant dream had been fashioned from hope, finished with joy, and presented to friends and family as an exciting alternative to settled life in the East. For a brief time, as the dust kicked up behind the oxen hooves and clouds piled high over a trackless plain, the adults felt free as children, while the children, too young to understand probabilities, welcomed the invigorating change and quickly fell into the spirit of things. Yet as the journey progressed, moods faltered, often shifting into doubt and fear. Children found their nights haunted by dark images. What would happen to them? And what, they wondered in dismal reflection, would morning bring?

MANY HAD TRAVELED west to regain their health—the dry air of the plains and deserts was a tonic for tubercular patients. Yet in their already weakened condition, consumptives fell prey to the rigors of the trail. Among the invalids in one party were Mr. Hicklen and his wife, both ill, with two children below the age of two—one an infant. One evening at supper, both Hicklen and his wife passed away, she dying five minutes after her husband. The next morning a fresh mound of earth marked their burial site. "On resuming [our] journey" wrote Luella Dickenson, "the teams and loose stock were driven over the grave that all signs might be obliterated, to prevent the Indians from disinterring the bodies for their clothing, which was their custom. The babies, Mary and Jimmy, were cared for in turns by the company all the way over."

Most orphans on the trail were given shelter, but not all. A miner traveling east from California happened upon a brother and sister guarding the wagon that held their parents—both dead from cholera. A steady stream of wagons had passed by the children daily, without a single offer of help. The angry miner realized that their party had abandoned the sick parents and left the children for dead, and he vowed to find the wagons. He helped the children bury their parents and finally caught up with the wagon train, which grudgingly accepted the children back. In another sad incident, a lone girl was found walking along the wagon trail, her shoes in tatters and her feet blistered. Crying, she told passersby that she no longer wanted to live. One tough-speaking woman told her rudely to stop "making such a fuss." Unbelievably, the party moved on, leaving the girl to limp along until another emigrant, John H. Clark, stopped to help:

> She was crying, and as I took her into my arms [I] discovered that her little feet were bleeding by coming in contact with the sharp flint stone upon the road. I says why do you cry, does your feet hurt you, see how they bleed. No (says she) nothing hurts me now. They buried my father and mother yesterday, and I don't want to live any longer. They took me away from my sweet mother and put her in the ground.

The West, in fact, harbored the good-hearted as well as the good-for-nothings, and diaries and journals record the compassionate outreach toward young and homeless orphans. The next day a more sympathetic group stopped, and a young woman who had lost her own child along the way became the young girl's new mother. "Such happiness as I saw beam on that child's face I hope never to forget," reported Clark.

The idea that a mother could pass away prompted deep sympathy and, also, a kind of caution. Children were orphaned when both parents died, or when a single parent was unable to care for them. The term *motherless child* prompted nostalgia in many. Widowers often felt incapable of raising their broods alone, sought out a stepmother, or decided to give up their children, believing that they would fare better in a functioning household. Ebenezer Pettigrew's loss of his wife, Nancy, was only the beginning. The three older boys had already been sent away to his brother Richard Muse Shepard's home because of the mother's difficult pregnancy.

> My dearest sons, Charles, William & James
>
> It is with the deepest anguish of heart, I inform you that your dearest Mother is no more, she closed her eyes in death, on the first day of this month at sunrise. She was taken in labour the evening before sunset, at 20 minutes of 12 oclock she was delivered of a daughter. . . . O my dear sons your loss is beyond all understanding and your dear father who in his weak & emaciated state of health knows not how to support it. He is undone forever.
>
> Your Affectionate father ER. Pettigrew

Pettigrew felt helpless to care for his children, and decided that the remaining four, the youngest children, would also have to be

Unidentified Colorado boy, ca. 1880s.

placed in a home. Reassured by his brother that the three eldest exhibited "cheerfulness" and "good feelings," Pettigrew made his unhappy decision on July 6, 1830—all the children would have to find new homes. His sister was the logical choice. With "humbel heart" he resigned his children over to their aunt, Mary Williams Bryan.

"LENDING" A CHILD to relatives to raise was a common event—often, one parent might die, or go west, and the child either fell upon the mercies of the community or was taken up by distant relatives. In the best cases, these guardians tried to keep the parent informed. But when many miles intervened, communication faltered. Mr. and Mrs. Hezekiah Hammond were two such adoptive parents, caring for a niece who was often "poorly," and trying to keep her mother apprised. In this 1846 letter they wrote to Sarah Hammond, they let her know that her daughter had been overtaken by "A fit of sickness . . . the last of februarey."

> I thout with worms and A cold but it proved to be the lung fever and the information in the bowels which set in and caused a hard fit of sickness sum of the time we thout she could not live we did all we could for her and employed the most skilful that this town afforded. . . . The girl continued with spels out of hur head, screaming out for her teacher, Miss Rasey. She cald for hur so much that she cum hear and staid 4 or 5 nites and took care of hur when she got so that she could walk a few stepps she was so pleased as you ever saw A child when that first lurnt to walk she is [now] very smart and has rode out wounce.

Families grew, were rearranged, recombined, sometimes with children from one group thrown in with another. Young Connie Willis was typical of the frontier extended family—she confided to a traveler that she was the "only one" of her "ma's first man's children. But ma married again after pa died and there were a lot of the second batch. When the mother died she left a baby only a few hours ol." As the oldest child, she never questioned her role of taking charge of the household and the tiny little baby.

As children who fell outside the boundaries of family life, orphans bore a certain stigma, and even in adulthood were still identified as orphan girls or boys. "You recollect Fanny the orphan girl whom I had awhile, & whom could not keep in my situation with her bad conduct?" queried Harriet Shaw of New Mexico. The girl's behavior was automatically pinned on her state of being orphaned, despite the fact, as Shaw later admitted, that Fort Defiance, New Mexico, was "no place to bring up a girl" among the many soldiers. Fanny, however, could hold her own.

Children were frequently left without families, due to illness or, often, mining accidents, such as an explosion in an underground silver mine in Utah that left "forty-six widows and hundreds of orphans penniless." Compassion quickly turned practical, as miners passed hat after hat, and in two days' time, according to the reverend Bert Foster, $952.70 was handed out. Miners had a reverence for family life and would commonly "adopt" children, or at least help them out until the children could be placed elsewhere. At a placer mine, a common sight was a donation box inscribed "For the Orphans" nailed to a tree.

Children had also been orphaned by the Civil War, and several homes were founded to meet their pressing needs. Annie Turner Wittenmyer, an Iowa crusader, recognized the desperate situation of orphaned children, and in 1863, responded to the plea of nearly five hundred soldiers in a Southern hospital to extend her "noble charity" to their wives and children, mothers and sisters, as *if* they were orphaned. "A severe winter is before them," the men pleaded. "We are rent with anxiety . . . succor them, and withhold your charity from us." Wittenmyer wrote letters, gave speeches, and buttonholed politicians, "convincing them of the usefulness of orphans' homes." Later critics charged that she misused public funds that should have gone to the orphans, but much of the controversy is lost in the dimness of history.

AS MORE HOMELESS children appeared, orphanages sprang up, the first being in San Francisco in 1852, even though there were relatively few children in the area. Children's agents were created by the Federal School Board in 1870 to look after needy urban children. Each district of a city would have one agent, and the agents would take troubled youth and direct them into industrial institutions to learn skilled trades, as well as "rough work to begin with." Often, orphanage founders were sympathetic souls—men or women such as May Arewright Hutton, an orphan herself, as was her husband. Sound investments had made her a millionaire, and when the huge, 225-pound woman decided to "give back," she founded a children's home, and considered herself mother to her many young residents.

State institutions housed youth of all ages, with the very youngest attending a "charity kindergarten" modeled on one launched at an orphan house in Philadelphia in 1879. So successful was that effort that "visitors from all parts of the country thronged the building to see for themselves what good, systematic training . . . could develop

Unidentified Colorado girl, ca. 1880s.

in little children under six years of age." Originally called "school gardens," these efforts at early education were promoted by a female philanthropist from Massachusetts, who paid the annual expense of twelve hundred dollars per school. "Children were gathered in from the streets, from three years old to six; profane, obscene, thieving, untruthful, quarrelsome, untidy, half-clothed and half-fed." In three weeks' time they were transformed into quiet, orderly, and affectionate children, whose talents included singing.

Such schools were rigorous in subject matter and discipline. The first classes included reading, writing, and "some other light studies" such as elementary geography and written arithmetic. One of their guidelines, however, implied a new thinking and direction: "Children should not be required to do right in order to please the teacher, or anyone else, as is sometimes done in some kindergartens."

Nevertheless, "poorhouse" children were characterized in literature as mistreated, left to live on a "wedge of bread" and a bit of water. A popular literary theme was that of the child inheritor, placed in an orphanage by mistake, who would grow up with the graceful and ladylike characteristics of her station while an imposter, a child of the streets, would be impetuous, self-willed, and bound for destruction. In most moral tales, the "good" child was always discovered and welcomed back. In life, the poorhouse children seldom fared so well.

Nor did Native American orphans. The state schools forced upon the children the mores of a culture they would never join, releasing them back to their families—they were sent to the schools even though their parents were alive—as cultural misfits, unhappy with both societies, adrift in a disapproving world. Protestant missionaries in particular tried to instill the elements of "civilized" behavior, believing in the need of proper dress, regular habits, and the alphabet. In the light of nineteenth-century thought, their efforts followed the most acceptable—if narrow—of tracks: Americanization through alteration, as practiced by the good-hearted Oregon missionary Narcissa Whitman, whose educational methods seem, at times, chilling. Her use of "it" in reference to a child is somewhat softened by her feelings being "greatly excited" by him. It is difficult to believe that Whitman, an educated woman, upheld the uninformed, early view that questioned whether Indians were people, or not.

Child in Pacific Grove, California. Photograph by C. K. Tuttle.

WAIILATPU, March 1, 1842.

My dear Jane and Edward—

. . . After attending to the duties of the morning, and as I was nearly done hearing my children read, two native women came in bringing a miserable looking child, a boy between three and four years old, and wished me to take him. He is nearly naked, and they said his mother had thrown him away and gone off with another Indian. His father is a Spaniard and is in the mountains. It has been living with its grandmother the winter past, who is an old and adulterous woman and has no compassion for it. Its mother has several others by different white men, and one by an Indian, who are treated miserably and scarcely subsist. My feelings were greatly excited for the poor child and felt a great dis-

Cheyenne River Agency St. John's William Welsh Memorial (Boarding) School for girls, South Dakota, ca. 1880s.

> position to take him. The care of such a child is very great at first—dirty, covered with body and head lice and starved—his clothing is a part of a skin dress that does not half cover his nakedness, and a small bit of skin over his shoulders.

She feared that her work would be interrupted in the midst of rearing him. What if the Indian grandmother returned, and the child was taken away?

Whitman had raised another orphan, Mary Ann, a child with a "mild disposition, was easily governed and makes but little trouble. The Lord has taken our own dear child away so that we may care for the poor outcasts of the country and suffering children. We confine them altogether to English and do not allow them to speak a word of Nez Perces."

In fairness, both Whitman and May Wynne Lamb, a young Kansas woman teaching school in Alaska from 1916 to 1919, understood that orphans cast out by tribe members were often turned into servants. Lamb was particularly disturbed by the fate of a "tiny child, snuggled close in one arm" of Mr. Kilbuck, the postman, who had somehow come by the orphan and knew that Lamb would be susceptible. He held the baby out and asked, "Can you take her for a few days?"

> This child, less than three years old, was an orphan whom he had found living with relatives in a downriver village near Goodnews Bay. Strangely enough, in this home she was unwanted, neglected, and most urgently in need of another home. Besides not being welcome, she had suffered inhuman treatment at the hands of a

mean, ignorant, and merciless aunt. It was scarcely believable but she had been placed purposely on a hot stove for punishment, a torturous treatment that had left a brand on her hips which she would carry all her life.

Since both her parents had died, she was obliged to make her home with relatives—the wicked aunt [in this family] was particularly heartless.

May was fascinated. Was she ready to be a mother? And, whether yes or no, what better way to find out? She plunged into the new experience willingly, adding childcare to her busy duties of teaching school. Days passed, and the child stayed on, with no efforts on the part of the postman to place her elsewhere.

She was called Lily. Just why she was christened with that name was most perplexing, since she resembled a lily in no way whatsoever. Her little baby head was covered with straight, black, coarse hairs, all in tangles and dirty from lack of care; her face was scared, sad, and flat, with a little pug nose; furthermore, her swarthy body was thin and frail from want of nourishing food. While she was shy and bashful, she seldom cried, but her somber face presented a dark picture of sadness. . . .

She continued to be my baby, winning her way deeper and deeper into the affections of my heart each day, and her appearance soon changed; food took away the emaciated look, and soap and water and clean, fresh clothes worked wonders for her appearance; then in time she overcame her fear, developing into a distinctive character with sweet, childish ways.

She gave us little trouble for a child of her years. Alice [her helper] complained because she wet her bed; this was, indeed, a

Fort Yates Boarding School classroom, ca. 1885. Photo by Frank B. Fiske, Fort Yates, North Dakota.

South Dakota orphanage founder Elizabeth Hazelton Bixby Sherrard with orphan babies, ca. 1880.

problem for immediate and speedy solution, for Alice did the laundry each week. It was icy cold weather and drying wet bedding in the kitchen did not fill the atmosphere with a very agreeable aroma. Whatever the cost, peace and harmonious relations were necessary, for if Alice went on strike we would be in a serious predicament.

Something had to be done, but I . . . didn't have the heart to execute a spanking, for her little body had already suffered enough welts. If she were well and if love and care with reason didn't bring results, then there would be no other course to follow but to let her sleep in her wet, uncomfortable bed, while nature took its course. . . . Ultimately, [she] graduated from that stage of life.

Even children in families might be haunted by an occasional, brief fear of abandonment, of being left behind in a strange land, an intense feeling far more frightening than they could ever explain. It took a stalwart youngster to uproot, time and again, during family migrations in the West. Perhaps, like Andrew Davis and his sister, quoted by historian Elliot West, they became "like little scared partridges, [who would] hover down as if trying to fill the least possible space."

Part 4

GROWING UP

Photo on previous page: Boy driving turkey cart to deliver vegetables, ca. 1900.

12

Children's Work

The mining country is no place for boys . . . there is a vast amount of bad talking and no schools at all.—*Edmund Booth*

While parents plowed and harvested, spun and sowed, their children turned into entrepreneurs, finding in the new land countless opportunities to trade, barter, scrounge, or sell, bringing back to the family whatever profits they could earn. They had no lack of opportunity. The prairies were lush with berries to be gathered, firewood to be chopped, or, in one case in Kansas, according to Blanche Beale Lowe:

> There were so many bones on the prairie the children easily gathered wagonloads to haul off to a trading place. The trader knew that Wichita businessmen needed bones to make things like umbrella handles, corset stays, buttons, and crochet hooks. Bones were even ground up for fertilizer. So when Grandpa came in with no money in his pocket, but a load of buffalo bones in his wagon, the trader was ready to do business. He got the bones, Grandpa got flour, medicines, coal oil, cattle feed, lead for bullets . . . many things the family needed. Mama said that finding bones to barter was about the luckiest thing that could have happened.

A team of horses was vital to trading—without them, families were unable to plow, clear fields, or haul wood—and farmers would often give in and obtain a dreaded mortgage, often as high as $150, to obtain them. Under such an obligation, children were particularly hard-pressed to help repay. "We had just finished threshing grain," wrote a young Nebraska boy, "so father began to haul it to market to be able to pay the mortgage within a week." For six consecutive days he hauled wheat to market twenty-four miles each day, starting with a load at four in the morning and returning at ten in the evening, accompanied by his willing son. The struggling family seemed sunk in misfortune, since, according to historian Rose Rosicky, prices for farm products were so low they received only "$1.80 for 100 lbs. of dressed hogs."

The family's economy depended upon each member—children no less than adults. Charles Svoboda, a young Czech settler in Nebraska, tried to harvest and sell wheat, but, along with his immigrant parents who had never farmed before, he found the land and its offerings formidable. "We labored night and day for over two weeks, cutting a good share of the wheat after it was half shattered. Stacks were not built right and got wet. . . . [L]oaded fifteen sacks of wheat on my spring wagon and set out for our nearest grain market thirty-two miles away. One of the grain buyers would not even look at it. [When I returned] I never shall forget the expression on my mother's face, when she realized that I had brought home neither money nor the provisions, so badly needed."

Boys pitching hay, ca. 1880. Photo from the Ola Garrison Collection.

Keturah Penton and her young sister, growing up in rural Ohio in the 1830s, made summer hats for her father and brothers, using "Rye straw braided and sewed" that she would "sell every summer . . . [for] a half dolar." Spry and enterprising, as well as worried about her family's well-being, at the age of ten Keturah "began to think about" earning her own living, as well as going to school in the winters. She "worked round in the summers when not needed in the corn field." She would "tend babys and wash dishes for which I got a dollar and a half a month but some of the time only 25 cents a week but I clothed my self."

Esther Whinery Wattles and her sisters, daughters of a farmer, learned to "spin and weave and to make up all our cloth for both boys and girls and our Father's and Mother's clothing." She and her sister Jane Ann, the "best spinner," shuttled chains of woven wool and flax, and such early enterprise led her to expect the same from her own children. Seven year olds could herd sheep, one boy even earning as much as forty dollars for a summer's work, while a young Iowa girl, appropriately named Alice Money Lawrence, paid by her father to work as a shepherd, managed to save a dollar and a half per week to finance one term at school. Hilda Rawlinson "came in and took care of the baby, the mother, the children . . . [and] did cooking, the housework, the washing, the ironing, the canning, the baking: everything that the mother did." As a teenager, she earned the considerable sum of five dollars a week.

Some were purely entrepreneurs, but many were forced into the workplace by family needs. When Emma Evans's father left their Mormon enclave to find work, her mother, Priscilla, was left in an unhappy situation. "During my husband's absence, we had considerable sickness," she wrote. "My little daughter, Mary, came near dying with scarlet fever. To help out, our eldest daughter, Emma, got a position as a clerk in the Co-op store. I appreciated that action of the Board very much, as before that time they had not been employing lady clerks and she was the first girl to work in that store."

Seymour Bennett had the chance to work as an adult, stacking milk bottles and making change in a grocery store at age twelve. Within a few months, he had done so well that his boss depended on him and even left him alone to run the store. "Two little girls" from Wyoming, "both on one horse," impressed homesteader Elinore Pruitt Stewart, who was helping a backwoodsman outfit his cabin for his mother's visit. The girls "had heard that a wagon-load of women were buying everything they could see, and . . . they told us they had come to sell us some blueing. When they got two dollars' worth sold, the blueing company would send them a big doll." No one needed blueing, but when the girls cheerfully offered to sell them a beautiful, red geranium instead, they settled on the sale.

Another young boy, perhaps a runaway, was traveling alone from Michigan when he ran out of money in Iowa. He worked as a milkman for a farmer, and after several month's of slapping cows' sides and jetting milk into buckets, he had earned the price of a cow—which he bought—plus eleven dollars. On his journey to California, the cow calved, the calf was sold as meat, and the milk from the lactating cow paid his way to the coast. Mornings, he would milk the cow, then lay his saddlebags across her back and journey down the road, selling the milk as he went. When offered $125 for the cow, he refused, figuring that the road to California was long, and, as a milk vendor, he would make more in sales than the price of the cow.

Other boys sold newspapers, and realized a tiny profit. Carried by ship, by wagon, or by packhorse from their origin in New York, the papers cost the boys fifty cents apiece, which a boy might sell for a dollar, if lucky. A dime from each sale was his to keep after returning the profits to the vendor and paying for the apples and peanuts they carried along to entice the miners into a sale. By the late 1800s, local presses brought down the price of the paper and reduced profits for the vendors.

In the gold fields, children often worked the mines along with their parents, or panned gold flakes from the mine tailings. Some, like Edith White, found unusual rocks and minerals. "Going into the mines . . . was a wonderful experience, because of the beautiful colored chalks I found there. These were pieces of soft rock in colors of pastel shades . . . and in the sluices that ran through the town from the mines . . . I found fine yellow clay which I could play at modeling." When not helping sluice water through the pans, screens, and wooden boxes, they roamed happily around the hillsides scrounging food, stripping bushes of berries, eating anything they could find that grew wild in the terrain, from camas and lotus root to wild apples or chestnuts. Tall tales might be spun about the "boy millionaires" of the Mother Lode, such as the mythic four-year-old Sammy Timmons, who went out to play behind the family's claim shacks in Placerville in 1858 and came home with a quartz boulder bearing nearly two hundred dollars' worth of gold, but most were simply legend. More common were the lives of children such as Hermann Scharmann, a German immigrant who helped his parents mine, was paid wages in gold dust, and "had saved a small quantity" as his share of the mining operations.

Other children, not quite so lucky as to receive wages, had to hustle for gold dust, paying a tiny commission to saloon owners to allow them to search the cracks of the wood floor for the precious flakes dropped by drunken miners. Wetting the heads of long pins, they would stick them through cracks in the planks to retrieve the precious fragments. The leather pouches miners used for carrying their gold often had broken seams or holes, and their transactions were usually so hasty that a sprinkle of gold dust would float down into the cracks. Miners also lavished gold on the saloon girls, who stuffed their bodices to overflowing with generous enticements, some of which wafted to the floor, to be scavenged by eager boys. The mining camps spawned all kinds of enterprise, as gangs of young boys would gather out behind the mining tent camps and stage prize-fights, place bets, and collect winnings, imitating the gambling behavior of adults. They collected discarded bottles in exchange for quarters, often earning up to five dollars a day.

Children in a rural orchard, ca. 1860s.

The code of the mines dictated that any man entering another man's sluice box would be shot on sight, but it amused the miners to have children scamper through and tidy up after them—they gave the children free reign. Miners were notoriously softhearted, and their sentiments overflowed at the thought of a needy child. Re-

Girl in the barnyard, ca. 1880s.

called an eleven-year-old girl, recently orphaned by the death of her guardian, an adult sister:

> Often the miners would take small nuggets of gold and ask me to guess the weight. "If you guess right, Martha, you can have it," was the usual offer, and in a short time I became so expert that I had accumulated a fair sized hoard of gold, and was in fair way to make my fortune.
>
> It was in Placerville that I found my first nugget. One day a miner gave me and the other children permission to dig on his claim, telling us we could have what we found. Diligently we set out to work, and carefully scooped up the soft dirt and then washed it, just as we had seen the men do so many times. I was the luckiest one of the group, and found a nugget worth five dollars. With this I bought a pair of shoes, of which I was sorely in need.

In the mining districts, roving groups of teenage immigrants from Germany or Czechoslovakia earned money performing as "hurdy-gurdy" dancers. Like gypsies, they flashed about in flamboyant costumes, dazzling the bemused miners, who were starved for diversion of any kind. The boys strummed out plaintive tunes on guitar, organ, and tambourine, while the girls modestly performed a waltz or an ethnic polka, dressed in lavish, traditional getups. The miners, enthralled by so much feminine exuberance, would toss the girls fifty-cent pieces for the price of a dance. Since dancing usually lasted for five hours or so, these "hardy, healthy looking girls . . . received shelter, food . . . and about $240 per annum and were hired by the various dance houses in [San Francisco] at the rate of $4 per night, up to 12 o'clock and $7 if retained until morning." Called "hurdy-gurdy girls," the young women were imported by contractors from their homes in Europe and sent to America, ostensibly to learn English, as well as to send money back. Usually no older than fourteen or fifteen, the girls strictly maintained their virtue even though they performed in dance halls and saloons, obliged to dance with anyone who would pay a quarter. The girls "drank a good deal"—up to fifty glasses a night, as they flung their brightly colored, checked German shawls about. Innocence was part of their allure, and to insure they kept it, the drinks "were two parts claret and a hundred parts sugar-water." Modest and old-worldly, the girls never paired off with miners, but would cluster together on their way home, acting as one another's chaperones as they danced out their three-year contracts. They would sail back to Germany, having earned a tidy nest egg.

THE YOUNG IMAGINATION never faltered when it came to earning money—and the grim reality of life in America in the mid-1800s was in sharp contrast to the ostentatious wealth of the growing number of prosperous elite. In the cities and the country, economic need drove young children into fourteen-hour days for scant wages, as well as putting them at risk of injury by heavy mining or factory machinery. While a percentage of the country thrived, many at the aspiring levels—the immigrants, small farmers, sluice miners, and their children—were forced into ever lower income levels. The Apprenticeship Law of 1858 allowed any "white" person under twenty-one and over fourteen to commit himself—this was for boys only—to a binding apprenticeship situation, receiving little or no pay, without the parents' approval. By 1868, the law had expanded to allow unpaid work—in which he or she was ostensibly learning a trade—for charitable societies, as long as the child worked no longer than eight hours a day. Even this stipulation was gotten around by the consent clause, in which the child could, indeed, work more hours as long as he or she "consented" to it. Yet somehow, apprenticeship did not jibe with the American spirit of independence, and by 1870, according to historian John Bauer, there were only 393 apprenticed youngsters of the 2,214 recorded as formally working for wages. Enterprise was necessary, since older youths searching for work in traditional venues often came up short. "All business is overstocked with young men who come out daily which renders it difficult to get employment and letters of introduction do no good," complained Edward Austin, a young man who had gone west to seek his fortune.

Child labor sprang from harsh precedent, in which fathers were given supreme authority over children, and many offspring of hard-driving, unkind, or even murderous parents resigned themselves to a youth spent in grim servitude, without church, society, or neighborhood to intervene. The belief that children were the property of their parents was common—Congregationalist missionary Narcissa

Utah farm girls milking cows, ca. 1880s. Photograph by G. E. Anderson.

Wyoming girl examining milk bucket, ca. 1880s.

Whitman voiced the outlook: "I am glad to see young Henry Johnson. He learns to bear the yoke so well, not in his youth, but in his infancy."

The yoke, however, was often misused, particularly when a parent was caught up in stern self-interest, or took advantage of youthful dependence, forcing a child to work undue hours under merciless conditions. One cruel and miserly father was a successful farmer in Washington, whose children simply provided more labor in his growing empire. His son was worked almost beyond his abilities with adult farm chores, and although beaten down by the father's ruthlessness, he still managed a bleak optimism. Traveler Mrs. Hugh Fraser, passing through on a visit, was haunted by the "grasping stinginess and downright cruelty" of the father, "either a stiff-necked Methodist or Hardshell Baptist."

Children routinely were assigned adult labor, although not without some hesitation on the part of the parents. The general age level for employment was fourteen until the 1930s. Even as late as 1930 there were more than two million children under the age of fourteen who worked, many in occupations involving large machinery or exposure to lead or to other industrial substances. In the work hierarchy, youngest children were usually spared, while older ones, seen as the parent's best support, were relied upon to take the parent's place.

America was a work-based land, and even privileged children were commended for earning, saving, and occasionally, for putting

Boys shining shoes, ca. 1900s. Photo by Buckwalter.

their own schemes into commercial effect. Affluence did not preclude moneymaking schemes for children, nor did it mean that money was handed out freely. "Alice and I delighted in spending days . . . scraping up funds. San Franciscan Annette Rosenshine was "continually on the alert for discarded clothing or broken household appliances to sell to the junkman . . . whose broken down horse and wagon, and hoarse singsong croak, 'any rags, bottles sacks!' was a familiar sound of the streets of San Francisco" since "an assortment of odds and ends might net a fair sum not to be despised."

Some work was sought, some was simply occupational. When children could substitute for adults, they did. When they could devise their own schemes for income, they did. But the random use of children in adult capacities seemed unusual to travelers—one British observer glimpsed a young girl on a river bank along the Columbia River, a remote and desolate spot. The boat had glided close to the bank and a bare-legged ten year old "sauntered down the path" to the beach, followed by a small, howling infant. The ship tossed a "thin and flabby mail-sack across the water to her." She was the postman! The traveler watched the girl carrying the bag and the baby struggle up the steep rock, the bag occasionally slipping from her grasp, perhaps thinking to himself how, in the great frontier of the New World, she embodied the rationalist notion of John Locke: that the children of plain people should begin useful work at the age of three.

13

Festivities and Favorite Times

Do they have Christmas out West? Well, they have it in their hearts, if no place else, and, after all, that is the place above all others where it should be.—*Rev. Cyrus Brady*

Memories of childhood call up family festivities, where warmth and bustle drew in swarms of neighbors and friends, who happily assembled for a logrolling, apple bobbing, housewarming, or husking bee. Churches were also social outposts, offering convivial events of every nature, from religious revival to sack races and ice cream socials. Even weddings drew crowds, particularly for the good-natured torment that came after in the form of the traditional charivari. For the wedding celebration, the young couple was pestered silly by the clanging of cowbells, or by whistles, horse fiddles, and a battery of tin pans, loud as thunder. Sometimes the chimney was plugged in the notorious "smoke 'em out" technique, or else the groom might be briefly kidnapped and spirited away—anything to keep the young couple from their marriage bed. Children delighted in watching all the behaviors they were so sternly advised against—what fun to be a grownup.

Adults tried to make pleasant memories for their children, with scraps and piecings, music and merrymaking, while children dreamed or danced or invented worlds of play. For them, the "cares of existence were not theirs to worry about," as one young woman noted, at least not for a little while.

The child's world began at home, hopefully a refuge where simple comforts came from family proximity, with relations of all kinds jumbled together, and beds, cots, and blankets in a welter across the plank floor. Children and animals dozed off around the hearth, making a semicircle of feet, hands, and paws turned toward the embers to roast, like potatoes. Sleep settled in when the fiddle finally died, or the long-winded bedtime tales trailed off to the end. Festivities were frequent, and apparently independent of budget or means. The Wilson family of Nallagh, Nebraska, was "down to almost nothing of life's goods" but inevitably had "more fun than the richest children on earth." Food was scarce, but somehow they had enough. The scant clothes they owned were always clean. Recalled Sylvia Dye:

> No prairie home ever had more laughter, singing, joking, dancing, and just plain gaiety than theirs. . . . Grandma Martha played her organ, sang, and her deep religion helped her believe everything would come out right. Somehow the Wilsons gave their children the necessities of life, the desire to read, to make music, to enjoy each other, everybody, and everything.

Jubilee time was birth time, when the innocent newcomer to a family setting attracted well-wishers from miles around, ready to celebrate the family's blessing. When Arizona military wife Martha Summerhays gave birth to "the first child born to an officer's family in Camp Apache . . . the greatest excitement prevailed." Sheep ranchers and cattlemen "gathered at the sutler's store to celebrate events with a round of drinks. They wanted to shake hands with and congratulate the new father. . . . Thus arrived the new recruit." The same ferment rose up at the christening of James Henry Gleason's infant son at his California hacienda on January 1, 1855. "A delightful time we have had for the last week!" Gleason exclaimed, welcoming the crowds that flooded his adobe house. Horses, carriages, and coaches arrived from "all parts" of the country, bringing guests determined to sample his "Turkeys, plum pudding, roast pigs, music, dancing, bull fighting and racing," as well as glimpse the new child. Always hospitable, Gleason practiced what he called "perfect looseness" in keeping up the level of gaiety.

Birthdays were occasion for merrymaking. "I remember my fifth birthday," wrote Californian Sarah Bixby Smith. "Aunt Martha made a wonderful cake, which contained a button, a thimble, a penny and a ring; and in some very satisfying way, the section containing the ring came to me. I had always wanted a ring. I was happy, happy, and then the very next day I lost it, making mud pies with Annie Allen."

In fact, nearly any occasion gave rise to merrymaking—including the rescue of an entire Dakota village from the ravages of a prairie fire. Survivors Anna Waltz, her infant baby, and husband decided that only a prairie-chicken dinner could "offset the tension" of the near disaster and "show the great thanksgiving in their hearts for God's intervening."

> With everyone sharing the task, it did not take long before the chickens were in the pan, frying and popping in the hot grease and being turned over and over until each piece was a rich golden brown and ready to eat. We carried it out to the table in the yard in huge kettles, and it was truly a feast. There was plenty of fluffy mashed potatoes and gravy, homemade pickles, heaps of homemade bread and rolls, butter, buffalo berry jelly, and chokecherry and wild plum jam. I think all the women brought as many kinds of homemade pickles and wild fruit jellies and jams as they could to show off their skills in culinary art—much to the satisfaction of everyone present. And the chicken! There was so much of it that after everyone had eaten all they could manage, every woman took enough home to last for several days.

Hospitality brightened up the frontier home, while in school or in town, "playacting" was popular, with rural dwellers so hungry for entertainment that any presentation—a game of charades, a lecture, a tableau vivant, even the simple recitation of psalms or verse—drew foot-stamping applause. As settlements burgeoned, people sought greater excitement than picnics and socials, and theater troupes sprang up, attracting rural socialites from far and wide to sit on scratchy, plank seats, breathing in culture along with spirals of fresh sawdust, swept up in heaps, that drifted like spun gold in the lamplight's glow. Flat kerosene lamps—the so-called stage footlights—played shadows up and down the walls, almost a pantomime of the onstage action. A dollar bought the sophisticated theatergoers "advance entry," while twenty-five cents would do for last-minute arrivals. In remote Fort Shaw, a military post near Sun Valley, Idaho, the "first professional stage performance in Montana" was the social locus of the entire state, according to Agnes B. Chowden, drawing performing arts fans from far and wide.

> Intimate theater took place nightly around the family hearth, when a careworn settler, suddenly softened in the fire's glow, would launch into a round of stories. As if sleepwalking, children were lured deep into the fabler's circle, a magic domain free of expectation, age, or gender—a good yarn was simply loved by all.

Musicians, euphonious, rowdy, or just loud, could transfix any gathering with a twang of strings and fiddle sawing, sending out a welter of plaintive tunes, from parlor to public dance halls. Weatherbeaten settlers, fortified with popcorn and cold lemonade, could overcome life's monotony with a good polka. "There were dancing parties where the grown-ups and the children danced together, square dances, waltzes, schotisches, mazurkas and polkas. In those days, up there in the mine the little girls all learned to dance not with little boys, but with friends of our fathers," recalled Edith White. For young Sylvia Dye, the "best part of the Nallagh dances" was seeing her folks "so happy," their cares briefly dispelled by a the wheedle of the bow, calling them to turkey trot or do-si-do. At dances, Sylvia could "play around" with her friends, knowing that the best part, the ride home, was yet to come.

> "I just loved to hear the snow go crunch, crunch under the wide-tired wagon wheels . . . from the back of the spring wagon or the lumber wagon [which] was such a nice place to sleep as we rode home. Lying on the quilt in the back of the wagon, which had been filled with fresh hay, was so soft. Our parents sat up front on the spring-wagon seat, drove the horses, and talked about the good times at the dance. In good weather we children just lay there listening to the folks talk, watching the stars and moon, sleeping and waking and sleeping as the wagon jiggled along with the wheels and horses' feet often slopping in the water as we forded the Cedar Creek and wet meadows. In winter we had several quilts over us and the hay below kept us warm. In fact it was so comfortable that I hated to get home and have to get out in the cold."

The sign that a fine social event was in the offing was when Katherine Elspeth Oliver's mother "would seat herself before [her melodeon] and play from memory." Neighbors drifted toward the Oliver house as if dazed, drawn by the haunting airs of "Annie Laurie," "Silver Threads Among the Gold," and others. Even bold digressions into opera failed to dim local ardor, and Sunday nights would commence early and end late, as her mother sat in the twilight, playing "far into the dark, the lamps unlighted," to an admiring, slightly spellbound group of neighbors.

Food also prompted revelry, with bounty of any sort automatically shared, whether a smoked hog or a covey of freshly caught quail. When Harriet Shaw and her husband lugged home a wagonload of ripe watermelons and musk melons to their rural New Mexico compound, she immediately "made a bee and asked in the neighbors to help eat them." By the next day, the only one of the overfed neighbors they could "raise by eleven o'clock" was "a little boy . . . weighing nine and a half pounds." Presumably, *after* eating melons.

CHRISTMAS BLEW IN on the crest of winter, with prairie lands so frozen and inhospitable none could stir outside except for the most important chores. As December advanced, adults suddenly thawed, like icicles, and tried to thrill and charm and weave magic spells for their children, however briefly. Strangers seemed close as kin, and above all, kindness flowed. The day stood hallowed and special to almost everyone, although the adult version was often stretched thin. The greater the anticipation, the greater the disappointment, it was feared, and starry-eyed children who had pinned their hopes on Santa could only believe that he *had lost his way* to Kansas or Nebraska or Texas—why else the barren space beneath the tree? When Mary Ronan prayed for a doll, she found her stocking dangling empty. How to understand? Holidays could seem a somber reminder of what she lacked rather than what she had, no matter how her parents tried to dress it up.

"Well Christmas has come round again, but I cannot say that I enjoyed it much," admitted Carrie Williams, a young mother in a Sierra mining town who was delighted to find mittens for her son's stocking for the economical price of only twenty-five cents. "They just fit the little toad," she exulted. Despite a bounty of roasted turkey, chicken, bread pudding "that was capital," and "plum cake not to be beat" prepared by her mother-in-law, Carrie couldn't help but notice her own dearth of gifts.

> I found a bundle of candy tied on the door knob of my room and on opening a drawer in the bureau found one of my old ragged stockings containing a beautiful embroidered hand kerchief. That was the amont of Christmas gifts that fell to my share. George had his Christmas tree full, and little Walla's stocking was filled to overflowing. The little toad was very much delighted when he saw the varieties of candy that it contained. Strange to say, he did not know enough about candy to know that it was to eat, never having had any before.

Yet wealth was in the eye of the beholder. When Santa finally made his way to Iowa, Sarah Gillespie found him a "very decent kind of a gentleman," who turned 1879 into a bumper year for benevolence.

[A]n Acc't Book or journal, 4 handkerchiefs one silk & linen finish with a very nice wreath of flowers around it. & 2 white ones . . . then the best of all was a set of cuffpins they are very nice they are a plain body with 2 tinted leaves on it colored & then I got a journal, 240 pages in it. . . . Frankie got a drum & Sarah got a trunk & Fred got a 2 wheeled bell & . . . Henry got a shirt, set of studs 4 handkerchiefs & journal.

True riches came not from lavished gifts, but from strength of family, which made Mormon midwife Rachel Emma Woolley Simmons a self-acknowledged "wealthy woman" as she recalled Christmas, 1884, when "nearly forty persons," including children and grandchildren, gathered together. "We enjoyed ourselves first class as usual . . . [and] there were twenty-nine pairs of stockings hung up and filled." Blanche Beale Lowe's most treasured memory was of a generous gift arranged by the entire family as a surprise for her younger sister, Florence. The girl was nearly twelve, loved music with a passion, and had taught herself to play, although just a little. In a moment of wild extravagance, the whole family "chipped in to buy [her] a pedal organ." To keep the gift secret, two uncles smuggled the huge instrument in from town late Christmas Eve, and slipped it secretly into the little parlor when Florence was asleep. All Blanche could remember about that Christmas morning was Florence crying, and "everybody happy."

Generosity abounded, and the more dire the circumstances, the more likely it was to be in evidence. Children learned the lessons of their parents, and, with little else to rely upon, could set their imaginations to work for the good. In the California mining frontier, just before Christmas, two young boys huddled with their gravely ill parents in a cold canvas tent near California's upper Feather River. "We kissed each other tenderly and talked for many hours of the former happy Christmas days we had spent back in our Brooklyn home," recalled one son, Hermann Sharmann, describing the miserable scene. He and his brother pooled their resources to buy the sick parents something cheerful, browsing the aisles at the general

North Dakota children at Christmas, ca. 1860. Photo by Frank B. Fiske, Fort Yates, North Dakota.

store and passing over knives, calico, and shiny gimcracks—even sardines and smoked herring. Then Jacob, the younger brother, cried out: "Look at this. Canned peaches! Could anything be so delicious?"

Instantly, they decided on peaches, and hiding the tin can, they set to work making a Christmas festival for their parents. They tacked a pine bough over their pallets, covered it with ribbon and trinkets and called it a Yule tree. Tenderly, they nursed their parents as if they were babies, brewing coffee, preparing flapjacks, even salting the food lightly with gunpowder, a common substitute for salt.

When everything was in readiness we set out an empty box between the pallets on which our parents lay. . . . We brought in the hot meal on tin plates and arranged everything neatly where father and mother could reach without getting up. . . . We came in, bearing the peaches.

To their sorrow, neither parent could touch the food.

> We both cried a little, but our mother comforted us and told us that we should eat the share for them. So we sat down and divided the peaches. . . . Our hunger and the rare treat before us made us forget the sorrow of the futile gift and we ate until not a trace of syrup was left inside the can.

Christmas morning dawned for Episcopal pastor Cyrus Brady in a particularly poignant way. Decked out in a long cassock and dangling the traditional cross, he was used to the odd looks and raised eyebrows of "plain" Methodists and Baptists who frowned upon ostentatious displays of gold, lace, ornate crosses, or vestments. As a long-skirted messenger of the "High Church," he might as well have been St. Nick himself, for all the looks he drew. But God's word was truth for him, and Brady's parish happened wherever he found a chance to minister. On one Christmas night, a snowbound group of travelers trapped in a stalled train—"three men, one woman, and two little children"—was a heaven-sent opportunity to spark compassion among a shivering group of strangers. Huddled around the dim stove was a "drummer" who sold trinkets, a cowboy, a prosperous cattle baron, and an impoverished widow who was giving up the "unequal struggle" of earning a living after the death of her husband and was returning to live with her mother.

> The poor little threadbare children had cherished anticipations of a joyous Christmas with their grandmother. From their talk we could hear that a Christmas tree had been promised them and all sorts of things. They were intensely disappointed . . . [and] they cried and sobbed. . . . Just before they went to sleep, the drummer said to me:
>
> "Say, parson, we've got to give those children some Christmas!" . . . The woman beamed at him gratefully. . . .
>
> The children were soon asleep. Then the rest of us engaged in earnest conversation. What should we give them?
>
> ". . . I would give my gun to the little girl," said the cow-boy, "though on general principles I don't like to give up a gun. You never know when you're goin' to need it, specially with strangers," he added, with a rather suspicious glance at me. I would not have harmed him for the world.
>
> "I'm in much the same fix," said the cattleman. "I've got a flask of prime old whiskey here, but it don't seem . . . appropriate for the occasion, though it's at the service of any of you gents." . . .
>
> "Never mind, boys," said the drummer. "You all come along with me to the baggage car."
>
> So off we trooped. He opened his trunks, and spread before us such a glittering array of trash and trinkets as almost took our breath. . . .
>
> I think we spent hours looking over the stock which the obliging man spread out all over the car for us. . . . The trainman caught the infection, too, and all hands finally went back to the coach with such a load of stuff as you never saw before. We filled the sock, and two seats besides, with it. The grateful mother was simply dazed.
>
> As we all stood about . . . the engineer remarked:
>
> "We've got to get some kind of a Christmas tree."
>
> So two of us ploughed off on the prairie—it had stopped snowing and was bright moonlight,—and wandered around until we found a good-sized piece of sage-brush, which we brought back and solemnly installed, and the woman decorated it with bunches of tissue-paper from the notion stock and clean waste from the engine. We hung the train lanterns around it.
>
> We were so excited that we actually could not sleep. The contagion of the season was strong upon us, and I know not which were the more delighted the next morning, the children or the amateur Santa Clauses, when they saw what the cow-boy called the "layout."
>
> Great goodness! Those children never did have, and probably never will have, such a Christmas again. And to see the thin face of that mother flush with unusual color when we handed her one of those monstrous red plush albums which we had purchased jointly, and in which we had all written our names in lieu of our photographs, and between the leaves of which the cattleman had generously slipped a hundred-dollar bill. . . . Her eyes filled with tears, and she fairly sobbed before us.
>
> During the morning we had a little service in the car . . . and

I am sure no more heartfelt body of worshippers ever poured forth their thanks . . . than those men, that woman, and the little children. . . .

"It feels just like church," said the cow-boy, gravely, to the cattleman. "Say, I'm all broke up.". . .

The train-hand . . . returned with the snow plough early in the afternoon . . . and he brought a whole cooked turkey with him, so the children had turkey, a Christmas tree, and Santa Claus to their heart's content. I did not get home until the day after Christmas.

But, after all, what a Christmas I had enjoyed!

As the seasons changed, weather varied and children grew, but different festivities marked out the calendar from year to year. "We had our holidays," recalled San Francisco youngster Nellie McGraw, whose large household was the hub of the endless social activities attendant to a fashionable mother and a father who was a prominent attorney in the city.

> First was New Year's day. We always had a festive dinner and . . . relatives [came]. The afternoon of New Year's day was devoted to

Mr. and Mrs. Alex Krueger fixing up Christmas tree. Photo by Alexander Krueger.

Children enjoying a picnic, ca. 1900.

receiving calls. The men did the calling and the women stayed at home to receive them and dispense light refreshments, but we children had little part of the day. . . .

After New Year's came Valentine's day and that was a big event. They had beautiful cards in those days. Some with both sides decorated. These would represent scenes of summer and winter and were frosted and edged about with fine silk fringe. Some were fashioned like a book and contained fitting sentiments for the day. These were also fringed and tied together with cunning cords and tassels to match the fringe. Others were of fancy paper lace surrounding a pretty picture. . . . There were "comics" insulting and mean, but we never had any of them, though the store windows were full of them. Father bought most of our valentines and provided each with a generous supply. Then in the evening after dinner we were allowed to go out and send them. It was quite a game to escape being caught—we slipped the card under the door, rang the bell and scampered away. We had to be pretty spry because ofttimes the child to whom the valentine was intended was on the other side of the door ready to spring and shout "I caught you" but if our name was not called we knew we had not been "caught." Sometimes we wore our mackintoshes—these were a fairly good disguise as they consisted of a long cape with a hood and in the darkness we usually managed to escape. We all had to be in the house by 8:30 but it was a lively exciting time while it lasted.

No July passed without fireworks erupting into the night sky, collapsing into a glittering afterwake that shimmered over balloons, basket dinners, and triple-layer cream cakes held aloft when carried to the red-checked picnic tables. The nation's birthday party caused lavish amounts of roast chicken, butter-soaked corn, and peach cobbler to vanish, as if by magic. On the Fourth, "every one dances, eats candy, sucks lemons, laughs, and makes merry," recalled Elinore Pruitt Stewart. Historian Joanna Stratton cites a Fourth of July held in Douglas, Kansas, in 1871:

> everybody is invited to come and bring filled baskets and buckets. There will be a prominent speaker present, who will tell of the big future in store for southern Kansas. Grand fire works at night! Eighteen dollars worth of sky rockets and other brilliant blazes will illuminate the night! There will also be a bunch of Osage Indians and cowboys to help make the program interesting. After the fireworks there will be a big platform dance, with music by the Hatfield Brothers.

"What a satisfying supply of fire-works!" said Sarah Bixby Smith of the family celebration in Los Angeles in the 1860s. "There were torpedoes, safe for babies, fire-crackers of all sizes, double-headed Dutchmen, Chinese bombs . . . pinwheels that flung out beauty from the top of the hitching post, dozens of roman candles with their streams of enveloping fire, and luscious shooting stars." "Our picnics usually led to some misadventure," recalled Nellie McGraw, whether it was the Fourth of July or a simple Sunday. Her mother would sew for weeks to get the family ready, cutting, hemming, and stitching "pretty percale dresses and trimming new straw hats and planning our lunch, which was packed in a basket so huge that we children could not lift it." A three-seated rig and a span of horses were hired to race the family to the ferryboat to cross the bay and then on to Redwood Canyon, or out to Orinda Park.

"We always had our colored eggs at Easter," recalled Frank Hoyt, of Lincoln, Nebraska. And to celebrate this major religious holiday, his mother, like others, "saved up all bits of Calico that would fade and at Easter wound them tightly around the eggs and boiled them hard." All "colored and striped," they were hidden in the prairie grass outdoors.

Frontier religious holidays differed from those enjoyed by European children, whose families had lived in close proximity for generations, and who were sent out in large groups on May Day, All Souls' Day, and Christmas Day to gather flowers, treats or candies, twigs or ribbons—whatever the history of the event dictated. On the frontier, mass events for children were impossible. They were isolated by vast distances, and came together at church socials and building bees only when adults had a reason for merrymaking.

Birthdays, too, were celebrated, but with less mention in diaries and journals. Perhaps the sheer number of children was prohibitive—who could bake that many cakes, or fulfill individual expectations for gifts that would never come? On Wednesday, June 8, 1853, pioneer Harriet Sherrill Ward noted her brother William's birthday—he was eleven years old. "Morning clouds soon cleared off pleasant. . . . No birthday is mentioned for young William. It can only be hoped that someone remembered it."

She might have added that, at eleven, young William was considered a man. Loved by his parents, his maturity was subtly acknowledged by withdrawing childish expectations. Like other pioneers, he was growing up with the country.

14

Hide-and-Seek and Other Games

It was glorious fun to go up on the Twin Peaks hills on a windy March day and fly our kites.—*Nellie McGraw*

We laid in the shade and made mansions out of the clouds.
—*Ethelyn Whalin Crawford*

At the first sound of "Wagons ho!" children swung down from their passenger perches to walk alongside the covered wagons, feet scuffing the dust, eyes darting in search of any diversion—a bush, a bone, a bird, a stone—to distract them from the weary miles ahead. Trailside treasures could be anything, from shiny green mesquite beans to a sparrow egg or an arrowhead, to use in a game of chance or competition. Even cow bladders had potential. When inflated, they bounced high as a balloon. "Blown-up bladders make wonderful playthings," said Sarah Bixby Smith, who had inured herself to the world of entrails by observing the "interesting insides" of slaughtered sheep on her California ranch. Likewise, no boy could pass up the bloated body of a dead ox, particularly one found festering near the Platte River in the summer of 1841. Stretched invitingly taut by the heat of the sun, the ox proved irresistible to a group of wagon train boys. Jumping and jostling, they crowded around, cheering one another on as they leapt, face down, onto its drumlike surface, bouncing as if on a trampoline. Suddenly, one boy sprinted forward, leaped into the air, and dove straight into the rotting carcass. A hush settled—how could the first American ox-bouncing contest have ended so horribly? Andy, the dripping contestant, was helped out of the ox and taken, presumably, to the nearest stream to wash.

Even scarcity became a game. Children had watched their mothers scavenge for food, using wild grapes for raisins, egg whites for milk, crackers for apples, sorghum for sugar, so they, too, learned to improvise. Leaves turned into party hats while the bleached vertebrae of dried cattle carcasses could be locked together, like blocks. Thick sap, weeping in dollops from deciduous trees, made substitute chewing gum, a habit forbidden by most parents, while pill boxes served as wagons filled with buttons for cargo. Two Kansas children harnessed large locusts to their toy wagons and herded them mercilessly about. Popcorn sheep and pecan cattle were easy to fashion, while twine, buttons, leather, bottles, boxes, or scraps of calico, part of every child's repertory, were the stuff of imagination. Even railroad tracks, in those settings after the establishment of the transcontinental railroad, were used—a child's ear, pressed to the metal, could detect the hum of an approaching train. Young emigrants from Nebraska turned muskmelon rinds inside out, strapped them to their feet, and skated around their cabin floor.

Young Wyoming girl balanced on stilts, ca. 1880s.

When siblings were forced into fellowship with one another, they usually spent the time embroiled in teasing, either good-natured or not. Rachel Emma Woolley Simmons, a young Utah girl, recalled that her brothers were kind to her, and "used to carry me in turn, and when we would come to a piece of ice, they would take me by the hand and slide me across it."

Games also had their fanciful side, often touching on superstition and fear, or resorting to the mythic, the magical, or the forbidden, such as the exotic art of fortune-telling. Oregon-bound Jesse Applegate and his young friends spent hours reading their coffee-cup fortunes from the dregs of a half-full cup of coffee, improbably turned mouth down. After the grounds had settled, they squinted into the muddy remains, searching for "pictures of future scenes" and wondering if the "future . . . in store for that train of courageous people" would include Indians, or not. In the same vein, young Iowan Sarah Gillespie would play "Telling What We Dreamed," surprised that she and her brother Henry often "dreamed just the same thing." Her mother could not remember dreams at all, while her Pa "dreamed that he saw a black cow" and considered it a good sign.

Magic aside, for most children the shadow world of the West was far removed from the goblins, trolls, and sprites of European fairytales. Who cared about gnomes when real wildcats padded nearby? Or Old World goblins in the face of a grizzly bear? Fear of witches gave way to fear of Indians, as children tried to manage their fright through games, to gain control over the wild unpredictability of frontier life. In "wolf across the river," or midnight tag, youngsters acted out the saga of hunter and hunted, recalling the exploits of their own parents as they practiced for life, playing either role. Arizona children, according to historian Elliot West, waited until dark to play "all the tigers are gone," in which the tiger-child would slip off among the boulders while the others spread out through the dark, squealing "all the tigers are gone!" The tiger, also fearful of the dark, would skulk along close to the others, finally selecting a victim to pounce upon and tag. Squeals of fear and surprise announced every pouncing. What game, played in the dark, would not call up ancestral fears? Being "it" seemed much like fate itself, in which parents, friends, oxen, animals—anything or anyone could be unhappily chosen. Games, like frontier life, called for vigilance.

While adults often made do in dugouts, lean-tos, and tents, children found their own refuge in the sand dunes, in packing crates, or in high-ceilinged barns, dim and dusty, that were cut through by shafts of sunlight and dancing dust motes. Huge and dark, the barn loomed up, home to childhood mystery and reverie, as well as to pranks and contests of all kinds. When Bethenia Owens ran joyously into a barn, carrying a baby that she was tending, a horde of young

Colorado girl playing in the water, ca. 1890.

children swept in behind her, eager to "swing, play hide and seek," and turn the haymow into a huge, slick slide. Barns were home to sleepy white owls and hornbills, as well as to snakes and ducks—animal and birdlife galore. What could be more intriguing to children? Even as a twelve year old, Bethenia could not resist the weathered knotholes of the barn:

> I was fond of hunting hen's eggs, which I seldom failed to find. One afternoon, I crawled under the barn, as I knew there were eggs there. The ground was hard and smooth, and so near the barn-floor that moving room was at a premium. About the center of the space, I found a nest full of eggs, and squeezed under till I could reach and gather them into my apron.

Games were the universal language of childhood, spoken by strangers, understood immediately, and joyfully taken up by all, whether a round of "one-eyed cat," or marbles, or dressing up a straw baby. In schoolyards and front yards, at town picnics or socials, children patted out rhythms and rhymes, seemingly simple, but, like adult oratory, or letters sent by Pony Express or even Indian smoke signals, they were comments upon life in the language of childhood. For traveling families, being on the move led to feelings of rootlessness, which adults solved by simply joining a church, a literary society, a quilting group, or a grange, soon feeling "right at home." Children had only school in common, besides the shared traditions of games and songs. When the Massachusetts child answered the riddle posed by an Iowa youngster, they spoke the same language. Games named the memorabilia of the ordinary. In Clarence V. Kellogg's rhyming game, daily events were set to music and used for hopscotch or jump rope.

Then the butcher began to hang the ox
the ox began to drink the water
the water began to quench the fire
the fire began to burn the stick
the stick began to beat the dog
the dog began to bite the pig
the pig began to jump the sty
and so the old lady got home that night

Like children anywhere, frontier youth used games to model their future roles as well as make sense of the world around them, fashioning toys to mimic familiar household objects—twig furniture, rags clothing, stick guns, and the like. Adult ceremonies—marriages, funerals, and religious oratory—were also staged in a spirit of fun and mockery.

Games divided genders, established temporary codes of behavior, or could bend and tweak friendships into combat or collusion, offering such complexity as life itself. Although expected behavior differed for girls and boys, neither was particularly disparaged during play. No matter how children conducted play at home, in the public realm sexes were separate—boys to one side, girls to the other. Boys exhibited an intense need to win and girls to socialize, although roles were sometimes switched. "I could do almost anything the boys could," said Sarah Bixby Smith. "I recall with a shudder my participation in the stabbing of fat frogs in a shallow pool. . . . I did draw the line at knocking down swallows' nests and feeding the baby birds to the cats." Girls might giggle, play hopscotch, and jump rope, while boys shot marbles, played shinny, spun tops, and took long, deliberate aim with a peeled birch branch slingshot.

Marbles delighted all children, giving focus to circles of tousled heads bent over a "null ring," or marble track, traced in the schoolyard dirt. As with most juvenile gambling, "they . . . played for keeps, not fun," recalled Jack O'Connor. Mothers viewed gambling with distaste, although chess and checkers were allowed.

I was playing bull ring one day and beating [Tom Barker] and pocketing his marbles. He became more and more frustrated. Finally when a marble I had shot from the ring went into an irrigation ditch he made up a rule that I had lost my turn because I had not recovered the marble. My sense of justice was outraged. I beat him up, picked up the marbles in the ring, and marched grandly off. When I was in the middle of the street a large stone whizzed past my head. I turned, and as I did so another large stone crashed into my nose. I fell like a brain-shot elephant. Tom Barker was a far better rock thrower than he was a marble player.

Wisconsin children Jennie, Edgar Krueger, and Effie Goetsch Carr playing with toys. Photo by Alexander Krueger.

To Nellie McGraw, the fourth child of thirteen, games enjoyed on the plank sidewalks of San Francisco's 21st and Valencia Streets were typical teenage sport. The boards of the sidewalk were set closely together but still allowed a "nice knot hole" for button flipping.

We had tops . . . for girls. They had the string fastened to the handle. We wound the tops just as the boys did theirs, and threw them but kept them off the ground while they spun till they died out. These were not very exciting and we preferred the boy's top. We were quite adept at jacks. . . . We threw one jack in the air and while it was descending we grabbed as many jacks in one hand as we could and held it open to catch the descending jack. . . . We jumped rope in many ways. . . .

We had Pinny Poppy show time, too. . . . We would cut a peep hole at one end of the [shoe] box, or if we intended an elaborate affair, one at each end and a partition across the middle so that

Postcard of child, ca. 1907.

Two children with doll, bottles, ca. 1860.

North Dakota children in the woods, ca. 1880s. Photo by Frank B. Fiske, Fort Yates, North Dakota.

there were two different scenes. Summer and winter scenes were popular, for the latter we had a floor of white cotton; the walls of the boxes were decorated with colored paper and pictures. We could buy charming little scenes such as a sleigh ride or a hay ride. . . . When our "show" was completed we covered the box with bright tissue paper which reflected a pretty glow on the scene. . . . We carried these shows around the schoolyard and allowed customers to look through the peep hole for pins. . . .

We made large families of paper dolls. We could buy pretty faces by the sheet or in smaller quantities and paste them to the bodies that we cut out. We kept them carefully in boxes. . . .

We made paper flowers too. . . . And of course we dressed dolls. We had a little doll's sewing machine worked with a crank that did fairly good work. . . .

Then there was kite season; for several weeks everybody was busy making kites. We collected light sticks for the frame, pasted colored tissue paper over the frame, and then ransacked the family rag bag for material for the tails. It was glorious fun to go up on the Twin Peaks hills on a windy March day and fly our kites. . . .

We had roller skating season when every child had a pair of roller skates but as our street was very steep, we had to look for a more level space. . . . The great excitement came when Mayor Phelan who had a large home and garden at Valencia and 16th

Collection of early American dolls, ca. 1900.

street had a paved sidewalk put in. It was wide and long and as good as the skating rink. We would get permission to go there and skate. The parents of the neighborhood little realized how the Mayor's household was suffering. Day after day probably fifty children congregated. Finally the gardener sent us home. That was the first paved sidewalk I remember in our district, though I believe some of the business blocks "downtown" were paved. That must have been about 1884.

What was fun? To fourteen-year-old Sarah Gillespie, jolly times were "wading in the slough," or drainage ditch, with her brother Henry, while Nellie McGraw found stilt season, when "most children made their own," about as delightful a scene as could be imagined. When not striding crazily about, children staggered and fell, bumping into walls and one another, delighted at the danger until finally, the parents took charge. "The foot rest was apt to break and throw the child," wrote Nellie. "So Father ordered ours from the carpenter shop—the uprights were nicely planed and the footrests were firmly screwed to the uprights. We liked ours rather high—the higher they were the more fun we got out of them."

For Sarah Bixby Smith, youthful delight was "the south yard where we built the big snow man; it was there that the sleigh upset when we turned in from the street with too much of a flourish . . . it was there under the apple trees that we turned somersaults." For added excitement, she and her friends would eye the croquet mallets, which served as "attractive crutches." To Sarah "it was as much fun playing lame as it was playing legitimate croquet."

Technology, fledgling as it was, offered such pleasures as the Edison phonograph, a newfangled gadget whose lily-shaped trumpet boomed out a sonorous declaration: "This is an Edison Record." Nickel telephones, a novelty afforded by the upper classes, gave children "a fine opportunity for many kinds of maneuvering," including such pranks as tricking the operator into thinking a coin had dropped in the slot.

To play was to "romp and race full of life & energy," as did Harriet Shaw's three youngsters as they staged "a grand battle" in her room "with their forts as strong as boards chairs & pillows could make them." Predictably, children's play reflected parents' attitudes, and in Texas and New Mexico, where secessionists as well as unionists lived side by side, children mirrored their parents' prejudices. Young Georgie Shaw, who "built quite a nice little house of mud with windows and doors all in Mexican style," allowed it to be knocked down by his brothers. When he surrendered, it was because he held a "secession fort."

Missionary Narcissa Whitman's daughters were likely to follow the traditions of the local Indian women. The girls had a "great disposition to take a piece of board or a stick and carry it around on their backs, if I would let them, for a baby." Worried that memories

Children playing at a Sunday picnic, ca. 1900.

Children sledding down Pennsylvania Street, Denver, Colorado, ca. 1910. Photo by Harry Rhoads.

of their own culture would fade away, she kept the girls housebound, "away from the natives," finally deciding to "change their taste a little" by fashioning traditional rag dolls from a "piece of cloth rolled up with eyes, nose and mouth marked on it with a pen." The dolls "answer[ed] every purpose. They caress them and carry them about the room at a great rate, and are as happy as need be. So much for my children." In many girls' bedrooms, beneath cots or bunks or wall beds, rag dolls slouched or sat, propped up in dollhouse crates or barrels, or staring at the knobby visage of the nearby corncob doll. Wrote Sarah Bixby:

> Elizabeth . . . was a doll almost as tall as I, that had been made by my great-grandmother . . . for her son's little girls. The doll came last to my mother, who was the youngest, and from her descended to me. Elizabeth had a cloth body, stuffed with cotton, white kid arms and hands and a papier-mache head. [She] . . . is now eighty or more years old, but looking as young as ever.

Pets, particularly dogs, were common, kept by homesteaders to act as sentries, but often serving as guardians, and company when everyone was away. "I remember . . . the first dog I saw laugh," wrote Katherine Davis. "I was sure and am yet, that he and other dogs actually laugh. I was not six, then, but I knew he was laughing because he was having such a good time playing with us. He crawled under the cabin and barked when the mountain lion screamed near us."

Play could turn dangerous, particularly if unsupervised. On one of Sarah Bixby Smith's ventures into the horse stable, she discovered a "very heavy little bottle standing on a dark ledge" containing mercury—the glittering, toxic globules like a viscous stream of silver. "Great was my joy to get a few drops in my hand, divide them into the tiniest globules, and then to watch them coalesce into one little silvery pool."

Sports was a joyous pastime, and the pioneer settlement of Ballagh, Nebraska, was no different than any other whistle-stop village, with its sandlot baseball team lauded as the most important organization in town. Fans filled buggies, carriages, and wagons and lined up on both sides of the ball diamond, screaming, "Wash 'em out, wring 'em out, hang them on the line to dry! We can beat Blake any ol' time. Sometimes the women would get a little angry and even nasty, but mostly, it was jolly chanting for their own teams."

Music, also, was a common legacy, and children were taught to sing and follow notes from their earliest years on. Blanche Beale Lowe's class "learned to read music by notes and syllables and to sing parts together." Her grandfather must have been the instructor, since he "used a pitch pipe until they somehow got a foot-pedal." One Texas mother, lacking a piano or even a mouth organ, assembled her children beneath the blazing summer sky with only a rough plank upon which she had sketched in the keys. As they "hit" the key, she would sing out the corresponding note, and after months and years of practice, each child managed to learn the scales.

Dances offered tantalizing glimpses of adult behavior, and reminded children that there was a life awaiting them where pleasures could be had free of parental sanction. "Perhaps you wonder what young people did for entertainment?" asked Loula Blair Schill of Illinois. "Our gang did not dance, but had a few parties in the year and jumped around to their favorite tune":

Happy is the Miller Boy
Who lived in the mill
The wheel goes around
With a right good will
One hand on the hopper,
The other in the sack
As ladies step forward,
Gents step back.

She admitted to "Skip to My Lou," as well as the ubiquitous kissing games such as post office, after which abundant food was enjoyed, from lemonade to oranges, perhaps even brown-sugar lick—candied brown sugar—to sweeten up the tart green skins of apples.

"Come to the circus!" rallied children of all ages, and parents, too, who in a flurry of balloons, peanuts, and popcorn would gape in startled delight at long-maned horses and bareback riders, or spangled trapeze artists and yawning lions. Brass band cacophony sounded, clowns cavorted, and sideshows beckoned, although the more seductive exhibits were strictly off limits to children. For fifty cents a box seat and twenty-five cents for an arena seat, the circus offered up its thrilling attractions. Where else could such untold oddities as "the Unrivalled Female Equestrian" or "The Homohippocal Amphitheater! Featuring Madamoisella Ida—The Fairy Equestrienne" be seen?

By the mid-1800s, circuses were widespread throughout the country, appearing predictably in dusty towns as long, horse-drawn trains, or else arriving by railcar or riverboat. Every circus was announced by a great cloud of dust, kicked up by a free, promotional parade that wound its way through town, blaring out the evening's schedule, from tableaux to tigers, flying men to fire-eaters, an un-

Electric car pulling a child's sled, Denver, Colorado, ca. 1910. Photo by Harry Rhoads.

Unidentified North Dakota children in front of barn, ca. 1870s. Photo by Frank Fiske, Fort Yates, North Dakota.

Unidentified boy; Paul Hughes and Kathryn Dial, dressed in wedding costume; Lawrence Deegans holding Bible, dressed as preacher; and L. P. Bishop, posed as San Antonio mayor. Practice for children's mock wedding, Travis Park Methodist Church, San Antonio, Texas, December 10, 1926. Photo by Paul Hughes.

likely pageant of high-hatted actors, sleek acrobats, artists and animals, parading and cavorting under the brightly striped, canvas top. The largest tents were those of Ringling Brothers and Barnum & Bailey, and swooped up to an incredible height of sixty-five feet. The father of Rachel Emma Woolley Simmons "believed strongly in circuses." He said they were educational, and took not only his own nine children, but those of the neighbors as well. "He would get us good seats, dole out popcorn and peanuts and then take a seat three or four steps higher, so he could look down on us, light a cigar and give himself up to silent enjoyment." Her sister wasn't content to be an observer.

> The story goes that when Father had taken us to the gardens and wandered into the pavilion to see what was going on he found a seat near the door in case he was too bored to sit the performance out. It was tumbling and somersaulting, etc. Sue was then three years old and watched very intently then dashed from her seat saying "Me do that" and proceeded to somersault the entire length of the aisle bringing up at the platform. Father never missed her and could not understand what all the laughter and applause was about!

But children eventually outgrew childhood play. Rachel became jaded by frequent attendance. "I can see the tents from my window," she wrote. "I don't think I will go again if there are forty elephants."

Part 5

Manners, Morals, Discipline, and the Great Beyond

Photo on previous page: Miss Evelen Hettinger (right) with unidentified friend in North Dakota, ca. 1880s.

15

Spare the Rod

The children Are Not Like children Raised in the States they have no Father And they Will Not Mind Me.—*Abigail Malick*

It is difficult to write with her in my arms, and it is too cold to tye her into a chair.—*Maria Silliman Church*

No one could imagine the mischief such a really good child could accomplish.—*Georgiana Kirby*

Early American discipline presumed that children should be invisible, women submissive, and men the natural, moral authority of the family. Well-thumbed copies of the King James Bible fell open naturally to Proverbs 6:20 and 23, with their injunctions "Keep your father's principle, my son. Do not spurn your mother's teaching" and "Correction and discipline are the way to life." In fact, "Spare the rod and spoil the child" was reaffirmed daily between overworked parents, although whom to spare and whom to spoil depended upon family size, general temperament, level of piety, and the child's own patterns of obedience. The young were considered lost to most traditional minds—small travelers in an indeterminate state able to be rescued, finally, by achieving adulthood, with every effort made to avoid vanity and low moral tone along the way. The ideology of child raising grew partially from Darwin's evolutionary theory, in which beings developed from lesser to greater, from imperfect to perfect, leaving children with a long way to go.

In fact, they should also pass through a "furnace of affliction," believed preacher J. H. Williams, since only when "tried in fire," as divine providence saw fit, would they have the strength to face the "worldly cares, trials, losses and vexations" of adulthood. Suffering, in fact, was actually "a godly effort" to "drive out the worthless and leave only those of purified character"—a moral purgative that would surely cleanse. If every boy could "restrain himself and become a man, a citizen, worthy of this great republic in which we live," he mused, wouldn't it be a better place for the next generation?

Viewed as property, children were to be maintained and organized, groomed and directed, with spankings, whippings, supperless nights, scoldings, ear pullings, or cuffings used to stem the tide of childhood folly. Failing that, purposeful indifference could always be invoked, with a parental icy chill providing just the right degree of chastening to curb young rowdiness.

Religious tradition supported household discipline, beginning on Sunday, when time-honored prohibitions against cooking, cleaning, card games, or any recreation, including hopscotch or marbles, were firmly in place. Frank Hoyt recalled his mother's embarrassment when an uncle came to visit from Nebraska City and noticed the wash boiling on the stove. "Margaret," he queried, "you wash on Sunday?" The pot was whisked off the stove, at least until the uncle had left. Western "blue laws" made it illegal even to hang laundry, and the sudden calm that descended over the Sunday home came like a deep sigh of relief, since it meant—at last!—a break from interminable chores. Restfully tranquil, the day would feature a leisurely walk home from church and lemonade sipped on the front porch. Sunday night, chicken would sizzle and corn pop—the makings of a peaceful, convivial evening.

Recalled Texan Tommie Clack:

> Saturdays were days to get ready for Sundays. Extra cooking was done [then] so there would be food ready for Sunday dinner when people got home after a two-hour sermon. Out here in West Texas we gave "holy" a somewhat different definition from what people did in older states. I know that my grandparents in Tennessee would not even have a fire going in a cookstove on a Sunday. We were certainly not that strict. Why, some West Texans would even go fishing on a Sunday, if they took a notion.

But the Sabbath offered no relief from family expectations. When discipline demanded, the rod or switch were ready at hand, to be wielded by any interested adult, related or not. In the communitarian stronghold of rural life, nearly anyone could be recruited into the loose-knit role of "family." The respect afforded parents extended to adults in general, and cuffs, slaps, and spankings were not unusual. Carrie Williams, a married woman in a Sierra mining town, wrote candidly about disciplining her child, Walla.

> Walla was extremely troublesome all day. In the evening he came to me, and I took him up and . . . when I went to put the young gentleman in the cradle he made decidedly a fuss, so I had to take him up then. I was so aggravated that I slapped him a little, at which he screamed lustily. His grandma came running in, pitying him up, and wanted to take him from me . . . giving me a down right talking to about my cruelty, as she called it. Perhaps I was hasty in what I done. It will be a lesson to me in future. . . . He could not sleep but kept waking every once in a while and crying. Then I began to think he had an ear ache, though he never had it before . . . he would not be still, so his grandma slapped him several times, which finally quieted his nerves.

Older children, seen as a natural bulwark to contain the exploding energies of younger siblings, were used to maintain order, and added balance to a growing family. A young married woman writing to Lucretia Mott at the National Women's Rights Convention in Cleveland, Ohio, on October 5, 1853, defended her right to bear numerous offspring, claiming that she had "less trouble" at home with her eleven children since the older ones always helped out. Despite such reasoning, even the lure of built-in child care failed to convince, and whether from prudence, mishap, or oversight, the birth rate declined by half in the latter part of the century, averaging 3.5 children per family by 1900. According to historian Barbara Ehrenreich, even the "best women felt they have not stamina enough."

With theories afoot and change in the air, little wonder that the demotic spirit of the founding fathers was applied to child rearing, as well. "God's angel is named freedom!" cried Andrew Jackson upon his 1828 election victory, proclaiming an American way of life without tyranny by a government. According to French observer Alexis de Tocqueville, "Jackson brought the notion of political rights to the level of the humblest citizen," which might well include women and children. In the West, children were viewed more democratically, and valued for their ability to contribute to the family well-being. In fact, the harsh "Selfe-Deniall and Selfe-Tryall" that passed as child rearing in the 1800s had been tempered, in the mid-1900s, with newfangled notions of encouragement and patient instruction—some even called it leniency, judging by occasional diary accounts.

In fact, discipline was seldom mentioned in western diaries and journals—either it was considered indiscreet, or so taken for granted that it received no mention. In fact, spankings fell into disfavor—diversions and blandishments were offered instead. "Mother would give us a certain number of lumps of sugar as a bribe or a reward," recalled

Edith Kitt. New consideration was given to the home setting, with the dawning thought that perhaps nurture *could* affect nature.

In a new land, new rules were forged. Some parents were harsh, others easygoing. But all felt freer to practice the discipline of choice because of the loose western ways and the necessities being more important than civilities in frontier life. Mothers might be severe disciplinarians or—in the new, western manner—"pals," such as the daughter of Elinore Pruitt Stewart, "Jerrine . . . a dear little pal," who accompanied Stewart hiking, camping, and riding around the mountains of Burnt Fork, Wyoming. Physical discipline, particularly when wielded by mothers, might be mysteriously lacking. Jesse Applegate recalled going against the maternal will and receiving a tentative "swipe across the shoulders with a switch" when he disobeyed. To satisfy her, he "dance[d] around" in mock distress, but the whole event seemed more ridiculous than painful, causing him to conclude that he'd "never known a mother to cause a child to suffer pain, however alarming her threats might be." In Ben Wallicek's west Texas family, they "just talked kindly . . . often saying such things as 'I like you.' "

Discipline was needed as much for safety concerns as moral uplift. A child who pledged not to swim or roam and return in time for supper was a trustworthy child, albeit somewhat unnatural, and in the parent's mind, secure from mishap. Discipline discouraged the dangers that kept parents wary.

The parents of Andrew Pamburn adopted a silent drill, best shown on the day he freed his pet bear cub, which promptly attacked the cow his mother was milking. The subsequent ruckus could only be imagined. "I expected severe castigation," Pambrun recalled, "but there was not a word spoken pro or con." Puzzled, he continued to wait for physical punishment, or anger, or . . . anything, only to find the next morning that the bear was gone. The parents had simply disposed of it. "I could not find him. He was no more."

When it came to vices, mothers took a dim view, even if it was play gambling, carried out without coins. San Franciscan Nellie McGraw might join in a "very absorbing" game of shooting buttons, even playing "for keeps" with money, but others were forbidden, since "some mothers wouldn't allow that as it was considered gambling." Nor could well-behaved children chew gum or stay out after 8:30 P.M.

In some schools, discipline was meted out in direct proportion to the child's degree of seasonal usefulness. In Oregon, children were few and their labor depended upon, which may have influenced the relative ease with which Jesse Applegate sailed through school, claiming that "only one" teacher ever struck him. Walt Whitman, who taught in seven different schools in seven towns between 1836 and 1841, disdained the use of "whipping sticks" and other corporeal punishments. "What nobleness can reside in a man who catches boys by the collar and cuffs their ears?" he wondered. "Or [gives] a whack of a ferrule?"

When discipline grew lax, it could also be due to an exhaustion too pervasive for a parent to overcome. "I can't keep my eyes open . . . for I have had them kept open by this scamp of a boy for several consecutive nights, and I feel used up completely," complained Civil War wife Mary Binckley to her husband, by letter, in 1865. Sleep was essential. She needed her strength to "travel out in various directions some 8 or 10 miles in search of corn and fodder" for the family.

Girls who lived in the shadowy world of enforced meekness hoped to be seen as "amiable," "docile," or both, and those who were particularly advantaged were groomed to reflect the parents' apparent social worth and were held to high account. "My language was criticized," complained Sarah Bixby Smith, after a sassy reply to her mother. "You bet your boots!" Worse, the girl sucked on her sunbonnet strings, and had her "tongue burned from the vinegar and cayenne pepper into which they had been dipped." Like most young girls, she despised the humble hat. "Those sunbonnets, with which my head was sheathed every time I started out into the airy out-of-doors, were my chief pests. I usually compromised my integrity by untying the strings as soon as I was out of sight." Doubling back the corners of the bonnet, she made it into a "sort of cocked hat," with the dangling strings secured into a bow on top, thus letting her "poor scratched ears out of captivity."

Sunbonnets, in fact, cast a shadow in nearly every girl's life, raising wails of complaint and prompting futile attempts to outwit authority and be rid of its scratchy confines. Like mares with blinders, girls anxiously swiveled their heads left to right, trying to take in the whole landscape, and feeling their freedom to be vastly impaired.

Bonnets ended up in bushes, behind rocks, and under haystacks, until finally, the frustrated mothers cut buttonholes in the bonnet tops, yanked the hair up through the holes, and braided it tightly to the head, securing it snugly in place.

THE NEMESIS OF discipline was disobedience, which cropped up in the normal child as readily as prevailed on the overland crossing—how else to keep the children safe? Although Rachel Emma Woolley Simmons had "one of the most indulgent of mothers," she still managed to disobey, and often went bathing with her friends despite the warnings received.

> We staid longer than usual and the night being dark I lost my way. I suppose I must have passed the wagons and not recognized them. The grass was very high and the dew very heavy. I was wet to my knees, but after what seemed to me a very long time, and after I had repented my disobedience, I found our wagons, and also found Father with a rope in his hand. . . . I received a very warm reception. I think it had the desired effect. I don't remember any more escapades of that kind during the rest of the journey. In consequence of getting so wet that night, I had a crick in my neck the next morning. My head was drawn on one side. I tried to make myself believe it was because Father had whipped me and thought he ought to be sorry, but it didn't seem to strike him that way. I had to lie in bed all day.
>
> Mother petted me some, I remember. Disagreeable results always follow disobedience whether in young or old.

Frontier discipline of the 1900s often stemmed more from temperament than policy, proving that life was nothing if not a study in contrasts. Puritan patriarch Jonathan Edwards's stern, fatherly eye observed his offspring daily, and, according to an onlooker, "when [the children] first discovered any considerable degree of self-will and stubbornness," he would attend to them until he had thoroughly subdued them and brought them to submit.

Even worse were abusive fathers, cowardly and themselves childish, who raged against their young children. Like the West itself, such men were dangerous but seldom punished, since a man's home was his own domain, and the era of children's rights had yet to be born. Many men were edgy in their parental roles, often keeping children at arms' length, viewing them as troublesome in their youth, often better left to the maternal sphere. Yet others could be gentle—such as the father of Mary Ellen Applegate, who never lifted his voice, but would simply say at some mistake: "Mary Ellen, I believe you would better not do that." Yet others turned over authority to their wives. In the family of Francis Prevaux, an Oakland, California, minister writing in 1858, the children were given a "trouncing from their mother," while Prevaux took to contemplation, wanting "none of this business" of discipline. Candidly, he admitted "I have not had spunk enough to attend to it."

In the hierarchy of discipline, fathers presided, mothers chimed in, and in the case of family proximity to an older relative, grandparents might come last, wielding a more traditional, stiff-backed authority, and holding their pesky offspring to a far more exacting standard than anything dreamed up by the parents. Life had taught them serious lessons, and like Grandma Tichenor, a spry elder who had only recently met her young granddaughter from San Francisco, they knew how to pass their lessons on. Young Nellie McGraw, born in 1874, the fourth of thirteen children and daughter of a prominent Pacific Coast attorney, had grown up far too sassy, Grandma decided. As a sharp disciplinarian, she would have none of the stylish new "sympathy and understanding." A child's moodiness was discouraged—who knew where the unchecked pout might lead? Grandma's hard-bitten marriage to a penniless itinerant preacher on the Illinois frontier had filled her with fortitude. Raising eight children, living in a shack in the wilds and traveling by mule across the Isthmus of Panama simply reinforced the fact that no rowdy youngster would defy her! Nellie found the go-around with her Granny memorable.

> It was at Port Orford that I made the acquaintance of Grandma Tichenor, and my memory of her is of a scrawny, quick-speaking, active, and very determined woman! I was learning to button my shoes. We wore high shoes with eight or ten buttons to each shoe. The nail for the button hook hung on the wall low enough for us

to reach it and hang the button hook back when we finished with it. It was quite a chore for me to manage the shoe buttons and when the task was completed I left the hook on the floor where I had been sitting. Grandma said: "Hang it up."

Her bossy tone brought out all my rebellion and sense of injury. I darted out the door. . . . Grandma followed and how she could run! I scooted out and around the flower beds, she racing and clutching at me and I escaping by too narrow a margin to feel comfortable. There was a well just outside the open gate, with a high square board curbing around it. I darted for it, Grandmother full tilt after me. We ran around and around and around that wall, till I began to realize that her reach was improving, and that my chances for escape were diminishing. There was a field a little way off and I made for it. It was surrounded by a board fence. The ground was rough and I gained on Grandma. The fence was a horizontal board fence such as we never see these days—I rolled under the fence and Grandma threw herself over it. We raced around and made for the well—again we raced around it and then I darted into the house and had just time to squeeze under Mother's rocking chair where she was sitting holding the baby. I, of course, thought that Mother would protect me, but she would make no move to settle the marathon.

Grandma dragged me out by the heels, but we were both too limp and breathless for comfort. We sat on the floor, our legs outstretched before us and our backs against the wall and gasped, and panted, and panted, and gasped. It was sometime before we had breath for speaking, and before we were sufficiently rested to get to our feet.

I think it was her mild voice, which was all she could summon at the time, that won the battle, as I was subdued enough to hang the button hook on the nail. From the vantage point of years, it seems a strenuous way in which to train a child.

I never saw Grandma after that visit, but as I grew older, I learned that she was a strenuous and courageous woman . . . [who] had lived through an Indian war and a fire that burned every house in the little town but hers. No wonder she felt capable of making a stubborn child hang a button hook on its nail!

The spoiled child was seldom seen in hardworking, frontier America, but cropped up increasingly in affluent, urban homes, the result of easy standards, broad horizons, newfound wealth, and impending social disarray. Presiding over mechanical toys, sporting sharp clothing and even a pony, such privileged offspring had servants to direct, and bore out the parents' need to establish lineage and class through its pampered heirs.

Church, school, and the general population discreetly scorned such misfit children, with much publishing effort devoted to eliminating "bad" childhood habits, from lying to thumb-sucking. Like a fruit gone rotten, the coddled child would not only "end up badly," but his slack habits might leach into others. Advice columns railed against lenient parents, some so spineless they used the "secret smile," later acknowledged by Margaret Mead, which was a subtle form of approval nervously "flashed" out from the parent's face in the midst of discipline—a debilitating double message. The image of the chastising parent, hand upraised, surreptitiously confiding by grin, seems bizarre. Yet such was testified to by many child experts, such as the Reverend Dr. Oscar P. Fitzgerald, whose favorite theme, the "innate depravity of childhood," was only proven by the new breed of spoiled young. To him, "one of the delusions of young people was the notion that other people are very deeply interested in all they do or say. It usually requires a long time to get free of this delusion."

Proper youngsters, thoughtful behavior—it made sense to adults, who were so careful of their young that even valentines were screened for hidden slights or unsuitable inferences. No child should bring unhappiness to another by substituting an insulting, comic valentine for the usual offerings of fancy paper lace. Although giggled and pored over, such novelties were too unkind for a Christian child to send. Still, a valentine could bear a "secret message," according to Nellie McGraw.

> I remember one of my sisters received one about 4 × 6 inches and a stiff back with a cunning little spelling book at the top and an appropriate verse as to how she could correct her spelling. Another sister had one with a small cube of soap attached. These I believe were sent by my father as Mother was very careful that we

never sent any that in any way emphasized a person's shortcomings.

Consideration was touted by female doctors, becoming the new field of social work, usually applied to orphan children, in which punitive viewpoints were softened, and practical care added to the general strategy of child rearing. "The average boy has a hard time in this world," wrote Dr. Mary P. Sawtelle. "He gets too many kicks and cuffs and rude rebuffs . . . and is rarely treated with common civility." She believed that "grown people are rarely ready to confess that they have been bad to the boys. . . . They only complain that the boys are bad to them." In the same spirit, Wyoming homesteader Eleanor Pruitt Stewart believed that "parents should praise their children more . . . the little things work hard for a few words of praise, and many of them never get their pay." Such behaviorists reasoned that if a mother had faith in her own child, then she would be "half inclined" to see good in other children as well—all to the social improvement.

Such newfangled notions drew mixed reactions. Benevolence was fine for orphans, but generally, why should children be rewarded when in a temper? Food was often offered as reward or withheld as discipline, with every household convinced of the merit of its own, food-related behavior.

While foods and fashions might vary, in every home there was a legacy of manners and decorum passed down through time and only slightly influenced by the family's living in the West. Family etiquette was observed through well-enforced table traditions. Don't eat with elbows askew! Don't blow your nose on the napkin! Don't shovel food into the mouth with knives or dump hot coffee into a saucer—blow on it and then drink! And worse, children must not clutch their forks like make-believe daggers or pick their teeth in public. Table manners meant demarcation in a basically rankless society, blurring the lines between the unpolished and impoverished, and the hopeful social aspirants. Although lack of lineage forestalled any aristocratic pretensions in America, any family could claim superiority by adding well-bred children to its credit.

Such children would naturally refrain from foot scuffing and hair pulling—every twitch and deviation of the nervous temperament was bad-mannered trouble. Tickling in particular led to self-indulgent, even promiscuous, behavior. One concerned mother in Nebraska wrote to a doctor at the Children's Bureau in 1915:

> I am so glad that you do not approve of this awful habit [of tickling]. . . . If I had the ability to lecture I certainly would on this subject. It seems to be a common thing for people to tickle babies around their sexual parts, these organs are sacred and should not be harmed. If a child grows up a degenerate whose fault is it? Can you tell me why there is not a law against this?

Thumb-sucking and oral manipulation were also outlawed, with mothers pinning the baby's hands down to keep the thumbs and fingers dry, or stuffing them into little mittens. Failing this, one mother resorted to wood splints as an arm restraint, or to strips of elastic to pin the child's pajama sleeves to the bed. Aluminum mittens were in use in the 1920s, as well as broad cardboard cuffs, to keep hands away from the mouth.

Restraint and right living were reinforced through storytelling, since few could resist the lure of a good fable, and anyone with a story to tell found a ready audience for a moral lesson. To assist the storyteller, Christian tract and book societies published a host of children's "how to live" books, including the popular *Bernie's White Chicken,* written by an inspirational author known simply as Pansy. As told, young Bernie's mother was an impoverished widow, his family destitute, and the only light on Bernie's dim horizon was his feathered sage, a white chicken who gave surprisingly rousing "Talks on Becoming a Missionary." Although limited to the language of "cut-cut-cut," the bird managed to convey its message and change Bernie's life forever.

No less inspiring—and a great boost to childish aspiration—was the writing of Parson Weems, who specialized in moralizing tracts and semifictionalized biographies of American heroes, including that of George Washington, originally published in 1802. The first four editions sold briskly, but by the fifth edition, Weems took aim at moral laxity by adding the tale of the cherry tree. "Truth, George . . . is the loveliest quality of youth. I would ride fifty miles, my son, to see the little boy whose heart is so honest, and his lips so pure, that we may depend on every word he says." With the words "Pa, do I ever tell lies?" any parent reading the book could point out the obvious rewards of virtue.

Widely read, highly sentimental domestic novels were aimed at older girls, offering high-minded heroines whose only recourse, after life's buffetings, was faith. In the 1850 book *The Wide, Wide World,* a quaint young girl reluctantly enters into the helter-skelter world of the male, challenging him professionally while her true, maidenly self secretly pleads for "rescue." Girls nurtured on such tracts were less inclined to challenge men in business, choosing instead the contemplative and quiet life.

Poorhouse children, or orphans, figured strongly in tract literature, along with children who conveniently died young. In such polemics, since the unfortunates would never grow into "good and useful" men and women, it was up to the young reader to do it for them.

16

Schools from the Ground Up

Our teachers had very little education and schools were not graded . . . often in the winter we slid on frozen ponds and slid down hill and snow balled each other.—*Martha Peitzke Paul*

Be pleasant, brave, and fond of books.—*Alfred E. Whitaker*

Education was highly prized by homesteaders, who not only "proved up" the land but their children as well, seeing the forward thrust of Manifest Destiny reflected in education as well as acreage. "They came, for the most part, from intelligent families," noted Kansas schoolmarm India Harris Simmons, and they wanted the same, or better, for their children.

"There was no school within many miles until 1876," wrote Nebraska pioneer Frank Cejda. "I saw no book and scarcely a newspaper. I had forgotten the letters of the alphabet." Idaho settler Agnes Reid sorrowed over the lack of a nearby schoolhouse, not to mention that of a town or village. "You asked me about school for the children. It seems about as unattainable as the moon," she wrote to her father, fearing that her offspring would run free as the prairie deer unless she enforced discipline and schooled them at home:

> Of course, we are teaching Freddie to read in the evenings. The books . . . sent and . . . given to him by friends . . . are supplying endless entertainment but when I really think of an education for them, here in the wilderness, it frightens me.

"We have been spelling and laughing this evening," wrote Mary Elizabeth Norton, a Kansas mother involved in home schooling. "It is a good thing to do both." California pioneer Edith White spent "evenings alone with our father and mother. Father read the novels of Charles Dickens aloud to us, and I recall distinctly our delight over *David Copperfield* and *Great Expectations*. . . . The books of Dickens are almost sacred to me because of those happy times of long ago." Harriet Shaw tried "to teach the children what I can every day," pleased that her son Georgie "reads very well & Hattie some though I do not urge her along as I should."

The intellectual curiosity that sprang from home schooling later ignited literary societies, public lectures, and various other kinds of oratory, including singing schools, where the "young of the prairie" were taught "notes and parts." Such fledgling schools served as churches as well as a meeting ground for festivities, playacting, elocutions, and spelling matches. When a "literary club was . . . in full force," as in Ballagh, North Dakota, "everyone in the community took part, singing, reciting long poems, or putting on plays," wrote Sylvia Dye. A spelling contest took a new turn when the owner of the leading hardware store in Abilene, Texas, offered a new "Charter Oak cookstove and an assortment of pots and pans" to the person who could fashion the most words out of the letters in "Charter Oak." The entire town was involved—Tommie Clack's mother could hardly contain her enthusiasm.

> Mother was sitting up nights . . . she wrote her words down on brown paper bags. We could not waste paper on trial efforts in what was a betting game. With our big new unabridged dictionary on her lap, pencil and sack in hand, she worked through many a night for the prize.

With over four hundred words, Tommie's mother won. Kitchen-table schooling led to community erudition, despite the circumstances.

"We'd sit around the table in the evenings when my father was home and he'd ask us questions, and he would say, 'now there are the reference books. Suppose you go look it up in one and you'll remember it,' " a young girl recalled. For Blanche Beale Lowe, "there was no foolishness around the dining table during the evening homework period." For the Lowes, like other pioneers, there was no questioning the popular maxim "love and thinking must go hand in hand."

Usually, mothers alone bore the burden of home education—a difficult task for women already vexed by the endless demands of cobbling shoes, stitching hems, hoeing fields, turning dresses—chores without number. J. H. Williams, worried about his wife's peckishness, confided to his oldest son, James, that she was surely ill due to having "too much to do to keep all in order for school."

Frontier class, Farnsworth, Nebraska, 1898.

BOOKS WERE A needed lifeline—where else could a wide-eyed frontier boy peruse the workings of a flying machine, or learn to spell "omnivore"? Reading matter was regularly lent out, with a typical collection including Thackery, Cooper, or Kipling, as well as the 1860 *Uncle John's Story for Good California Children, Cousin Phebe's Chats With the Children,* and such odd icons as *Jack the Fraid Boy, Chatterbox,* or *Harper's Young People.*

"Books bring you face to face with . . . thoughts to enlighten and instruct you," enthused a popular writer. Male literary heroes abounded, as well as enough heroines and female authors in circulation to keep girls intrigued. Some attempts were made for cross-cultural enlightenment—occasionally a fictional family was surprised to discover a Mexican or South American member. Author Daisy Smortcut even treated monstrosities, with her *Princess Sweet-pea and Gottleib the Hunchback.*

Carrie Williams's son, Walla, enjoyed two primers brought home by his father, one "the history of Jack Horner and his Christmas pie, with which Walla is very much delighted. The other is a primer printed on linen with the alphabet in great large letters." A most treasured addition to an antislavery homestead might be a classic such as *Uncle Tom's Cabin,* with its strong moral invective, to be read aloud in the family circle, or *Little Women,* sent by a friend or relative, which was devoured cover to cover, passed about the family circle, then lent to friends. Dime novels were popular among the young and anathema to parents. "They render the imagination unclean and destroy domestic peace." But novel or classic, reading out loud in the family setting was the primary entertainment of the nineteenth-century American family.

Shared books provided endless material for conversation. Somehow, the news of a new release traveled through the territories, and the literate would write their reviews in letters home. "I am much obliged for the Haunted House," wrote Eleanor Williams to her son, James. "Dickens always gives a surprise. . . . It is quite interesting but not equal to his other stories I have read. The characters do not seem to live as they do in some others." Books were her effort to "make her children intelligent, since they had few other advantages."

KITCHEN-TABLE SCHOOLING WAS limited, and after a year or so, even the most gifted instructors found that a more formalized scholarship would benefit a rambunctious brood of school-age children. Perhaps the most telling proclamation of support for an "outside" education had to do with simple exhaustion. To pioneer Margaret Hecox, "it was a great relief to us tired mothers to be rid of the care of our older children for several hours a day."

A first step toward actual school was the frontier "blab school," such as the one attended by Abraham Lincoln as a child, which drew students of all ages to a central location to study aloud and recite together. Vocal harmony was one thing, but blab school efforts had a distinct roughness in reading ability, resulting in uneven spelling and punctuation. As a result, rural adults often wrote haltingly, their shorthand reflecting brief years of spotty and incomplete "schoolin'," usually under the roof of the most primitive of structures, the one-room schoolhouse. Ostensibly it was a public school, in which all ages clustered together and where "each in turn would come to the front of the room to recite when his class was called," according to Tommie Clack. Here "a younger child could learn much, listening to the older children as they read, or watching them as they did their arithmetic. It was not a bad way to learn more yourself, listening to others." Furthermore, she recalled, "while the older students recited, the younger ones amused themselves by writing on the blackboard, by drawing on paper or by modeling horned frogs . . . from clay."

State by state, constitutions were drawn up to provide that a school for at least three months' duration be established in every district, with a superintendent of public instruction elected every three years. In California, the first was drawn up in Monterey in 1849, and by 1874, according to historian John Bauer, a movement required California children from eight to fourteen to attend classes at least two-thirds of the school year.

Such schools demanded taxes—an odd notion to those independents who bartered, rather than bought, and had few resources and many objections to paying anyone. Where families were few and tax funds scarce, the number of schools would drop, causing John C. Pelton to open the first free public school in San Francisco in 1849, despite the high costs of renting a building and the scant number of children. You are "slightly insane," his friends advised, according to historian John Bauer, but he proceeded anyway. Within four months he had 130 students and had taken in over two hundred dollars in donations, and the next year the school was taken over by the city as a public school. The free aspect was not a draw, since oddly, California's major cities did not enroll many students. In the sum total of San Francisco's school districts, only 45 of 409 children attended school in 1855, while in Los Angeles, only 178 of 821 school-age children actually attended classes between 1854 and 1855. In one ten-year period, only one person in thirteen in the state had attended school of any kind. Either the schools were too remote or schooling interfered with children's work.

States fluctuated in numbers of schools, with Colorado having the highest number by the early 1900s—fourteen per every thousand students. Also devoted to education were Montana and Nebraska, while the lowest number of public schools were in New Mexico and Arizona—five and zero respectively. "Those early schools were unbelievably crowded," wrote Tommie Clack. "The southside school [in Abilene, Texas] opened for primary and intermediate students with 85 pupils in one room and 100 in the other. A year later it had 283 students."

Typically, a public school might begin in a back shed, a sod dugout or even a saloon, but eventually, buildings were needed, books bought, and the children of the area informed. Clearly, any county with a decent schoolhouse would attract the greatest number of families, although the term *decent* was always in question. A typical

Teacher Rose N. Meeham with her class in Montara, California, September 21, 1893.

classroom was usually so primitive that children often gathered on the cold dirt floor, or perched on broken boxes within a drafty frame structure, under a canvas or twig ceiling. Some were taught in chicken coops or brush lean-tos, some in a clapboard house, while others made do in barns, stores, even a packing shed. Students outside of early Los Angeles sweltered in a lean-to built of wild mustard stalks, shaded by the spreading branches of a giant oak. One school convened in the cabin of an abandoned ship, one in a cow shed, another in a tent made of blue-jean material, sewn by "Grandma" Bascom, who built it all alone with her own hands, using only a "good stout needle." In Abilene, Texas, an "attic was converted into a classroom. It was always dark and gloomy, for the only light came through the attic's low windows. . . . It was quite impossible to read from the blackboards in the semi-darkness," recalled Tommie Clack.

The first American schoolhouse built at the Santa Clara mission in California in 1846 had a fire built on a rude platform of stones set in the middle of the floor, while the smoke wafted through a hole in the tile roof. Sylvia Dye described a schoolhouse in Ballagh, Nebraska, so cold that the students never left the heated radius of the coal-burning stove. Jesse Applegate attended one school made of rough-hewn logs with a fireplace and flue built of rocks, clay, and sticks. The "children used to pick clay out of the logs and eat it," he mused.

"Bring your own box" was the furniture requirement for many

schools, with students providing nearly everything from home. Children were expected to provide their own copybooks, as well as any books that the family might own. Instead of paper, they used slates or boards—the ubiquitous blackboard was often a rough plank coated with black paint—a faded and stained map, a globe, and a dictionary. In California, Mrs. Isabell, a teacher, printed letters on the back of her hand with a lead pencil. When paper was finally found in the Ballagh school, they dipped pens into inkwells cut into the rough desktops. Sylvia Dye used "dip pens . . . that were always dropping a gob of ink just about the time we had a nice page of work completed. I think it was about second grade we had lead pencils and were allowed to have pen and ink around the fourth grade."

One school had such rough wooden seats that even the most squirming students settled down—who wanted to be impaled on a splinter? The seats in Martha Peitzke Paul's Iowa schoolhouse "were long benches placed on three sides of the room," without desks or table to work on. Incredibly, when a writing assignment was made, the children would "turn and face the wall" to balance their tablets.

"I finished algebra and philosophy before my seventeenth birthday, last March," wrote Emma Shepard Hill. "Since I finished algebra, I have taken up geometry, chemistry, and rhetoric. I think I shall like them all." Science projects might involve heating an oven to warm an egg for a successful hatching, or, as she pointed out: "It is a curious experiment to put a healthy bivalve into a dish of water deeply colored with indigo, and see it gradually grow lighter and finally become perfectly clear, as the creature absorbs every particle of the coloring substance." She concluded that cockles were interesting, but more so when "fried in a batter of bread crumbs."

Generations of Americans grew up using the Palmer Method of penmanship, which taught them to grasp the stylus loosely and write with the whole arm, not just the fingers. Papers were messy and ink splattered, if the writers even had ink. But as children pored over old geography texts, their boundaries grew far beyond the cornfields, and the knowledge of the stars, the universe, and names of foreign lands set many rural children to dreaming of finding more books to read or even of leaving and going further west.

Students in better-outfitted schools might have *McGuffey's* readers, the *Sanders First Reader,* and the *Webster Spelling Book.* Also used were *Ray's Arithmetic* and *Pinneo's Grammar.* Music was encouraged, no matter the availability of instruments. In a class attended by Blanche Beale Lowe, "We learned to read music by notes and syllables and to sing parts together," while her Grandpa, who must have been the music instructor, "used a pitch pipe until they somehow got a foot-pedal."

SCHOOLS WERE NEARLY always crude and inadequate. Teacher Nellie Carnahan Robinson's one-room school near Lavender, Colorado, was located, appropriately enough, in Disappointment Valley.

> I was amazed when I saw the schoolhouse, but I made no comments. I am sure there was not another schoolhouse in the whole country as primitive as this one. There couldn't have been. It was made of logs and had been built in a day by the men in the settlement. The dimensions were about fourteen by sixteen feet. The logs were chinked and daubed with adobe mud. In many places the mud had fallen out. If a child wanted to look at anyone passing, he would peek between the logs. . . . On some days we had occasional showers of dirt when a wood rat would be prowling around.

Typically, a privy had room enough for only two at a time, with the boys' privy lurking on the west side of the barn, the girls' on the east. Lacking toilet paper, children used handfuls of pages from the Sears Roebuck catalog, spending time to appraise the merchandise and puzzle out the prices. "In winter, the wind blew up the holes we sat on and nearly froze our bottoms. Some called this little "comfort station" a back house, and some called it the "not so nice," but no matter how crude it posed no hardship, since all the children had the same at home. "Teacher, too," recalled one girl.

Parents were fiercely supportive of their children's scholarly efforts. "There was no foolishness around the dining table during the evening homework period, and none when Papa and Mama looked over our monthly report cards. If you had a bad mark in deportment, watch out. Pap and Mama had had so little chance to go to school they weren't going to let us waste our chance. Papa always signed our report cards when he was in town," recalled Blanche Beale Lowe.

Settlers who balked at the idea of state or county taxation loosened up when it came to hiring teachers—no one could be expected to do such grueling work for free. Clearly, teachers must be paid to enlist, and the farmers and ranchers accustomed to bartering for seed and paying pennies for milk or dress goods would "buy" a teacher for their children. Such was the subscription system, in which individual families would pledge a certain amount to pay for education. Five families might raise ten dollars to hire an instructor for a month, but often, classes were pay-as-you-go. When Dora Bryant and her nine siblings marched off to class in western Oklahoma, they brought a nickel to class daily to pay the teacher. Generally, the teacher boarded with one of the farm families for the duration of her work. Recalled Czech immigrant Charles Zulek of schooling in Nebraska in 1856:

> Father loaded my brother Joseph and me in a wagon and also our bed, bedclothes, provisions, and clothing. The teacher and pupils lodged in the same room. We stayed there for one term and then moved our bed and bedding back home again, repeating the operating during each term. It was called a "subscription school" because each neighbor subscribed . . . to pay the teacher.

Education often bowed to necessity, since chores were unilateral, and "children's work" meant whatever work had to be done. Studies dipped during harvest and picked up after, then flagged again during planting time. To maintain even the skeleton of a schedule, rural schools ended up with two terms a year, summer and winter, since education must "combine the practical and the useful . . . for we are a working people," wrote the Reverend W. A. Scott in 1855. Children in Murfreesborow, Tennessee, in the 1860s, attended school for only eighty days of the year and not during cotton-picking time, recalled Ida and Ada Boyd, twins from the area. As part of the farm economy, according to Joyce Taylor, "[Life] was all about the same—raise corn in the summer and go to school in the winter." "I began to attend as a beginner, and continued until I was twenty-one," said Frank Cejda of Nebraska. "But never more than three months in the year, in the winter, for I had to run the farm." Distance also meant difficulty, and the further away the school, the less it was attended.

"Her Daily Duty," Okanogan, Washington, ca. 1900. Photo by Frank Maisuka.

Often, girls stuck to their studies in the one-room schoolhouse, while boys drifted away, usually to remain at home to help with the heavy field work. A disproportionate number of educated young rural women rose up, and fewer such men.

Although some might have enjoyed the freedom *not* to study, others deeply regretted the loss. Martha Ann Minto rued the fact that she "did not go to school more than three months" in her entire life—nor had most of her friends. "We could outlive our destitution & everything else of the kind," she sighed, but not the fact that "we could not get an education so early." She was not alone. Many frontier folk were unable to read, while others, keenly aware of their ignorance, tried to catch up by joining in a class, or hiring a tutor. Thus was Albert, an adult from Ballagh, North Dakota, compelled to knock on the door of Sarah Ballagh, daughter of the town founder and known for her fine European education, to ask if he could learn to read and write along with her class of youngsters. "Of course the children laughed at the big man who was having such a time trying to learn the simple ABC's," wrote Sarah's niece. "But Sarah was very patient and said he could learn if he would stay at it. But no sooner than school started, Albert would remember some undone chore at home. He would say, "Golly me, I forgot to turn out the cows." He would dash out the door, jump on the bareback mule, and gallop off for home—about forty miles away. After a few tries, he gave up on "learnin'."

PRIVATE SCHOOLS, CALLED lyceums, seminaries, academies, classical school, or a ladies academy, were run by nuns, educators, or religious groups, and cost considerably more. They attracted the children of the up-and-coming western parents who might have preferred to send their children east, but, instead, turned to the institutes that existed in cities along the West Coast, where board and tuition might cost as much as one hundred dollars, including money for fuel, bedding, and washing. In day schools, such as the Select School for Young Ladies in Iowa, French, fancy work, and music, as well as an academic curriculum, were offered for three to five dollars per month, along with the proviso "never run, jump, scream, scramble, and push in order to get a good seat. . . . Don't whisper . . . don't wear a tall headdress; don't keep seats . . . don't step on people's dresses going downstairs, [and] take copious notes," according to Mrs. Farrar, from *The Young Lady's Friend.*

Not all private schools were suitable, whether the student could pay or not. Annette Rosenshine's stint in private school "for a short time" was unhappy. She felt "ashamed of [my] untidy thick sandwiches . . . so I took refuge in the toilet to swallow my lunch. I was terribly frightened when one of the older girls, finding me there, gravely told me that eating in a toilet was a sin." However, she delighted in owning a school desk and chair—a cozy arrangement provided by each mother. She had "never had such a piece of furniture that gave me such pleasure" and admired "all the little pigeon holes necessary to hold [such] treasures as a primer and slate."

Or, the private school might rile up the parent as well. In California's Santa Cruz district, Georgiana Kirby was dissatisfied that "the rowdies again have matters in their own hands and a low-bred [supervisor] will again vent his spite on the children of the district." Not one to take her children's education lightly, Kirby launched the appropriate campaigns against him, taking "the first steps towards procuring liberal Unitarian teaching for those of us who cannot accept the sorry Methodism. I long to be teaching somebody myself, but there is not sufficient appreciation of the higher sort of culture to make any parent anxious."

Academy subjects were the same spelling, geography, and arithmetic found in European schools, although the newness of America called for modern languages rather than classical. In class, the students bent over their spellers, writing books, and readers, some with five-syllable "puzzlers" enclosed. One young girl, a trained pianist, was so eager to learn she even "read the hymn-book by letter from cover to cover many times." One teacher, reported the *Santa Barbara Post* in June 1869, even "called the children to their feet, and then and there proposed putting them through a course of calisthenics!"

A liberating spirit was footloose on the frontier, and swept up girls, particularly, in a sense of new freedom, as they were encouraged to complete at least primary and secondary education, part of the necessary enhancement of a young girl's mind. Unfortunately, such support crumbled when it came to college, and many reverted quickly to the idea that women's brains were physiologically too small to encompass difficult subjects, and their bodies too weak to absorb philosophy, history, mathematics, and chemistry in a college setting. So deep-seated was this belief that few women enrolled in college in the mid-1800s.

As for the handicapped—there are few records of actual schools for those so disadvantaged. One young woman wrote that her brother, Tom, had been sent to a "school for backward children at Boulder, MT" until they could no longer take care of him. "He needed help to dress himself, eat at the table, and move about. He could not communicate except by signs and by spelling with the hands in the deaf alphabet. Attempts to teach him lip reading were unsuccessful." The family finally decided to keep him at home and "Anita Wells, a teacher at Boulder, spent one or two summers with us. She taught Tom reading and some arithmetic and showed my mother how she could continue with Tom during the rest of the year."

17

Schoolhouse Days

The worst set of children I ever saw or heard tell of. [I] am almost afraid that I never can bring them under subjection.—*Montana schoolteacher*

Dear Aunt, I would like to tell you something the snow is very deep. It is an inch deep & would like to see you very much indeed. I would like to have you teach here the snow is all gone now.—*Georgie M. Shaw, age 7*

I consider teaching an eternity job.—*Lannie Frost Perigo*

I found myself presiding over an interesting group of juveniles of all ages and while in the capacity of school teacher I made some interesting acquaintance.—*Martha Spence Heywood*

Teachers are badly paid—worse than any laboring class," a magazine article in 1862 announced. "A first-class bootblack obtains almost as much." People were scandalized to discover that the city pedagogue's monthly salary of around thirty dollars was matched by most day laborers, including cooks and housekeepers, while a rural instructor might earn as little as six dollars per month for a female, and twelve dollars per month for a male, plus room and board. Since classes were in session only a few months of the year, instructors lived the entire year on the income of six months' work.

Many teachers were dedicated to education and viewed such low pay as penance. They considered themselves intellectual missionaries to the heathen—which, in a way, they were. Frontier children were tenacious and tough, weaned on adult work, inspired by mature expectations, and filled with a self-reliance that led to intense territoriality. Fights broke out like grassfires, desks flew open and were overturned, girls cried, hair was pulled and faces scratched. Boys, seemingly addicted to mischief, considered themselves honorable if they tailored down their tormenting of smaller children, or refrained from gouging eyes, kicking felled victims, or using a rock on the same-sized opponent. The schoolyard, like a bullring, was filled with the prancing and posturing of adolescence, resounding with a barrage of fights, body blows, feints, and jabs. Parents could seldom fathom the actual state of a prairie classroom, preferring, like one optimistic father in 1858, to believe "the children are all very ardent in their studies, they have a very good and orderly school and are doing well." J. H. Williams, facing the facts about his local school, knew the teacher would soon lose heart and leave. He vowed to do whatever he could to "keep him on."

Barely out of school themselves, young instructors realized the scant advantage they had over their students and were thankful, daily,

School children pledging allegiance to the flag, Monterey, California, ca. 1880.

to be on the business side of the desk. For one, they received wages in cash *without* having to work in the fields. They also had the satisfaction of helping to shape America's future out of the gangling miscellany of frontier youth. Yet young instructors were inexperienced, and found it difficult to hold attention. "Of my sixteen pupils, there were three who were more advanced than myself, but I took their books home with me nights, and, with the help of my brother-in-law, managed to prepare the lessons beforehand. They never suspected my incompetency," wrote Bethenia Owens, a divorced eighteen year old who took up pedagogy to support her son. India Harris Simmons, a young Kansas schoolmarm, opened her first class in October 1888 with nineteen pupils. With peeling, homemade slates, box desks, and only an apple and a ball to illustrate "mathematical" geography, the young teacher found herself distracted. The endless, rolling prairie worked the same effect upon her as on the children. "It really was very lonely," she wrote. "Sometimes [the pupils] and the teacher as well, paused in their engrossing pursuit of knowledge to look through the open door at a speck of black on a distant swell of ground, hoping that it might chance to be a human being riding or driving their way, being disappointed later to see that it was no more than a clump of soap weeds which some mirage or some play of light or shadow had magnified and lifted into view." Loula Blair Schill lived on a "relinquishment," or land parcel, four miles from Bloomington, Illinois. After teaching six pupils nearly her own age, she decided "It wasn't easy [teaching] your own sisters and especially that cut-up John. He claims I pulled one of his ears loose. . . . I know he deserved it." When a fifteen-year-old Californian organized his first primary school, he found the children "good and manageable," but welcomed his rescue by an older, more experienced teacher, who set up a class nearby and invited him to attend.

Educators taught for the love of it, for the challenge, for the salary, for the thrill of independence, or for the vision. "Who can tell how far-reaching may be the ideals implanted in the heart and mind of a little child?" wrote one Kansas instructor. With laundry work netting comparable pay of $1 to $1.50 per week, a teacher had to be drawn to more than salary.

Most were young girls, but some came to the profession through motherhood, finding the two jobs eerily similar. Colorado matriarch Pearl Price Robertson had a nine-month-old baby at home, as well as a desire to use her mind. She had spent "long winter months" thinking about teaching, and finally summoned the courage to apply.

> I washed and pressed my one dress, mended the only shoes I possessed, and in a shabby black coat and khaki hat I went to town to write the examinations for a Montana teacher's certificate. Timidly at first, then glowingly as I warmed to my subjects, I wrote and wrote, and then feverishly awaited the returns from Helena. When I was once more the happy possessor of a teacher's certificate I went to my local board of trustees and asked for a position and they were too surprised to say, "no."

Three years later, she taught her own and her neighbors' children, and considered this time as "some of the happiest hours" of her life.

> In that tiny prairie schoolhouse I zealously tried, out of my own knowledge and experience, to bring beauty and joy into the lives of the thirty-three children whose only experiences had been

those of the drab life on the bleak prairie. All the love I put into my work there has been returned to me a thousandfold. The money I earned helped to feed and clothe my family and started my boy to high school.

Teaching was difficult. Young women often stayed only a year or so before they married and moved away. One young Kansas teacher, seated behind a box in a dugout, taught "thirteen months without a vacation and almost the same group of pupils" before finally quitting. If she had waited long enough, the school system would finally have lumbered along to lend support through the County Normal System, which offered teachers further education from experts in the field.

And the schoolmarm? Such women were tough, stern, and able to take surprises. Daily they might drill students on the "rights, duties and dignity of American citizenship," aware that if moral uplift was ignored, discipline would slide. When four-year-old Jesse Applegate was switched by a teacher for his failure to distinguish between *B, P, Q,* and *D,* the frightened boy "grabbed the stick, broke it, jumped out the door, ran home, and never returned to that class." Said Jesse: "This was the only time I was ever struck in school, and don't remember that I was ever insulted in school by a teacher but this one time."

Rules were needed—and not only for the children. In 1840, Chloe Clark Willson, the "first teacher on Puget Sound," had to self-monitor in order to remain tolerant and even civil. Closing her eyes, she would remind herself mentally how overworked the poor, farm children really were, how burdened with schoolwork—perhaps there was even domestic stress. In a flash of insight, anticipating child psychologists of the next decades, she wondered if it wasn't her job to make school fit their schedules—or, at the very least, make it palatable? As if in a trance, she would repeat these self-admonishments:

Never give a command which you do not intend shall be obeyed.
When you do give a command inwardly enforce its obedience.
Never punish when a child has not intentionally done wrong.
Never think your child is too young to obey.
Guard against too much severity.
Always control yourself.
Never show a want of resolution.
As parents be united in governing.
Do not talk about children in their presence.
Do not make exhibition of their manners.
Do not be continually finding fault.
Never punish by exhibiting imaginary fury.
Parents must have deep pity.
The mother must take her child by the hand and be its guide to the Savior.

Teachers frequently resorted to such behavioral reminders. The catalog of the Abilene, Texas, schools for 1907–8 prohibited teachers from reading newspapers, books, or periodicals that "do not bear directly upon the work of the school" from 8:30 in the morning to 3:30 in the afternoon. *A Teacher's Handbook* from the Denver School District Number One, Arapahoe County, Colorado, published in the early 1900s, was universally addressed to "her," since most teachers were female.

Discipline

Do not send your pupils to the Principal for peccadilloes. Discipline them yourself.

Keeping the class that is not reciting busy does not mean that they be employed in meaningless work. The task should be both profitable and disciplinary. It is easy to keep the "off class" busy guessing conundrums and solving aimless problems, but this is not credit to the teacher, and harmful to the pupils.

Remember that you can never exhibit vexation in your room without losing the pupils' respect: they detect immediately such exhibitions, however slight. . . .

When a pupil is noted for persistence in impudent language, or intentional disrespect or willful disobedience, the teacher having exhausted all her skill, let the Principal of the school first try the power of persuasion, then reprimand; that failing to produce the desired reform, let the pupil be interviewed by the Superintendent. Careful memoranda of days, dates, doings and sayings of the culprit should be kept by the teacher.

> When these means prove of no avail . . . [at] the last resort—the rod be applied.
>
> Avoid espionage through others as a means of discipline.
>
> It is manifestly unjust to punish the entire school on account of the misdemeanors of the majority.
>
> Hold the pupils responsible for what you see, not for what others say they saw.

The same handbook prompted a teacher to ask the following questions:

> Are all the pupils busy at their work?
> Are two studying from the same book?
> Is the teacher interrupted by questions during recitation?
> Are the pupils addicted to snickering?
> Is the floor clean?
> Are the desks spotted with ink?
> Are the lips moving during study?

Better yet, ask "are they awake?" since only the comatose would forgo a schoolchild's greatest delight—teasing. Children teased mercilessly. They teased fellow students, themselves, the teacher. They pulled pigtails, broke chalk, and hooked spitballs, trying to break the tension. No teacher escaped, no matter how many rules were in place—as Arizona schoolmarm Angeline Mitchell Brown discovered. Her class of twenty-five children in the Tonto District, west of Prescott, Arizona, were rapt with attention one day—and no wonder. "I felt something tugging at my dress as if there was a weight on it—shook it and went on with my class; presently feeling it again I looked down & there lying on my dress skirt in a ray of sunlight was as hideous a reptile as I've ever seen. He was black & yellow & tawney & had a body like a monstrous lizard & a 'spiky' looking tail & a head like a snake & was over a foot long—Lord!" She flung herself to her feet, gathering her dress. With a "yell you could hear a mile," she jumped up on the stool, while the children laughed and shouted in delight, exclaiming, "Why, teacher, that's nothing but a Gila Monster!" If only, she thought, a teacher could elevate character, teach capitalization, and smile at the day's "monsters," his or her accomplishments would be great, indeed.

If young and attractive, the schoolmarm might stir up deep feelings of interest from her male students, while to the girls, she was like a glamorous older sister. Adolescent minds, already askew with disorderly and sybaritic musings, grew dizzy in her presence. In one case, all the boys in seventh grade "were mad about" a young Arizona schoolmarm, and to show their devotion "made her life hell." The love-struck boys flipped grasshoppers down her neck, hid toads and large spiders in her desk, glued her seat during recess, then shuffled the books on her shelf so that a mere touch would bring them tumbling down. She constantly ducked the bombardment of rubber bands loosed by the dazzled youngsters, at their wit's end of inspiration. "I thought she was the most beautiful lady I had ever seen and would willingly have memorized my entire primer for her," one student sighed.

Male instructors also had a powerful effect on the students. "My love for my handsome, kind and intelligent teacher knew no bounds," sighed Bethenia Owens, recalling her adolescent years. "I found many opportunities of being in his society." He was fond of the young girl, admired her ability to watch a brood of babies and young children as well as study, and would sometimes visit Bethenia's father, or simply drop by to visit. When he had to leave Clatsop, Washington, Bethenia suffered.

> He took my little hand in his, and I went with him through the gate . . . then he said: "Now, little one, you must go back. You are a nice little girl, and some day you will make a fine woman; but you must remember and study your book hard, and when you get to be a woman everybody will love you, and don't forget your first teacher, will you?"

She ran behind the barn to sob out her grief, and missed him for a very long time. Later, whenever some family member was angry with her, the phrase would blurt out, "I wish the teacher had you

Children in front of school in Farnsworth, Nebraska, 1898.

with him." Bethenia would stop, sigh, and stare into space. All she could reply was "I wish he had, too!" Teaching called for great personal equanimity and attracted principled young women who, in an earlier era that had a greater Catholic population, might have taken to the convent. Even in the late 1880s, their morality was part of their contract, and potential hires were grilled about card playing and dancing, and whether or not they would stay over on the weekends and teach Sunday school. Nor was smoking allowed. Teachers, also, were drawn by the idea of service and believed, at least at first, that any amount of effort was worth rewards in heaven. Mary Sears, unseasoned and devout, from Greenwich, Massachusetts, hoped that her stint of teaching in rural Rochester, Ohio, from 1859 to 1860 would at least be meditative. At twenty, she was already older than most pedagogues, as well as more naive. "With God's help," she confided to her journal, "[she] would make great advancement in the Divine road":

January 29, 1859

> On Monday the directors of the School in this district came to engage me to take the school for two coming months. . . . I was at once filled with hopes and fears, but trusting all in the hands of God, I came to feel that all would end right, that for some wise

Kids washing up at day nursery, Pueblo, Colorado, ca. 1910.

purpose it was so ordered that I should going to the school. . . . I pray fervently [that] I may be prospered in my School.

January 31, 1859

Monday Eve. In school one day, oh, my feelings at this time! School appeared very well, but I see that 'twill not be any easy task to put and keep them all in shape. . . . Came home tonight with a violent head ache and feel near sick.

March 12, 1859

Monday the scholars began to see what they could do oh, how trying they were. To provoke me the boys brought a mouse into school to disturb us. As I could not learn which one did it, and knowing all had some to do with it, I punished all the boys which greatly offended some and their parents.

March 18, 1859

Friday. The boys and some girls destroyed my ferule (purse) refused to obey me, etc. etc. completely disheartened I went to Mr. Peets, one of the directors, to spend the night.

March 19, 1859

Saturday. Directors in School—terrible times—expelled one boy. No School this afternoon. Felt almost dead when I reached home. . . .

March 27, 1859

This begins the last week of my school. Happy shall I be when 'tis all over with. I almost dread to enter upon the untried scenes of the week however I go relying wholy upon God's Omnipotent Arm for strength and I know I cannot fall while he sustains me.

It took a lot to manage a rowdy gaggle of twenty children clustered, hivelike, in the tiny room, all ages together, without adequate books, bristling with boredom and excess energy. Desperately, she turned to games, songs, and learning mnemonics, having heard that play was increasingly used by parents and reformers to reach the young. Somehow, it seemed ineffective. Although not in the same setting, a student, Sarah Gillespie, clearly showed what a teacher's efforts, and life in a classroom was like in 1879, from a student's point of view:

Go to school. The Boys act like very bad boys. Henry was sitting astride the fence & . . . Will Vanasltyne & Fred Chapman come up on 1 side & the other on the other side & caught hold of his legs. H did not like that so he hit Fred on the head & that made him let go & Will still hung on so Henry went after him & told Wm that if he did not want to get into trouble to leave him alone & then Will pitched onto him & I told the teacher & she started out there but they ran & H went to the steps & sat down, we stood where we were a few minutes, & then we (teacher & we girls) started back to the schoolhouse & then those boys went back where Henry was the teacher said it won't be well for them to touch Henry & every time the teacher would start to go out there & call them they would Run . . . teacher gave the boys a little speech & then she called them out one at a time & whipped them over the head & legs & she whipped little Charlie Vanalstyne in his seat.

The teacher's authority was utterly undermined when Mrs. Vanalstyne stormed in the next day and summoned her "out on the stoop & had a real talk with her." The teacher returned crying, and for the rest of the day refused to say a word to Charlie or to the rest of the boys. "Great mischief" had been done to the school. "The clock pendulums were hidden, the chairs all inverted & the organ meddled with and a light broken. The principal called the school to order, asking who had been at the school between 5 o'clock and 7 o'clock P.M. or who knew who was there, and everyone answered no Sir to both questions."

Tough teachers, it seemed, commanded no more respect than their weaker fellows. Florence McCune, a sixteen year old who lived with her family on the corner of Broadway and Seventeenth Streets in Denver, wrote of her school days at Wolfe Hall during the mid-1870s.

Thursday, January 8, 1874. Miss Eloise [Sargent, teacher of Grammar, Geography and Gymnastics] was as cross as a bear all day today. I thought she would "split her shirt" if she wasn't careful. This afternoon I was sent out of the Composition class for whispering.

Monday, January 12, 1874. . . . Miss Eloise gave Fannie & I a blowing up for not having on our Gymnastic dresses. She also sent us out of class for whispering she has been cross as a bear all day.

Friday January 16, 1874. We had a real hard lesson in Mental Arithmetic but I was perfect. At recess we had a funeral at Wolfe Hall. Emma Oakes was minister. . . . The scene was a very sad one. The dear departed, was Davies University Arithmetic. . . .

Monday, February 2, 1874. I just got to school in time this morning. I did four of my examples this morning before going to school. Did not have them right. I missed five in Mental Arithmetic this morning. . . . Was perfect in the rest of my lessons today.

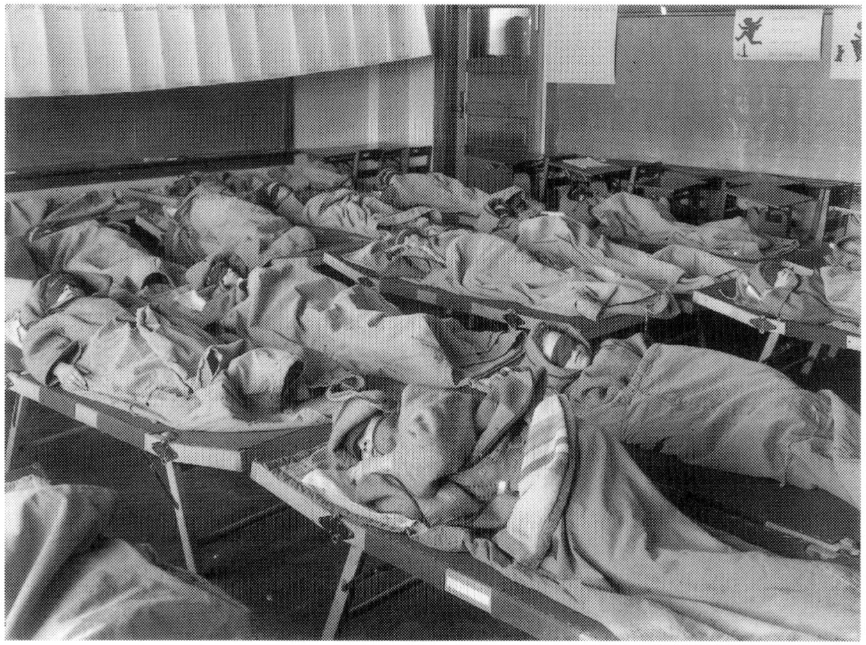

"Enforced" nap time for Denver, Colorado, elementary school students, ca. 1910.

Solutions were sought. To ease the tension, some schools tried to segregate according to sex, as in Lincoln Junior High School in Abilene, Texas. According to Tommie Clack, "a high board fence separated the playground for the boys from the playground for the girls. Stiles were placed at the ends of the walks from the school to the street. Boys were directed to use the south stile . . . girls the north. This rule was sometimes abused."

The students took no field trips—they already knew how to weigh meat, spin wool, or figure prices at the general store, and since few rural children had aspirations beyond their own community, there was little disappointment in career choices. Boys would be men who were members of a community, girls would be wives and mothers. In all, the educational system of the early 1900s prepared the pupil for the world in which he, and she, was living.

18

The Rugged Cross

We children all thought it was a happy day when Preaching day came for we all expected a good time and a chicken dinner.—*Keturah Penton*

You always ought to know what you ought to do. Of course, you don't always do it. Nobody does. That's human nature. But at least you always ought to know what's right. I reckon that's what religion is for.
—*Jack Dempsey*

Keep good heart, and don't get it too full of the world, groceries & c. Such things are of little use in heaven.—*Calvin B. West, writing to his sister Sally, April 23, 1853*

Then there was that time that Reverend Storm baptized a child by the wrong name.—*Barbara Levorson*

"If God had intended man to go West, he wouldn't have put up the Rocky Mountains" was a popular saying, quoted by those opposed to emigration, expansion, and the dread Manifest Destiny, which inevitably took loved ones away from their ancestral homes. But the answering maxim, "Progress, Civilization and Christianity," proved stronger, leading hordes of adventurers, mountain men, homesteaders, and merchants west over the Rockies, and giving them, upon arrival, much to be thankful for.

Faith was integral to early America, and religious revivals during the Great Awakenings, which fell indiscriminately upon believers of all denominations during the late 1700s and the early 1800s, drew a greater turnout than the Fourth of July, as thousands of Baptists, Methodists, and Presbyterians, whose dust could be seen for miles as they came by foot, horseback, or buggy, gathered to worship, rejoice, be healed and believe. Camp meetings presaged the future political rally, while the churches, always having served as community centers, would lead to future granges, co-ops, and farm associations. It took hope to go west, belief to stay there, and faith to institute a growing sense of independence. Such hardy self-reliance formed the roots of religion and capitalism, as many cried out, "Sir, what must we do to be saved?"

"This country needs much Christian exertion," exclaimed Abigail Smith of Kansas to her brother and sister in 1844, sensing a fall-off in local church attendance. Like others, she kept a wary eye on the spiritual climate, ever ready to revive spirits that might flag. Any homestead without a dog-eared King James drew comment. "[Two] or 3 children but no Bible!" exclaimed a startled young girl after paying a visit to a lax family. In addition to the bible, *Pilgrim's Progress, McGuffey's Reader,* or Bible society tracts would constitute approved family reading material. In most communities, denomination mattered less than simple determination. "There wasn't any organized church in French Corral," wrote Edith White of California. "Once a month a Methodist Presiding elder preached in the school-house, and one of our townsmen conducted a Sunday school."

Children learned early the lesson of compassion, as well as to exhibit the best behavior in the worst circumstances. Everywhere were opportunities to help. "I had an ambition to save up four hundred dollars with which to buy entrance to an old ladies' home," recalled a Wyoming midwife, Mrs. Mortimer. "Just before I got the full amount saved up, I found that Eddie Carwell wanted to enter the ministry. I had just enough, so I gave it to him." In Nebraska, the Czech settlers pooled every penny to help one another with local disasters—burned barns, collapsed sod huts, grasshopper-ridden crops and the like. Francis Prevaux and his family daily discovered a "small grocery store" stocked with delicacies, from ginger to tapioca, on his doorstep each week, sent by an unnamed benefactor. In Utah, according to Hannah Crosby, lack of food reaped a wealth of sharing.

> One day there came a man asking for a loan of flour, even a very small amount . . . his children had tasted no bread for three days. My mother was concerned for her own, and was quick to make answer that there was but flour enough for one small baking. I remember how sad the man looked and turned away saying it was useless for him to go farther. My father called him back, as he had been talking with my mother [and I] suppose he had been weighing the question of starvation for his own children and he said to him, "my children can suffer no more than yours. If starvation comes, we'll starve together. You may have half the flour we have." And picking up the flour sack he dipped into the man's sack fully one half.

Hannah's mother was rewarded some weeks later by finding a sack of flour behind the door, mysterious and unexplained. What friend would be apt to send flour? Was the church distributing to the poor? The generosity went unconfessed, and the children spent days guessing, with the only conclusion being, according to Hannah's father, that "no one but God would provide us with flour at this time."

From careworn hearts came quick and generous responses, for everyone understood that bounties given were also returned, thanks to mysterious, though immutable laws. "Everyone's heart was in the right place when it came to doing something," said Edith White, a child growing up in California's gold country. "My parents were always ready to help their neighbors in trouble." Charity took place without fanfare. Reticules were quietly emptied, pockets turned out, and cigar-box banks plundered to help those in need. Harriet Shaw, after sending a young relative money for the "great many little expenses that people do not think of and which embarrass the student in his course," added, "do not tell anyone that I give so much. Others may be inclined to give him less." When Captain A. C. Farnsworth heard that Bethenia Owens, the daughter of a friend, was taking in washing, picking blackberries, and ironing to finance her medical studies, he announced, "I am alone in this world. I have more money than I need, and I think I cannot do better with it than help you." She cried at his "generous, unselfish offer," but for the good of her own hard-won individualism, refused. Bethenia's spirit had always demanded self-sufficiency—even as a young girl she was determined to help herself.

Such stories were commonplace, and the examples set by parents were deeply understood by the children. As Edith White recalled:

> Mother organized many a community Christmas tree. She went around to the storekeepers and miners taking up subscriptions and then rode on horseback to Grass Valley to buy the presents. She had a friend named Mrs. Black who was a rollicking sort of young person, and they went on these excursions together. She kept every person in mind, and tried to get just the right thing. Later the purchases would be delivered by stage coach, and Mother would superintend the decoration of the tree and the naming of the presents. No one was forgotten and we were like

one big family—this community of 500. But my mother never neglected her family in spite of her services to the community. Her capable hands could turn off work faster than any other person I ever knew.

In the Czech settlements in Nebraska, mutual helpfulness was "the redeeming feature of those hard times," as exigency "made brothers of all and sisters of the women. They were like one family. If one was in . . . trouble, the others sacrificed to help." Family might well include strangers, too, as the family of Frank Cejda discovered. Cejda's father, joining the tide of Germans, Swedes, and Norwegians rushing to claim homestead parcels in Nebraska, found that he lacked the full fourteen dollar fee—he was horrified to find himself two dollars short. Panicked, he looked around for another Czech, or a friendly face—but he recognized no one at the County Land Office. Suddenly and mysteriously, his application went through. Not a word was spoken, but he suspected that "the Registrar of the U.S. Land Office, a kindly man, paid it."

Families generously tried to help one another, no matter how distant the members. Typical was Harriet Shaw, a missionary wife in Fort Defiance, New Mexico, who collected fifteen dollars to send to her sister in Vermont. When her husband, Milton, added "more to it" and "sent it in a draft," Harriet was matter-of-fact about his generosity. "[Milton] always noticed that when he gives, the Lord always paid him back double." Such generosity was noticed by children, too. When Bethenia Owens's father joined the Clatsop Volunteers to retaliate against a murderous band of Indians, suddenly, a Mr. McDonald "stepped forward." "I am a single man," he said, "and have no one to care for me. . . . I will go in your place." As fate would have it, McDonald was killed, leaving a model of sacrifice equaled only in Scripture, and never forgotten by the Owens family, each member of which vowed to measure up to this offering.

Church-raised children, bible-versed, were part of a culture in which "Are you saved?" was as routine as "How's the weather?" Saved from what? a newcomer might wonder. Saved from plague? Floods? But the life in question was spiritual, not temporal, as children discovered at a very early age. Harriet Shaw voiced every Christian mother's concern when speaking of her son, Georgie. "I feel very anxious for his early conversion," she worried, but rejoiced when the boy began to "ask . . . questions about Jesus his crucifixion & his second coming, which shows his little mind is thinking."

Christian children were Bible bred and Bible versed, and, like their parents and church elders, could often retort wittily with sayings that were scriptural. One California six year old, cited by historian Eliot West, when locked in her room as punishment, thundered out the psalm "Open the door for the children, Tenderly gather them in." Alice Clarissa Whitman, the young daughter of two Oregon missionaries, "every morning at worship [sings] her verse and . . . is very much disappointed if we do not give the tunes she is acquainted with." As a youngster of only four years old, Lorenzo Dow "suddenly fell into a muse about God," even forgetting to play. "My companion observing, desired to know the cause; I asked him if he ever said his prayers . . . to which he replied, no. Then, said I. 'You are wicked and I will not play with you. So, I quit his company and went into the house.' "

Children might rebel, reject their faith, or, like Edward Austin, devote far more time to metaphysical contemplation than normal. He mused frequently over how to "interpret temptation," finally deciding that on "so free and open" a frontier, temptation "simply did not exist," since temptation was "enticement to the forbidden," and, on the frontier, nothing was forbidden. "If we . . . do anything that is wrong, that is wicked, not temptation."

As a child's life unfolded, faith might show its various facets, at times inspiring, or else seeming like tedium and obligation. Californian Sarah Bixby Smith admitted that her "restlessness" too often led to disaster.

> My parents had gone to the chancel carrying my little sister Anne for her christening, leaving me in the pew. It was a strange performance. The minister took the baby in his arms, and then put something from a silver bowl on her forehead, and began to pray. I must know what was in the bowl! Everybody had shut-eyes, so there was a good chance for me to find out without troubling anyone. I darted forward and managed to discover that the mysterious something was water, for I spilled it over myself.

To children, church often seemed a prolonged ordeal. "Ministers never thought about keeping to any sort of schedule," wrote twelve-year-old Tommie Clack. "And when they started preaching they sometimes did not know when their sermon was over, for they loved the sound of their own voices. Babies had good time, for they slept through it all." Emma Shepard Hill complained to her friend Estelle that "Prayer meeting nights seem to come whenever there is good skating or sled riding; and I always have to go to prayer meeting, no matter what the other girls and boys are doing." For Hill, the prayers seemed longest on those nights she was allowed to "go skating afterwards." For Barbara Levorson, growing up as a Norwegian Luthern in central North Dakota, church was "the agony of sitting still for three hours" while the Reverend Storm "scolded and pounded the pulpit with his fists."

> I wriggled restlessly . . . and mama bade me sit still. I committed to memory every daisy [on] the other girls' hats. I wriggled forward and backward and mama said: "Du skall sitte stille." I gazed with longing at the prairie outside the windows. I counted the flies buzzing on the window panes. . . . By now the other girls were staring at me. Soon they would be asleep. Why couldn't I sleep, too?

Little wonder that frontier children, tiring of their usual games, would mimic a church service and turn it into play. Augusta Dodge Thomas related how Kansas pranksters in the 1870s enjoyed the diversion of "Heaven and Hell," which placed God and Gabriel atop the haystacks, while Satan was relegated to the musty corn cellar. Oddly, when Gabriel blew his buffalo horn, the dead who popped back to life seemed identical to those recently buried in the hay. As "God" recounted the sinner's evil deeds, he thundered out a list of why that individual would never, *ever* inherit the kingdom. Then "the offending children . . . slid down into the shed (Hell) and were burned by Guy, the Devil, who threw broom corn chaff all over them, as the substance nearest to fire." Thomas believed that "if it wasn't eternal, it at least lasted until we changed our clothes."

Mrs. Albert Manwaring and children, Springville, Utah, 1903. Photo by G. E. Anderson.

BAPTISM LAUNCHED A new believer onto the old path and took place rain or shine, even in winter's icy grip. A young Czech, Charles Zulek, recalled an immersion in Nebraska when "a hole was cut in the ice, it being freezing weather. The people were then baptized in the water and they had to walk to town in the cold. The woman who was baptized first was never well afterward." Immersion scarcely dampened revival spirits, and a "happy visiting time" was had by all. Rickety buckboards, filled with ardent believers, rocked toward the weeklong camp meetings, where all convened beneath starry skies, to sing, revel, share food and neighborly companionship in old-fashioned festivity that few could resist. For camp organizer H. C. Bailey, "it was no small job to prepare food and provide sleeping room for from five to eight hundred people and their horses."

Mother and children in Sunday best.

Those who failed to attend "meeting" knew that, sooner or later, a traveling preacher would pay a call. "As soon as we got settled the Methodist itenerate found us, and our home became a preaching place again," wrote Keturah Penton. "We had preaching at our house on week days, most of the time on Tuesdays," while Sundays were for "Prayr meeting and class with occasionally a sermon from some good old Local Preacher."

> The preacher would join with us and tell us Bible Storys and then explain them to us while we all cracked Nuts and Poped corn. Then when we began to tire they always had a fund of aneckdotes to tell and they would draw us out till we would ask some questions. Then he would turn the conversation and ask the older one some question and then would pass it around to all the children and before we knew it we would answer questions in the catechism, so we learned to love and reverence the preacher and we children all thought it was a happy day when Preaching day came for we all expected a good time and a chicken dinner.

"Good times" might turn into stormy recrimination if the preacher was a brimstone type, generally Baptist, Methodist, or perhaps Presbyterian. According to young Keturah Penton, "The preachers were . . . lay[ing] a firm foundation for the generations that followed," and no matter how they raged, "the members stood by them and helped them all they could." Latter-Day Saint patriarch Brigham Young impressed a young Mormon, Martha Heywood, when he "preach[ed] an out and outer sermon on gold, merchants, lazy women and men who want nothing but fine clothes—sowing seeds for their own destruction." Frippery was forbidden in fundamentalist sects, since lace flounces and gold eyeglasses were usually Satan's bulwarks, considered to be the devil's own. Ohioan Keturah Penton's family had only a "change of Raiment for the Sabbath, for we did not have to have a change for every day." Rather than parade finery, "We went there to try to do some work for the Master that would tell in the years to come." Extraordinarily devout, Keturah judged other children by their "reverence for the Place of Worship" and was sure "every body young and old [would] take a deep interest in Church work." On the more frivolous side were young girls such as Sarah Gillespie, who, despite her cares, considered church the single social event of the week. Pleased, she recalled: "I went to Sunday School Congregationalist & wore my new suit of clothes."

The firmest foundations were built at home, claimed noted fighter Jack Dempsey, who grew up in the early 1900s in Manassa, Colorado. His father believed that "religion showed what you ought to do," not necessarily what you *did* do. Observed the son, "any inconsistency between his religion and his manner of living never bothered him," although young Dempsey was exhorted to "do right," to begin every evening with family prayers, to never lie, and to always behave. "For us children there were many rules and precepts. Things to do, and things not to do. If you didn't do as you were supposed to, you were weak, but if you behaved yourself properly you were strong. It was up to you."

Maintaining faith seemed difficult at times. The freedom engendered by democracy and the confusion of new sects, beliefs, and denominational subsets made it difficult to keep up. Religion seemed as much on the move as the people to whom it ministered. Even the Friends, thought a stable and peace-loving group, fragmented, leaving one young Ohio girl, Esther Whinery Wattles, to follow her family's choice. The split occurred in 1827 as a "division among the Hicksites and the Orthodox." Esther was too young to know why her father and stepmother went with the Hicksites, her uncles with the Orthodox. "Their children were not allowed to play with us after the division," she wrote. Each group had disowned the other.

Absentee fathers were not immune to worries about their children's religious upbringing, and some tried to administer moral lessons by mail. A letter would take three months to arrive. Who knew what mischief might occur in the meantime? Such fears bothered William Dresser, who wrote to his young children Albert and Charley in Madison, Wisconsin, from the gold fields of California.

Sac City March 13 1853

My Dear Boys

I wish to talk with you about what kind of boys you are, and why you are different from other children, Why are you not Pagons? Why do you like to have your food cooked? How is it you would not like to eat a piece of an other boy, or a slice from an old dead woman? What is the reason that some boys have a beaw and arrow, and you a spelling book? That they are dressed in skins and you in cloth? You live in a house and they in a hole in the ground?

A good while ago, a good many generations back, Missionaries taught our forefathers the truith of the bible, at that time our forefathers lived, as other heathens do now, and the influences of the gospel is to make men better, to be industrious, to love one another, to mak us be kind to each other, it makes us wise, & as far as we live upt to it makes us good, the the differnece between you and other boys who are Pagons is that you are living under the influence of the Religion of Jesus Christ and because they have not the knowledge of the true God they are making there own Gods, and some are very poor ones I assure you, and some are very costly, very dear to keep

Now if the Bible makes us so much better, if it does us so much good, it must be very good itself. It gives us good muthers and good frends and neighbours and by its influence we learn how to live, and how to live comfortable, Thus it is that our kind of people live comfortable in good howses, dress neetly and have good food, and the most of the people in the world have not the knowledge of God, a few have and you are among that happy few. . . .

Now when the wise men first went to see Jesus they took very costly Francincenc, and gold and Myrrh, when you go to him you need not take Myrrh for . . . He don't neet it for he rose from the dead and assended into heaven, but try to so live as to allways to remember him and know that he is at the right hand of God and sees all we do. . . .

I hope you will all be good children recolect that you have a father in California who prays for you every day and that Jesus is in heaven pleading for you, give my love to Mother & Grand Mother I remain my Dear boys your ever affectionate Father

Wm Dresser

Religion in the West had much to do with the miracle of place, found in the majesty of plains, mountains, and rivers so achingly beautiful that the viewer could only marvel. It was a hard life, but one with spiritual rewards. "When you think of me you must think of me as one who is truly happy," wrote Elinore Pruitt Stewart, a true optimist and hardy Wyoming homesteader. "I want many things I haven't got but I don't want them enough to be discontented and not enjoy the many blessings that are mine."

19

Feelin' Poorly

I have a great aversion to Doctors for children and therefore venture to doctor [them] myself.—*Mary Anderson*

She was taken with [a fit of sickness] the last of february I thout with worms and A cold but it proved to be the lung fever and information in the bowels.—*Sarah Hammond describing the condition of her niece, Ellenburgh*

With many strikes against them, the Wilsons survived without medication, and very little of life's goods.—*Sylvia Dye*

European emigrants landed in America in part to escape plague and pestilence, to "weed out" the frailties of the Old World, according to settler Agnes Reid. Yet even in the new land, communicable diseases were rampant, as slop jars, contagion, and airborne filth competed with human and animal wastes that when trodden underfoot, released germs that swirled through the air, if stirred by any movement at all. Flies blanketed walls and windows. Tents, privies, and kitchens shared the same space and often, the same water in heedless, congested towns without apparent sanitation. Even the mainstay of family life—dorm-style bunking, all in one bed—created a dense and contagious environment, with a single dingy mattress as the bearer of one another's infections.

Disease struck randomly and often, as with the Ohio family of Esther Whinery Wattles, the eighth of thirteen children who "all lived" until the youngest turned fourteen. Then "a bilious typhus fever came and took two brothers and [the] youngest sister, all within two weeks of each other, and the remainder of them dropped out one by one." By 1879, the death rate in the country was so steep that the connection between filth and disease could no longer be ignored. In lowland settlement areas, water that stood in puddles and clogged streams offered tranquil breeding grounds to legions of mosquitoes, giving the risk of malaria to every passerby. In Wisconsin in 1841, malaria killed eighty of the six hundred residents of Lake Muskego, and before the last third of the century, annual death rates from malaria ran as high as 5.7 per 10,000, according to historian Ronald Numbers. The death-swath cut through the Mississippi Valley into Canada—one of the chief causes of morbidity in the late nineteenth century. Few children advanced to adulthood without having witnessed or been struck by one disease or another.

Wrote Agnes Reid:

Early in September our little golden-haired Jimmie was stricken with a terrible fever, something of the nature of typhoid, yet the doctor gave it some other unpronounceable name, and for four months he lay, feeble, moaning, unconscious. After the first few days he never recognized any of us, but would open his mouth like a little bird when anyone came to the bed. Every two hours we fed him from a spoon, either medicine or liquid nourishment, and every six hours bathed him.

Some days I would feel hopeful and meet the doctor with, "Oh, he is better today, doctor!" but the doctor would look at him and shake his head. His solemn, "No change" would shatter my rising hopes. I have never lost a child but it seemed to me that we must have suffered more than we would to have really given him up. There was his pitiable little skeleton ever before us, almost accusingly, as much as to say we were not doing enough. There was the endless, nerve-wracking care of him, and there was even the conviction that we must lose him after all. . . .

We never really knew when the change did come, but gradually, so gradually, he began to mend. Then we were able to release the doctor from his self-imposed contract. He had made over a hundred trips on horseback, a distance of 2 1/2 miles, and we poor, poverty-stricken home-builders had only one hundred dollars to offer him. . . . We insisted however, that he take all we had, to prove in some measure our gratitude to him. I even said, "Why doctor, you have saved our child," and he came back with, "Saved your child, no, my good woman, all my knowledge of medicine could never have saved that child, had it not been for your nursing and your strict observance of my directions. Doctors could save great many more children if they were only blessed with mothers like you."

The effects of overcrowding and lack of ventilation were obvious in the shanty towns and urban centers of the Midwest and Far West, resulting in high death rates for young children. Entire families were felled by ague, also known as pestilential or intermittent fever. If not ill themselves, settlers watched brothers and sisters, parents, friends, and relatives succumb to every manner of shaking, swooning, and sweating. So common was the illness, particularly in low-lying, swampy areas, that specific "shakin' " times were set aside from chores, with turns staggered so that farmwork could proceed. "Shakin' " time was different for everyone—some had only a moment's tremor, others fell to stamping and knocking and could hardly keep their footing. "When the fever came up, [John] was so flighty he did not realize what to do and could do nothing," wrote Esther Wattles. "Ague was so prevalent that our [entire] family was sick," recalled Rachel Emma Woolley Simmons, a young Utah girl.

I can remember being in our trundle bed with my brother and all shaking until it seemed as if our teeth would come out. The chill would last for hours, then the fever was just as hard as the chill. There was no one to wait upon us but Uncle John, and in time he was taken sick so father had to pay a man a bit or 12 1/2 cents for every pail of water that was brought into the house, and I don't suppose it was a few for a family of eight persons all burning up with the fever.

Equally disabled was the family of Kansas homesteader Miriam Colt, whose son Willie lay on an Indian blanket near the door, calling for water while the grandmother lay "on her bed in the other room . . . very sick." The grandfather also was "on a blanket on the floor; his fever . . . raging," while Miriam's daughter, Lydia, "has got up and is sitting on her trunk; looks weak and sad." Overland traveler Emma Shepard Hill's younger brother had "chills and fever for some time, and since leaving Fort Kearney," causing the family to "abandon the tent and [sleep] in the wagon. . . . Now that he was sick he must have the comfortable bed."

Those whom illness overlooked might suffer other setbacks. Skin ruptured, bones broke, and "felons," or boils, would appear as if by magic. Elizabeth Cabot's son had an "eruption," for which he wore a truss. An abscess formed in Rebecca [Heywood's] abdomen & "broke at the navel." Said her father, matter-of-factly, "Rebecca's abscess occasionally runs a little . . . but that does not allarm us." "Allarm," it seems, was reserved for the deathbed. As she began to gain in "strength and flesh," they could see that things were better with their daughter's health, although the worst thing about her extended illness and convalescence was "so much washing" of the bedclothes. "There was so little of her, so wasted was she, that it was a marvel to us how so much stench could be produced," her father noted as he and his wife oversaw the girl's bed rest, gave cool alcohol rubs alternated with hot compresses, and fed her soft food.

"Children are running the streets completely covered with smallpox, & no more attention is paid to it than to any common sickness," wrote Harriet Shaw of Socorro, New Mexico, who had fortunately received "vaccine matter" from her mother in Vermont and was "ready to have the children vaccinated again." The disease lasted for weeks and afflicted Americans in epidemic numbers. A Californian, James Henry Gleason, described ten days of the pestilence that beset his home in Monterey in 1852—incurred through the Californian tradition of hospitality. A diseased visitor had died while staying with them, infecting several of Gleason's young children—and he could hardly sleep for fear of their demise. "It is impossible for me to describe to you in words the distress beneath that roof about Christmas time and the anxiety felt by the sick and well. I had never been amongst it before."

From 1904 until about 1912, Sylvia Dye missed school each winter because of pneumonia. Carrie Williams's son, "Darling little Walla," often had a "fever [that] continued all night until falling asleep." She tried everything, then finally "gave him some oil . . . and he immediately vomited it up." Finally, they bathed him "to his hips in a tub of warm water," then "took him out and put his feet in a pan of strong mustard water" despite his "kicking and screaming." Puzzled and anxious, she had only her own diagnosis to rely upon and thought it was a cold. Frank, the son of Francis Prevaux, was often ill with a "very severe cold, accompanied with a distressing cough." His father worried: "Last night, it seemed almost as though he would go frantic, such was the trying character of his cough. I very often fear he will not live to grow up." The wheezing, snuffling, and frequent spitting carried on in Oakland, California, 1858, made clear that "colds are very prevalent in this community."

Children were also beset by swollen joints, summer complaint (acute diarrhea), pneumonia, scarlatina, mumps, measles, headache, heartburn, cankers and chilblains, bruises and bronchitis, coughs and croup, earache and eyestrain, blistered feet, even jaundice. A ruptured appendix could result in deadly peritonitis, and the few who managed to survive were left with massive abdominal lesions that touched off wails of pain at each movement.

While living with her aunt, "a very large girl for hur age" named Irena was afflicted with the St. Vitus's dance—a mysterious affliction often referred to in literature, yet a mystery to early medicine. Her odd, jerky movements and fever never seemed to turn more serious. Her aunt wrote: "Hur helth is much better now then it was last winter she is troubled in cold." If and when a doctor did arrive, the results could be equally harrowing—who could know? One frontier physician became expert at the quick, tabletop removal of tonsils and adenoids—an easy job, according to one young patient. "[He] painted my throat with some mildly anesthetic solution, promising me a dime for an ice-cream soda if I didn't howl too loud, putting a knee against my chest and his left arm around my head to hold me immobile, and then cutting out the growth with a scalpel in his free right hand." What caused the tonsil to flare up? No one knew, but overheated schools, filled with hot, stifling gas were blamed.

To ward off illness, mothers gave children as many herb teas, "potions," and nostrums as the budget could afford. "Let me know whether you took your vomit, whether you have got your pills and whether you have begun Lent," intoned Abigail Adams in 1764, reciting a daily litany of medical admonitions to her children. Agnes Reid, like others, employed the only other precautionary measure possible in prevaccine times—isolation. "I regretted to take my tiny infant among people where might lurk the germs of every dread disease." To physician Urling Coe, "illness was often rooted in poverty, attacking mostly [those] who live on coarse food and in open houses." He had faith that the well-to-do and the well-fed were "seldom sick." Recalled young Marian Russell, traveling by wagon train to Santa Fe with her lively, adventuresome mother.

> In those days homeopathic remedies were used almost exclusively . . . poultices for Will's aching chest were made from ground mustard mixed with water and spread on red flannel. His earache was treated by a drop of sweet oil and the sedative smoke from a pipe.
>
> The boil on my back mother brought to a head quickly by an application of soft soap and sugar. A whole clove was inserted in a tooth that started aching. Smelling salts were handy for folks who felt faint. Burns were covered quickly with dry baking soda.

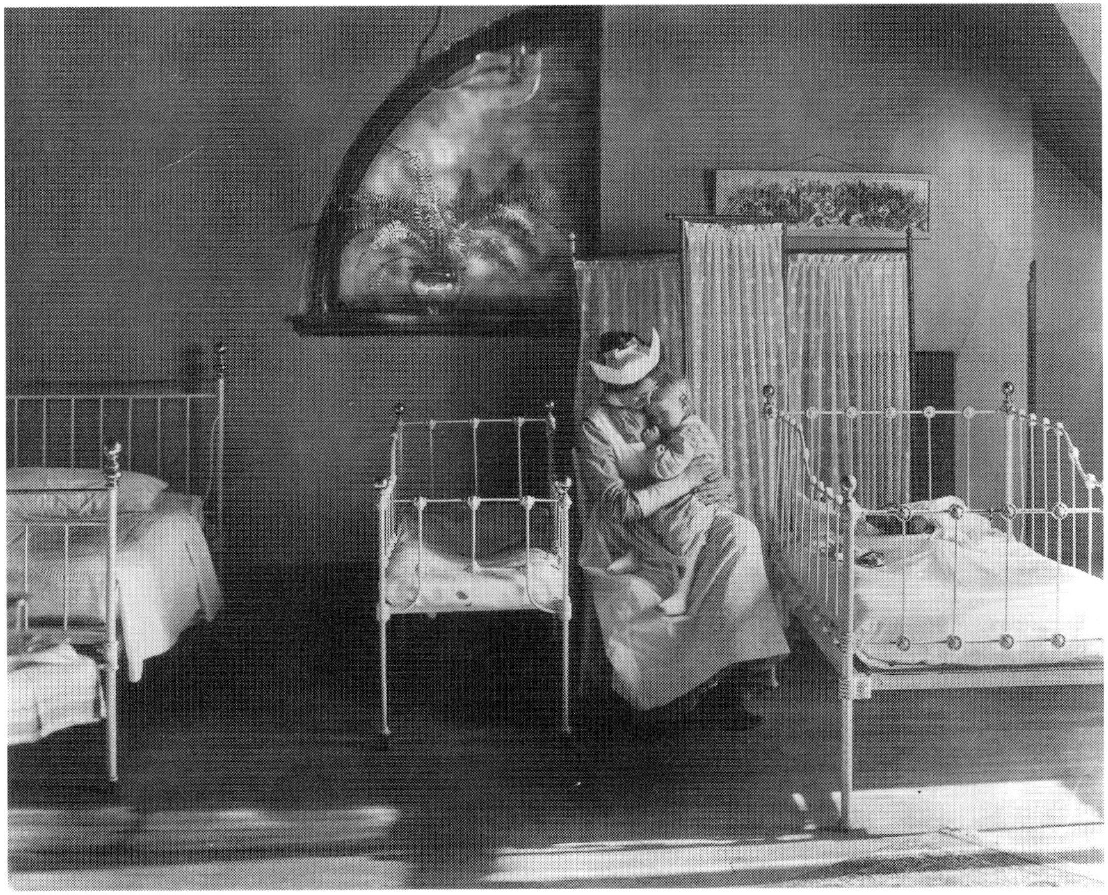

Children's ward, Northwestern Hospital for Women and Children, Minneapolis, ca. 1900.

Neuralgia yielded to a pillow filled with hops and heated hot in the oven. Stomach ache was treated by liberal portions of pennyroyal tea or hot ginger. Cough syrup [was] made from the bark of the wild choke cherry infused with honey. . . . Puff balls were kept to stop bleeding . . . ten-penny nails, about six to a bottle of strong vinegar, made a blood tonic. The vinegar dissolved the nails. Take a teaspoonful of the tonic each night before retiring, it would put iron in your blood and curl in your hair.

As if disease was not enough, frontier families were plagued by other signs of decline as well—not the least of which was teeth. "I would like to care for baby so as to give him good teeth," wrote an anxious mother in 1922. "The two oldest haven't any enamel . . . at all and one of the girls teeth look kind of yellow."

Even dogs were a threat, as recounted by Mrs. N.W., writing from Texas in 1916 to the chief of the Children's Bureau. "Last March [my son] was bitten in the forehead by a dog, making a very deep hole directly over his right eye. . . . It had become intensely hot in June when I noticed a small knot in his left eye." She tried to cure the inflammation herself using boiled towels, boric acid, and hot applications of baking soda in water, but his "clear, pretty eyes" turned lashless and infected—she was unable to solve the problem at home.

"No person need die of lockjaw," advised an early journal—little comfort to those afflicted—who had, no doubt, used the common remedy of hot wood ashes "as warm as can be borne" pressed to the afflicted area. Yet few survived the muscle-rending effects of this common disease.

Most parents dreaded calling in professionals because the cost was prohibitive. In fact, settlers and frontier families were willing to countenance the most terrible afflictions before voicing a medical need. "We are all in a state of partial anxiety about doctors and nurses," wrote Georgiana Kirby of Rancho La Salud, near Santa Cruz, California. "Those here of the former class being bunglers, giving calomel to a confined woman and losing healthy patients frequently, and most of the latter being filled more or less with old women's superstitions as regards the treatment of new-born babies." She added: "I hate the idea of a doctor."

Many doctors were obviously quacks who, between dosing or leeching—either by using ticks to suck blood or by delicately cutting the veins—would reduce a patient almost to the point of death in the arcane belief that the "less life there was left . . . the less disease there would be." One in particular, a "rough looking man with long whiskers," arrived by muleback to help young Edward Breen, whose left leg was broken between the knee and the ankle after his horse stumbled into a badger burrow. Obviously self-made, the "doc" "examined the boy's leg and proceeded to unroll a small bundle. . . . Out of this came a short meat saw and a long bladed knife. The boy set up a loud cry when he sensed what was to be done and finally after a long discussion convinced his parents that he should keep his leg." The "doc" was disgusted that his services had not been used. He was given five dollars and sent back to the fort, muttering. The doctors, even when certified, might wreak more havoc than nature itself—no wonder the frontier family dreaded medical encounters.

In the unfortunate case of a South Dakota girl, neither nature or medicine could make a difference:

> The girl was driving some cattle over to a waterhole when she stepped on a big rattlesnake in her bare feet and was badly bitten. This was terrifying for we all knew the great danger.
>
> When we reached the village, the mother and child were just arriving, with the father driving them in the wagon. Fortunately, the auto stage had not left, so we climbed from buggy and wagon, jumped in the stage, and were ready to start. The girl was in terrible pain by this time, and her mother was very much upset. The parents had done all they could for the child, but professional medical aid was imperative.
>
> The stage driver, realizing the urgency of the situation, certainly did his best to get us to the doctor with as much speed as the trails would permit. The journey was hard on both mother and child. I kept trying to comfort them, but the mother was so frantic and the girl in such pain that the going was pretty hard.
>
> It was long after sundown when the driver drove up to the doctor's office. After examining the foot and treating it, the doctor said he would do all in his power to save the foot. . . . "Very serious," he said. "Very serious, indeed. If she could have had an antidote for the poison immediately, it might have helped, but the poison has been in her blood so many hours that it is very dangerous." . . . The mother did not want the foot taken off, and I surely sympathized with her, but the child's leg was turning black up to the knee, and she was in agony.

Finally seeing the danger, the mother gave her consent to have the foot amputated. It was done the same day, but not soon enough. The poison had penetrated so far up the leg that it was necessary to take not only the foot, but the leg almost to the knee—a terrible shock to both mother and child. After the operation, her agony was relieved and she seemed glad to be free of the terrible suffering.

> One day . . . there was a letter . . . from the mother. They had taken their child on to the hospital. [T]he leg seemed to keep rotting more and more. At last, after several operations with the leg finally being taken off way above the knee, the child died. They were heartbroken and were not coming back to this country. They asked the neighbors to have a sale of their cattle and personal things and to send them the proceeds. They never wanted to see this desolate country again.

Jesse Applegate's medical encounter was less traumatic, but distasteful nonetheless. "In those days nothing was accepted as medicine unless it were offensive to the taste, and disagreeable to the stomach, and the more offensive and nauseating, the greater its medicinal virtues were supposed to be." Indian Fizic was the name for a common remedy brewed from the plant equecaqune, its use learned from the Indians. Brewed from the root, it was drunk hot and black—but not willingly. Applegate was "seized by the nose, and when, in gasping for breath, his mouth flew open, the physic was poured down his throat." Then unable to stand, he was put to bed in a fit of violent trembling, mostly from "nastiness," not fever.

Illness made way for nurturing and being nurtured. It eventually paved the way for medical advances, as its tolls mounted and science tried to intervene. It separated out special time for healing, reading, and for quiet. It brought family members, some normally quiet and withdrawn, to confess love for one another—like any other aspect of frontier life, virtue was intertwined with its bleaker aspects. Gradually, even the most remote homesteaders turned to filters to purify drinking water, and learned how to dispose of waste. It was no secret that a shovelful of dirt, pitched into the privy, would discourage flies, while flowing water stirred up and drowned mosquito larvae. Whenever pure water from the mountains was channeled into town, typhoid fever practically disappeared from the city. Thus, better sanitation helped lower the spread of disease and of parents' heartbreak.

20

Passing On

The home seems so cold and dreary without a baby's voice.—*Mrs. W. D.*

The yard is full of children, but as I say many times, there is none that can take the place of those that are gone, each child has its own place in the hearts of those that love it and it has to fill its own place.—*Rachel Emma Woolley Simmons*

Four months later we buried our baby and it was then that I knew how helpless I was when it came to knowing what a mother should know.
—*Mrs. W.D., writing to the Children's Bureau*

Another little girl has been given and taken, and now there are seven here, and four awaiting us on the other side.—*Sarah Hale*

The minute I heard the news I burst in a flood of tears and grief. . . . So the world goes—one minute in good health and the next in eternity.
—*Abigail Malick*

On the frontier, animals might stagger and die, men reel and cough and take to their beds, and siblings sink to their pallets or chest-of-drawer beds, eyes closed in eternal sleep. So predictable was death that men, women, and children developed a near-terrifying insensitivity to its presence. Death surrounded them, death dwelled with them, and most particularly, death took away their children. The overland crossing in particular was marked by infant and child losses, with many felled as they tumbled beneath the wagon wheels, or pitched out of the wagon bed. Burial sites were simply the quotidian consequence of an ambitious undertaking, and the plains across were dotted with grave markers—rough-hewn crosses that sprang up like wildflowers across the empty land. Death and loss seemed, at times, like some terrible, slow-moving play, each scene enacted before a wide-eyed audience of children, so spellbound by the grim scenes that detachment was the only possible response. So common were the leave-takings that death seemed a kind of game, with children singing out the growing numbers of Indian burial platforms or pioneer gravestones sighted as if playing a round of tag. A youngster, cited by Elliot West, counted thirty-two marked graves in fourteen miles, while another child reached nearly 375 before stopping. A third boy counted to 478 by the time his party had reached the Humboldt Sinks—an incredible tally, considering that most of the mounds had been ravaged by wolves and were indistinguishable from the landscape, save for a litter of bones, or occasional tatters of cloth idling in the breeze. Burial sites bore archeological evidence of the past, and stood as silent reminders of the harshness of the land and life's dreadful brevity. One "fresh made grave" sported a feather bed on top. According to young Jack O'Connor:

> [We] . . . had noted that between the two buttes that stood between the town and the Salt River was a collection of mounts that looked as if they might be graves. What genius first decided to dig into them I cannot remember, but wherever he was discovered that they actually were graves and that they were full of human bones and skulls of all sizes. The graves were shallow, since the ground was very rocky. We used to go at night carrying picks, shovels, and old barn lanterns to dig into them. The only things we saved were the skulls. These we soaked in water, scrubbed with brushes and Old Dutch Cleanser until they were clean and sometimes white. I kept a very good one and displayed . . . in my room . . . [then] gave it to a friend and his mother threw it away.

Maria Elliot, in July 1859, was matter-of-fact about the "skeleton of a papoose . . . done up in a red handkerchief . . . [and] very much dried and shriveled up." Ada Millington Jones, in June 1862, seemed indifferent to "two Indian graves . . . so old they had fallen down and scarcely anything remained but a few pieces of beads. We girls went out there and got a few beads which we strung." She complained, however, that "there weren't enough."

When death struck close, however, there was always startled response. Osseon Dodge remembered his mother's reaction to his brother's death—it stayed with him for years. "Her cry was not human. Then it seemed she would never get her breath again." Mary Ackley's mother, in whose ears rang the sad good-bye of friends and relatives, had said, "child, you will wish yourself back many a time," echoing the sentiments of those left behind: "I will see you no more . . . we will never meet again." "I have stared [death] in the face," said young Martha Ann Minto, whose memory harkened back to a lonely hillside grave where her brother was buried, and the haunting sound of her mother's lament, "Oh, my boy, my boy! How can I leave him there?"

Infants might pass as predictably as night succeeded day, and like the passing day, might only be known as "Tuesday's Child," since lives so truncated went without names. Worse was if the baby survived for several years, giving the false hope of a promising future. Since Agnes Reid had fallen so instantly in love with her twin girls, it took much longer to recover from their loss.

> We had named them Finetta and Heneaga for my two best friends and they lie buried on the bench that rises north of the house. . . . Their little coffins had to be made of what material we could find for we have been at such an expense. . . .
>
> During the life of the babies I slept with both of them and with little Charlie, who was just past two, and Francis in a trundle bed by the side of me. Nels felt that he could not be robbed of his rest or he would be unable to carry on his work, so for that five months I had the care of the four and I never knew what it was to sleep two hours at a time. Then when I could see the first one failing I was reconciled that she must go but I was sure that we would raise the other, and even after she died, the children and I consoled each other that the cradle was not empty as it would be in most homes when a baby had died. But when the second one had to, all that I had borne during the months seemed to curse me. When I looked at her little dead face I wanted to scream and run away from it all.

Her husband, Nels, tried to help her through the emotional trauma.

> [J]ust when I would have broken down, Nels put his hand on my shoulder and said, "Bear up, Emma, for my sake." Bear up, I surely did. For weeks and weeks I never slept a night and everyone feared I was losing my mind. It seemed to me that I had no mind to lose. Nels would take me for long rides in the buggy or on horseback, miles and miles and miles to try to tire me so I would sleep but the nerves that had been strained so long would not let go. I have seen him hold a ticking watch at my ear for two hours at a time with the hope that the monotony would bring me sleep and rest, but sleep was, it seemed to me, out of the question and

> all the time I had never shed a tear over the loss of my darling babies. Oh . . . those dreadful weeks are too terrible to recount.

What kept children alive? What made them die? A mother agonized in a letter to the U.S. Children's Bureau in 1916.

> He was an angel, never cried, too good I guess to be left on earth. I washed and put his night drawers on and put him to bed well & healthy. He played about the floor that night, laughing and as happy as could be. I nursed him at 3 o'clock in the morning and I awoke at 7 am and found him dead along side of me. You can think how I feel. I cry night and day for my big fat baby, [taken] from me like that.

How to contend with so much sorrow? For the lonely survivors, grief equaled the worst kind of despair, coming far from the comfort of a familiar church, family members, and friends. At any death, losses were mourned, lives recounted, minutes reviewed. A Wyoming woman, Mrs. Mortimer, "would have died of grief [at the death of her son] if I hadn't had to work so hard." Her husband, however, went "crazy with grief" and fell into a fever while she "hardened her heart" against her maker. But as the years passed and her husband became more and more "worn out and pale," she finally decided she was not going to stay and bury him too. Selling their belongings, they moved west, where she encountered a sympathetic Mexican woman, whom she told about her son. Like balm, the Mexican woman's words "showed her the way" to peace. "I wept for hours, but peace had come and has stayed." She accepted the loss of her son and vowed to "go to others' help every time there has been a chance."

"It is the Lord that hath done it," decided Narcissa Whitman, believing that the accidental drowning of her daughter was a "privilege" that demanded "praise and gratitude to God that He has so mercifully sustained" her and "preserved and sustained her soul."

With so much death afoot, survivors were forced to "toughen up." Some invoked faith, others turned philosophical. It helped to be matter-of-fact. "Mary Ann will soon . . . be . . . numbered with the dead," a woman simply observed in 1846. Said Rachel Emma Woollery Simmons:

> It never seems to make any difference to us who are left behind—we lose our nearest and dearest friends and our little darlings, but the world wags on just the same. We have to care for the living, go through the same routine of work as though nothing had happened, but as time wears on, owing to a wise Providence, our hearts are healed and our love becomes a tender memory, for we know that they are better where they are than in this world of trial and cares. We wouldn't have them back, still we miss their society, the council of the old and the prattle of the little ones, but our loss is their gain.

Death in Victorian times was not so gently accepted by all. There were instances of special "sitters" being hired to watch by the graveside in case the corpse reawoke—what could be more terrifying than to be buried alive? Although no such instance has been recorded, the hope for reunion, and even resurrection, was met in one case described by Benjamin Lakin, 1819.

> One day Brother Charles Climers children being brought in that had fallen from the upper floor and had been taken up as dead. There were none of the family at home, they being at meetings but the Children they took up the childe and shook it and hollowed over it but it still lay as dead. One of the children a boy (perhaps about 1 or 2 years old) made one of the other children take the Chile out of the door and hold it up and he took a gun and shot over it which brought it to immediately. Perhaps the report of the gun like an electric shock gave motion to the heart and set the blood in circulation. But how strange that a child of that age, even had he heard of such a thing before should have had the presence of mind to use the means.

But for most, there was no reviving. Death brought burial, forcing the bereaved to undergo the fateful repetition of a sorrowful, or sometimes joyous, rite. "A funeral was a wonderful sight to me. In those days the lodges came out in full regalia and had one or two brass bands playing funeral dirges and march," said Frances E. Albright, 1863. But more likely, it was a humble affair, sometimes with a rough pine box, but always with the need to embellish and to signify the degree of a family's love. When Army wife Katherine Gibson Fougera's friend lost her son, the women were at a loss. There were no coffins available, so a soldier offered to cut, fashion, and hammer a pine box for the child's burial. The rough-hewn surface disturbed the mother—it should be lined with "something soft to take away . . . the crudeness." After searching the commissary and scrounging through her own belongings, Katherine went to a trunk and "reverently lifted [out] my wedding dress. It was lovely, and my choicest treasure, but it had to be sacrificed. I padded the inside of the lid, then covered it all with soft satin pleating." Working all night, she replaced the ugly lead nails with "white-headed tacks" donated by a soldier for a funeral that had "neither service nor clergyman" but comforted the mother nonetheless.

"Do you remember I wrote you of a little baby boy dying?" queried Elinore Pruitt Stewart, another bereaved mother. "That was my own little Jamie, our first little son. For a long time my heart was crushed. He was such a sweet, beautiful boy. . . . He died of erysipelas. I held him in my arms till the last agony was over. Then I dressed [him] for the grave. Clyde is a carpenter so I wanted him to make a little coffin. He did . . . and I lined and padded it, trimmed and covered it."

When the Millington family lost George, their twenty-month-old infant, they refused to leave him alone on a lonely prairie, insisting on hiring a man to escort the body to Carson City, Nevada. It cost thirty-five dollars for the hired man, but the corpse traveled free. The family vowed to bury his remains in California once they had settled.

> We couldn't bear to leave his little body among the sands of this wilderness surrounded by Indians and wolves. Isaac cut the letters [on the coffin lid] so that it will be easier to identify him when we come back. We all gathered around his bed in the tent to watch him die.

Other cultures had other ways, and one result of the intermingling of races and groups in the West was the opportunity to observe the differences, contemplate their meanings, and modify sentiments accordingly. In Catholic regions, observed James Larkin on a trip to

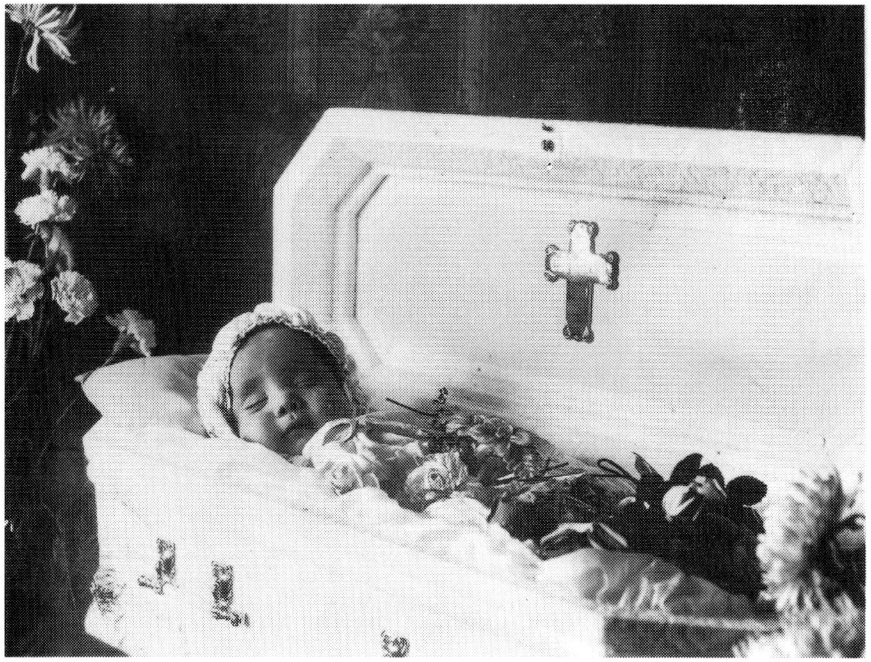

Infant in burial casket, ca. 1900s.

Santa Fe in 1857, death prompted an oddly casual kind of behavior. Was it the religion, he wondered, or a kind of pragmatism? "There passed before our house today the funeral of a child perhaps three years old. The dead body was exposed in an open bier carried by four women, some of them laughing and talking. It was dressed in the usual clothing, its face was plainly visible. A small boy preceded the bier."

Equally festive was a Chinese funeral. Marked by pomp and finery, it was a "wonderful sight" to Frances E. Albright, a child growing up in Virginia City, Montana, in 1863:

> Three or four hundred Chinamen marching and throwing little sheets of red paper, burning joss sticks and firecrackers to keep the devils away; they also had a band playing their strange music. Some of them had beautiful silk clothes, and each had a white sash over his shoulder, and all wore wooden shoes. There were many

Woman mourning "R. Tibb" near Jacksonville, Oregon, ca. 1870.

flags and banners, also several wagons of hired women who wailed and turned around to laugh.

In Anglo-American, frontier culture, survivors clung to their memories, allowing the deceased, particularly if a child, to live on in imagination, its presence hovering, like a guardian angel, in the form of postmortem photographs that hung from the plank walls and wallpapered rooms of every frontier dwelling. Also called "American Memorial" photos, they portrayed the "sleeping beauties" arranged neatly, like wax dolls, with flowers or prayer books clutched in hand. The delicately retouched photos glowed with pink cheeks, or in winding cloths of satiny blue. Like icons, the children in the memorial photos gazed fixedly from cabin walls, overseeing the families they had left behind. The memory of the child could live on in its memorabilia, as well. One woman kept a dead child's miniature rocking chair in her living room for forty years after the child's death.

If in a city, the baby's casket might grace a mortuary's front bay window. Kophin's of San Francisco made a bronze casket lined with white satin, with "such rare finish and furnish that it actually looked . . . inviting," causing passing mothers to shudder and hurry by.

Most puzzling, however, were children's attitudes. No one could ever, really, understand how children thought of death, or what impact it had. For example, in an account cited by Emmy Werner, San Francisco schoolteacher Sally Brown was telling her story of being wounded by a Mojave arrow. Four companions had died in the raid, and another dozen were wounded. The children tried to absorb the information, based on what they knew about death. One finally piped up, asking: "Did you live?" In another instance, young children at an army fort noticed Katherine Gibson Fougera leafing through a picture album. She stopped at a photograph of her father.

The small boy, pointing to the picture, asked, "Who's he?"
"My father," I replied.
"Where is he?"
"He's dead."
"Who killed him?" demanded the boy.

In the West, sickness and accident were "natural" deaths. The children looked puzzled, then the girl spoke up. "Nobody killed him. He just died his own self."

Part 6

ETHNIC AMERICANS

Photo on previous page: Two Indian papooses, ca. 1880s.

21

Many Cultures, Many Ways

I wonder if there is any difference between [the Chinese and the Indians] socially?—*Claire Hofer Hewes*

America's cultural diversity threw belief, habits, and tolerance into startling disarray, forcing people of every culture to cope or fight in surprising new ways. Whether disturbing or intriguing, such variety proved that, from language to lore, fashion to faith, the ways in which the nation's "melting pot" churned up new versions of family life could only be marveled at.

Differences abounded, particularly between whites and Indians, and even when agreements were struck, the terms were always in question. The tribes had little concept of what they were bargaining for—or of what they had supposedly given away. Treaties, once signed, were often broken, since the U.S. government often overrode its own policies, while Native Americans, democratic and members of loose-knit tribes, were not compelled to accept the mandates of their leaders and would often act independently.

Frontier families were morbidly fascinated by Native Americans. At first encounter, they were convinced that any Indian, friendly or not, was simply waiting for a chance to steal stock. Kansas settler Miriam Colt even feared that her children would be stolen. "They point to my boy and make signs that he is pretty. 'Chintu-chinka,' they call boy, and 'che-me chinka,' girl. As time passed and families "settled in," the terror lessened. Familiarity bred tolerance, and the children who trembled at the thought of "wild Indians" gradually felt more at ease, at least with those Indians who wandered into camp. Shyly, children would dig in their pockets and produce items to trade, whether pins for moccasins, or bent nails for a feather.

Hired by white families, Indian servants sometimes exchanged lore, food, customs, and affection with their Anglo employers, just as Anglos became more familiar, and comfortable, with their Indian neighbors. Sophia Martinez's aunt, a wash woman in the white families, would carry the girl along to work with her in a basket. "That's the way she raised me, among the whites. And they used to take me out of the basket and feed me milk." To "give service" was an unspoken mandate, and children found themselves forced along on zealous "visits to the heathen," mimicking the parents' actions as they learned the rule of charity. Young Helen Meilleur of Washington territory, began with Dinah, a crippled, elderly Indian woman who lived nearby.

> A small aluminum pot with a tight lid and a pail for safe carrying had somehow become Dinah's kettle. When Mother cooked our large midday meal a portion went into this pot to stay warm on the back of the coal range until Dinah [came] close to the back

Clara Archambault and unidentified North Dakota Indian girl, ca. 1889. Photo by Frank B. Fiske, Fort Yates, North Dakota.

gate. Then I ran out and thrust the pail into her hand. This maneuver was like passing the baton in a slow motion relay race because it had to be accomplished without impeding her progress. If she had stopped at our gate it could have been construed as begging action.

Later in the day I would find the empty kettle, scoured clean with sand and sea water, just outside the gate.

Indian tenderness was returned, overflowing even, to white children, since Indians believed that any young person, even a "ghost child," was innocent. It was not unusual for an Indian to intervene in Anglo family affairs, even if only offering to hold a baby, or stroke a child's blonde hair. In one case, an Indian woman strode into the rowdy household of a Montana mining family, where the youngest child was customarily "tied to a high chair and neglected" each day during harvest. According to Mrs. T. A. Wickes, who lived nearby, the "stern-faced squaw, working in the garden, entered the kitchen, took the child—the frightened mother knowing it was unsafe to protest—and with reproachful look at the mother bore it to the potato patch, where the contented child cried no more that day."

In another incident, army wife Martha Summerhayes was surprised by a "delegation of several squaws, wives of chiefs," who came to pay a formal call after the birth of her son.

> They brought me some finely woven baskets, and a beautiful pappoose-basket or cradle, such as they carry their own babies in. This was made of the lightest wood, and covered with the finest skin of fawn, tanned with birch bark by their own hands, and embroidered in blue beads; it was their best work. I admired it, and tried to express to them my thanks. These squaws took my baby (he was lying beside me on the bed) then, cooing and chuckling, they looked about the room, until they found a small pillow, which they laid into the basket-cradle, then put my baby in, drew the flaps together, and laced him into it; then stood it up, and laid it down, and laughed again in their gentle manner, and finally soothed him to sleep. I was quite touched by the friendliness of it.

Children cared for by Indian women readily learned their language. Alice Clarissa, the daughter of missionary Narcissa Whitman, "talks both Nez Perce and English quite fluently, and is much inclined to read her book with the children of the family, and sings all our Nez Perces hymns and several in English."

Indians, for their part, were intrigued by the trappings of the Anglo's sedentary existence, their use of indoor furniture, and would marvel and laugh at such mysteries as a ticking clock. Several squaws laughed "until the tears rolled down their cheeks" at the sight of a hoop skirt, and were similarly moved by the flounce of female petticoats. One chief thrust a finger straight through a loaf of bread, amazed at its soft texture, but generally, foods of the whites were shunned. Said Kiowa Jim Whitewolf: "I had never drunk milk much before. I didn't like it."

Anglo children, with their light eyes and sandy hair, seemed a marvel to some Indians. As in the case of any other desirable object, Indians were often prompted to barter.

"Trade?" gestured a squaw to a young army wife, pointing to the woman's baby. The mother laughed, thinking it a joke. Laughter, to the Indians, was a sign of assent. Suddenly, the mother realized that the Indian woman had laid her own infant on the ground and was moving toward her, arms outstretched. *She wanted to take the baby!* The young woman held her child tightly and waited for the soldiers to come. She had insulted the Indians, however, and the next day, a group of warriors appeared and demanded the white baby. The discussion raged on until other items could be substituted. Blankets were handed out, as well as large amounts of conciliatory sugar.

Another Indian, a chief from the feared Sioux tribe of Red Cloud, made an astounding proposition "to buy" the baby of military wife Elizabeth Burt. She could hardly believe her ears.

> "Ten ponies?"
>
> "No indeed."
>
> "Twenty?"
>
> Then we began to feel he really meant this as a bona fide proposition. What a monstrous idea!
>
> "Thirty ponies?"
>
> "No—no—no!" And my dear boy was tightly clasped in my arms and carried into the tent.
>
> After this, when an Indian appeared, a terrible fear seized me that our boy might be stolen and we held a closer watch over him than ever.

Indians, in turn, feared that white missionaries would snatch away their children, convert them, and keep them in mission schools until adolescence—a frequent occurrence. When missionary Harriet Shaw spied the little daughter of a chief, she longed to "adopt" the girl.

> I loved the little girl so much that I wanted to take her as my own. She should share my affections with my own loved little ones. We made her presents & he promised to bring her again. O that I could have her as my own, & educate her for a missionary among her tribe, but how could I ask a parent to part with his child? He is an old man & seems to dote on her, & she is as pretty a child as I ever saw in the states except her filth. O I did love her so much.

Little wonder they were afraid. Indian boarding school children were often felled by "foreign" diseases, such as smallpox and measles. Indian youth invited, lured, or forced into the Christian missionary or government day schools, were forced to accommodate, by changing their dress, learning English, and trying, however reluctantly, to "civilize" themselves. In a poignant example, missionary Mary Collins of the Dakota Territory marveled at the efforts of a group of young Sioux men who joined the YMCA, or the Young Men's Society, as it was called before it merged with the national group.

> Hearing a wagon coming down the road, I looked up to see six young men sitting in the chairs and an attempt had been made to dress in white man's clothes. Indian youth seldom ride in a wagon, always on horseback. One had a suit of clothes, and had divided it among the others. One had on a hat, another a pair of boots, another a vest, one a shirt, and another a coat, and another a pair of trousers. I at once knew it must be some formal occasion and [was told] "We are going down to Flying-By's to organize a young men's society."

With so much diversity, racial intermingling was inevitable, and the hushed tones that accompanied the scandalous breath of miscegenation was not lost on young children. In the Pacific Northwest, such breeding flourished, and the half-Indian children that tumbled about, playing outside the gates of the fur-trading forts, had usually come from the union of a footloose trapper and an Indian mother. As the children grew, and a western education was desired for the boys, a schoolteacher was usually imported. In 1859, one came to Fort Simpson, in western Canada, to teach the Espikelot boys in their local Tsimshean language. Over two hundred students crowded into the building to attend the Indian day school. Suddenly Cushwat, a local Indian boy, "got drunk and broke all the windows and doors." Then other Indians broke into the school, "plundering it" of its furniture. As a further distraction, tribal wits, seeing the large audience, insisted on performing feats of medicine juggling while class was in session. The Indian children, the teacher complained, did not respond to the same verbal prompts as their counterparts, giving answers that were incoherent, or worse, dreamy and fanciful and indirect. The Indians called upon animals and spirits as reference and measured distance in a circular, associative way. Puzzled frowns greeted any linear concept of time and its odd dependence on months, days, and years. They preferred "when the hen lays eggs," "when the corn falls down," or "on the day the apple tree blooms."

Mulattoes were common—the mixed-blood offspring of plantation owners and farm slaves who migrated west after emancipation, whose lighter skin tone bore evidence of their dual ancestry. In the case of mixed roots, the question of whom to shun and whom to embrace was a matter of skin color. Light-skinned blacks, particularly those from out of the country, were considered to be of a higher class than those of a darker-skin, even within the black community.

White children must have been puzzled at the mixed racial messages. While emancipated black Americans were soundly shunned in any social setting, the supposed drawing on their culture, as seen in variety shows, drew a popular response. "Most exciting of all [was] an occasional . . . minstrel show," recalled Edith White of Nevada County, California. "The entertainment consisted in banjo-playing, clog dancing and jokes, as well as songs. . . . The performers were always white men blacked-up. They traveled from town to town."

SEEMINGLY, WHITES HAD a system to determine the place of all other ethnic groups and races, depending on their skin color and their state of "colonization." Mexicans were seen by Anglo-Americans as "conquered" and thus unacceptable, yet South Americans were readily drawn into the flow of American life. Popular literature for children tried to sort out racial standing through such works as "The Jaina," an 1896 story, cited by historian Jim Silverman, in which the new multicultural child is presented. As the child of a blonde, German mother and a dark, Peruvian father, she is, perhaps, one of the first attempts to answer the questions children surely must have had. Such candor was daring indeed, since different races were safer when portrayed in their own, "exotic" lands, not as living intermarried on American shores.

Children were naturally drawn to the exotic, and to many, the sight of a Chinese vegetable vendor with his swinging baskets of fresh greens, polished fruit, and tangled root vegetables provoked wonder. Was such food palatable? What *was* chop suey? Others emulated the racial fear of adults—as did the rowdy Jack O'Connor, who delighted himself and his friends by shouting into a Chinese restaurant a gibberish phrase, "cheely-moka-helo." "I have no idea," O Connor admitted, "what it meant, if anything," although he hoped it was an insult in Chinese. He could hardly wait for the "fun" to begin as the man "rushed to the door with a knife or cleaver and chased us down the alley."

There was no end to surprises when it came to observing Chinese life, at least not for a young Texas girl, Tommie Clack.

> It was a Wednesday afternoon. Our mothers were cleaning the lamp globes. . . . Maude Tarpley [and I] were on our way to see the Chinese, the foreigners in our midst. These were mystery people. We wanted to know about them. Perhaps they had come to Abilene as workers on the railroad, and had stayed to make their living washing shirts for the cowboys . . . washing them and starching them until they were ever so stiff, then ironing the garments. . . . It was an unforgettable sight that we saw as we peered through the tiny windows. There were the men with their long queues hanging down their backs. . . . On a long ironing board lay the stiffly starched shirts and from a tin cup [each] would take a big mouthful of water and spurt it all over the garments to be ironed. Imagine spitting on laundry to get it ready to iron! Next Sunday men would wear their shirts with fronts and cuffs stiff as a board and shiny as a well-honed razor. How

Ellen Su Moon dressed for her graduation, San Francisco, ca. 1899.

did we small girls feel? Well, we had learned that all that glamour in those shirts had come from a Chinese mouth. It was a sobering discovery. . . . Somehow, I never again took another stroll down the[re] before prayer meeting.

Despite such harassment, the Chinese vendors loved to bestow gifts to the Anglo children, such as "chopsticks and a little bowl" overflowing with brightly wrapped pieces of candy. The "strange, dark smelly shops" of the Orientals were among Annette Rosenshine's "early exciting experiences" on Chinese New Year in San Francisco. She shivered in excitement as "a long table was placed against the wall . . . covered with all kinds of Chinese delicacies—ginger, nuts, and various kinds of sweet meats, all tastefully arranged." Although the Chinese wives were never to be seen, the men were eager hosts, passing out "many kinds of candies and wine." Everyone was entertained by the "little Chinese children decked out in their colorful costumes."

Obed G. Wilson, a miner in the Sierra, had his heart touched by two Indian children he found shivering in the snow, hungry and frightened, whose father was wounded and unable to hunt. He took them in and love blossomed. Whenever he returned to his cabin, the children "dropped their spoons ran to meet [him] and pranced around [him]." Even after their father recovered and the children left, they returned regularly, ever "eager to please," to replenish his woodpile with "dry oak limbs and pine knots at the cabin door." In return, the miner spent "most . . . evenings" teaching them pidgin English, using grimace, grunt, and finger-waggling to convey his thoughts. The girl was thrilled by handfuls of "brilliant" fabric, and he gave "beads, rings and tinsel" to her family. The generosity was reciprocal. When he mentioned casually that wild plums might taste delicious, the boy, Togie, hunted for the fruit, returning "late in the evening with nearly a bushel of delicious plums, two rabbits and one grouse."

ALTHOUGH CHILDREN WERE cautioned against "mingling" by parents and by custom, there still remained one avenue open for meeting other races—Sunday school. Here doors were flung open to any interested child, since volunteers and teachers sought any and all converts, from Indians to the occasional Celestial, the popular term for Asians. Asians were so eager to be educated that many would stop passersby on the street and beg the meaning of English words. When a Presbyterian school opened in 1870, young Chinese students flocked to the classes, becoming as familiar with the Bible as with *McGuffey's First Reader.* Education was highly prized, and many Asian dry goods stores had a backroom language school that was well attended by local children.

Black children were not seen in segregated Sunday schools, but they did make an appearance in the public schools of early states, with the greatest numbers in California, although seldom in white classes. Any who dared were often rudely expelled. In Arizona, even as late as 1920, Irene King noted the state law in which "they had to provide separate schools and maybe they had one Black, so they just hung up a sheet. Now if anyone from the state department walked in this little person knew how to go behind that sheet and then they were separated. . . . If no one was checking on them, they just went [with the rest.]"

Yet black families were paying taxes for education, and when a young black girl was turned away from school in San Francisco in 1858, the resulting furor brought about a revised school law, calling for separate but equal facilities in California. The minority tax base was considerable, and the city government responded to black lobbying efforts by finally building a black school. Yet the school proved inferior, and finally, in 1875, public schools in California were thrown open to black children. A teacher observed the students' behavior and went out to help the newcomers acclimate.

> On the first day of their entry, fearing trouble, I preceded the ranks out into the yard. No sooner had some of our boys caught sight of the new students than they raised a cry . . . and I commenced chasing them. I caught the first offender and gave him a good thrashing. Within a month the colored boys had overcome their timidity and were dashing around with the others, having as good a time as any.

Children of all races were exposed to one another, either in passing, in school, in situations of barter and trade—the list was endless. "It was a gala day for us children when Peddler Marks came to town. He was a Jew," stated Edith White. Her matter-of-factness may have reflected the tolerance of her parents, or their veiled racism. Where ignorance and fear reigned, there were strict divisions. Where charity, compassion, and education took root, the children might turn toward tolerance—a theme repeated not only in the West, but throughout the nation.

22

Native Americans

> What a fright we all got one morning to hear some white people were coming. Every one ran as best they could.—*Sarah Winnemucca*

> I soon managed to eat berries and chew gum at the same time. After a while I learned to chew tobacco and then I did not eat any berries. Later on I got to like tobacco very much and I probably used up more value (in tobacco) than I would have done had I eaten the berries.—*S.B., Winnebago boy*

Indian women soothed their unborn children by gentle singing as they peacefully "walked" the fetus, letting the serene rhythms of nature lull both mother and child into a spirit of repose. Birth usually took place in just as calm a manner, prompting favorable comparisons between them and Euro-American women. "Had the Indians no dropsical swelling? Morning sickness?" Adriaen Van der Donck, an early traveler on the continent in 1641, believed that Native American women were "seldom sick from childbirth, suffer no inconveniences from the same, nor do any of them die on such occasions," while another male observer, Col. Philippe Regis de Trobrian, called native childbirth "extraordinary." He saw women work right until labor's onset, then resume their chores the day after, without complaint, an impressive display of stoicism unlike civilized birth, which seemed to offer the delivering mother "long torture, medical attendance, intervention of chloroform, puerperal fever, two weeks in bed, thirty days in the bedroom, and such precaution." Historian Edna Patterson wrote that such births "physically and morally . . . corrupted the work of nature: As a result, white women weakened and often died, while Indian mothers gathered up their babies and vigorously went on their way."

Such vitality startled army officers, whose admiration might quickly turn to embarrassment if accused of undue interest, causing them to quickly point out that such "ease" was only animal-like, after all. Yet no culture or discipline could alleviate childbirth's misery, as witnessed by an officer in Custer's Seventh Cavalry, and who later described it to his wife, Katherine Fougera.

> One sizzling hot day . . . my husband saw a very young squaw drop out of line and steal behind a bush. A bit curious, he waited a short distance away to see what she was up to. Imagine his surprise to see her emerge holding in her arms a brand-new papoose. Having caught up with the others, she plodded through the scorching dust as though nothing had happened. The perspiration, though, was pouring down her face, and the newborn brave was wailing. . . . No matter what race, creed, or color, the agony of childbearing is the same all over the world. A great pity welled

in Frank's heart for the young savage mother and her baby, he stopped one of the gvt. wagons and made her get in it, seeing to it that they both were given plenty of water. The woman drank long and forced some down the throat of the wee one, but she said nothing.

An account from the journals of Lewis and Clark describe the details of Sacajawea's delivery.

11th February Monday 1805

about five o Clock this evening one of the wives of Charbono [Sacajawea] was delivered of a fine boy. it is worthy of remark that this was the first child which this woman had born, and as is common in such cases her labour was tedious and the pain violent; Mr. Jessome informed me that he had frequently administered a small portion of the rattle of the rattle-snake, which he assured me had never failed to produce the desired effect, that of hastening the birth of the child; having the rattle of a snake by me I gave it to him and he administered two rings of it to the woman broken in small pieces with the fingers and added to a small quantity of water. Whether this medicine was truly the cause or not I shall not undertake to determine, but I was informed that she had not taken it more than ten minutes before she brought forth.

Sunday June 16th 1805

I reached the camp found the Indian woman extremely ill and much reduced by her indisposition, this gave me some concern as well for the poor object herself, then with a young child in her arms, as from the consideration of her being our only dependence for a friendly negotiation with the Snake Indians on whom we depend for horses to assist us in our portage from the Missouri to the Columbia river.

. . . One of the small canoes was left below this rapid in order to pass and repass the river for the purpose of hunting as well as to procure the water of the Sulpher spring, the virtues of which I now resolved to try on the Indian woman. . . . I found that two dozes of barks and opium which I had given her since my arrival had produced an alteration in her pulse for the better; they were

Mother with baby in cradleboard, ca. 1880.

> now much fuller and more regular. I caused her to drink the mineral water altogether. She complains principally of the lower region of the abdomen, I therefore continued the cataplasms of barks and laudanum which had been previously used by my friend Capt. Clark. I believe her disorder originated principally from an obstruction of the mensis in consequence of taking could.
>
> Monday June 17th 1805
>
> . . . The Indian woman much better today; I have still continued the same course of medicine; she is free from pain clear of fever, her pulse regular, and eats as heartily as I am willing to permit her of broiled buffaloe well seasoned with pepper and salt and rich soupe of the same meat; I think therefore that there is every rational hope of her recovery.

Women could take little time from their vital work of hulling, hauling, rooting, sifting, drying, and gathering, to deliver a child. Even in advanced stages of pregnancy, Blackfoot women, swollen and uncomfortable, would strap themselves into broad, adjustable rawhide belts that allowed them to ride horseback and bend over at the same time, gathering food.

Surprises were avoided. Since tribes were migratory, a certain delivery date would help a woman plan the location of the birthing hut, as well as informing them whether or not they would deliver during a new moon—a sign of luck. A swath of brilliant moonlight would "pull" the child into existence, hence the Navajo saying "A child is born when the moon is straight overhead."

Lore, myth, and carefully proscribed taboos prevailed, usually dictating which foods at what temperature and in which amounts to eat during pregnancy. Although most women ate meat, Kiowa Apaches refused to eat it from the bone, seeing a difficult birth in the clinging shreds. Nor could they eat fat, since it resembled the "white stuff" covering the baby. Young children could not be placed on the lap of a pregnant woman, as it would "harden" the baby inside. Mothers were to urinate downstream. The afterbirth, a fearful thing, must be hidden, with the umbilical cord disposed of ritually. Sitting in the sun after the child's birth was forbidden since the afterbirth might be affected.

An Indian woman's term of delivery was served in a conical, hive-shaped birth hut, fashioned from twigs or grass and ideally near a stream for washing up. The Nevada Paiutes believed the tiny "Moon House" protected others from the "contamination" of a birth ordeal. A woman without a hut delivered within the home tents, or hogans, forcing the men to sleep elsewhere. Two primary fears were falling asleep, which would leave a woman defenseless and prey to evil spirits, or cold, which might cause her death. To insure warmth, fire-warmed stones were gently laid over the Modoc woman's abdomen and alongside the bed, while handfuls of hot kelp pressed along the mother's stomach and back kept the Pacific Coast Kwakiutl mother warm. Heated sand, spread between cloths, made an instant hot blanket, while California tribal women, according to historian Julie Goldsmith, lay atop a pit lined with heated rocks and ashes and were buried in the warm sand.

Contractions were quickened with corn smut or with blue cohosh, called squawroot. Cottonroot bark, rich in vitamin E, also had strong oxytocic, or contraction-causing properties. Soothing teas were imbibed during pregnancy and after delivery, with the Cherokees using a strong brew of partridgeberry, or squaw vine, while Zuni women turned to a brew of roasted cedar twigs.

Births took place in squatting, or crouching position, with a woman pulling grimly on a rope or leather strap to force the child out. As the baby emerged, great care was taken to keep him clean. Many, like the Northern Plains Osages, wiped the infant clean with handfuls of absorbent moss while the healing aroma of a burning sagebrush, kindled in a shallow pit, purified and scented the air. The birthing ground should be warm to greet the emerging child—the fire was damped into embers, covered with woven rye grass, then laid over with a clean quilt or cloth made from pounded and woven sagebrush bark. As the mother crouched on her hands and knees and pushed, the baby dropped down. If all the rules were followed—the ground heated, the drinking water warmed—a birth would go well. The postpartum mother would stay sequestered in the Moon House for nearly a month, then rejoined the tribe dressed in fresh clothes, her face painted with white clay—delighted to eat a full meal after her monthlong fast.

Children meant prestige, and the more children, the greater the

Lizzie Quintana and Jessie Arche "playing house" in Washington State, 1899.

parents' honor. So integral was parenthood that in many tribes, a man was not an adult unless he had fathered children—except for twins. According to historian Edna Patterson, that occurrence ranged from being mildly embarrassing evidence of excessive sexual intercourse to breaking a taboo, in which case one of the pair would be killed at birth. Infanticide was commonly practiced, particularly when a mother died in childbirth. If twins lived after the mother's death, they must be immediately separated, since it was believed that one would suck the life away from the other.

Fertility was governed by cycles of famine and plenty, with births limited to only what a tribe could bear. Parents who failed at birth control were held in low esteem, since natural abortifacients abounded. Ergot, a dark fungus growth that covered rye grass, could powerfully convulse the uterus into violent expulsion. A more gentle means, although still effective, was aromatic, wild geranium root tea, sipped while lying in a trench filled with warm ashes. Juniper berry tea was effective if drunk a cup at a time, three days in a row. Conversely, a woman who feared miscarriage could drink black haw-bark decoction to soothe the uterus.

DEATH STRUCK SWIFTLY and unexpectedly. In the native world, cycles of demise and rebirth were seen in lunar rhythms and yearly seasons. Families lived with death, expected death, and faced it bravely, taking the pragmatic approach of the Santa Domingo pueblo tribe in New Mexico, who believed that:

> The child is dead. If . . . people did not die, the world would fill up and there would be no place for you to live.

More wisdom was offered in the excerpt from the tribe's "Song of a Child's Spirit."

> *When a cloud comes this way, you will say, That is he . . . !"*

"Naming" brought the child into a family fraternity of secrecy, since names were never spoken aloud to prevent their lighthearted use in songs and stories, and worse, spells being cast upon that person through the use of the name. Girls were named after household items, and boys after animals and birds, with the appellations celebrated by joyful parents, who would host an elaborate naming ceremony, showering friends and family with gifts. Poor children, however, went officially unnamed, at least until someone could afford to give a feast. Without the official celebration, they were known by nickname only.

A child's life and fate was often determined by omens—whatever item fell into a child's reach and attracted its attention would determine his future path. Dreams were also portents. In the words of an unnamed Winnebago Indian, called only "S.B.":

> Father and mother had four children and after that I was born, it is said. An uncle of mother's who was named White-Cloud, said to her, "You are to give birth to a child who will not be an ordinary person." Thus he spoke to her. It was then my mother gave

birth to me. As soon as I was born and was being washed—as my neck was being washed—I laughed out loudly.

I was a good-tempered boy, it is said. At boyhood my father told me to fast and I obeyed. In the winter every morning I would crush charcoal and blacken my face with it. I would rise very early and do it. As soon as the sun rose I would go outside and sit looking at the sun and I would cry to the spirits.

Thus I acted until I became conscious.

Strength, piety and endurance were sought—children should be able to face dire circumstances, and to do so, learned to fast at an early age. Each year the fasting became more extreme, until by childhood's end, twenty-four hours could pass without food, or with only a minimum break. Recalled by S.B.:

At first I broke my fast at noon and then, after a while, I fasted all night. From the fall of the year until spring I fasted throughout the day until nightfall, when I would eat. After a while I was able to pass the night without eating and after a while I was able to go through two nights (and days) without eating any food. Then my mother went out in the wilderness and built a small lodge. This, she told me, she built for me to fast in, for my elder brother and myself, whenever we had to fast through the night.

Tribal life, always communal, meant that the tending of children was shared by all clan members, with patrilineal women playing an important role in the actual birth, as well as the naming rites. One might become a "ceremonial mother" and develop a close, long-lasting relationship with the child. Nearly half of the North American Indian groups were matrilineal, bestowing greater status to the woman's line and making her brother superior to her husband, with children calling the maternal uncle "father." Hopi children addressed both a mother and her sisters by the kinship term for mother, *inqu'u.* The offspring of sisters were called *iti'i,* or kinship siblings, and would naturally be adopted by the surviving sister.

"We are taught to love everybody," said Paiute Sarah Winnemucca. "We don't need to be taught to love our fathers and mothers. We love them without being told to." A young Cheyenne girl, trying to describe her parents' devotion to her, said, "They treated me as if I were a male member of the family. They took the greatest pains to have me well dressed—even my saddle was decorated." In their close-knit, supportive world, to be humble was the greatest virtue, and both children and adults disliked being singled out for praise.

The degree and intensity of a parent's love defies cultural comparison. Expressions might differ within cultures, but tenderness of heart is most certainly the same. If a Native American child was lost or stolen, the parents mourned continually, never forgetting, hoping for the child's return, and constantly planning the means of retrieval. When Oglala chief Red Fish's daughter was captured by enemy Crows, his grief was boundless. Taking eighty "fine buffalo robes and his best horse" to Fort Pierre, he begged Jesuit missionary Father de Smet, traveling through the Midwest in 1849, to invoke the white God's help. "I am a most unhappy father! I have lost my beloved daughter. . . . Speak to the Master of Life in my favor, and I will still preserve hope of seeing my child."

In another case, Stephen Powers, an early traveler in California, observed the tenderness of a Miwok father toward his son.

I have seen a father coddle and teeter his baby in [the water] for an hour with the greatest patience; then carry him down to the river, laughing good-naturedly; gently dip the [child] in the waves all over, then lay him on the moist, warm sand. The treatment . . . stopped the [child's] squalling all at once."

In a touching example of father-son intimacy, S.B., the Winnebago boy, wrote of his parent's role in his fasting ceremony. The father came each night to encourage his son in the arduous task, showing a deep degree of emotion and intimacy to the boy.

The second night, rather late in the night, my father came and opened the war-bundle and taking a gourd out began to sing. I stood beside him without any clothing on me except the breech-clout, and holding tobacco in each hand I uttered my cry to the spirits as my father sang. He sang war bundle songs and he wept as he sang. I also wept as I uttered my cry to the spirits. When he was finished he told me some sacred stories, and then went home.

Gender emphasis varied by tribe. Among the strongly matrilineal Zuni, girls were preferred, which forced the father to stay away during the delivery for fear that the baby might "catch" his unfortunate gender, prompting a favorite admonition: "Don't sleep or you will have a boy!" Brothers and sisters, however, shared a particular kind of relationship. "[They] hardly spoke to each other because of the deep respect they held. . . . There was no joking around. . . . Brothers would never kid their sisters. If someone said something [funny] about a sister or brother . . . [the brother] would have to leave the room in order not to show disrespect," according to Laura Black Bear Miles, a Cheyenne from Red Moon, Oklahoma. No brother would ever call his sister a liar, and a sister lent her brother continual support.

Respect, in fact, was sought in every situation, and was demanded of children, who learned quickly that adults must be catered to, obeyed, have their privacy respected, and be given the warmest place near the fire on a cold day. Conversely, adults could not borrow or remove a child's possessions without asking permission, since they were inviolate, and thus, secure. Respect afforded a child his individuality, which resulted in the child's own generosity. Moral emphasis also included giving, and children learned early that any stroke of good fortune must be shared with the neediest family members, since to hoard or overconsume wealth was considered unbalanced. To be a part of life's natural flow, plenty must be released back into the world. Yet realistically, children had individual temperaments, leading to different behavior, bad and good. Life took different shapes in different people, lending particular interest to the account of S.B., who wrestled with selfishness in his life:

> We were three boys, of whom I was the youngest, and at night we used to sleep together. In cold weather we used to fight as to who was to sleep in the middle for whoever got that place was warm . . . it became a habit with me to take the covers away from the other person.

Food deserved deep respect, and if it was heedlessly eaten a mother would quietly take the rest away, since polite tradition dictated light, although often continuous, eating in as peaceful a setting as possible. Favorite dishes, such as savory corn pemmican made of compressed juneberries, suet, and dried, ground corn, were nibbled discreetly with eyes cast down, the eater careful not to appear greedy. Less savory dishes, such as boiled prairie turnips, were eaten slowly not for ceremony, but because the taste was flat and washy. Children observed silence at meals, yet interestingly, the same rambunctious spirit seen in all children translated into Native American means and manners, at least according to the writings of the Winnebago boy S.B.

> We always ate out of one dish. Sometimes we did not have enough food on hand and then I would always try to get enough by eating very fast. In this way I always succeeded in depriving the others of their proper portion. Sometimes, on the other hand, I would purposely eat slowly, and then when the others were finished, I would say that I had not been given enough and so I would get some of their food. In this way I developed a habit (that I still have), for I am a fast eater. Even when I grew up, whenever I ate with other people, I always finished sooner than they.

As for discipline? Each tribe wielded its own threats, the worst being that an unruly child would magically turn into a huge, heavy boulder—an unteachable rock child, an outcast, even likely to be killed. For Hopi youth, the specter of the child-eating kachina, Soyoko, was terrifying, since it loved to eavesdrop on parents' complaints and then concoct a revenge. Children lucky enough *not* to be eaten had other punishments in store.

Education came from testing the air, studying the ground, interpreting the patterned track of a wary animal, and sniffing a lingering scent for identification and for determining the possibility of danger. Teachers were many, each with specific talents to impart to the new generation, taking handfuls of meal or other food as payment. A recognized fisherman would teach boys how to fashion a net and how to throw a spear neatly into the water after tracking the fish, anticipating every turn in advance. Typically, the teacher of tracking, weaving, fishing, or hunting could be found at the center of an eager ring of children, who were working hard to memorize the myths, songs, and rituals.

Rigorous mental and physical training began at the age of three or four. For safety's sake, children had to memorize every hillock, river, rock, and tree of their immediate terrain, learning by instinct the boundaries of the tribal territory. How else to keep from getting lost, kidnapped, or killed? Marksmanship was critical. White settlers were continually amazed at the speed and skill demonstrated by Indians, such as the Snake youth who could, according to historian John Bauer, "hit a mark at fifteen paces" with an arrow. One settler dared three boys to hit his hat, which he balanced in the air, taunting them with the distant target. The boys looked knowingly at one another, took casual aim, and smiled as the arrows spiraled down, piercing the hat squarely in the crown. Indian youths delighted in shooting down gold coins flipped into the air—particularly if the target was the reward. They hunted small game, and if a squirrel was spied ducking and scampering, the boys streaked toward it without hesitating, aimed in midrun, fired, and usually hit it—following the technique of "ready, then fire," or intuitive aiming. Hunger was the only reason to kill, and the entire animal must be used, with no part destroyed or wasted. Every child learned self-control—what else was reasonable?

Girls learned adult rituals through "tiny play," or games that imitated grown-up customs. Recalled one Cheyenne woman, as cited by ethnologist Truman Michaelson:

> Our mothers made rag dolls of women, men, boys, girls, and babies. We used forked sticks to represent ponies, and we mounted the tiny people on the fork of the sticks, pretending to move camp. Sometimes a baby would be born; or a marriage would take place—in fact anything that we knew about older people. In this play we did not allow any boys to play with us girls. We had rag dolls to represent boys.
>
> After a time as I became a little older we played "large play." This play consisted of real people, namely boys and girls. The boys would go out hunting (really, go to their tipis) and bring meat and other food. We girls would pitch our tipis and make ready everything as if it were a real camp life. Some of the boys would go on the warpath, and always came home victorious. . . . We girls would sing war songs. . . . Sometimes we had the Sun Dance. In this play we didn't use real food, but baked mud bread and used leaves for dishes. . . . we would have our [play] children's ears pierced and gave away horses. Some of the boys would have their breasts pierced with cactus thorns, others dragged buffalo skulls (which were really chunks of dead wood).

North Dakota Indian father with children, ca. 1899. Photo by Frank B. Fiske.

Games sharpened skill and alacrity, and were enjoyed by lines of children who jostled and pushed one another, their polished oak sticks thrust high, surging upward toward the stuffed buckskin balls. In one game, boys chewed green clover into a dense, wet mass, then spat the pellets to the next person, who caught them by mouth. As thinly disguised endurance tests, games were a way for strength and courage to be tried. Even hair pulling taught youngsters restraint and to not cry.

Children were honed and toughened, strained and stretched. How else to endure the freezing winters, long seasonal marches, drought, and food deprivation? In a test of strength, Cheyenne boys were drilled with sharp bone needles and forbidden to cry during the process. They were plunged into icy water, stung with ants and centipedes, and forced to run for miles under the scorching sun with only a mouthful of water, which they were forbidden to swallow. Blackfoot boys as young as three began each day, summer or winter, with a plunge in the river. If no water was nearby, they rolled in the snow naked, then shivered in the weight of their stiff buckskin clothes. This icy wake-up inured them to the cold, giving them the strength to hunt in severe winter temperatures "without freezing even their fingertips."

"Be brave! Be honest, be virtuous, be industrious, be generous, do not quarrel!" Cheyenne children were exhorted. Unremitting sermonizing reinforced tribal values, and even at day's end, the lessons continued during story time. Children thrilled to fireside tales of adventure as they shared strips of broiled buffalo tongue or cooked puppy or berry pemmican, savoring the food while held in thrall by adult tales of hunting, war, discovery, love, and conquest.

MANHOOD SEEMED ELUSIVE at times, yet the paths leading to it were ritually set. A southwestern youth of the Maricopa or other Arizona tribes would reach maturity by drinking a thick concoction of jimson weed during his vision quest, which caused an explosion of carnival-like, vivid hallucinations. Alone, hungry, and cold, the boy would crouch in a handmade shelter far from the tribe's encampment, tuned only to the wheeling lights of a private world, awaiting cues from the spirit world. S.B. was frustrated after three days of fasting and waiting without any spirit contact. "That morning I told my elder brother that I had been blessed by spirits and that I was going home to eat. However I was not telling the truth. I was hungry and I also knew that on the following night we were going to have a feast. . . . So I went home."

Young girls initiated into womanhood represented the fecundity that seemed to burst up from the earth, itself a living entity, fertile as a woman. The Eastern Dakota purity ceremony began when a young girl came forward, touched a round stone, and swore that she was pure. If truthful, the stone stayed still. If she had lied, it wobbled and toppled over.

In most tribes, chastity was preserved at all costs, insured by parental closeness.

> I had a bed of my own in my parents' tipi [consisting] of willow head and foot uprights. My own bags were placed against the wall of the tipi. The wall of the bed also included buffalo hides. My pillows were decorated with porcupine quills. My bed was always placed farthest from the door of the tipi, the place of honor. . . . My mother would always tell me that the . . . object of my owning my own bed was to keep me at home, and to keep me from being away at night with my girl chum.

And no wonder. S.B., so intent on stealing covers from his brothers and inventing his spirit blessing, wreaked havoc at the lodges of young girls, who were carefully guarded at all times. One mother was so worried about her daughter that she slept with her at night.

> We nevertheless bothered her all the time just out of meanness. One night we went there and kept her awake almost all night. However, just about dawn she fell asleep, so we—there were several of us—pulled up the whole lodge, poles and everything, and threw the poles in the thicket. The next morning the two were found sleeping in the open . . . and the mother was criticized for being over careful.

No child went without chores, and American Indians, continually on the move, attuned to seasons, sun, and game routes, naturally fell into the rhythm of work. During the Montana heat of June and July, Assiniboin children would uproot wild turnips with a pointed stick, the boys scouting out the roots, then signaling back to a contingent of diggers—aunts, sisters, and grandmothers, many with dim eyesight from a lifetime of campfire smoke, who needed the clear-eyed youngsters to help them gather. In summer, juneberries hung in patient clusters, ready to be swiped by hungry bears or children. Grandmothers dried the berries and used them to stuff berry bags, shaped like mock fawns and made of tanned deer skin, still covered with hair, its holes sealed, and set on wobbly legs. Children eagerly gathered cherries, sucking the sweet runoff after crushing them on rocks. The pulp was squeezed into patties and left to dry in the sun. Even the youngest hunters could stalk wild turkey, sage hen, mourning dove, quail, owl, and eagles, or at least gather *pigli,* the soft, yellow caterpillars, which they turned over quickly to their mothers to clean. The head was pulled down between thumb and first finger, and the bodies split open and cleaned. The remains were braided into a three-foot-long rope, cooked, and dried between two stone slabs.

ONE OF THE gravest threats to afflict young Indian children was the slave trade. "My mother used to hide me or make me hide whenever the white people came because we had heard of Indian children who had been kidnapped. We usually hid in the bushes," said Pomo Elsie Allen. "What a fright we all got one morning to hear some white people were coming. Every one ran as best they could," recalled Paiute Sarah Winnemucca. And no wonder. Kidnapping had begun with the Spanish padres, who kept young children confined in the California missions where they worked as servants by day and were kept locked in their dorm rooms at night. Girls were imprisoned from the age of nine until maturity, or until they married or managed to escape. Slavery was also carried out by warring tribes, by the French, who used Indian slaves as guides to the Great Plains and as labor on Louisiana plantations, and by California miners, who commonly stole Indian children for sluice and pick work in the mines, barely allowing them food and clothing as payment. Slave raids in northern California, facilitated by the Vagabond Act of 1850, which allowed "loitering" Indians to be forced into lifelong indenture, exterminated vast numbers of Indian adults and scattered their young.

In the mid-1890s, federal officials, pondering the fate of so many Native American orphans, as well as uneducated children living with their parents, opened reservation boarding schools, or day schools, for elementary students, staffed by volunteer Protestant missionaries, whose cultural blunders were due more to ignorance than vengeance. In South Dakota, reservation school field matrons were married women who tried to view the Indian children as their own. The day a child was taken to Indian school was a tragic day, filled with the premonition of death, since countless Indian children had died at the mission schools from white-borne epidemics. Parents were convinced that any child who left for the schools would either die or lose their Indian heritage. The entire school population fled when Cayuse chief Waileptuleek's three children succumbed to fever at Oregon's Mission Manual Labor School. An Oregon mission school founded by Rev. Spalding fared better, with "a hundred, both old and young . . . in attendance. As soon as one had learned something more than the others, they would gather around him, while he

Arizona Navajo "Desert Madonna," ca. 1860.

would become their teacher." By 1839, 150 children, and as many more adults, attended. Among the Cayuse, "more were ready to attend school than the mission family could supply with books."

By the end of the Sioux War of 1877, the major Indian wars had been fought and the "enemy" virtually defeated, allowing a new Indian policy to arise. Anglos were content that the hunting days of the Native American had passed. Indian children needed agriculture, industrial skills, and general education to prepare for citizenship. By 1908, the Supreme Court decision of *Quick Bear* v. *Leupp* granted reservation Indians more autonomy, allowing them to send their children to the school of choice and to designate the family's share of tribal education funds to be transferred to that school's treasury.

The history of white and Native American interaction is one of fear, misunderstanding, and an ultimate destruction that weighed most heavily upon the children of those lost or vanquished tribes. Children were a tribe's wealth—they embraced the future with the knowledge and tools of the past. The frontier and its wide-open policy of Manifest Destiny, however, did not embrace the Native American.

23

Growing Up Black

De suckin' mothers was given light wuk.—*"Grammaw," slave narrative*

Marly Bright, Marly Bright
Three score and ten;
Kin you git up by candlelight?
Yes, lift your legs
Are long and limber and light
—*Singing game from Texas*

Just as strife raged during the Civil War, so the new states and territories of the West were thrown into turmoil by the question of "freedom or not" for blacks. In 1861, before the war, every black living in Texas, Oklahoma, and Utah was legally a slave, given the proslavery legislation of those states and territories. In Texas, there were 250,000 blacks by 1865, living in circumstances little different than the plantation regimen in the South—a harsh, daily schedule of picking cotton, harvesting, planting, chopping, and tending livestock, with little concessions made to age or gender. Women and children were expected to toil daily in the hot sun, and even on small farms their labor was involuntary and unrewarded.

Even neutral states such as California were plunged into dissension because of the number of slaveholders who emigrated west, taking along their family slaves and claiming rights of ownership. After emancipation, slavery was still violently defended in California and Oregon, and briefly promoted in New Mexico, although always countered by abolitionists. Interestingly, one of the strongest antislavery forces in the West proved to be miners, who admired independence and were irked by the use of slave labor to compete in mining.

After the Civil War, increasingly large numbers of blacks began to emigrate west. In 1879–80, an estimated twenty thousand ragged men, women, and children from Mississippi and Texas caught the "Kansas fever" and swept into the state, intoxicated by the idea of freedom. Families hoping to settle and farm came up the Mississippi by riverboat or slowly walked up the Chisholm Trail to Kansas—the place where John Brown had first struck out against slavery. Called the Exodusters, most relocated on homesteads in Kansas, while some drifted further west as cowboys and others enlisted as soldiers. Among the Kansas emigrants was John Solomon Lewis and his family, who were so delighted to reach their destination that they "held a little prayer meeting" upon arrival. Said Lewis: "I looked on the ground and I says this is free ground. Then I looked on the heavens, and I says them is free and beautiful heavens. Then I looked within my heart, and I says to myself, I wonder why I was never free before?"

Black family posed at dinner table, ca. 1880s.

For them, the burden of life under slavery was gone, with its desperation of mothers torn away from children and the ongoing agony of the separated family. In *The American Slave: A Composite Autobiography,* an extensive series of oral histories taken from 1936 to 1938, story after story recounts the personal depredations and loathing suffered during the years of slavery. No more would the "wail of many a child for its mother and mothers for her child" be heard, as described by ex-slave William Robinson. No more would plantation children be "rotated," with one child replacing another as each was taken to market and sold. "I come pretty near to bein' tuk away from my maw," said Henry Cheatam in an interview. "When de slaves was bein' divided, I was goin' to have to go [to Texas] when somebody hollered 'freedom,' an' I sure was glad 'cause I could stay with my mammy now." Women who bore children in slavery under threat of punishment, or for the trifling reward of a calico dress and a silver dollar, could now bear children in freedom.

In slavery's place, however, came the realization that emancipation did not mean integration, and that lingering, deep prejudice would plunge black Americans into lives of grinding poverty. Their farming efforts, at least in Kansas, were often unsuccessful, and families faced a daily struggle to keep their children supplied with "milk, rice, pot-licker, vegetables and corn dumplings."

Black children in the West grew up on subsistence farms, in one-room houses or sod caves dug in the river banks. Life began with the Docterin' Woman, who was called upon for home deliveries. She swaddled a newborn in a colorful, patterned quilt, secured it tightly with safety pins, and cautioned, "Don't move this quilt. Don't move the pins." A prevalent superstition, rooted in African lore, warned that evil spirits always traveled in a straight line and could be deflected by the bright jumble of mixed-up quilt patterns. As children grew, they learned to card, spin, weave, and work in the fields—whatever work had to be done. Dressed in homespun or flannel, they worked from sunup to sundown, spurred on by the great family hope of land ownership. But conditions were harsh—the first predominantly black western town of Nicodemus, Kansas, lost most of its wheat crop to a winter blizzard. Many were starving, and were given food by the neighboring Osage Indians from the tribe's scant rations, received at Fort Ogallala. For income, black children picked up buffalo bones on the prairie and sold them for six dollars per ton, while their parents tried to negotiate with resentful neighbors over property rights—few surveyors would come out to survey the homestead plots of the black settlers. Even if a child grew up emancipated, he or she would still face segregation and deep prejudice, which in turn, plunged black Americans into ever-deeper levels of family and social affinity.

Faith figured strongly in the black childhood, whether the child was born in slavery, lived an urban life after emancipation, or was part of a free family living on a farm. Religion was experiential, visionary, and community-based. Participation was a joyous outpouring of song, call and response, Bible verses, encouragement—even faith healings. "We walked until our shoes were worn out, and our feet became sore and cracked open and bled until you could see the whole print of our feet with blood on the ground," wrote Jane Manning on her way to Utah. "We stopped and united in prayer to the Lord, we asked God . . . to heal our feet and our prayers were answered." Such faith was needed, given the fact that blacks throughout the West, long after the end of the Civil War, were still sunk in a mire of prejudice.

As the number of black migrants increased, community tolerance declined. Moving west had been a mass effort to escape the restrictions of Jim Crow. Yet even antislavery states refused to extend full rights and privileges to black residents. Prohibitive laws and regulations followed them, particularly in Oregon and California. In 1830, there were thirteen thousand freed slaves in the territories. The number reached nearly fifty thousand by 1870. Oregon passed a stringent antiblack exclusion act in 1844, and resentments brewed in every community where black women, who worked as domestics, looked for work traditionally held by the Chinese. By 1890 California had a black population that was the largest of any in the states, including the southern states. Yet in California, blacks were unable to testify in courts, which made them voiceless victims of countless crimes. In Iowa, an early law limited the state's schools to whites only, although after emancipation there is some evidence in the census that black children were being admitted in spite of the exclusions. In most states or territories, the black population was so small that black pupils were grudgingly allowed in the classes—except in Kansas and California, where black students were forbidden from attending classes with whites. In angry response, black, middle-class taxpayers flooded the legislature with petitions. Black leaders established newspapers to explain civil rights, and black parents prepared to fight for their children's education.

Ex-slaves were obsessed by the idea of education—both theirs, and their children's. An account in Delilah L. Beasley's *The Negro Trail Blazers of California* tells of the educational odyssey of Biddy Mason, an uneducated slave girl and single mother of three daughters who came west with a slave-owning Mormon family before the Civil War. Once in California, she was struck by the number of free blacks, and in 1856, petitioned for freedom for herself and her family. After a long struggle she obtained her papers, and then attended public school in Oakland, along with her children. The sons of her second marriage were also educated, studying by night at a business college because they were not allowed to be seen by day.

For Daniel Rogers, education was also a firm goal. His first attempt to reach California was thwarted because his wife lacked her "freedom paper," and on his second try, he successfully took his family of ten children across the plains by wagon and ox team. When settled, he immediately applied to the school board of the township for a school for his children, as well as a teacher. The board was so slow in its response that his oldest daughter married and gave birth to several children before classes began. Finally, the mounting numbers of black children forced the board to open the school doors for the children of the town's two black families, who, according to Beasley, "still lived in Watsonville and were anxious for an education." Eventually the board of education "secured the services of a young white girl . . . a Miss Knowlton, who because of her own . . . spirit of the Abolitionist, gave so much of her personal interest to the welfare of the children that they became devoted to her."

Part of the educational dilemma was finding teachers. White instructors willing to teach black children were usually Quakers or other abolitionists, and their roles were so contrary to usual white behavior that they drew notice. Esther Whinery Wattles recalled meeting an acquaintance, Hiram Gilmore, who, she noted, was "engaged in teaching at a colored high school." He encouraged men to work "among the colored people" in Cincinnati and urged women to join the Ladies Antislavery Society. Even if teachers were willing to teach black children, they were often thwarted by school policies that demanded all-white classes, or worse, the segregating of isolated black students behind blankets or partitions. Midwestern instructor Georgiana Kirby was shocked at the school's request to judge the color of her pupils' skin and to segregate them by means of tinted cards.

EDUCATIONAL DIFFICULTIES CROSSED all economic lines for black Americans. Not only did poor children suffer, but also those of the rising middle class. Attending school was expensive—even for an educated woman such as Pauline Williamson, who arrived in Oakland, California, in 1885 to establish a better life for herself and her son, Harry. Despite her nursing skills, middle-class parents, and an aunt who was willing to take them in, Pauline was unable to provide needed child care, pay for books, and keep up with the cost of Harry's clothes. She wrote to her sister, May:

> It will be some work getting myself educated, but my greatest drawback will be Harry. You see . . . there are a great number of days when [Mrs. Thomas] is ailing and she is easily worried, and very nervous. . . . You know Harry's disposition, and although he really tried . . . to be good, when I am gone away to work he will be troublesome. Aunt Susan is too old to take any care of him, and he needs a good deal of looking after and keeping out of mischief . . . you well know what the care of a child of that age is, then he will not always mind as readily as he should. . . . Should I try to send him away to a good school and let him stay there until he gets older? He really needs the guidance of a man. . . . With only three old women, I don't see how it will work.

The struggle to provide even the most basic necessities seemed overwhelming. "Harry will need a pair of shoes," she wrote. "I can make his old over coat do, and I had some clothes given me which I have cut over for him." Clinging to the margins of middle-class respectability, she tried to keep her son in school, but had overlooked an even greater drawback—his own reluctance to be there, at least for a while:

> School seems to disagree with him. He has been out . . . for a week, and I do not think he will go back again until after vacation . . . he is working. . . . He goes to work at six o'clock in the morning and gets home a little after eight at night . . . he is in a private family boarding house as a bell boy, he gets three dollars a week, one day he made 25 cents and yesterday he made 45 cents. . . . He is perfectly crazy about earning some money.

Middle-class black children were set high goals by their parents, who were beginning to achieve success in their own pursuits. Florence Sanderson, the daughter of the famed minister and educator Jeremiah Sanderson, had to show signs of progress in every area. She wrote to him in 1868:

> Don't laugh at this letter because it is my first letter, and I tried to do my best. In your letter . . . yesterday you [wanted] a specimen of my penmanship, and I have tried to do so to the best of my ability.

Progress grappled with prejudice—even education could not dispel the influence of racism. One of the worst examples, noted by historian Jim Silverman, is a fairy tale by Florence Crocker, in which the black son of a house servant yearns to be white like the children of his employer. On an outing at a lake, he gazes out at the swans, admiring their white feathers. When he falls in the water and nearly drowns, he begs to be turned into a swan. His wish is granted, and he is transformed—but into a *black* one. Incredibly, he is seen floating away with little Bessie, the white child, on his back. Further narrative perambulations reinforce the value of white over black.

Eventually, societies began to form in the frontier black communities, generally around the churches. Children increasingly attended school. Bazaars and church functions raised money for education and investments, and, as time went on, some fortunes were slowly amassed. Children could be raised with more ease and protection, yet always within the shadow of the white community, which limited opportunity and spread judgment for years to come.

According to Delilah L. Beasley's informative compilation of records from diaries and papers from the Bancroft Library, published in 1919, California was full of success stories. Wrote Beasley,

Moses Speese family near Westerville, Custer County, Nebraska, 1888.

"it should be inspiring because [so many] never for a moment lost [their] great ambition to better not only [personal] conditions, but that of their race. In fact, the Colored Convention of California, which had met as early as the 1890s, decreed "we intend to disprove the allegation that we are naturally inferior. The colored people of Nevada County possess property to the amount of $3,000,000 in mining claims, water, ditch stock and real estate." Laborers, artisans, ministers and merchants tended toward an upward mobility as soon as they had the income to acquire property. There were numerous, prospering black farmers and ranchers, including Mr. and Mrs. Lewis Washington Brunson, who started by vending vegetables and who, by 1917, were harvesting potatoes from ten fertile acres. "They killed one hog in the fall, and after saving enough meat to last them for two years, they rendered from this same hog ninety pounds of lard. Mr. Brunson is most happily married to Miss Mary Calbert. . . . He owns a Buick auto of the latest model, five head of horses and all the latest models of farm implements." Vocations and lifestyles in the middle-class black community were varied, from those of poetess, modiste, civic worker, and author to the inventor of a toilet cream, a cateress, songstress, hotelier, furniture dealers, and members of women's clubs and charities. Governor Stockton of California was given a banquet in his honor at the home of William

Leidsdorff, a wealthy pioneer of mixed racial ancestry, including black, who owned the first steamer to pass through the Golden Gate.

How to understand the role of blacks in the political, economic, and social development of the West and to fathom their struggle for equality has been history's task. To understand their children, as well, has proved more difficult. Growing up without national heroes, outside the circle of white society, they formed close bonds within their own, tight-knit communities. They moved where there was work—railroads, mines, farms—and thrived where there were laws against the introduction of slavery. As their children grew, so did their traditions, creating a legacy for the scions of slavery, and their children to come.

24

Asians in the New Land

> A man is not a success unless he is married and has a family, because to fail in this is to fail in life.—*Japanese proverb*

Asians who came to Washington, Oregon, and California stirred up particular animosity among western Americans. They were seen as strikebreakers who worked for low wages in dangerous situations and whose habits of careful economy were antithetical to the spendthrift style of the rowdy miners. They were hated for being foreign, caricatured as smoking opium, speaking unintelligibly in singsong Chinese, and for having heathen gods, joss houses, and gambling dens—not to mention their residence in squalid, fire-prone shacks and shanties in the confines of their special quarters in the ghettos of Chinatown. Worse, the wealthy Chinese merchants wore bracelets and brocaded, fur-lined gowns as women did, and indicated their leisure status with fingernails that were three-inches long. "Give us white men for a white man's country!" cried a banner headline in Boise, Idaho, a sentiment echoed throughout the country as such unseemly decadence was decried. In reality, the greatest complaint lodged against the "social nuisance" of the Chinese was their frugality—they worked for two dollars a day while American miners demanded four, saving nearly every penny toward their return home. As noncitizens without civil and legal rights, the unfortunate "Celestials" were swindled, beaten, and robbed at every turn. Their inability to testify in court led to the phrase "He doesn't have a Chinaman's chance."

Chinese children were rarely seen on the streets of mining towns or those along the Pacific Coast. Most had been left behind, as men indentured themselves to Chinese "companies" to work, hopefully sending money home to their families. In 1868 the Burlingame Treaty between the United States and China provided for free emigration and immigration to citizens of both countries, and promised to alien residents all the rights enjoyed by citizens. An 1870 law stated that Chinese women wishing to emigrate to America had to prove "correct habits and good character" to the United States commissioner of immigration—they could purchase tickets only if they won approval. After the Exclusion Act of 1882, the only women admitted were wives of merchants, officials, students, or teachers. The sum total of Chinese women in the United States in 1900 was 4,522. Legislation prohibited the hundred thousand Chinese living here from becoming citizens, owning land, working in California corporations, or attending white schools.

By the 1900s, more Chinese children could be seen, the boys with their long, braided queues, hurrying along to avoid the taunts of "Girls! Girls!"—an image not helped by the baggy silk pantaloons that flapped in the breeze. Embarrassed and frightened, they pleaded

Unidentified Chinese family in Idaho, ca. 1890s.

with their parents for permission to wrap their braids around their heads to hide their traditional hair under the coolie hat.

Although glimpsed on the streets, Chinese children were rarely seen in school, even though in San Francisco the board of education allowed Chinese students into the evening school's foreign classes as early as 1859. Only boys, however, became students. "I no educate my daughter," said one Chinese man. 'Women don't need education." He understood that if Chinese girls and women were educated, they could no longer be kept in traditional female seclusion and domesticity. The Chinese transported to California the practices of having several wives and of women and young girls being forced to have bound "lily" feet. American missionaries tried to prevail against this practice. "I am happy to say that I have now but eighteen little-footed girls, as I have been able to persuade parents against the cruel practice of bandaging their children's feet," stated Emma R. Cable in a report on the Chinese Mission Home.

A number of children were smuggled into the country to be sold as slaves or held until they were old enough to become prostitutes, and the mistreatment of them as chattel stands in odd contrast to the historic value that the Chinese place on family ties. Many must have come from families in desperate poverty or were orphans. Girls were considered more expendable than boys. Stories of their horrible fates have been documented by the Presbyterian missionaries who ran a Mission Home Day School.

> Little five year old Ah Seen was brought from China to San Francisco, by a Chinese woman, in the autumn of 1884. The woman had no certificate, as required by the Custom Officials, and being refused a landing, abandoned the child . . . she was left entirely alone in the hold of the ship . . . she was so dazed and sick that she could hardly speak, and seemed to have no interest in any thing. . . . Her body was covered with ugly sores. After having a bath, and a clean suit of clothes, she was given food and then put to bed, where she slept for nearly two days. With the use of simple remedies she began to improve in health, but for weeks she was silent, only speaking when spoken to.

Smuggled children were routinely used as slaves. "We came to a door which stood ajar; pushing it open and stepping within, the first sight to greet our eyes was little Yute Ying seated on the floor sewing buttons on to factory garments which were piled by the dozens around her." The Presbyterian women carried her out of the "degradation and misery" in one of thousands of rescues of Chinatown children in San Francisco between 1870 and 1890. In another account:

> Mae Seen [was] smuggled across the ocean with other girls in the coal bunkers of a Pacific mail liner, and landed under darkness of night by means of a coal bucket in which she was swung over the side of the ship onto a barge, from that into a boat, and rowed over to the Alameda flats, landed there and hidden in Oakland for months; then sold to a woman well-known among those who deal in human merchandise.

In hundreds of primary accounts, the individual stories of rescued girls are told. No child could be rescued unless she called for it, either by prearranged signal, or running away from her owners. The story of Chin Mui is typical.

> Chin Mui was born in 1869, of Chinese parents, in what she calls the "Indian country" among the California mines. Her father, Ah Lok, was a miner. Her mother, A'Gunn, a lover of bad whiskey. The father was kind to her, but the mother neglected her for drink. One little brother was a great deal more kindly treated, but he was a boy, and was attractive, too. There were frequent whiskey quarrels in the family when Ah Lok refused to replenish the bottle. . . . At last Ah Lok took Chin Mui to the Ophir Mine, and gave her to an old miner, named Ah Gos. Here the child's suffering really began. Ah How and his cruel old wife beat her upon every pretext, without mercy.
>
> One day she was sent to buy some food, when failing to find the place, she was gone a long time, and returned without the food. In anger, the woman shut her in a chicken-coop as punishment.
>
> Three days she was kept there without food. When released, the fear and exposure had paralyzed the optic nerve, and she was totally blind. She was then six years old. For one year longer she lived with the old miner, receiving no better treatment. As she was now a burden, her father was sent for to take her away. He may have had a little natural affection for the child, since he brought her to a physician in San Francisco, who pronounced her hopelessly blind. Upon hearing this, Ah Lok left her with friends for a few days, and went to visit at another place. This was, doubtless, a plan to get rid of his child, and his friends evidently thought so too, for they at once turned her out on the street. How long she wandered about she cannot tell.
>
> One evening, a Chinese interpreter of the courts, while walking through an alley, heard one woman call to her friend across the street, "Do you want to buy a girl?" "For how much?" Was the reply: "Oh, not much, for nothing."
>
> Thinking this strange, inquiry was made, and in finding it a case of need, he told "Spanish Charlie," a mongrel Chinaman, to care for the child. Charlie, being kindly disposed, brought the little thing to the home, 933 Sacramento Street.

This is Chin Mui's desolate life, as we know it, up to May 28, 1858, when she became an inmate of the home.

In more stable homes, children knew that just as they were dependent when young, so their parents would be when old, and the tight network of interdependency made them stay closely together. If a father went off to work the mines, the son would go too. Who else would care for him if something went awry? Many expected to return to China to live again, and it took time to realize that they would stay here for life.

Wealth was counted in generations, and the respect given to elders came from their venerable link with the past. Obeisances were made to ancestors, including parents, and it was the Chinese custom for the first-born son to take care of his parents and to look after the rest of the family.

When the missionary women would visit a home, their first plea was for the education of the children, and peripherally, for the cleaning up and enhancing of the home. They urged Westernization on the Chinese, in the form of papering the walls and carpeting the floors. One missionary was delighted to find progress on one of her visits:

> Imagine our delight upon the next visit to find on the walls gilt paper, pictures, the wood work grained, a beautiful Brussels carpet, and in the center of the room, a table on the cover of which lay the books, with chairs surrounding it—all ready for teachings.

A typical household might consist of "two wives, one of them little-footed, seven children . . . and two servant girls." Often, parents did not speak English, and insisted that children speak Chinese at all times. Insular people, they followed the proverb, "Each sweeps the snow from before his own door; none cares about the frost on another's roof." Parents insisted on keeping daughters home. They stayed in another room when the mission women came to teach—until the singing. "This proves too much for the mothers, they timidly open the door and come in, and are soon followed by two servant girls, one with a baby on her back."

In Chinatowns across the country, immigrant families lived with all generations crowded into one dark, smoke-filled room, with a few bricks to cook by and matting on the dirt floor. Nevertheless, the care of parents and grandparents was a moral obligation. To them, Americans, with their lack of respect for elders and head-

Chinese child watching the passing scene, Sacramento, California, ca. 1870.

strong independence, were barbarians, who, when they ate in restaurants, their settings looked afterward like a "wolf's den," and where, of all things, "men and women sat together with their shoes touching."

Chinese children grew up with the ethic of filial piety. To learn to honor a parent was the first step toward traits that would naturally follow, such as obeying a ruler, venerating elders, and caring for the young. Such interdependence formed the essence of China's greatness, was woven into the fiber of a family network, and, the emigrants hoped, imported to the narrow streets and incense-wafting rooms of Chinatowns throughout the New World.

Children were indulged with small gifts at every chance. The Chinese loved youth and lavished gifts upon them, whether the children were Chinese or white. In the spring, kites filled the air over Chinatown. Built as elaborate replicas of birds, spiders, and butterflies, they often emitted a loud buzz as they dipped and swooped, due to a small air device attached to the head of the kite. This airy carnival tantalized the white children, drawn by the mad swoops and dips of the wind-borne shapes. On Chinese New Year, elaborate floats with bright paper and flashing gold accents would trundle down the streets, surrounded by men dressed as dragons, to the sound of exploding firecrackers. Drums, horns, and cymbals clashed and clanged, while cut paper resembling money drifted to the ground. Chinese holidays were celebrated and all religious practices observed, although Confucianism and Buddhism were ethical and social practices as well as religious.

"Going to work on Gold Mountain" was heard in Chinese villages—most of them Cantonese from the far south, who were unable to speak Mandarin—where single men or eldest sons would straighten their queues and set off down a dusty trail, through forests of tung trees, and occasional loquat, to the ocean, to find passage to the land of opportunity. In China, there were no more "iron rice bowls," or permanent jobs, for them—the villages were dying from hunger. The desire to be in America, to reap its rewards in order to send money home to debt-ridden families, was so strong it gave rise to a generation of "paper sons," or young men who would give up their family name in order to emigrate to America. As the "son" of an American father—one who profited from selling his patrimony—the boy could avoid the Exclusion Act and emigrate to America. Authorities anticipated the paper sons, and interrogations could last for several days. If the son failed to remember details of family and village life, he would be turned back.

Yet, like the American innovation of chop suey, the Chinese who lived in Chinatown dwellings, huddled in dim rooms, saving their

Chinese elder counsels young boy, ca. 1870.

pennies, or those who had families and lived as merchants or mine workers, slowly became Americanized. Children who had grown up amid idols, to the scent of burning peanut oil in a teakwood lantern, eventually grew accustomed to such indecent American customs as public displays of shaking hands, brushing cheeks, and even . . . kissing. Chinese placed the highest value on social propriety and cultural refinement. Chinese etiquette forbade physical contact with unrelated women.

Other transitions took place in America, where the pace of life excluded the thoughtful contemplation of the past and lessened many of the Chinese traditions, including the belief in ghosts. In such a busy land as America, children going to school, vending vegetables and poking tiny needles into embroidery hoops had no time for specters, unlike children in China. Wrote Fei Xiaotong, in recalling his boyhood in China in the early 1900s:

> When I was a boy . . . we lived in a big old building . . . [with] dark room that had never seen sunlight . . . in these dark and desolate rooms, there were more places for ghosts than for people . . . not a day passed when people did not talk of ghosts to scare or amuse us children . . . to a child like me brought up in a small town, people and ghosts were equally concrete and real . . . because I grew up half in a world of ghosts, I was particularly interested in them.

Chinese children in America were caught between two values—the slow, painstaking life of form and ritual, and the quick-paced life in America, in which risks were taken, schedules overturned, elders superceded, and the past ignored. Somehow, they had to satisfy their parents' respect for the past with the brash, new culture of which they were a part. It was a long, arduous struggle for the Chinese to become respected by whites. They were seen only as laundry operators or servants. Families taught their children that they were strangers in this land and must work hard and be patient if they were ever to make a place for themselves.

THE JAPANESE WHO came to the West arrived some years after the Gold Rush of 1849, too late to be considered pioneers, except in their role in the fledgling agriculture industry in California, Oregon, and Washington. Called "Issei," or first-generation pioneers, their children had to bridge a cultural gap between the traditions of a feudal society and a capitalist one. Between 1868 and 1907, 275,000 Japanese immigrated to America.

Conditions in Japan were ripe for emigration. Centuries of primogeniture insured that the oldest son, the *chonan,* would inherit the family holdings, leaving his brothers to either marry into another family with land, seek an apprenticeship in some trade, or "go somewhere" to seek their own fortune. Crop failures caused rice riots and prompted even more to seek a new life in America.

Those who arrived came from a history of deprivation. "My parents never bought a toy for me when I was a child. I had a knife, so I made my toys with it. Even now I make almost everything by myself. I was surprised that the children in this country couldn't make anything by themselves," recalled Miunejiro Shibata.

Deprived or not, the Japanese daughter was adept in sewing, flower arrangements, playing *samisen,* a three-stringed Japanese musical instrument, and the art of kindling a fire with a blowpipe to cook the daily rice. Girls traditionally wore silk kimonos, which fluttered and caught the light like the wings of butterflies. In America, they adopted more discreet dress, often a simple, dark gown cut American-style, or a high-waisted, high-collared dress with pinafore. "I was immediately outfitted with Western clothing at Hara's clothing store," wrote one young girl, upon arriving in the United States.

In a typical Japanese farming family, day was greeted with a flower offering at the family shrine, where a sutra was recited. "We couldn't eat breakfast till we worshipped at the altar," recalled Mrs. Kamechiyo Takahashi.

There were few Japanese women in the country in 1900—the entire Japanese population in 1900 was only 24,326, of which only 985 were women. By 1920, the number of Japanese women had risen to 22,193, which made family life possible.

Traditional Japanese marriage, or *omiai-kekkon,* was an arranged union, in which both families carefully considered the qualities and prospects of the pair and, after much expense, they were wed. In America, it was impossible to find women locally, so men sent their photographs home to their villages, to "court" a bride by image. The woman would send her photo in return, and if both families approved the match, a wedding took place. In Japan, both parties did not have to be physically present for the wedding—the faraway husband's photograph served as bridegroom, the bride's name was entered in her husband's register at the local government office, and the couple, married by proxy, were legally wed.

Once here, the brides often discovered that the men they had married were entirely different from the photographs—often, unfortunately so. One woman, longingly thinking of her marriage-to-be, resolved that "the heart of Japanese woman had to be sublime . . . [it] had to be as beautiful as Mt. Fuji."

Picture-bride marriages were anathema to established social customs in the United States, causing intense racism to spring up against the Japanese immigrants, most of whom lived in small fishing enclaves along the coast, or worked in fruit groves or on vegetable farms. Prejudice caused children to be excluded from San Francisco schools. In their defense, a message from President Theodore Roosevelt was delivered in San Francisco in 1906 on the situation affecting the Japanese.

> I call your especial attention to the very small number of Japanese children who attend school, to the testimony as to the brightness, cleanliness, and good behavior of these Japanese children in schools, and to the fact that, owing to their being scattered throughout the city, the requirement for them all to go to one special school is impossible. . . . There would be no objection whatever to excluding from the schools any Japanese on the score of age. It is obviously not desirable that young men should go to school with children. The number of Japanese attending the public schools in San Francisco is very small—my earnest hope is that . . . the citizens of San Francisco will refuse to deprive these young children of education and will permit them to go to the schools.

Typically, a Japanese immigrant home of the early 1900s was "fashioned out of boards and leaked, [without] eaves to drain the rain." One woman's family "passed the night with raincoats over our beds" to stay dry. Such huts were without water or electricity, and were lit by oil lamps, with water drawn from a nearby well. Individual sleeping areas were made by "stretching a rope across the room and hanging clothes from it."

Chinese family crossing street in Sacramento, California, ca. 1870.

The world of a Japanese American infant was spent in the protective embrace of a back sling worn by the mother as she worked. Snug and secure, the baby rode about the onion and garlic and lettuce fields as the mother hoed and weeded. Their houses were small, narrow, wooden shacks, just like chicken coops. When land leases expired, according to Juhei Kono, they "had a horse pull their house and move it on to another field to work." Seasonal work moved them from the onion fields, to digging potatoes, cutting celery, or picking grapes on the Sacramento Delta. Young children would scare the birds away from the newly thrown seed. Older children tried to earn money, sometimes by working in nearby orchards and fields.

In winter, they wore woolen shirts and jackets, cut from one pattern that circulated from house to house and was altered to fit different sizes. Lacking heaters, the flimsy shacks were warmed only by a tin stove. The children were wrapped in futons, with a *yuntampo,* or wrapped water bottle, placed at the foot of the sleeping mat.

Children were precious, celebrated by traditional days for each gender—Boy day and Girl day. The family tree was held as reverent, and a particular *kanji* from the Kanji system, a formal style of writing Japanese characters, was chosen for the name of the children. The name was particularly important for boys, when it came to stating the full name. If families were religious, the children would learn *Shiso Gogyo,* a book of strict moral lessons, including the works of Confucius. Many learned it by heart, since it was believed helpful for leading a good life.

One young boy heard the epithet "Japs!" when he landed in San Francisco in 1905, and knew from that moment on the meaning of prejudice in America. Japan had won the war with Russia, and their strong military presence caused fear among Americans who were already prejudiced against Asians. "They even picked up horse dung off the street and threw it at us. I was baptized with horse dung," wrote Nisuke Mitsumori. He and other Japanese youngsters "never went out at night" and even during the day felt insecure because of the gangs of American youth who harassed them. Many children, in adulthood, looked back to the difficult times spent as strangers in the land of America. Yet their families had advanced in America—buying land, farming independently, and becoming respected members of their communities.

25

Niños de España

Life in the grand ranchos was enjoyed by a wealthy class of Spanish and Mexican *haciendados,* or Mexican landowners—aristocrats who considered themselves white and extended their hospitality to all of like kind. They had inherited their land and wealth from their ancestors and lived in good-natured indolence and luxury—at least by the shocked descriptions of hard-driven New Englanders who had followed the gold rush to California or moved to New Mexico to farm. To them, such ease seemed sinful—they had not witnessed the taming and settling of the land, and seemed ignorant of the daily labor that went into maintaining stock, planting and harvesting fields, and supplying food for large numbers of workers and family. Europeans understood the more leisurely aspects of Spanish life, and those amenities were seen as "the way of life," lived out in houses that were, according to a French traveler, Charles Marryat, "open to all . . . as the time passed in continual fiestas, in which pleasure succeeded pleasure, music to dancing."

By 1842, ninety-two ranchos stretched from San Diego to San Luis Obispo, and from there north. One hacienda, La Guajome, was so large that its owner, Don Cuevas, "could stand at any corner . . . and see in any direction, the [2219] acres that he owned." Like a fortress, each adobe sprawled atop the mesa, affording a panoramic view across miles of treeless flats, broken only by an occasional willow, or the lush grape cuttings from Spain that sprang up in the mild coastal climate. Everywhere, orchards of oranges, olives, pomegranates, and lemons spilled out a seasonal abundance. The ranchos were usually built near a stream, while those that were "dry" heard the gentle "swish" of windmills as they dredged up water from the reluctant aquifers below.

Ranch life was often interrupted by Indian raids, and every hacienda was built of three-foot-thick adobe walls, solid as a fortress, with windows recessed in deep sills, slightly slanted, smaller outside than in, to offer protection from arrow flurries. Tiny panes of glass were set side by side, so if one was shattered by an arrow, the rest would remain. As a last measure, heavy wooden shutters could be swung shut.

A cool inner patio, through which the light breezes would play, housed hundreds of potted geraniums as well as the household's children, who tumbled about, happy and cared for by Indian servants. As described by Arcadia Bandini:

> I think on quiet days, when no winds blew, just the soft breezes murmuring all around the big house, and through the orange orchard . . . I loved to breathe in the whole clean smell everywhere around with the pungent heavy odor of orange blossoms. Hearing the soft grinding of the mill, as it slowly turned around and the droning of the flies or bees. . . . What peace.

Each rancho was a buzzing hive of crafts and workmanship—a place where buttons and belt buckles were pounded out of silver coins, and local tule reeds and buffalo grass were dried, dyed, and woven into small baskets. Sheep shearing took place as regularly as the weekly Saturday-night bath, and brandings were a spectacular event.

✧ ✧ ✧ ✧

THE POWERFUL RANCHERO families, backbone of the California culture, were part of a sprawling lineage of interrelated families, noted for kindness and easy hospitality, who met frequently, danced, dined, rode horseback over the rolling hills, wed one another's family members, and, in general, staked out "fiesta" as the highlight of nearly every week. Children growing up amid such revelry could remember the *fandangos,* the Lenten festivities, and the *cascarones,* or "egg frolics," held during a betrothal ceremony for an older brother or sister. Eggs were carefully sucked or dripped clean, then filled either with perfume, gold dust, or paper confetti, and finally sealed with a dollop of wax. All fun broke out as the eggs were hurled back and forth, the idea being to crack the shell on the head of the intended, or whoever happened in the way. On Shrove Tuesday, ash-filled eggs were also aimed and cracked as a signal of repentance.

In later years, the Spanish love of horses and riding, the mainstay of Californian as well as Mexican culture, meant that to be a *charro,* or horseman, was the dream of every young boy. Taking place in Mexican communities, this festive rodeo prompted parades where young boys learned by imitation, as elders flung artful lariats or performed elegant riding tricks. Twelve was the minimum age for participation, but often boys had already practiced for years. Complete mastery of the horse was required—from full-force galloping to instant, taut-reined stops where the horse quivered into eerie stillness after a series of crouching movements, seemingly impossible for such a large beast. Bull tailings were the most popular sport, and young Hispanic boys were wild to try their luck at this tricky endeavor. In the *coleadero,* the tail was grabbed, wrapped around the boy's boot, then luck invoked as the horse was spurred into a frenzy of speed to outrun the bull and flip it off balance. In more extreme maneuvers, boys leaped from one horse to another at top speed—the dangerous *paso de muerte.*

The entire family was drawn into the *charreada,* with girls dreaming of wearing the queen's *mantilla,* or at least becoming a *charra,* or lady rider. Everyone admired the finely crafted *charro* attire—saddles, hats, vests and pants glittering with silver.

The *charro* tradition was as deeply rooted in Mexican culture as faith itself. Children saw in it the pagentry and discipline of Catholic ceremonies—the omnipresent cornerstone of weekly and seasonal festivities. Catechism and the Act of Contrition were as deeply embedded in memory as a parent's names. The church calendar formed the backdrop to all festivities of the year.

Originally, each rancho had its own priest, but as time went on, the families would convene at the nearest church, usually a tiny mission without pews, seats, or kneel-boards. Servants ran ahead with pillows and chairs to fluff and arrange for the "patrona." Children were marched off to catechism and the sacraments. On Lenten Fridays, they prayed the Way of the Cross, with one boy selected to carry the lamp, lighting the gloom enough so the padre could actually see through the gloom to read his prayers. Souls in purgatory were a constant, solemn presence, for whom children were instructed to pray. On Saturdays, the church bell would ring out at sunset, summoning parents and children to recite the rosary. Feasts were numerous—children would rise in the morning, sleepily wondering if today was the feast of St. John the Baptist, St. Peter, St. James, or St. Ann. The padres, according to traveler Charles Marryat, were "good lenient, lazy and kind-hearted fellows, funny yet moral, thundering against vice and love, yet giving light penances and entire absolution."

Christmas was a delicious, exuberant round of festivities, stretching from December 12 through January 6, the Day of the Magi. Children waited for *Las Posadas,* a drama based on the night journey of the Holy Family, in which they formed a long procession, with candles, animals, and adults, to wander from one rancho or house to another, seeking Christ's shelter. As in the Nativity, they were turned away time and again, until finally, the appointed family would throw open its doors and a folk fiesta began.

Young girls in Spanish homes looked forward to a time-honored tradition—that of dressing up the life-size, religious statues in churches, treating them as if they were large dolls. In one case, when a Mexican church burned in Ysleta Mission near Santa Fe in 1907,

Spanish girls: (left to right) Isabel del Valle, Felicidad Abadie, Matilde Rimpau, Josefa del Valle, Frances Alexander, Alice Bowers, Sofia Rimpau, Rosa del Valle; and James del Valle, ca. 1860.

the statue of the Virgin was wearing the dress of Concha Paz Fernandez, daughter of one of the devout families of the church.

Hispanic children were bound to long-held traditions of behavior. Young girls were not permitted out alone, even on household errands. If paying a visit, they had to take along a younger sister or brother, knowing that their mother was watching them as they strolled along, fretting about the daughter's innocence. Arcadia Bandini, a child of La Guajome in southern California, spent hours trying to figure out ways to dodge the careful attentions of her Indian nurse, Paula, in order to see the slaughtering of cows—anything to "get a closer look."

> I would shiver in fright and glee, as the men would lead the big ponderous mooing animal and tie its head firmly to one tree . . . then the animal would really begin its lowing, and I'd begin to shiver, as the hind legs were roped to the second tree. . . . At the sight of the blood, I would scream and yell with fright.

Spanish parental tradition was absolute hierarchy, as strong parental discipline demanded complete obedience and humility in children, both boys and girls. Childhood was brief for Californio belles—customarily, they were betrothed by ten or twelve, and by their early teens, wed. Girls of the most tender age were given prenuptial gifts instead of toys and encouraged to think in matronly directions. In one account, Don Teodoso Yorba of Rancho Santa Ana gathered his young grandchildren about, then opened a huge chest of stiffened, mottled calf skins, gleaming with gold nails. Waves of camphor wafted out from a bed of finely woven shawls, gold chains, bracelets, dresses, and brooches of precious stones. According to historian Norine Dresser, the children, still young enough for dolls,

Veranda of unidentified early California mission, ca. 1860s. Photo by Park.

could then contemplate their future fate as married women, a puzzling task.

Boys led a freer life, and were allowed to join the older men in some exploits—drinking with them, playing games of chance, and laughing at ribald stories. Boys gravitated naturally to cockfights, races, fandangos, hunting, fishing, and sailing.

But childish high spirits could not be entirely dictated by gender. Children were children, and both boys and girls sought out mischief with the same assiduous spirit.

> Who could forget pomegranate season? Then we would be all discolored, from face and hand to our clothes, which would be simply ruined for good, as this juice is one that nothing . . . removes, only by eating away the material. As for face and hands, even lemon straight, or with salt, would not whiten up again. We were mottled for several days with a sickening bluish-tan complexion. I . . . loved granados, hard as they were to peel. A bite into the tough skin was our way to start peeling. A bitter mouthful, those skins were, but forgotten at once when one sees the beautiful clear shine on the ruby-red kernels of the fruit itself, so juicy and delicious to eat.

As California and New Mexico were Americanized, the leisurely ways of the rancheros began to fade. As a civilization, they had inherited—not earned—great wealth, and they traded only in gold. As California became more overrun with Anglos, paper money came into trade. The Mexican Californians had little respect for the new paper currency. What to do with it? The stuff, according to Arcadia Bandini, was "unsanitary, easily blew away, was lost or dropped, not heard." Her grandmother, mistress of the sprawling ranch, would stuff the offensive paper in her petticoat pockets, and often dropped it when bustling about. Her careless fiscal habits were the basis of an often-told family story:

> It was [her] habit, if short of paper in the outhouse, to use some from her pocket, never bothering to notice the figure printed in the corner, and the rush would be on as soon as she was out of sight. I'll bet it was the only time some of my relatives really worked.

Although family tales continued to be told, the families themselves—great, sprawling numbers of children and adults closely bound by lineage and experience—found their lives quickly changed. As more Americans flooded into the gold-rich lands of California, they needed lumber for ships and land to settle, and many would boldly squat on land-grant territory, daring the Spaniards to drive them off. Piece by piece, the great ranches were broken down, rights were revoked, and the graceful, sunny life of the early Californians was taken away.

References

Introduction

Nannie Alderson: Nannie Alderson and Helena Huntington-Smith. *A Bride Goes West* (Lincoln: University of Nebraska Press, 1969).

Isabella Bird: Isabella L. Bird, *A Lady's Life in the Rocky Mountains* (New York: Putnam, 1879–80; previously published in *Leisure House* magazine, 1878).

Maggie Brown: Lillian Schlissel, Byrd Gibbens, and Elizabeth Hampsten, *Far From Home: Families of the Westward Journey* (New York: Shocken Books, 1989).

Solomon Butcher: Pam Conrad, *Prairie Visions: The Life and Times of Solomon Butcher* (New York: Scholastic, 1991).

Daniel Chaplin: Catherine M. Scholten, *Childbearing in American Society: 1650–1850* (New York: New York University Press, 1985).

Ethan Allen Crawford: Lucy Crawford, *Lucy Crawford's History of the White Mountains,* Stearns Morse, ed. (Boston: Appalachian Mountain Club, 1978).

Sarah Hale: Sarah Hale, *Ladies' Magazine* (1836).

Martha Heywood: Martha Spense Heywood, *Not by Bread Alone: The Journal of Martha Spense Heywood, 1850–56,* Juanita Brooks, ed. (Salt Lake City, Utah: Utah State Historical Society, 1978).

"infant depravity": Robert Sunley, "Early Nineteenth-Century American Literature on Child Rearing," in *Childhood in Contemporary Cultures,* Margaret Mead and Martha Wolfenstein, eds. (Chicago: University of Chicago Press, 1955).

"land of independence": Edwin C. Guillet, *The Great Migration* (Toronto: Thomas Nelson and Sons, 1937).

Martha Ann Minto: Martha Ann Minto, "Mrs. Minto's Narrative & Conversation," manuscript (Berkeley: University of California, Bancroft Library).

Mrs. G.H.: Molly Ladd-Taylor, *Raising a Baby the Government Way: Mothers' Letters to the Children's Bureau, 1915–1932* (New Brunswick, N.J., and London: Rutgers University Press, 1942).

Mrs. Mortimer: Elinore Pruitt Stewart: Elinore Pruitt Stewart, *Letters on an Elk Hunt* (Lincoln: University of Nebraska Press, 1979).

Bethenia Owens: Bethenia Owens, *Dr. Owens-Adair, Some of Her Life Experiences* (Portland, Ore.: Mann and Beach, 1906).

Francis Prevaux: Francis Prevaux, "Letters, 1858," manuscript (Berkeley: University of California, Bancroft Library).

Agnes Reid: Agnes Just Reid, *Letters of Long Ago* (Salt Lake City, Utah: Tanner Trust Fund, 1973).

Annette Rosenshine: Annette Rosenshine, "Life Is Not a Paragraph," typescript (Berkeley: University of California, Bancroft Library).

Harriet Shaw: Harriet Bidwell Shaw, "The Letters of Mrs. Harriet Bidwell Shaw" (Santa Fe: Dorothy Woodward Collection, New Mexico Records Center and Archives).

Elinore Pruitt Stewart: Elinore Pruitt Stewart, *Letters on an Elk Hunt* (Lincoln: University of Nebraska Press, 1979).

Esther Whinery Wattles: Esther Whinery Wattles, "Reminiscences," typescript (personal collection of Ruth Arps).

Connie Willis: Alberta Hannum, *Look Back With Love* (New York: Vanguard Press, 1969).

Chapter 1: Going West

Mary Ackley: Mary Ackley, *Crossing the Plains and Early Days in California: Memories of Girlhood in California's Golden Age* (privately printed, 1928).

Mary Ellen Applegate: Mary Ellen Applegate, "On to Oregon," manuscript (Berkeley: University of California, Bancroft Library).

"Between 1840 and 1860": Elliot West, *Growing Up with the Country: Childhood on the Far Western Frontier* (Albuquerque: University of New Mexico Press, 1989).

Elisha Brooks: Glenda Riley. *Frontierswomen: The Iowa Experience* (Ames: Iowa State University Press, 1981).

"child of Nature": George McCowen, "Diary," typescript (Sacramento: California State Library).

Conestoga with eight holes cut: Dee Brown, *The Gentle Tamers* (New York: Bantam Books, Inc., 1974).

Elizabeth Custer: Elizabeth B. Custer, *Tenting on the Plains.* (Williamstown, Mass.: Corner House Publishers, 1973).

William Dangerfield: William Dangerfield, "Intimate views of childhood," William Dangerfield Letters, February 14, 1853.

Depression: Margaret Banks, "Stories From the Attic," in *Daughters of Dakota,* Vol. II, Sally Roesch Wagner, ed. (Yankton, S. Dak.: Daughters of Dakota, 1990).

Donner Party: Patrick Breen, "The Diary of Patrick Breen, 1846–47," manuscript (Berkeley: University of California, Bancroft Library).

Elizabeth Dixon Greer: Elizabeth Dixon Greer, "Diary 1847" (Oregon Pioneer Association, Thirty-fifth Annual Session).

Maggie Hall: Lillian Schlissel, *Women's Diaries of the Westward Journey* (New York: Schocken Books, 1982; 1992).

Kate Heath: Kate Heath, "A Child's Journey Through Arizona and New Mexico," *The Californian* 3 (January 1881).

Lucy Ann Henderson: Lucy Ann Henderson, "Young Adventure," Rodney Strong, ed., *Nevada Historical Society Quarterly* (summer 1973).

Sallie Hester: "The Diary of a Pioneer Girl: The Adventures of Sallie Hester, Aged Twelve, in a Trip Overland in 1849," *The Argonaut* 98 (September 12 and 25, 1925).

Emma Shepard Hill: Emma Shepard Hill, *A Dangerous Crossing and What Happened on the Other Side* (Denver, Colo.: Bradford, Robinson Printing Co., 1924).

"Hold fast or you will be run over again": John H. Clark, "A Trip Across the Plains in 1852," typescript diary (Sacramento: California State Library).

Elizabeth Hull: Elinore Pruitt Stewart, *Letters to a Woman Homesteader,* copyright 1913 and 1914 by *Atlantic Monthly,* copyright 1914 and 1942 by Elinore Pruitt Stewart.

Ada Millington Jones: Ada Millington Jones, "Journal Kept While Crossing the Plains," 1862, manuscript CF-II, photocopy (Berkeley: University of California, Bancroft Library).

Elizabeth Keegan: Lillian Schlissel, *Women's Diaries of the Westward Journey* (New York: Schocken Books, 1982; 1992).

Elizabeth Lord: William Dangerfield, "Intimate views of childhood," William Dangerfield Letters, February 14, 1853.

Blanche Beale Lowe: Blanche Beale Lowe, "Growing Up in Kansas," *Kansas History,* vol. 8, no. 1 (spring 1985).

Richard Martin May: Richard Martin May, "The May Family Genealogy," manuscript (Berkeley: University of California, Bancroft Library).

Eliza McAuley: Emmy E. Werner, *Pioneer Children on the Journey West* (Boulder, Colo.: Westview Press, 1995).

Number of children through Fort Laramie: John H. Bauer, *Growing Up With California: A History of California Children* (Los Angeles: Will Kramer, 1978).

Virginia Reed: Virginia Reed, letter to her cousin, May 16, 1847, Virginia E.B. Reed Letters, 1847–1901, BANC MSS 89/127c (Berkeley: University of California, Bancroft Library).

Mary Ronan: Mary Ronan, *Frontier Woman: The Story of Mary Ronan as Told to Margaret Ronan,* H. G. Merriam, ed. (Missoula: University of Montana Press, 1973).

Mrs. Francis H. Sawyer: Mrs. Francis H. Sawyer, "Overland to California, Notes from a Journal . . . May 9 to August 17, 1852" (Chicago: Newberry Library).

Hermann J. Scharmann: Hermann J. Scharmann, *Christmas in the Gold Fields, 1848* (San Francisco: California Historical Society, 1959).

Susan Thompson: Lillian Schlissel, *Women's Diaries of the Westward Journey* (New York: Schocken Books, 1982; 1992).

Rebecca Woodson: Rebecca Hildreth Nutting Woodson, "Recollections," 1850–58, manuscript (Berkeley: University of California, Bancroft Library).

Chapter 2: Be Fruitful, Be Fearful

Ferdinand Bayard: Ferdinard de Bayard, *Travels of a French Man,* cited in Claire Fox, *The Fence and the River* (University of Minnesota Press, 1999).

Elizabeth Cabot: Elizabeth Cabot, *More Than Common Powers of Perception: The Diary of Elizabeth Rogers Mason Cabot,* P.A.M. Taylor, ed. (Boston: Beacon Press, 1991).

Rachel Calof: Rachel Bella Calof, *Rachel Calof's Story* (Bloomington: Indiana University Press, 1995).

Urling Coe: Urling Coe, M.D., *Frontier Doctor* (New York: Macmillan Co., 1939).

Dr. S. Josephine Baker, Mrs. G.B., Mrs. W.M.: Molly Ladd-Taylor, *Raising a Baby the Government Way: Mothers' Letters to the Children's Bureau, 1915–1932* (New Brunswick, N.J., and London: Rutgers University Press, 1942).

Priscilla Evans: Priscilla Merriman Evans, in *Heart Throbs of the West,* Kate B. Carter, ed. (Salt Lake City, Utah: Daughters of the Utah Pioneers, 1958).

Mary Hallock Foote: Mary Hallock Foote, *A Victorian Gentlewoman in the Far West,* Rodman W. Paul, ed. (San Marino, Calif.: Huntington Library, 1972).

Martha Heywood: Martha Spense Heywood, *Not by Bread Alone: The Journal of Martha Spense Heywood, 1850–56,* Juanita Brooks, ed. (Salt Lake City, Utah: Utah State Historical Society, 1978).

Georgiana Kirby: Georgiana Bruce Kirby, *Georgiana: The Journal of Georgiana Bruce Kirby, 1852–1860* (Santa Cruz, Calif.: Santa Cruz Historical Trust, 1987).

Mrs. Caroline Kirkland: Mrs. Caroline Matilda Kirkland, *A New Home, or Life in the Clearings* (G. P. Putnam's Sons: New York, 1953).

Mary Kincaid: Judith Walzer Leavitt, *Brought to Bed: Childbearing in America, 1750 to 1950* (New York: Oxford University Press, 1986).

Judith Walzer Leavitt: Judith Walzer Leavitt, *Brought to Bed: Childbearing in America, 1750 to 1950* (New York: Oxford University Press, 1986).

Little Charley Malick: Charley Malick, "Malick Family Correspondence, 1848–1869" (New Haven, Conn.: Yale University Beinecke Library).

Mrs. O'Shaugnessy: Elinore Pruitt Stewart, *Letters on an Elk Hunt* (Lincoln: University of Nebraska Press, 1979).

Josephine Peabody: Josephine Preston Peabody, *Diary and Letters of Josephine Preston Peabody,* Christina Hopkinson Baker, ed. (Boston: Riverside Press, 1925).

Annette Rosenshine: Annette Rosenshine, "Life Is Not a Paragraph," typescript (Berkeley: University of California, Bancroft Library).

Harriet Shaw: Harriet Bidwell Shaw, "The Letters of Mrs. Harriet Bidwell Shaw" (Santa Fe: Dorothy Woodward Collection, New Mexico Records Center and Archives).

Sarah Bixby Smith: Sarah Bixby Smith, *Adobe Days* (Fresno, Calif.: Valley Publishers, 1974).

Chapter 3: Lyin' In

Mary Ackley: Mary Ackley. *Crossing the Plains and Early Days in California: Memories of Girlhood in California's Golden Age* (privately printed, 1928).

"Can you give me any information": Molly Ladd-Taylor, *Raising a Baby the Government Way: Mothers' Letters to the Children's Bureau, 1915–1932* (New Brunswick, N.J., and London: Rutgers University Press, 1942).

Childbirth in Hot Creek, Nevada: Maria Trumbell Silliman Church Papers, 1829–1858 (New York: New York Public Library).

Goddfried Duden, *Report on a Journey to the Western States of North America* (Columbia: State Historical Society of Missouri and University of Missouri Press, 1980).

Sarah Farrell: Julie Roy Jeffrey, *Frontier Women* (New York: Hill and Wang, 1979).

"Feelin' poorly": Judith Walzer Leavitt, *Brought to Bed: Childbearing in America, 1750 to 1950* (New York: Oxford University Press, 1986).

Katherine Fougera: Katherine Gibson Fougera, *With Custer's Cavalry* (Lincoln: University of Nebraska Press, 1968).

Emily French: Emily French, *The Diary of a Hard-Worked Woman,* Janet Lecompte, ed. (Lincoln: University of Nebraska Press, 1968).

Fubbister: Sylvia Van Kirk, *Many Tender Ties: Women in Fur-Trade Society, 1670–1870* (Norman: University of Oklahoma Press, 1987).

George Gregory: George Gregory, *Medical Morals Male* (New York: published by the author, 1853).

Lillian Heath: Lillian Heath as told to Neal E. Miller, "The History of 111 West Lincoln Way," 1954, manuscript 296A (Laramie: Wyoming Historical Society).

Martha Spense Heywood: Martha Spence Heywood. *Not by Bread Alone: The Journal of Martha Spence Heywood, 1850–56,* Juanita Brooks, ed. (Salt Lake City, Utah: Utah State Historical Society, 1978).

Martha Morrison Minto: Martha Ann Minto, "Mrs. Minto's Narrative & Conversation," manuscript (Berkeley: University of California, Bancroft Library).

Mrs. Moss: Mabelle Eppard Martin, "From Texas to California in 1849: Diary of C.C. Cox," *Southwestern Historical Quarterly* 29 (January 1926).

Margaret Archer Murray: Margaret E. Archer Murray, "Memoir of the William Archer Family," *Annals of Iowa,* vol. 39, no. 5 (summer 1968) quoted in Glenda Riley, *The Female Frontier: A Comparative View of Women on the Prairie and the Plains* (Lawrence: University of Kansas Press, 1988).

Audrey Oldland: Julie Jones Eddy, *Homesteading Women: An Oral History of Colorado, 1890–1950* (New York: Twayne Publishers, 1995).

Bethenia Owens, *Dr. Owens-Adair, Some of Her Life Experiences* (Portland, Ore.: Mann and Beach, 1906).

Hilda Rawlinson: Julie Jones-Eddy, *Homesteading Women: An Oral History of Colorado, 1890–1950* (New York: Twayne Publishers, 1995).

Agnes Just Reid: Agnes Just Reid, *Letters of Long Ago* (Salt Lake City, Utah: Tanner Trust Fund, 1997).

Russian immigrant woman: Lillian Schlissel, Byrd Gibbens, and Elizabeth Hampsten, *Far From Home: Families of the Westward Journey* (New York: Schocken Books, 1990).

Harriet Shaw: Harriet Bidwell Shaw, "The Letters of Mrs. Harriet Bidwell Shaw" (Santa Fe: Dorothy Woodward Collection, New Mexico Records Center and Archives).

Elinore Pruitt Stewart: Elinore Pruitt Stewart, *Letters to a Woman Homesteader,* copyright 1913 and 1914 by *Atlantic Monthly,* copyright 1914 and 1942 by Elinore Pruitt Stewart.

Charlene Perkins Stetson: Charlene Perkins Stetson, Katherine S. Day Collection, 1905–1935 (Hartford, Conn.: Stowe-Day Library).

"vitalization": Regina Markell Morantz-Sanchez, *Sympathy and Science: Women Physicians in American Medicine* (New York: Oxford University Press, 1985).

Chapter 4: Tin Bottles and Baby Care

Isabella Bird: Isabella L. Bird, *A Lady's Life in the Rocky Mountains* (New York: Putnam 1879–80; previously published in *Leisure House* magazine, 1878).

Pauline Diede: Pauline Diede, *Homesteading on the Knife River Plains,* Elizabeth Hampsten, ed. (Bismarck, N. Dak.: North Dakota Germans from Russians Heritage Society, 1983).

Sylvia Dye: Sylvia Dye, *Sandhill Stories: Life on the Prairie 1875–1925* (El Cerrito, Calif.: Parthenon Publications, 1980).

"everybody was willing to tend a baby": M. H. Field, "Grandma Bascom's Story of San Jose in '49," *Overland Monthly* 9 (May 1887).

Mary Hallock Foote: Mary Hallock Foote, *A Victorian Gentlewoman in the Far West,* Rodman W. Paul, ed. (San Marino, Calif.: Huntington Library, 1972).

Francina: Sarah Bixby Smith, *Adobe Days* (Fresno, Calif.: Valley Publishers, 1974).

Emily French: Emily French, *The Diary of a Hard-Worked Woman,* Janet Lecompte, ed. (Lincoln: University of Nebraska Press, 1968).

Sarah Gillespie: Sarah Gillepsie, "I Am A Good Girl, 1877–1879," diary, *The Pacific Historian* (February 1962).

Isaac Goldberg: Isaac Goldberg, *Arizona Citizen,* October 19, 1878, quoted in Floyd S. Fierman, *Roots and Boots: From Crypto-Jew in New Spain to Community Leader in the Southwest* (Hoboken, N.J.: KTAV Publishing House, 1982).

Georgiana Kirby: Georgiana Bruce Kirby, *Georgiana: The Journal of Georgiana Bruce Kirby, 1852–1860* (Santa Cruz, Calif.: Santa Cruz Historical Trust, 1987).

Mrs. Caroline Kirkland: Mrs. Caroline Matilda Kirkland, *A New Home, or Life in the Clearings* (New York: G. P. Putnam's Sons: 1953).

Abigail Malick: Abigail Malick, "Malick Family Correspondence, 1848–1869" (New Haven, Conn.: Yale University Beinecke Library).

Mother to the Children's Bureau in 1910, Mrs. E.M., Mrs. N.W., Mrs. E.M., Tillie Mae W., Iowa mother worried about food: Molly Ladd-Taylor, *Raising a Baby the Government Way: Mothers' Letters to the Children's Bureau, 1915–1932* (New Brunswick, N.J., and London: Rutgers University Press, 1942).

Bethenia Owens: Bethenia Owens, *Dr. Owens-Adair, Some of Her Life Experiences* (Portland, Ore.: Mann and Beach, 1906).

Matilda Peitzke Paul: Matilda Peitzke Paul, "Diary, 1938," manuscript (Iowa City: Iowa State Historical Society), quoted in Glenda Riley, *The Female Frontier: A Comparative View of Women on the Prairie and the Plains* (Lawrence: University of Kansas Press, 1988).

Josephine Peabody: Josephine Preston Peabody. *Diary and Letters of Josephine Preston Peabody,* Christina Hopkinson Baker, ed. (Boston: Riverside Press, 1925).

Keturah Penton: Keturah Penton, quoted in Cathy Luchetti, *Women of the West* (1982; reprint, New York: Orion/Crown, 1992; originally in collection of Mrs. Donald A. Belknap and Reva Barrett).

Agnes Reid: Agnes Just Reid, *Letters of Long Ago* (Salt Lake City, Utah: Tanner Trust Fund, 1973).

Annette Rosenshine: Annette Rosenshine, "Life Is Not a Paragraph," typescript (Berkeley: Bancroft Library, University of California).

Harriet Shaw: Harriet Bidwell Shaw, "The Letters of Mrs. Harriet Bidwell Shaw" (Santa Fe: Dorothy Woodward Collection, New Mexico Records Center and Archives).

Lydia Sigourney: Lydia Howard Sigourney, *Letters to Mothers* (New York: Harper & Brothers, 1839).

Elinore Pruitt Stewart: Elinore Pruitt Stewart, *Letters on an Elk Hunt* (Lincoln: University of Nebraska Press, 1979).

Anna Waltz: Anna Langhorne Waltz, "West River Pioneer: A Woman's Story, 1911–1915," *South Dakota History,* vol. 17, no. 2 (summer 1987).

Chapter 5: No More Babies for Me!

Urling Coe: Urling Coe, M.D., *Frontier Doctor* (New York: Macmillan Co., 1939).

Contraceptive sources: Dr. A. M. Mauriceau, *The Married Woman's Private Medical Companion* (New York: privately printed, 1849).

Martha Farnsworth: Martha Farnsworth, *Plains Woman: The Diary of Martha Farnsworth, 1892–1922,* Marlene Springer and Haskell Springer, eds. (Bloomington: Indiana University Press, 1985).

Emily French: Emily French, *The Diary of a Hard-Worked Woman,* Janet Lecompte, ed. (Lincoln: University of Nebraska Press, 1968).

Dr. Mary Glassen: Elizabeth Hampsten, *Read This Only to Yourself: The Private Writings of Midwestern Women, 1880–1910* (Bloomington: Indiana University Press, 1982).

Malinda Jenkins: Malinda Jenkins as told to Jesse Lilienthal, *The Gambler's Wife: The Life of Malinda Jenkins* (Boston: Houghton Mifflin, 1933).

Gwendoline Kinkaid: Elizabeth Hampsten, *Read This Only to Yourself: The Private Writings of Midwestern Women, 1880–1910* (Bloomington: Indiana University Press, 1982).

Midwife sources: Lucy Ann Henderson, "Young Adventure," Rodney Strong, ed., *Nevada Historical Society Quarterly* (summer 1973); Thomas Ewell, *Letters to Ladies, Detailing Important Information, Concerning Themselves and Infants* (Philadelphia: n.p., 1817).

Mrs. H.H., Mrs. E.S., "My soul rebelled": Molly Ladd-Taylor, *Raising a Baby the Government Way: Mothers' Letters to the Children's Bureau, 1915–1932.* (New Brunswick, N.J., and London: Rutgers University Press, 1942).

Agnes Reid: Agnes Just Reid, *Letters of Long Ago* (Salt Lake City, Utah: Tanner Trust Fund, 1973).

Rose Williams, Lettie Mosher: Elizabeth Hampsten, *Read This Only to Yourself: The Private Writings of Midwestern Women, 1880–1910* (Bloomington: Indiana University Press, 1982).

Margaret Sanger: Margaret Sanger, *The Autobiography of Margaret Sanger* (New York: Dover Publications, 1938).

Sarah Everett Hale, Mary Ann Humble Case, Katharine Hohn Reimann, Mary Vian Holyoke: Judith Walzer Leavitt, *Brought to Bed: Childbearing in America,* 1750 to 1950 (New York: Oxford University Press, 1986).

Harriet Shaw: Harriet Bidwell Shaw, "The Letters of Mrs. Harriet Bidwell Shaw" (Santa Fe: Dorothy Woodward Collection, New Mexico State Records Center and Archives).

Daniel Scott Smith: Daniel Scott Smith, "Population, Family and Society in Hingham, Massachusetts, 1635–1880," master's thesis (Berkeley: University of California, 1973).

Judity Turner: Judith Walzer Leavitt, *Brought to Bed: Childbearing in America, 1750 to 1950* (New York: Oxford University Press, 1986).

Chapter 6: For the Love of a Family

Margaret Archer: Glenda Riley, *Frontierswomen: The Iowa Experience* (Ames: Iowa State University Press, 1981).

Sophia Gelhorn Boylan: Sophia Gelhorn Boylan, "My Life Story, 1867–1883" (Iowa City: Iowa State Historical Society), quoted in Glenda Riley, *The Female Frontier: A Comparative View of Women on the Prairie and the Plains* (Lawrence: University of Kansas Press, 1988).

Angie Mitchell Brown: Angeline Mitchell Brown, "Diary of a Schoolteacher on the Arizona Frontier," September 5, 1880, to February 10, 1881 (Prescott, Arizona: Angie M. Brown Collection, Sharlot Hall Museum).

Elizabeth Burt: Elizabeth Johnston Burt, "40 Years as an Army Wife," manuscript (Washington, D.C., Library of Congress).

Frank Cejda: Rose Rosicky, *A History of Czechs (Bohemians) in Nebraska* (Omaha: Czech Historical Society of Nebraska, 1929).

Tommie Clack: Tommie Clack and Mollie Clack, *Pioneer Days . . . Two Views* (Abilene, Tex.: Reporter Publishing Co., 1979).

Katherine Davis: Katherine Davis, "Memoirs" (Santa Fe: New Mexico State Records Center and Archives).

Rachel Bella Kahn: Linda Mack Schloff, *"And Prairie Dogs Weren't Kosher": Jewish Women in the Upper Midwest Since 1855* (St. Paul: Minnesota Historical Press, 1996).

Mrs. Anna Kalal: Rose Rosicky, *A History of Czechs (Bohemians) in Nebraska* (Omaha: Czech Historical Society of Nebraska, 1929).

Caroline Kirkland: Mrs. Caroline Matilda Kirkland, *A New Home, or Life in the Clearings* (New York: G. P. Putnam's Sons, 1953).

Mrs. Marsh: Julia M. Carpenter, "My Journey West," manuscript (Berkeley: University of California, Bancroft Library).

Bethenia Owens: Bethenia Owens, *Dr. Owens-Adair, Some of Her Life Experiences* (Portland, Ore.: Mann and Beach, 1906).

Keturah Penton: Keturah Penton, quoted in Cathy Luchetti, *Women of the West* (1982; reprint, New York: Orion/Crown, 1992; originally in collection of Mrs. Donald A. Belknap and Reva Barrett).

Agnes Reid: Agnes Just Reid, *Letters of Long Ago* (Salt Lake City, Utah: Tanner Trust Fund, 1997).

Stephen Riggs: Mary Gay Humphreys, *Missionary Explorers Among the American Indians* (New York: Charles Scribner's Sons, 1913).

Marian Russell: Marian Russell, *Land of Enchantment: Memoirs of Marian Russell Along the Santa Fe Trail* (Evanston, Ill.: Branding Iron Press, 1954).

Mollie Dorsey Sanford: Mollie Dorsey Sanford, *Mollie: The Journal of Mollie Dorsey Sanford in Nebraska and Colorado Territories, 1857–1866* (Lincoln: University of Nebraska Press, 1959).

Harriet Shaw: Harriet Bidwell Shaw, "The Letters of Mrs. Harriet Bidwell Shaw" (Santa Fe: Dorothy Woodward Collection, New Mexico State Records Center and Archives).

Rachel Emma Woolley Simmons: Rachel Emma Woolley Simmons, "Journal of Rachel Emma Woolley Simmons," in *Heart Throbs of the West,* Kate B. Carter, ed. (Salt Lake City, Utah: Daughters of the Utah Pioneers, 1958).

Sarah Bixby Smith: Sarah Bixby Smith, *Adobe Days* (Fresno, Calif.: Valley Publishers, 1974).

Flora Spiegelburg: Flora Spiegelburg, Spiegelburg Brothers Papers (Santa Fe: New Mexico State Records Center and Archives).

Elinore Pruitt Stewart: Elinore Pruitt Stewart, *Letters on an Elk Hunt* (Lincoln: University of Nebraska Press, 1979).

Martha Summerhays: Martha Summerhays, *Vanished Arizona* (original edition, 1908; reprint, Philadelphia: J. B. Lippincott Co., 1963).

Anna Waltz: Anna Langhorne Waltz, "West River Pioneer: A Woman's Story, 1911–1915," *South Dakota History,* vol. 17, no. 2 (summer 1987).

Esther Wattles: Esther Whinery Wattles, "Reminiscences," typescript (personal collection of Ruth Arps).

Jeanette Wrottenbert: Linda Mack Schloff, *"And Prairie Dogs Weren't Kosher": Jewish Women in the Upper Midwest Since 1855,* (St. Paul: Minnesota Historical Press, 1996).

Sarah York: Sarah Butler York, "Experiences of a Pioneer Arizona Woman," *Arizona Historical Review,* vol. 1, no. 2 (July 1928).

Chapter 7: A Father's View

Mary Ellen Applegate: Mary Ellen Applegate, "On to Oregon," manuscript (Berkeley: University of California, Bancroft Library).

John Barrows: John R. Barrows, "A Wisconsin Youth in Montana, 1880–1883," in *Way Out West: Recollections and Tales*, H. G. Merriam, ed. (Norman: University of Oklahoma Press, 1969).

Henry S. Bloom: Henry S. Bloom, letters, February 23, 1851, February 22, 1851 (Berkeley: University of California, Bancroft Library).

Thomas Booth: Edmund Booth, *Forty Niner: The Life Story of a Deaf Pioneer* (Stockton, Calif.: San Joaquin Pioneer and Historical Society, 1953).

Tommie Clack: Tommie Clack and Mollie Clack, *Pioneer Days . . . Two Views* (Abilene, Tex.: Reporter Publishing Co., 1979).

David de Wolf: David de Wolf, "Diary and Letters, 1849–1850" (San Marino, Calif.: Henry E. Huntington Library).

William Dresser: Dresser Family Papers, "Letter from W. Dresser to Sarah," "Letter from W. Dresser to Albert and Charles," "Letter from Sarah Dresser to Her Husband, William," 1848, typescript (Berkeley: University of California, Bancroft Library).

Sylvia Dye: Sylvia Dye, *Sandhill Stories: Life on the Prairie 1875–1925* (El Cerrito, Calif.: Parthenon Publications, 1980).

Anne Ellis: Anne Ellis, *The Life of an Ordinary Woman* (Boston: Houghton Mifflin, 1990).

Floy Emhoff: Glenda Riley, *Frontierswomen: The Iowa Experience* (Ames: Iowa State University Press, 1981).

Edward Fitch: Nyle Miller, Edgar Langsdorf, and Robert E. Richmond, *Kansas in Newspaper* (Topeka: Kansas State Historical Society, 1963).

James Henry Gleason: James Henry Gleason, *Beloved Sister: The Letters of James Henry Gleason, 1841–1859* (Glendale, Calif.: Arthur H. Clark Co., 1978).

Maggie Hall: Maggie Hall, letters (Berkeley: University of California, Bancroft Library).

Howard Havens: Howard Havens, letters (Berkeley: University of California, Bancroft Library).

Lucy Ann Henderson: Lucy Ann Henderson, "Young Adventure," Rodney Strong, ed., *Nevada Historical Society Quarterly* (summer 1973).

Edith Stratton Kitt: Edith Stratton Kitt, *Pioneering in Arizona: The Reminiscences of Emerson Oliver Stratton and Edith Stratton,* John Alexander Carrol, ed. (Tucson: Arizona Pioneers' Historical Society, 1964).

Mary McNair Mathews: Mary McNair Mathews, *Ten Years in Nevada or, Life on the Pacific Coast* (Buffalo: Baker, Jones & Co., 1888).

Nellie McGraw: Nellie Tichenor McGraw Hedgpeth, "My Early Days in San Francisco," *The Pacific Historian* (February 1962).

Dave Mortimer: Elinore Pruitt Stewart, *Letters on an Elk Hunt* (Lincoln: University of Nebraska Press, 1979).

Jack O'Connor: Jack O'Connor, *Horse and Buggy West* (New York: Alfred A. Knopf, 1969).

Francis Prevaux: Francis Prevaux, "Letters, 1858," manuscript (Berkeley: University of California, Bancroft Library).

Annie Pierce: George S. Smith, *The Life and Times of George Foster Pierce, D.D.* (Sparta, Ga.: Hancock Publishing Co., 1888).

Agnes Reid: Agnes Just Reid, *Letters of Long Ago* (Salt Lake City, Utah: Tanner Trust Fund, 1973).

Milton Shaw: Harriet Bidwell Shaw, "The Letters of Mrs. Harriet Bidwell Shaw" (Santa Fe, N.M.: Dorothy Woodward Collection, New Mexico Records Center and Archives).

Sarah Bixby Smith: Sarah Bixby Smith, *Adobe Days* (Fresno, Calif.: Valley Publishers, 1974).

Lorenzo Waugh: Lorenzo Waugh, *Autobiography* (San Francisco: Francis, Valentine and Co., 1888).

Carrie Williams: Carrie Williams, diary, Gold Flat, Nevada County, California, 1858–64 (New Haven, Conn.: Western Americana Collection, Beinecke Rare Book and Manuscript Library, Yale University).

Chapter 8: Family Discord

Abigail Bailey: Abigail Bailey, *Religion and Domestic Violence in Early New England: The Memoirs of Abigail Abbot Bailey,* Ann Taves, ed. (Bloomington: Indiana University Press, 1989).

Helen Carpenter: Helen Carpenter, journal (Berkeley: University of California, Bancroft Library).

Mrs. Hugh Fraser: Mrs. Hugh Fraser, *My Life and Times* (London: privately printed, 1880).

Mrs. H.B., North Carolina woman: Molly Ladd-Taylor, *Raising a Baby the Government Way: Mothers' Letters to the Children's Bureau, 1915–1932* (New Brunswick, N.J., and London: Rutgers University Press, 1942).

Bethenia Owens: Bethenia Owens, *Dr. Owens-Adair, Some of Her Life Experiences* (Portland, Ore.: Mann and Beach, 1906).

Andrew Pambrun: Andrew Pambrun, *Sixty Years on the Frontier in the Pacific Northwest* (Fairfield, Wash.: Ye Galleon Press, 1978).

Francis Prevaux: Francis Prevaux, "Letters, 1858," manuscript (Berkeley: University of California, Bancroft Library).

Milton and Harriet Shaw: Harriet Bidwell Shaw, "The Letters of Mrs. Harriet Bidwell Shaw" (Santa Fe: Dorothy Woodward Collection, New Mexico Records Center and Archives).

J. H. Williams: Ambrose P. Dietz, A.M., *Our Boys: A Collection of Original Literary Offerings* (San Francisco: A. L. Bancroft and Co., 1879).

Mr. Wilson: Helen Carpenter, journal (Berkeley: University of California, Bancroft Library).

Chapter 9: Rural Lives

Mary Jane Anderson: Mary Jane Anderson, "John Anderson Papers, 1864–1904" (Harrisburg, Pa.: Pennsylvania State Archives).

Jesse Applegate: Jesse Applegate, *Jesse A. Applegate's Recollections* (Roseburg, Ore.: Press of Review Publishing, 1914).

Ada Boyd and Ida Boyd: Joyce L. Taylor, "A Profile of Three American Women, 1888–1893," master's thesis (San Diego State University, 1983).

Sophia Gelhorn Boylan: Sophia Gelhorn Boylan, "My Life Story, 1867–1883" (Iowa City: Iowa State Historical Society), quoted in Glenda Riley, *The Female Frontier: A Comparative View of Women on the Prairie and the Plains* (Lawrence: University of Kansas Press, 1988).

Frank Cejda, C. V. Svoboda: Rose Rosicky, *A History of Czechs (Bohemians) in Nebraska* (Omaha: Czech Historical Society of Nebraska, 1929).

Lavina Gates Chapman: Joanna Stratton, *Pioneer Women* (New York: Simon & Schuster, 1981).

Tommie Clack: Tommie Clack and Mollie Clack, *Pioneer Days . . . Two Views* (Abilene, Tex.: Reporter Publishing Co., 1979).

Miriam Colt: Miriam Davis Colt, *Went to Kansas* (L. Ingalls & Co., 1862).

Ethelyn Whalin Crawford: Julie Jones-Eddy, *Homesteading Women: An Oral History of Colorado, 1890–1950* (New York: Twayne Publishers, 1995).

Sylvia Dye, *Sandhill Stories: Life on the Prairie, 1875–1925* (El Cerrito, Calif.: Parthenon Publications, 1980).

Priscilla Merriman Evans: Priscilla Merriman Evans, in *Heart Throbs of the West,* Kate B. Carter, ed. (Salt Lake City, Utah: Daughters of the Utah Pioneers, 1958).

Emily Hawley Gillespie: Emily Hawley Gillespie, *"A Secret to be Buried": The Diary of Emily Hawley Gillespie, 1858–1888,* Judy Nolte Lensink, ed. (Iowa City: University of Iowa Press, 1989).

Sarah Gillespie: Sarah Gillespie, "I Am A Good Girl, 1877–1879," diary, *The Pacific Historian* (February 1962).

Oma Jensen Graham: Julie Jones Eddy, *Homesteading Women: An Oral History of Colorado, 1890–1950* (New York: Twayne Publishers, 1995).

Anna Biggs Heaney: Joanna Stratton, *Pioneer Women* (New York: Simon & Schuster, 1981).

Emma Shepard Hill: Emma Shepard Hill, *A Dangerous Crossing and What Happened on the Other Side* (Denver, Colo.: Bradford, Robinson Printing Co., 1924).

Mrs. Caroline Kirkland: Mrs. Caroline Matilda Kirkland, *A New Home, or Life in the Clearings* (New York: G. P. Putnam's Sons, 1953).

Edith Kitt: Edith Stratton Kitt *Pioneering in Arizona: The Reminiscences of Emerson Oliver Stratton and Edith Stratton,* John Alexander Carrol, ed. (Tucson: Arizona Pioneers' Historical Society, 1964).

Blanche Beale Lowe: Blanche Beale Lowe, "Growing Up in Kansas," *Kansas History,* vol. 8, no. 1 (spring 1985).

Sadie Martin: Sadie Martin, "Nothing Seemed Permanent on the Desert," in *So Much to Be Done: Women Settlers on the Mining and Ranching Frontier,* Ruth B. Moynihan, Susan Armitage, and Christiane Fischer Dichamp, eds. (Lincoln: University of Nebraska Press, 1990).

Martha Ann Minto: Martha Ann Minto, "Mrs. Minto's Narrative & Conversation," manuscript (Berkeley: University of California, Bancroft Library).

Susan Newcomb: Susan Newcomb, diary, January 31, 1871 (Lubbock: Southwest Collection, Texas Tech University.)

Audrey Oldland: Julie Jones-Eddy, *Homesteading Women: An Oral History of Colorado, 1890–1950* (New York: Twayne Publishers, 1995).

Jack O'Connor: Jack O'Connor, *Horse and Buggy West* (New York: Alfred A. Knopf, 1969).

Matilda Peitzke Paul: Matilda Peitzke Paul, "Diary, 1938," manuscript (Iowa City: Iowa State Historical Society), quoted in Glenda Riley, *The Female Frontier: A Comparative View of Women on the Prairie and the Plains* (Lawrence: University of Kansas Press, 1988).

Mr. Parrish: Hubert Bancroft interview, conducted by Mrs. Hubert Bancroft (Berkeley: University of California, Bancroft Library).

Keturah Penton: Keturah Penton, quoted in Cathy Luchetti, *Women of the West* (1982; reprint, New York: Orion/Crown, 1992; originally in collection of Mrs. Donald A. Belknap and Reva Barrett).

Nels Reid: Agnes Just Reid, *Letters of Long Ago* (Salt Lake City, Utah: Tanner Trust Fund, 1973).

Rachel Emma Woolley Simmons: Rachel Emma Woolley Simmons, "Journal of Rachel Emma Woolley Simmons," in *Heart Throbs of the West,* Kate B. Carter, ed., (Salt Lake City, Utah: Daughters of the Utah Pioneers, 1958).

Sarah Bixby Smith: Sarah Bixby Smith, *Adobe Days* (Fresno, Calif.: Valley Publishers, 1974).

Elinore Pruitt Stewart: Elinore Pruitt Stewart, *Letters on an Elk Hunt* (Lincoln: University of Nebraska Press, 1979).

Herbert Stubbs: Joseph Brown, *Crossing the Plains in 1849* (Marysville, Calif.: privately printed, 1916).

Edith White: "Memories of Pioneer Childhood and Youth in French Corral and North San Juan, Nevada County, California. With a Brief Narrative of Later Life," told by Edith White, emigrant of 1859, to Linne Marsh Wolfe, 1936 (n.p.), quoted in *Let Them Speak for Themselves: Women in the American West, 1849–1900,* Christiane Fischer, ed. (New York: E. P. Dutton, 1978).

Connie Willis: Alberta Hannum, *Look Back With Love* (New York: Vanguard Press, 1969).

Chapter 10: Prairie Hardships

Mary Ackley: Mary Ackley, *Crossing the Plains and Early Days in California: Memories of Girlhood in California's Golden Age* (privately printed, 1928).

Jesse Applegate: Jesse Applegate, *Jesse A. Applegate's Recollections* (Roseburg, Ore.: Press of Review Publishing, 1914).

Jane Bell: Jane Bell, letter from Oroville, California, October 31, 1859, manuscript (Berkeley: University of California, Bancroft Library).

Isabella Bird: Isabella L. Bird, *A Lady's Life in the Rocky Mountains* (New York: Putnam, 1879–80; previously published in *Leisure House* magazine, 1878).

John Breen: John Breen, "Pioneer Memoirs of John Breen: Who Came to California Overland in 1846 as a Member of the Donner Party." Hubert Howe Bancroft interview.

Frank Cejda: Rose Rosicky, *A History of Czechs (Bohemians) in Nebraska* (Omaha: Czech Historical Society of Nebraska, 1929).

Tommie Clack: Tommie Clack and Mollie Clack, *Pioneer Days . . . Two Views* (Abilene, Tex.: Reporter Publishing Company, 1979).

Arthur James Cowan: Mrs. Arthur Cowan, "Journal, 1895," typescript of manuscript (Missoula: Montana State Historical Society).

May Crowder: May Lacey Crowder, "Pioneer Life in Palo Alto County," *Iowa Journal of History and Politics* 46, 2 (Apr. 1948)

"dig her grave six feet": Elliot West, *Growing Up with the Country: Childhood on the Far Western Frontier* (Albuquerque: University of New Mexico Press, 1989).

Sylvia Dye: Sylvia Dye, *Sandhill Stories: Life on the Prairie 1875–1925* (El Cerrito, Calif.: Parthenon Publications, 1980).

Melora Espy: Joanna Stratton, *Pioneer Women* (New York: Simon & Schuster, 1981).

Sarah Gillespie: Sarah Gillepsie, "I Am A Good Girl, 1877–1879," diary, *The Pacific Historian* (February 1962).

Martha Heywood: Martha Spense Heywood, *Not by Bread Alone: The Journal of Martha Spense Heywood, 1850–56,* Juanita Brooks, ed. (Salt Lake City, Utah: Utah State Historical Society, 1978).

Emily Shepard Hill: Emma Shepard Hill, *A Dangerous Crossing and What Happened on the Other Side* (Denver, Colo.: Bradford, Robinson Printing Co., 1924).

Edith Kitt: Edith Stratton Kitt, *Pioneering in Arizona: The Reminiscences of Emerson Oliver Stratton and Edith Stratton,* John Alexander Carrol, ed. (Tucson: Arizona Pioneers' Historical Society, 1984).

Mary Gettys Lockard: Joanna Stratton, *Pioneer Women* (New York: Simon & Schuster, 1981).

Blanche Beale Lowe: Blanche Beale Lowe, "Growing Up in Kansas," *Kansas History,* vol. 8, no. 1 (spring, 1985).

Abigail Malick: Abigail Malick, "Malick Family Correspondence, 1848–1869" (New Haven, Conn.: Yale University Beinecke Library).

Fitch Hyatt Marean: Fitch Hyatt Marean, "Letter to the Editor, July 18, 1914," in "Historical Sketches of Main," *Whitney Point Reporter,* August 23, 1919.

Mrs. Mortimer: Elinore Pruitt Stewart, *Letters on an Elk Hunt* (Lincoln: University of Nebraska Press, 1979).

Bethenia Owens: Bethenia Owens, *Dr. Owens-Adair, Some of Her Life Experiences* (Portland, Ore.: Mann and Beach, 1906).

Keturah Penton: Keturah Penton, quoted in Cathy Luchetti, *Women of the West* (1982; reprint, New York: Orion/Crown, 1992; originally in collection of Mrs. Donald A. Belknap and Reva Barrett).

Pearl Price Robertson: Pearl Price Robertson, "Journal of a Ranch Wife

1932–35," *Frontier,* vol. 13, no. 3, p. 215, cited in H. G. Merriam, *Way Out West: Recollections and Tales* (Norman: University of Oklahoma Press, 1969).

Annette Rosenshine: Annette Rosenshine, "Life Is Not a Paragraph," typescript (Berkeley: University of California, Bancroft Library).

DeWitt Seaver: Charles D. Ferguson, *The Experiences of a Forty-Niner* (Cleveland: Williams Publishing Co., 1888).

Sarah Bixby Smith: Sarah Bixby Smith, *Adobe Days* (Fresno, Calif.: Valley Publishers, 1974).

Elinore Pruitt Stewart: Elinore Pruitt Stewart, *Letters of a Woman Homesteader,* coopyright 1913 by *Atlantic Monthly,* copyright 1914 and 1942 by Elinore Pruitt Stewart.

Esther Whinery Wattles: Esther Whinery Wattles, "Reminiscences," typescript (personal collection of Ruth Arps).

Anna Waltz: Anna Langhorne Waltz, "West River Pioneer: A Woman's Story, 1911–1915," *South Dakota History,* vol. 17, no. 2, (summer 1987).

Chapter 11: Motherless Children

Mary Ackley: Mary Ackley, *Crossing the Plains and Early Days in California: Memories of Girlhood in California's Golden Age* (privately printed, 1928).

Abigail Bailey: Abigail Bailey, *Religion and Domestic Violence in Early New England: The Memoirs of Abigail Abbot Bailey,* Ann Taves, ed. (Bloomington: Indiana University Press, 1989).

"Charity kindergartens": Ambrose P. Deitz, A.M., *Our Boys: A Collection of Original Literary Offerings* (San Francisco: A. L. Bancroft and Co., 1879).

John H. Clark: John H. Clark, "A Trip Across the Plains in 1852," typescript diary (Sacramento: California State Library).

Mary Collins: Mary C. Collins, Mary C. Collins Papers (Pierre: South Dakota State Historical Society).

Luella Dickenson: Luella Dickenson, *Reminiscences of a Trip Across the Plains in 1846 and Early Days in California* (privately printed, 1904).

Mr. and Mrs. Hezekiah Hammond: Hammond Family Letters (Oakland, Calif.: Virginia Turner private collection).

May Wynne Lamb: May Wynne Lamb, *Life in Alaska: The Reminiscences of a Kansas Woman, 1916–1919,* Dorothy Wynne Zimmerman, ed. (Lincoln and London: University of Nebraska Press, 1988).

Ebeneezer Pettigrew: Ebeneezer Pettigrew, Pettigrew Papers (Raleigh: North Carolina Division of Archives and History).

Agnes Reid: Agnes Just Reid, *Letters of Long Ago* (Salt Lake City, Utah: Tanner Trust Fund, 1973).

Harriet Shaw. "The Letters of Mrs. Harriet Bidwell Shaw." (Santa Fe: Dorothy Woodward Collection, New Mexico Records Center and Archives).

Elliot West: Elliot West, *Growing Up with the Country: Childhood on the Far Western Frontier* (Albuquerque: University of New Mexico Press, 1989).

Narcissa Whitman: Narcissa Whitman, *Marcus and Narcissa Whitman and the Opening of Old Oregon* Clifford M. Drury, ed. (Glendale, Calif.: A. H. Clark Co., 1973).

Carrie Williams: Carrie Williams, diary, Gold Flat, Nevada County, California, 1858–64 (New Haven, Conn.: Western Americana Collection, Beinecke Rare Book and Manuscript Library, Yale University).

Connie Willis: Elinore Pruitt Stewart, *Letters on an Elk Hunt* (Lincoln: University of Nebraska Press, 1979).

Annie Turner Wittenmyer: Annie Turner Wittenmyer, Annie Turner Wittenmyer Papers (Washington, D.C.: Library of Congress, Manuscript Division).

Chapter 12: Children's Work

John Bauer: John H. Bauer, *Growing Up With California: A History of California Children* (Los Angeles: Will Kramer, 1978).

"Boy millionaire": Charles Peters, *The Autobiography of Charles Peters* (Sacramento, Calif.: privately printed, 1915).

Edmund Booth: Edmund Booth, *Forty Niner: The Life Story of a Deaf Pioneer* (Stockton, Calif.: San Joaquin Pioneer and Historical Society, 1953).

Priscilla Evans: Priscilla Merriman Evans: *Heart Throbs of the West,* Kate B. Carter, ed. (Salt Lake City, Utah: Daughters of the Utah Pioneers, 1958).

Mrs. Hugh Fraser: Cushwat: Helen Meilleur, *A Pour of Rain* (Victoria, B.C., Canada: Sono Nis Press, 1980).

"Hurdy-gurdy" dancers: "Dance Girls," *Alta California* (San Francisco), October 19, 1857.

Blanche Beale Lowe: Blanche Beale Lowe, "Growing Up in Kansas," *Kansas History,* vol. 8, no. 1 (spring 1985).

Orphan: Martha A. Gentry, " 'A Child's Experience in '49,' as Related by Mrs. Martha A. Gentry of Oakland, Calif., to Jennie E. Ross," *Overland Monthly,* 63 (April 1914).

Keturah Penton: Keturah Penton, quoted in Cathy Luchetti, *Women of the West* (1982; reprint, New York: Orion/Crown, 1992; originally in collection of Mrs. Donald A. Belknap and Reva Barrett).

Hilda Rawlinson: Julie Jones-Eddy, *Homesteading Women: An Oral History of Colorado, 1890–1915* (New York: Twayne Publishers, 1995).

Annette Rosenshine: Annette Rosenshine, "Life Is Not a Paragraph," typescript (Berkeley: University of California, Bancroft Library).

Hermann Scharmann: Hermann J. Scharmann, *Hermann J. Scharmann's Overland Journey to California* (New York: Staats Zeitung, 1852).

Elinore Pruitt Stewart: Elinore Pruitt Stewart, *Letters on an Elk Hunt* (Lincoln: University of Nebraska Press, 1979).

Charles Svoboda: Rose Rosicky, *A History of Czechs (Bohemians) in Nebraska* (Omaha: Czech Historical Society of Nebraska, 1929).

Esther Whinery Wattles: Esther Whinery Wattles, "Reminiscences," typescript (personal collection of Ruth Arps).

Edith White: "Memories of Pioneer Childhood and Youth in French Corral and North San Juan, Nevada County, California. With a Brief Narrative of Later Life," told by Edith White, emigrant of 1859, to Linne Marsh Wolfe, 1936 (n.p.), quoted in *Let Them Speak for Themselves: Women in the American West, 1849–1900,* Christiane Fischer, ed. (New York: E. P. Dutton, 1978).

Narcissa Whitman: Narcissa Whitman, *Marcus and Narcissa Whitman and the*

Opening of Old Oregon, Clifford M. Drury, ed. (Glendale, Calif.: A. H. Clark Co., 1973).

Chapter 13: Festivities and Favorite Times

Cyrus Brady: Rev. Cyrus Townsend Brady, *Recollections of a Missionary in the Great West* (New York: Charles Scribner's Sons, 1900).

Agnes B. Chowden: H. G. Merriam, *Way Out West: Recollections and Tales* (Norman: University of Oklahoma Press, 1969).

Sylvia Dye: Sylvia Dye, *Sandhill Stories: Life on the Prairie, 1875–1925* (El Cerrito, Calif.: Parthenon Publications, 1980).

Sarah Gillespie: Sarah Gillepsie, "I Am A Good Girl, 1877–1879," diary, *The Pacific Historian* (February 1962).

James Henry Gleason: James Henry Gleason. *Beloved Sister: The Letters of James Henry Gleason, 1841–1859* (Glendale, Calif.: Arthur H. Clark Co., 1978).

Frank Hoyt: "Hoyt-Bobenmeyer & Thompson Family History" (Lincoln, Nebr.: private papers).

Blanche Beale Lowe: Blanche Beale Lowe, "Growing Up in Kansas," *Kansas History,* vol. 8, no. 1, (spring 1985).

Nellie McGraw: Nellie Tichenor McGraw Hedgpeth, "My Early Days in San Francisco," *The Pacific Historian* (February 1962).

Katherine Elspeth Oliver: Joanna Stratton, *Pioneer Women* (New York: Simon & Schuster, 1981).

Hermann J. Scharmann: Hermann J. Scharmann, "Stories," *San Francisco Call,* December 10, 1909.

Harriet Shaw: Harriet Shaw, "The Letters of Mrs. Harriet Bidwell Shaw" (Santa Fe: Dorothy Woodward Collection, New Mexico Records Center and Archives).

Rachel Emma Woolley Simmons: Rachel Emma Woolley Simmons, "Journal of Rachel Emma Woolley Simmons," in *Heart Throbs of the West,* Kate B. Carter, ed. (Salt Lake City, Utah: Daughters of the Utah Pioneers, 1958).

Sarah Bixby Smith: Sarah Bixby Smith, *Adobe Days* (Fresno, Calif.: Valley Publishers, 1974).

Elinore Pruitt Stewart: Elinore Pruitt Stewart, *Letters on an Elk Hunt* (Lincoln: University of Nebraska Press, 1979).

Joanna Stratton: Joanna Stratton, *Pioneer Women* (New York: Simon & Schuster, 1981).

Martha Summerhays: Martha Summerhays, *Vanished Arizona* (original edition, 1908; reprint, Philadelphia: J. B. Lippincott Co., 1963).

Anna Waltz: Anna Langhorne Waltz, "West River Pioneer: A Woman's Story, 1911–1915," *South Dakota History,* vol. 17, no. 2 (summer 1987).

Harriet Sherrill Ward: D. B. Ward, *Across the Plains in 1853* (Seattle, Wash.: Ward, 1911).

Edith White: "Memories of Pioneer Childhood and Youth in French Corral and North San Juan, Nevada County, California. With a Brief Narrative of Later Life," told by Edith White, emigrant of 1859, to Linne Marsh Wolfe, 1936 (n.p.), quoted in *Let Them Speak for Themselves: Women in the American West, 1849–1900,* Christiane Fischer, ed. (New York: E. P. Dutton, 1978).

Carrie Williams: Carrie Williams, diary, Gold Flat, Nevada County, California, 1858–64 (New Haven, Conn.: Western Americana Collection, Beinecke Rare Book and Manuscript Library, Yale University).

Chapter 14: Hide-and-Seek and Other Games

Jesse Applegate: *Jesse A. Applegate's Recollections* (Roseburg, Ore.: Press of Review Publishing, 1914).

Ethelyn Whalin Crawford: Julie Jones-Eddy, *Homesteading Women: An Oral History of Colorado, 1890–1950* (New York: Twayne Publishers, 1995).

Katherine Davis: Katherine Davis, "Memoirs," (Santa Fe, N.M.: New Mexico Records Center and Archives).

Sarah Gillespie: Sarah Gillepsie, "I Am A Good Girl, 1877–1879," diary, *The Pacific Historian* (February 1962).

Clarence V. Kellogg: Clarence V. Kellogg, *Early Day Life in the California Mining Camps* (privately published, 1866).

Blanche Beale Lowe: Blanche Beale Lowe, "Growing Up in Kansas," *Kansas History,* vol. 8, no. 1 (spring 1985).

Nellie McGraw: Nellie Tichenor McGraw Hedgpeth, "My Early Days in San Francisco," *The Pacific Historian* (February 1962).

Jack O'Connor: Jack O'Connor, *Horse and Buggy West* (New York: Alfred A. Knopf, 1969).

Bethenia Owens: Bethenia Owens, *Dr. Owens-Adair, Some of Her Life Experiences* (Portland, Ore.: Mann and Beach, 1906).

Ox contest: Elliot West, *Growing Up with the Country: Childhood on the Far Western Frontier* (Albuquerque: University of New Mexico Press, 1989).

Loula Blair Schill: Loula Blair Schill, manuscript (San Francisco, Calif.: David Brownell Collection).

Harriet Shaw: Harriet Bidwell Shaw, "The Letters of Mrs. Harriet Bidwell Shaw" (Santa Fe: Dorothy Woodward Collection, New Mexico Records Center and Archives).

Rachel Emma Woolley Simmons: Rachel Emma Woolley Simmons, "Journal of Rachel Emma Woolley Simmons," in *Heart Throbs of the West,* Kate B. Carter, ed. (Salt Lake City, Utah: Daughters of the Utah Pioneers, 1958).

Sarah Bixby Smith: Sarah Bixby Smith, *Adobe Days* (Fresno, Calif.: Valley Publishers, 1974).

Narcissa Whitman: *Marcus and Narcissa Whitman and the Opening of Old Oregon,* Clifford M. Drury, ed. (Glendale, Calif.: A. H. Clark Co., 1973).

Chapter 15: Spare the Rod

Mary Ellen Applegate: Mary Ellen Applegate, "On to Oregon," manuscript (Berkeley: University of California, Bancroft Library).

Bernie's White Chicken: Pansy, *Bernie's White Chicken* (Cincinnati: Western Tract Co., 1888).

Mary Binckley: Mary Binckley, "John Milton Binckley Papers, 1816–1943" (Washington, D.C.: Library of Congress Manuscript Collection).

Postcard of unidentified girl, ca. 1907.

Maria Silliman Church: Maria Silliman Church, "Maria Trumbell Silliman Church Papers, 1829–1858" (New York: New York Public Library).

Tommie Clack: Tommie Clack and Mollie Clack, *Pioneer Days . . . Two Views* (Abilene, Tex.: Reporter Publishing Company, 1979).

Discipline, general views: Thomas A. Bailey, *The American Spirit* (Boston: D. C. Heath & Co., 1963); Sacvan Bercovitch, *The Puritan Origins of the American Self* (New Haven and London: Yale University Press, 1975); Alexis de Tocqueville, *Democracy in America,* Richard Heffner, ed. (New York: Mentor Books, 1955).

Jonathan Edwards: Jonathan Edwards, *Memoir of the Rev. Jonathan Edwards, Compiled Originally by Sam Hopkins,* John Hawksley, ed. (London: n.p., 1815).

Reverend Oscar P. Fitzgerald: Oscar P. Fitzgerald, *California Sketches,* (Nashville, Tenn.: privately printed, 1880).

Frank Hoyt: "Hoyt-Bobenmeyer & Thompson Family History" (Lincoln, Nebr.: private papers).

Georgiana Kirby: Georgiana Bruce Kirby, *Georgiana: The Journal of Georgiana Bruce Kirby, 1852–1860.* (Santa Cruz, Calif.: Santa Cruz Historical Trust, 1987).

Edith Kitt: Edith Stratton Kitt, *Pioneering in Arizona: The Reminiscences of Emerson Oliver Stratton and Edith Stratton,* John Alexander Carrol, ed. (Tucson: Arizona Pioneers' Historical Society, 1964).

Abigail Malick: Abigail Malick, "Malick Family Correspondence, 1848–1869" (New Haven, Conn.: Yale University Beinecke Library).

Nellie McGraw: Nellie Tichenor McGraw Hedgpeth, "My Early Days in San Francisco," *The Pacific Historian* (February 1962).

Lucretia Mott: Lucretia Mott, "The Laws in Relation to Women," in *Lucretia Mott: Her Complete Speeches and Sermons,* Dana Greene, ed. (New York and Toronto: Edwin Mellen Press, 1980).

Nebraska mother writing to Children's Bureau: Molly Ladd-Taylor, *Raising a Baby the Government Way: Mothers' Letters to the Children's Bureau, 1915–1932* (New Brunswick, N.J., and London: Rutgers University Press, 1942).

Lucretia Mott: Lucretia Mott, "The Laws in Relation to Women," in *Lucretia Mott: Her Complete Speeches and Sermons,* Dana Greene,, ed. (New York and Toronto: Edwin Mellen Press, 1980).

Andrew Pamburn: Andrew Pamburn, *Sixty Years on the Frontier in the Pacific Northwest* (Fairfield, Wash.: Ye Galleon Press, 1978).

Francis Prevaux: Francis Prevaux, "Letters, 1858," manuscript (Berkeley: University of California, Bancroft Library).

Dr. Mary P. Sawtelle: Margaret Austin, M.D., "History of Women in Medicine: A Symposium," *Bulletin of the Medical Library Association,* vol. 44, (January 1956).

"secret smile": Robert Sunley, "Early Nineteenth-Century American Literature on Child Rearing," in *Childhood in Contemporary Cultures,* Margaret Mead and Martha Wolfenstein, eds. (Chicago: University of Chicago Press, 1955).

Rachel Emma Woolley Simmons: Rachel Emma Woolley Simmons, "Journal of Rachel Emma Woolley Simmons," in *Heart Throbs of the West,* Kate B. Carter, ed. (Salt Lake City, Utah: Daughters of the Utah Pioneers, 1958).

Sarah Bixby Smith: Sarah Bixby Smith, *Adobe Days* (Fresno, Calif.: Valley Publishers, 1974).

"stamina enough": Barbara Ehrenreich, *For Her Own Good: 150 Years of Experts' Advice to Women* (New York: Anchor Books, 1978).

Elinore Pruitt Stewart: Elinore Pruitt Stewart, *Letters on an Elk Hunt* (Lincoln: University of Nebraska Press, 1979).

Ben Wallicek: Ben Wallicek interview, Oral History Collection (Lubbock, Tex.: SWT/Texas Tech College).

George Washington: M. L. Weems, *A History of the Life and Death, Virtues and Exploits of General George Washington* (Elizabeth-town, N.J.: Shepard Kollock, 1802).

Walt Whitman: John H. Bauer, *Growing Up With California: A History of California Children* (Los Angeles: Will Kramer, 1978).

Carrie Williams: Carrie Williams, diary, Gold Flat, Nevada County, California, 1858–64 (New Haven, Conn.: Western Americana Collection, Beinecke Rare Book and Manuscript Library, Yale University).

J. H . Williams: Ambrose P. Deitz, A.M., *Our Boys: A Collection of Original Literary Offerings* (San Francisco: A. L. Bancroft and Co., 1879).

Chapter 16: Schools from the Ground Up

Jesse Applegate: Jesse Applegate, *Jesse A. Applegate's Recollections* (Roseburg, Ore.: Press of Review Publishing, 1914).

Frank Cejda: Rose Rosicky, *A History of Czechs (Bohemians) in Nebraska* (Omaha: Czech Historical Society of Nebraska, 1929).

Tommie Clack: Tommie Clack and Mollie Clack, *Pioneer Days . . . Two Views* (Abilene, Tex.: Reporter Publishing Co., 1979).

Ida and Ada Boyd: Joyce L. Taylor, "A Profile of Three American Women, 1888–1983," master's thesis (San Diego State University, 1983).

Sylvia Dye: Sylvia Dye, *Sandhill Stories: Life on the Prairie, 1875–1925* (El Cerrito, Calif.: Parthenon Publications, 1980).

Mrs. Farrar: Mrs. Farrar, *The Young Lady's Friend* (Boston: n.p., 1836).

Free public school: John H. Bauer, *Growing Up With California: A History of California Children* (Los Angeles: Will Kramer, 1978).

Margaret Hecox: Margaret Hecox, "The Story of Margaret M. Hecox," Marie Valhasky, ed., *Overland Monthly* (May 1892).

Emma Shepard Hill: Emma Shepard Hill, *A Dangerous Crossing and What Happened on the Other Side* (Denver: Bradford, Robinson Printing Co., 1924).

Georgiana Kirby: Georgiana Bruce Kirby, *Georgiana: The Journal of Georgiana Bruce Kirby, 1852–1860.* (Santa Cruz, Calif.: Santa Cruz Historical Trust, 1987).

Blanche Beale Lowe: Blanche Beale Lowe, "Growing Up in Kansas," *Kansas History,* vol. 8, no. 1, (spring 1985).

Martha Ann Minto: Martha Ann Minto, "Mrs. Minto's Narrative & Conversation," manuscript (Berkeley: University of California, Bancroft Library).

Mary Elizabeth Norton: Mary Elizabeth Norton, "Norton Family Diaries," January 26, 1880 (Topeka: Kansas State Historical Society).

Martha Peitzke Paul: Martha Peitzke Paul, "Diary, 1938," manuscript (Iowa City: Iowa State Historical Society), quoted in Glenda Riley, *The Female Frontier: A Comparative View of Women on the Prairie and the Plains* (Lawrence: University of Kansas Press, 1988).

Agnes Reid: Agnes Just Reid, *Letters of Long Ago* (Salt Lake City, Utah: Tanner Trust Fund, 1973).

Nellie Carnahan Robinson: Nellie Carnahan Robinson, "The Recollections of a Schoolteacher in the Disappointment Creek Valley," Michael B. Husband, ed., *The Colorado Magazine,* vol. 51 (spring 1974).

Annette Rosenshine: Annette Rosenshine, "Life Is Not a Paragraph," typescript (Berkeley: University of California, Bancroft Library).

Harriet Shaw: Harriet Bidwell Shaw "The Letters of Mrs. Harriet Bidwell Shaw," (Santa Fe: Dorothy Woodward Collection, New Mexico Records Center and Archives).

India Harris Simmons: Joanna Stratton, *Pioneer Women* (New York: Simon & Schuster, 1981).

Alfred E. Whitaker: Alfred E. Whitaker, *Mercantile Library Association Records* (San Francisco, Calif.: Francis & Valentine, Printer, 1874).

Edith White: "Memories of Pioneer Childhood and Youth in French Corral and North San Juan, Nevada County, California. With a Brief Narrative of Later Life," told by Edith White, emigrant of 1859, to Linne Marsh Wolfe, 1936 (n.p.), quoted in *Let Them Speak for Themselves: Women in the American West, 1849–1900,* Christiane Fischer, ed. (New York: E. P. Dutton, 1978).

Carrie Williams: Carrie Williams, diary, Gold Flat, Nevada County, California, 1858–64 (New Haven, Conn.: Western Americana Collection, Beinecke Rare Book and Manuscript Library, Yale University).

Eleanor Williams: Josiah Butler Williams, "Family Papers" (Ithaca, N.Y.: Cornell University, Department of Manuscripts and University Archives).

J. H. Williams: Ambrose P. Deitz, A.M. *Our Boys: A Collection of Original Literary Offerings* (San Francisco: A. L. Bancroft and Co., 1879).

Charles Zulek: Rose Rosicky, *A History of Czechs (Bohemians) in Nebraska* (Omaha: Czech Historical Society of Nebraska, 1929).

Chapter 17: Schoolhouse Days

Jesse Applegate: Jesse Applegate, *Jesse A. Applegate's Recollections* (Roseburg, Ore.: Press of Review Publishing, 1914).

Angeline Mitchell Brown: Angeline Mitchell Brown, "Diary of a Schoolteacher on the Arizona Frontier," September 5, 1880, to February 10, 1881 (Prescott, Arizona: Angie M. Brown Collection, Sharlot Hall Museum).

"Discipline": *A Teacher's Handbook* (Arapahoe County, Colo.: Denver School District Number One, ca. 1900).

Tommie Clack: Tommie Clack and Mollie Clack, *Pioneer Days . . . Two Views* (Abilene, Tex.: Reporter Publishing Co., 1979).

Sarah Gillespie: Sarah Gillepsie, "I Am A Good Girl, 1877–1879," diary, *The Pacific Historian,* (February 1962).

Martha Spence Heywood: Martha Spense Heywood, *Not by Bread Alone,* Juanita Brooks, ed. (Salt Lake City, Utah: Utah State Historical Society, 1978).

Florence McCune: Florence McCune, "Diary, 1872–1885, A Colorado Reader" (Denver: Colorado Historical Society).

Montana schoolteacher: Fannie Thornburg, Campbell Family Papers, 1836–1920 (Bozeman, Mont.: Montana State University Library Special Collections).

Monthly salary statistic: Glenda Riley, *Frontierswomen: The Iowa Experience* (Ames: Iowa State University Press, 1981).

Bethenia Owens: Bethenia Owens, *Dr. Owens-Adair, Some of Her Life Experiences* (Portland, Ore.: Mann and Beach, 1906).

Lani Frost Perigo: Joanna Stratton, *Pioneer Women.* (New York: Simon & Schuster, 1981).

Pearl Price Robertson: Pearl Price Robertson, "Journal of a Ranch Wife, 1932–35," *Frontier,* vol. 13, no. 3, cited in *Way Out West: Reminiscences and Tales,* H. G. Merriam, ed. (Norman: University of Oklahoma Press, 1969).

Loula Blair Schill: Loula Blair Schill, manuscript (San Francisco, Calif.: David Brownell Collection).

Mary Sears: Mary Sears, "A Young Woman in the Midwest: The Journal of Mary Sears, 1859–1860" *Ohio Historical Quarterly,* vol. 65 (1975).

Georgie M. Shaw: Harriet Shaw, "The Letters of Mrs. Harriet Bidwell Shaw" (Santa Fe, N.M.: Dorothy Woodward Collection, New Mexico Records Center and Archives).

India Harris Simmons: Joanna Stratton, *Pioneer Women* (New York: Simon & Schuster, 1981).

J. H. Williams: Ambrose P. Dietz, A.M., *Our Boys: A Collection of Original Literary Offerings* (San Francisco, Calif.: A. L. Bancroft and Co., 1879).

Chloe Clark Willson: Chloe Clark Willson, *The Journal of Henry Bridgeman Brewer, Sept 3, 1839 to Feb. 13, 1843* (Fairfield, Wash: Ye Galleon Press, 1986).

Chapter 18: The Rugged Cross

Edward Austin: Edward Austin, "Letters, 1849" (Berkeley: University of California, Bancroft Library).

H. C. Bailey: H. C. Bailey "California in '53," reminiscence, typescript (Berkeley: University of California, Bancroft Library).

Frank Cejda: Rose Rosicky, *A History of Czechs (Bohemians) in Nebraska* (Omaha: Czech Historical Society of Nebraska, 1929).

Tommie Clack: Tommie Clack and Mollie Clack, *Pioneer Days . . . Two Views* (Abilene, Tex.: Reporter Publishing Company, 1979).

Hannah Crosby: Hannah Crosby, *Sketch of the Life of Hannah A. Crosby, Daughter of Edward and Emily Abbot Bunker* (Historical Records Survey and Federal Writer's Project: Utah Works Administration, 1935–39).

Jack Dempsey: Jack Dempsey, *Round by Round: An Autobiography,* in collaboration with Myron M. Stearns (New York: Whittlesey House, 1940).

Lorenzo Dow: Lorenzo Dow, *The Dealings of God, Man and the Devil* (St. Louis, Mo.: n.p., 1849).

William Dresser: Dresser Family Papers, "Letter from W. Dresser to Sarah," "Letter from W. Dresser to Albert and Charles," 1848, typescript (Berkeley: University of California, Bancroft Library).

Captain A. C. Farnsworth: Bethenia Owens, *Dr. Owens-Adair, Some of Her Life Experiences* (Portland, Ore.: Mann and Beach, 1906).

Sarah Gillespie: Sarah Gillespie, "I Am A Good Girl, 1877–1879," diary, *The Pacific Historian* (February 1962).

Martha Heywood: Martha Spense Heywood, *Not by Bread Alone,* Juanita Brooks, ed. (Salt Lake City, Utah: Utah State Historical Society, 1978).

Emma Shepard Hill: Emma Shepard Hill, *A Dangerous Crossing and What Happened on the Other Side* (Denver: Bradford, Robinson Printing Co., 1924).

"lax family," "Open the door for the children": Elliot West, *Growing Up with the Country: Childhood on the Far Western Frontier* (Albuquerque: University of New Mexico Press, 1989).

Barbara Levorson: Barbara Levorson, *The Quiet Conquest* (Hawley, Minn.: *Hawley Herald,* 1974).

Mrs. Mortimer: Elinore Pruitt Stewart, *Letters on an Elk Hunt* (Lincoln: University of Nebraska Press, 1979).

Bethenia Owens: Bethenia Owens, *Dr. Owens-Adair, Some of Her Life Experiences* (Portland, Ore.: Mann and Beach, 1906).

Keturah Penton: Keturah Penton, quoted in Cathy Luchetti, *Women of the West* (1982; reprint, New York: Orion/Crown, 1992; originally in collection of Mrs. Donald A. Belknap and Reva Barrett).

Francis Prevaux: Francis Prevaux, "Letters, 1858," manuscript (Berkeley: University of California, Bancroft Library).

"Progress, Civilization and Christianity": Glenda Riley, *Frontierswomen: The Iowa Experience* (Ames: Iowa State University Press, 1981).

Harriet Shaw: Harriet Bidwell Shaw, "The Letters of Mrs. Harriet Bidwell Shaw" (Santa Fe: Dorothy Woodward Collection, New Mexico Records Center and Archives).

Abigail Smith: Mrs. E. Clark, manuscript, late 1800s (Spokane, Wash.: Spokane Public Library).

Sarah Bixby Smith: Sarah Bixby Smith, *Adobe Days* (Fresno, Calif.: Valley Publishers, 1974).

Elinore Pruitt Stewart: Elinore Pruitt Stewart, *Letters of a Woman Homesteader,* copyright 1913 and 1914 by *Atlantic Monthly,* copyright 1914 and 1942 by Elinore Pruitt Stewart.

Augusta Dodge Thomas: Augusta Dodge Thomas, "Prairie Children: An Autobiography," reminiscence (Topeka: Kansas State Historical Society).

Esther Whinery Wattles: Esther Whinery Wattles, "Reminiscences," typescript (personal collection of Ruth Arps).

Calvin B. West: Reginald R. Stuart and Grace D. Stuart, "Calvin B. West of the Umpqua," *The Pacific Historian,* vol. 4, no. 5 (July 1962).

Edith White: "Memories of Pioneer Childhood and Youth in French Corral and North San Juan, Nevada County, California. With a Brief Narrative of Later Life," told by Edith White, emigrant of 1859, to Linne Marsh Wolfe, 1936 (n.p.), quoted in *Let Them Speak for Themselves: Women in the American West, 1849–1900,* Christiane Fischer, ed. (New York: E. P. Dutton, 1978).

Alice Clarissa Whitman: Narcissa Whitman, *Marcus and Narcissa Whitman and the Opening of Old Oregon,* Clifford M. Drury, ed. (Glendale, Calif.: A. H. Clark Co., 1973).

Charles Zulek: Rose Rosicky, *A History of Czechs (Bohemians) in Nebraska* (Omaha: Czech Historical Society of Nebraska, 1929).

Chapter 19: Feelin' Poorly

Abigail Adams: Abigail Adams, *The Adams-Jefferson Letters: The Complete Correspondence Between Thomas Jefferson and Abigail and John Adams,* Lester J. Cappon, ed. (Chapel Hill: University of North Carolina Press, 1998).

Mary Anderson: Mary Anderson, "John Anderson Papers, 1864–1904" (Harrisburg, Pa.: Pennsylvania State Archives).

Jesse Applegate: Jesse Applegate, "Jesse A. Applegate's Recollections" (Roseburg, Ore.: Press of Review Publishing, 1914).

Edward Breen: Edward Breen, cited in Emmy E. Werner, *Pioneer Children on the Journey West* (Boulder, Colo.: Westview Press, 1995); and in Patrick Breen, "The Diary of Patrick Breen, 1846–1847," manuscript (Berkeley: University of California, Bancroft Library).

Urling Coe: Urling Coe, M.D., *Frontier Doctor* (New York: Macmillan Co., 1939).

Miriam Colt: Miriam Davis Colt, *Went to Kansas* (Philadelphia: L. Ingalls & Co., 1862).

Sylvia Dye: Sylvia Dye, *Sandhill Stories: Life on the Prairie, 1875–1925* (El Cerrito, Calif.: Parthenon Publications, 1980).

James Henry Gleason: James Henry Gleason, *Beloved Sister: The Letters of James Henry Gleason, 1841–1859* (Glendale, Calif.: Arthur H. Clark Co., 1978).

Sarah Hammond: Sarah Hammond, Hammond Family Letters (Oakland, Calif.: Virginia Turner private collection).

Emma Shepard Hill: Emma Shepard Hill, *A Dangerous Crossing and What Happened on the Other Side* (Denver: Bradford, Robinson Printing Co., 1924).

Georgiana Kirby: Georgiana Bruce Kirby, *Georgiana: The Journal of Georgiana Bruce Kirby, 1852–1860* (Santa Cruz, Calif.: Santa Cruz Historical Trust, 1987).

Mrs. N.W.: Molly Ladd-Taylor, *Raising a Baby the Government Way: Mothers' Letters to the Children's Bureau 1915–1932* (New Brunswick, N.J., and London: Rutgers University Press, 1942).

Francis Prevaux: Francis Prevaux, "Letters, 1858," manuscript (Berkeley: University of California, Bancroft Library).

Agnes Reid: Agnes Just Reid, *Letters of Long Ago* (Salt Lake City, Utah: Tanner Trust Fund, 1973).

Marian Russell: Marian Russell, *Land of Enchantment: Memoirs of Marian Russell Along the Santa Fe Trail* (Evanston, Ill: Branding Iron Press, 1954).

Harriet Shaw: Harriet Bidwell Shaw, "The Letters of Mrs. Harriet Bidwell Shaw" (Santa Fe: Dorothy Woodward Collection, New Mexico Records Center and Archives).

Rachel Emma Woolley Simmons: Rachel Emma Woolley Simmons, "Journal of Rachel Emma Woolley Simmons," in *Heart Throbs of the West,* Kate B. Carter, ed. (Salt Lake City, Utah: Daughters of the Utah Pioneers, 1958).

Statistics of Wisconsin deaths: Ronald L. Numbers and Judith Walter Leavitt, *Wisconsin Medicine: Historical Perspectives* (Madison: University of Wisconsin Press, 1981).

Summer complaint and other childhood diseases: Sally G. McMillen, *Motherhood in the Old South* (Baton Rouge and London: Louisiana State University Press, 1990); Anna Garretson to her cousin, Jan. 29, 1886, Anna Garretson Papers (Chapel Hill, N.C.: Southern Historical Collection).

Esther Whinery Wattles: Esther Whinery Wattles, "Reminiscences," typescript (personal collection of Ruth Arps).

Carrie Williams: Carrie Williams, diary, Gold Flat, Nevada County, California, 1858–64 (New Haven, Conn.: Western Americana Collection, Beinecke Rare Book and Manuscript Library, Yale University).

Chapter 20: Passing On

Mary Ackley: Mary Ackley, *Crossing the Plains and Early Days in California: Memories of Girlhood in California's Golden Age* (privately printed, 1928).

Frances E. Albright: H. G. Merriam, *Way Out West: Recollections and Tales* (Norman: University of Oklahoma Press, 1969).

Sally Brown: Emmy E. Werner, *Pioneer Children on the Journey West* (Boulder, Colo.: Westview Press, 1995).

Counting graves: Elliot West, *Growing Up with the Country: Childhood on the Far Western Frontier* (Albuquerque: University of New Mexico Press, 1989).

Osseon Dodge: Augusta Dodge Thomas, "Prairie Children: An Autobiography," reminiscence (Topeka: Kansas State Historical Society).

Maria Elliot: Phoebe Elliot to William Elliott, July 26, 1833, in "Elliot-Gonzales Letters," quoted in Sally G. McMillen, *Motherhood in the Old South* (Baton Rouge and London: Louisiana State University Press, 1990).

Katherine Gibson Fougera: Katherine Gibson Fougera, *With Custer's Cavalry* (Lincoln: University of Nebraska Press, 1968).

Sarah Hale: Sarah Hale, *Ladies' Magazine* (1841).

Ada Millington Jones: Ada Millington Jones, "Journal Kept While Crossing the Plains," 1862, manuscript CF-II, photocopy (Berkeley: University of California, Bancroft Library).

Benjamin Lakin: Charles A. Johnson, *The Frontier Camp Meeting: Religion's Harvest Time* (Dallas, Tex.: Southern Methodist University Press, 1956).

James Larkin: James Ross Larkin, *Reluctant Frontiersman: James Ross Larkin on the Santa Fe Trail, 1856–1857,* Barton H. Barbour, ed. (Albuquereque: University of New Mexico Press, 1990).

Abigail Malick: Abigail Malick, Malick Family Correspondence, 1848–1869 (New Haven, Conn.: Yale University Beinecke Library).

Martha Ann Minto: Martha Ann Minto, "Mrs. Minto's Narrative & Conversation," manuscript (Berkeley: University of California, Bancroft Library).

Mrs. Mortimer: Elinore Pruitt Stewart, *Letters on an Elk Hunt* (Lincoln: University of Nebraska Press, 1979).

Mother writing to Children's Bureau, 1916: Molly Ladd-Taylor, *Raising a Baby the Government Way: Mothers' Letters to the Children's Bureau 1915–1932* (New Brunswick, N.J., and London: Rutgers University Press, 1942).

Mrs. W.D.: Molly Ladd-Taylor, *Raising a Baby the Government Way: Mothers' Letters to the Children's Bureau, 1915–1932* (New Brunswick, N.J., and London: Rutgers University Press, 1942).

Agnes Reid: Agnes Just Reid, *Letters of Long Ago* (Salt Lake City, Utah: Tanner Trust Fund, 1997).

Rachel Emma Woolley Simmons: Rachel Emma Wooley Simmons, "Journal of Rachel Emma Woolley Simmons," in *Heart Throbs of the West,* Kate B. Carter, ed. (Salt Lake City, Utah: Daughters of the Utah Pioneers, 1958).

Elinore Pruitt Stewart: Elinore Pruitt Stewart, *Letters on an Elk Hunt* (Lincoln: University of Nebraska Press, 1979).

Narcissa Whitman: Narcissa Whitman, *Marcus and Narcissa Whitman and the Opening of Old Oregon,* Clifford M. Drury, ed. (Glendale, Calif.: A. H. Clark Co., 1973).

Chapter 21: Many Cultures, Many Ways

Elizabeth Burt: Elizabeth Johnston Burt, "40 Years as an Army Wife," manuscript (Washington, D.C.: Library of Congress).

Tommie Clack: Tommie Clack and Mollie Clack, *Pioneer Days . . . Two Views* (Abilene, Tex.: Reporter Publishing Co., 1979).

Mary Collins: Richmond L. Clow, "Mary C. Collins, Missionary to the Western Sioux," *South Dakota Historical Collections,* vol. 41 (1892).

Miriam Colt: Miriam Davis Colt, *Went to Kansas* (L. Ingalls & Co., 1862).

Cushwat: Helen Meilleur, *A Pour of Rain* (Victoria, B.C., Canada: Sono Nis Press, 1980).

Claire Hofer Hewes: Claire Hofer Hewes, "Reminiscences, 1898," typescript (Reno, Nev.: University of Nevada Library, Special Collections Department).

Irene King: Mary Logan Rothschild and Pamela Claire Hronek, *Doing What the Day Brought: An Oral History of Arizona Women* (Tucson: University of Arizona Press, 1992).

Sophia Martinez: Elizabeth Colson, *Autobiographies of Three Pomo Women* (Berkeley: Berkeley Archeological Research Facility, University of California, 1974).

Helen Meilleur: Helen Meilleur, *A Pour of Rain* (Victoria, B.C., Canada: Sono Nis Press, 1980).

Jack O'Connor: Jack O'Connor, *Horse and Buggy West* (New York: Alfred A. Knopf, 1969).

Opening California schools to blacks: John H. Bauer, *Growing Up With California: A History of California Children* (Los Angeles: Will Kramer, 1978).

Annette Rosenshine: Annette Rosenshine, "Life Is Not a Paragraph," typescript (Berkeley: University of California, Bancroft Library).

Harriet Shaw: Harriet Bidwell Shaw, "The Letters of Mrs. Harriet Bidwell Shaw," (Santa Fe: Dorothy Woodward Collection, New Mexico Records Center and Archives).

Martha Summerhays: Martha Summerhays, *Vanished Arizona* (original edition, 1908; reprint, Philadelphia: J. B. Lippincott Co., 1963).

Narcissa Whitman: Narcissa Whitman, *Marcus and Narcissa Whitman and the Opening of Old Oregon* Clifford M. Drury, ed. (Glendale, Calif.: A. H. Clark Co., 1973).

Edith White: "Memories of Pioneer Childhood and Youth in French Corral and North San Juan, Nevada County, California. With a Brief Narrative of Later Life," told by Edith White, emigrant of 1859, to Linne Marsh Wolfe, 1936 (n.p.), quoted in *Let Them Speak for Themselves: Women in the American West, 1849–1900,* Christiane Fischer, ed. (New York: E. P. Dutton, 1978).

Jim Whitewolf: Jim Whitewolf, *Jim Whitewolf: The Life of a Kiowa Apache Indian,* Charles S. Brant, ed. (New York: Dover Publications, 1969).

Mrs. T. A. Wickes: Mrs. T. A. Wickes, "The Pioneer Woman of Montana," *Frontier,* vol. 10, no. 4, p. 337, cited in H. G. Merriam, *Way Out West: Recollections and Tales* (Norman: University of Oklahoma Press, 1969).

Obed G. Wilson: John H. Bauer, *Growing Up With California: A History of California Children* (Los Angeles: Will Kramer, 1978).

Chapter 22: Native Americans

Elsie Allen: Victoria Brady, Sarah Crome, and Lyn Reese, "Resist! Survival Tactics of Indian Women," *California History* (spring, 1984).

California mission Indians, the value of children: Maynard Geiger, O.F.M., *Mission Santa Barbara* (Santa Barbara: Franciscan Fathers of California, 1965); Guadalupe Vallejo, "Ranch and Mission Days in Alta California," *Century Magazine* 41 (December 1890).

Cheyenne traditions: Truman Michaelson, "Narrative of a Southern Cheyenne Woman," *Smithsonian Miscellaneous Collections,* vol. 87, no. 5. (1932).

"Child is born": Clay Lockett, "Midwives and Childbirth Among the Navajo," *Plateau* 12 (1939).

Childbirth lore: Judith Goldsmith, *Childbirth Wisdom from the World's Oldest Societies* (New York: Congdon & Weed, Inc., 1987).

Father de Smet: Rev. P. J. de Smet, *Western Missions and Missionaries: A Series of Letters* (New York: Mentor Books, 1955).

"Fawn" filled with juneberries: James Willard Schultz, *Blackfeet and Buffalo: Memories of Life Among the Indians,* Keith C. Seele, ed. (Norman: University of Oklahoma Press, 1981).

Katherine Fougera: Katherine Gibson Fougera, *With Custer's Cavalry* (Lincoln: University of Nebraska Press, 1968).

Herbs for childbirth: Judith Goldsmith, *Childbirth Wisdom from the World's Oldest Societies* (New York: Congdon & Weed, Inc., 1987).

Kiowa customs: *Social Anthropology of North American Tribes,* Fred Eggan, ed. (Chicago and London: University of Chicago Press, 1937.)

Lewis and Clark: *Original Journals of the Lewis and Clark Expedition, 1804–1806,* Reuben Gold Thwaites, ed. (New York: n.p., 1904).

Laura Black Bear Miles: Laura Black Bear Miles, oral history (private collection of Victor Orange).

Miwok father and son: John H. Bauer, *Growing Up With California: A History of California Children.* (Los Angeles: Will Kramer, 1978).

Partridgeberry tea: Matilda Coxe Stevenson, "The Zuni Indians," in *Twenty-third Annual Report of the Bureau of American Ethnology for the Years 1901–1902* (Washington, D.C.: U.S. Government Printing Office, 1904).

Edna Patterson: Edna B. Patterson, *Sagebrush Doctors* (Springville, Utah: Art City Publishing Co., 1972).

Protestant missionaries: Susan Peterson, " 'Holy Women' and Housekeepers: Women Teachers on South Dakota Reservations, 1885–1910," *South Dakota History,* vol. 13, no. 3 (fall 1983).

Santa Domingo tribe: in *The Winged Serpent: American Indian Prose and Poetry,* Margot Astrov, ed. (original edition, 1946; reprint, Boston: Beacon Press, 1992).

S.B.: Paul Radin, *The Autobiography of a Winnebago Indian* (Berkeley: University of California Publication in American Archaeology and Ethnology, 1920).

Col. Philippe Regis de Trobrian: Edna B. Patterson, *Sagebrush Doctors* (Springville, Utah: Art City Publishing Co., 1972).

Twins: Edna B. Patterson, *Sagebrush Doctors* (Springville, Utah: Art City Publishing Co., 1972).

Vagabond Act: Victoria Brady, Sarah Crome, and Lyn Reese, "Resist! Survival Tactics of Indian Women," *California History* (spring 1984).

Adriaen Van der Donck: Judith Goldsmith, *Childbirth Wisdom from the World's Oldest Societies* (New York: Congdon & Weed, Inc., 1987).

Sarah Winnemucca: Sarah Winnemucca, *Life Among the Piutes: Their Wrongs and Claims,* Mrs. Horace Mann, ed. (Boston: Cupples, Upham & Co.; New York: G. P. Putnam's Sons, 1883).

Chapter 23: Growing Up Black

Deliliah Beasley: Delilah L. Beasley, *The Negro Trail Blazers of California* (Los Angeles: Times Mirror Co., 1919).

Mr. and Mrs. Lewis Washington Brunson: Delilah L. Beasley, *The Negro Trail Blazers of California* (Los Angeles: Times Mirror Co., 1919).

Florence Crocker: Florence Crocker, *Who Made Oakland?* (Oakland, Calif.: C. Dalton, 1925).

Exoduster statistics: Nell Irvin Painter, *Exodusters: Black Migration to Kansas after Reconstruction* (New York: Alfred A. Knopf, 1976).

"Grammaw," "Marly Bright": *The American Slave: A Composite Autobiography*, George P. Rawick, ed. (Westport, Conn.: Greenwood Publishing Co., 1972).

Georgiana Kirby: Georgiana Bruce Kirby, *Georgiana: The Journal of Georgiana Bruce Kirby, 1852–1860* (Santa Cruz, Calif.: Santa Cruz Historical Trust, 1987).

John Solomon Lewis: Nell Irvin Painter, *Exodusters: Black Migration to Kansas after Reconstruction* (New York: Alfred A. Knopf, 1976).

Jane Manning: Jane Elizabeth Manning, "Sketch of My Life and Experience" (Salt Lake City, Utah: LDS Archives).

Number of pre–Civil War slaves in the West: Quintard Taylor, *In Search of the Racial Frontier: African Americans in the American West, 1528–1990* (New York: W. W. Norton and Co., 1998); Randolph Campbell, *An Empire for Slavery: The Peculiar Institution in Texas, 1821–1856* (Baton Rouge: Louisiana State University Press, 1989).

Florence Sanderson: Florence Sanderson, Jeremiah Sanderson Papers (Berkeley: University of California, Bancroft Library).

Esther Whinery Wattles: Esther Whinery Wattles, "Reminiscences," typescript (personal collection of Ruth Arps).

Pauline Williamson: Pauline Lyons Williamson, letters (New York: Lyons-Williamson Collection, Schomberg Center for Research in Black Culture, New York Public Library).

Chapter 24: Asians in the New Land

". . . as beautiful as Mt. Fuji": Kazuo Ito, *Hokubei Hyakunen Sekura* (Seattle, Wash.: n.p., 1969), quoted in Emma Gee, "Issei: The First Women," in *Counterpoint: Perspectives on Asian America,* Emma Gee, ed. (Berkeley: University of California, Asian American Studies Center, 1976).

Emma R. Cable: "Report of the Occidental Board of the Women's Foreign Missions: Howard Street Presbyterian (Chinese) Church, 1884–86."

Chinese in mining camps: "The Chinese," *Idaho* (Idaho City) *World,* September 30, 1865; Betty Derig, "Celestials in the Diggings," *Idaho Yesterdays* (fall 1972).

Chinese man against education: "Report of the Occidental Board of the Women's Foreign Missions: Howard Street Presbyterian (Chinese) Church, 1884–86."

Chinese women emigrating to America: Ruthanne Lum McCunn, *Chinese American Portraits: Personal Histories, 1828–1988* (San Francisco: Chronicle Books, 1988).

Exclusion Act: Bill Hosokawa, *The Quiet Americans* (New York: William Morrow and Co., 1969).

Fei Xiaotong: Fei Xiaotong, quoted in *Land Without Ghosts: Chinese Impressions of America from the Mid-Nineteenth Century to the Present,* R. David Arkush and Leo O. Lee, eds. (Berkeley: University of California Press, 1989).

North Dakota boy from Fort Berthold Indian Reservation, ca. 1910.

Issei, Japanese statistics: cited in *The Issei: Portrait of a Pioneer,* Eileen Sunada Sarasohn, ed. (Palo Alto, Calif.: Pacific Books, 1983).

Japanese proverb: unidentified.

Mae Seen, Chin Mui, Ah Seen: "Report of the Occidental Board of the Women's Foreign Missions: Howard Street Presbyterian (Chinese) Church, 1884–86."

Miunejiro Shibata, Mrs. Kamechiyo Takahashi, Juhei Kono, Nisuke Mitsumori: quoted in *The Issei: Portrait of a Pioneer,* Eileen Sunada Sarasohn, ed. (Palo Alto, Calif.: Pacific Books, 1983).

President's address: Theodore Roosevelt, quoted in John H. Bauer, *Growing Up With California: A History of California Children* (Los Angeles: Will Kramer, 1978).

Chapter 25: Niños de España

Arcadia Bandini, "pomegranate season": Sarah Bixby Smith, *Adobe Days* (Fresno, Calif.: Valley Publishers, 1974).

Marriage practices: Norine Dresser, "Marriage Customs in Early California," *The Californians* (November/December 1991).

Charles Marryat: Captain Charles Marryat, *Travels and Adventures of Monsieur Violet* (New York: Harper & Brothers, 1843).

Ninety-two ranchos: Charles Churchill "The Chroniclers, Part II. Alfred Robinson: A Yankee Parses Paradise," *The Californians* (March/April 1992).

Photograph Credits

p. 1 Colorado Historical Society, Buckwalter, #234
p. 4 Colorado Historical Society, Dean, #F-34015.
p. 9 Utah State Historical Society, C-239 #9
p. 16 Colorado Historical Society, Mrs. Harold Writer Collection
p. 18 Sharlot Hall Museum, PO 1869p
p. 21 Colorado Historical Society, #F3592
p. 24 Florida State Archives
p. 27 Oregon Historical Society, CN #015512
p. 29 National Archives
p. 34 Historical Society of North Dakota, photo by Cournoyer Fiske
p. 36 Florida State Archives, #4360
p. 41 Colorado Historical Society, photo by Tonnesen Sisters, #F-28,655
p. 42 State Historical Society of North Dakota, Fiske #2930
p. 43 Private collection of Susan Derenne Coerr, San Francisco, Calif.
p. 44 Colorado Historical Society
p. 45 California State Library, box 992, folder 8
p. 48 Colorado Historical Society, 1914, #F11,437
p. 50 Denver Public Library Western History Department, Harry Rhoads, #15776 Rh-377
p. 51 Colorado Historical Society, #F32,230
p. 52 State Historical Society of North Dakota, Fiske # 3831
p. 53 State Historical Society of North Dakota, Fiske #1759
p. 54 State Historical Society of North Dakota, Fiske # 3831
p. 55 State Historical Society of North Dakota, Fiske #2618
p. 56 Peter Palmquist
p. 60 Utah State Historical Society, #921
p. 61 Utah State Historical Society, #917.8 r.42
p. 63 Kansas State Historical Society, Topeka, Kans., #17251-1
p. 67 South Dakota Historical Society
p. 69 University of Wisconsin–Lacrosse Murphy Library
p. 73 State Historical Society of North Dakota
p. 74 State Historical Society of North Dakota
p. 76 Sharlot Hall Museum, #PO 8584
p. 77 State Historical Society of North Dakota
p. 78 Sharlot Hall Museum, # PO 1819p
p. 79 University of Washington Library, Barnes #1890
p. 81 State Historical Society of Wisconsin, Whi #(835) 60
p. 82 Colorado Historical Society
p. 91 Idaho Historical Society
p. 95 National Archives, West # 93
p. 96 State Historical Society of North Dakota
p. 97 Sharlot Hall Museum, # PO-175-P
p. 98 Nebraska State Historical Society, Solomon D. Butcher Collection, #B983-1416
p. 99 Montana Historical Society
p. 102 State Historical Society of North Dakota, Fiske #530
p. 103 Wyoming State Museum
p. 104 Denver Public Library Western History Department, #X-61479
p. 105 Seaver Center for Western History Research, Natural History Museum of Los Angeles County, J. E. Whitney #1488
p. 106 National Archives, West #162
p. 107 Denver Public Library, Harry Rhoads #Rh-426
p. 108 Private collection of Virginia Turner
p. 109 Bayview Bank and Museum, #1809
p. 110 Colorado Historical Society, #F-38, 181
p. 116 Colorado Historical Society, #F-38, 181

p. 117 Bayview Bank & Museum, C. K. Tuttle, #OCM-M00803
p. 118 South Dakota Historical Society
p. 119 State Historical Society of North Dakota, Fiske #5158
p. 120 South Dakota State Historical Society
p. 121 State Historical Society of Wisconsin, Whi x3 23265
p. 124 Colorado Historical Society, Ola Garrison Collection #54
p. 125 National Archives, West #102
p. 126 National Archives, West #109
p. 127 Rell Francis Collection, Springville, Utah
p. 128 Sharlot Hall Museum, #PO 1455pb
p. 128 Colorado Historical Society, Buckwalter, #719
p. 133 State Historical Society of North Dakota, Fiske #2704
p. 135 State Historical Society of Wisconsin, Alexander Krueger #WHI K91 167
p. 136 University of Wisconsin La Cross–Murphy Library
p. 139 Sharlot Hall Museum, #PO 904 pa
p. 140 Colorado Historical Society
p. 141 State Historical Society of Wisconsin, Alexander Krueger, #Whi K91 165
p. 142 Colorado Historical Society
p. 142 University of Wisconsin–La Crosse
p. 143 State Historical Society of North Dakota, Fiske #2503
p. 144 University of Washington Libraries, #WW 14455
p. 145 Seaver Center for Western History Research, Natural History Museum of Los Angeles
p. 146 Denver Public Library Western History Department, Harry Rhoads #563
p. 147 Denver Public Library Western History Department, Harry Rhoads #167
p. 147 State Historical Society of North Dakota, Fiske #2682
p. 148 University of Texas, The Institute of Texan Cultures, *The San Antonio Light* Collection, Paul Hughes #0723-B
p. 149 State Historical Society of North Dakota
p. 159 Private collection of Virginia Turner, Oakland, Calif.
p. 161 Bayview Bank and Museum, San Francisco, Calif.
p. 163 National Archives, West #188
p. 166 California State Library, #8394
p. 169 Private collection of Virginia Turner, Oakland, Calif.
p. 170 Denver Public Library Western History Department
p. 171 Denver Public Library Western History Department, #Rh-671
p. 175 Rell Francis Collection, Springville, Utah
p. 176 Denver Public Library Western History Department, #fr6499
p. 181 Minnesota Historical Society, #R32 p. 14
p. 188 Southern Oregon Historical Society, Peter Britt
p. 189 Peter Palmquist Collection, Arcada, Calif.
p. 189 The National Archives
p. 192 State Historical Society of North Dakota, Fiske # 2837
p. 195 Seaver Center for Western History Research, Natural History Museum of Los Angeles County
p. 198 National Archives, #111-SC-85780
p. 200 Eastern Washington State Historical Society, 1899 #474X
p. 203 State Historical Society of North Dakota, Fiske #41-336
p. 205 Denver Public Library Western History Department, #X-330067
p. 208 Keystone-Mast Collection, University of California at Riverside, #WX7408
p. 211 Nebraska State Historical Society, Solomon D. Butcher Collection, #B983-1345
p. 214 Idaho State Historical Society
p. 216 Louis J. Stellman Collection at the California State Library, #10, 902a
p. 217 Louis J. Stellman Collection at the California State Library, #10, 911B
p. 219 Louis J. Stellman Collection at the California State Library, #10, 882A
p. 223 Seaver Center for Western History Research, Natural History Museum of Los Angeles County
p. 224 Bancroft Library, University of California, Berkeley
p. 236 Colorado Historical Society, #F-50,510
p. 241 State Historical Society of North Dakota, #41-190

INDEX

Page numbers in *italics* refer to illustrations.

D

E

F

G

H

I

J

K

L

M

N